Church History

Twenty Centuries
of Catholic Christianity

John C. Dwyer

Paulist Press † New York † Mahwah

Cover design by Morris Berman

Library of Congress
Catalog Card Number: 84-62561

ISBN: 0-8091-3830-1

Published by Paulist Press
997 Macarthur Boulevard
Mahwah, New Jersey 07430

Printed and bound in the
United States of America

Contents

Foreword

My purpose in writing this book has not been simply to chronicle events but rather to draw a brief but accurate picture of the church in its historical reality and ambiguity, and to suggest ways of judging this ambiguity from the standpoint of the original revelation in Jesus and the reception of that revelation by his first followers.

It is precisely the normative character of the church of the earliest days which makes church history different from purely secular history and it is also this factor which should keep the church historian honest. The believing Christian has no obligation to defend what churchmen are doing or have done at any particular moment of history, and he or she has no obligation to subscribe to a given model of the founding of the church by Jesus. Christian faith does not really consist in the acceptance of dogmas, and it consists even less in the assertion of facts which properly belong in the domain of secular historical science. Faith is not a substitute for critical intelligence; it is the willingness to let God define himself on his own terms and therefore it is the willingness to let God define himself in history. God is revealed in human weakness as well as human strength, in human ignorance as well as in human wisdom. It is for this reason that genuine faith is never concerned with marshalling so-called historical evidence in favor of predetermined positions. Here, as in all other areas of life, genuine faith is liberating.

In this book, I have, more than is usually the case, emphasized the role of theology in the life of the church. The study

1

of church history makes it clear that theology is not an esoteric pastime for a clerical leisure class but an extremely important factor in explaining the growth and change of the church from the beginning. Since theology is the attempt to make accurate use of human language in order to speak about God, it would be very surprising if this were not the case.

In a highly condensed work of this type, practically every line could be amply footnoted. However, this would clutter the text and I do not believe that it would serve any useful purpose. The judgments which I make are rarely traceable to a single source; they are the result of a few decades of reading and reflection, and for most of these judgments I am indebted, at least indirectly, to many more authors and sources than could be listed in even a lengthy footnote.

The mistakes of the past are, if anything, more informative than the successes, and although I have made no attempt to write "revisionist" history, I have made some rather negative judgments about events such as the Constantinian Settlement, the mass conversions, the Crusades, the Council of Trent's neglect of the legitimate concerns of the Reformers and its consequent "Latinizing" of the Catholic church, and the pontificates of Pius IX, Pius X, and Pius XII.

In each case, I have tried to present the event in a way which will be helpful to us as we try to make intelligent judgments about the unique tasks which face us today. For it is this, after all, which is the purpose of church history as a theological discipline. The Christian is summoned by the word of God to face an ever-changing world, and to evaluate its challenges, its possibilities, and its dangers. In the past, Christians have accepted some of these challenges and have rejected others; they have capitalized on some of the possibilities and they have let others pass them by; they have seen and guarded against some dangers, and they have closed their eyes and have fallen prey to others. Perhaps more than in other areas of life, the old adage is true of church history: those who do not understand the past are condemned to repeat it.

My thanks to all who have helped in the writing of this book, especially my students, (former and present), whose critical questioning has made teaching them such a joy and inspiration. All of my present and past students at St. Bernard's Graduate School of Theology and Ministry in Albany have contributed to this revision, but the following made comments which shaped the final chapter, and they deserve special mention: JoAnn Crowley, Nancirose Halse, Lorrie Lyons, John Madden, Chris Ringwald, Mike Rivest, Mike Sheppeck, Joanne Stankavage, and Ray Sullivan. Don Brophy at Paulist Press made some very valuable suggestions. Finally, as all of our friends know so well, without the presence of my wife, Odile, none of this would have come to pass. This second edition of the book was finished in what is, for us, the most beautiful place in the world, Platte Clove, NY.

John C. Dwyer

1

From the Beginning
to the Year 100

1.1 INTRODUCTION: THE IMPORTANCE OF THE FIRST CENTURY FOR THE CHURCH OF LATER TIMES

The history of the church begins with the history of Jesus. This is true, even though the church did not really exist during Jesus' earthly life, but was at most foreshadowed by certain things that he said and did. It is also true, even though the question of whether Jesus founded a church is difficult to answer, because the answer depends very much on the picture which one associates with the phrase "founding a church." Church history begins with Jesus, because "church" is always minimally but essentially the group of those who take Jesus and his life with absolute seriousness, and who find in him a new understanding of the word "God" and a new grasp of what it means to be human. (And, incidentally, this is precisely what it means to call Jesus "the Christ.")

1.2 WHAT WE KNOW ABOUT JESUS

The story of Jesus' life is a very difficult one to write, and this is due mainly to the character of the sources. Jesus himself wrote nothing, and secular historians of his own time give us no information about him. From about ninety years after his death, his name begins to appear, sometimes in garbled form, in the work of some Roman historians and other writers. Taken together, these works provide us with barely enough information to enable us to state with certainty that Jesus existed. On the other hand, we have documents called "Gospels" which appear to give information about his life, or at least part of it, but they were written by his followers, many years after his death. These documents are, by the admission of their writers, religious propaganda, in the sense that they were written to bring others to faith in Jesus as the Christ. The writing of the Gospels is itself an event of church history of the latter half of the first century, but at this point it is the relationship of these Gospels to Jesus and to the events of his life which interests us.

1.21 The Gospels and the Life of Jesus

The Gospels are not "lives of Jesus." Rather, they are records of early Christian preaching, beginning about a generation after Jesus' death; as such they are expressions of faith in Jesus, as this faith was experienced in a number of early communities. What the Gospels tell us, immediately and directly, is how these communities *experienced* Jesus from three to six decades after his death. The Gospel writers and those for whom they wrote were trying to live as Christians and to share their faith with others. They wrote Gospels to solve problems of *their* day and *their* time, and they tried to achieve this goal by telling stories of what Jesus *had done*, of what people *thought he had done*, of what he *might have done*, or perhaps *would have done*, if he had had to confront the same problems they were facing in the years after his death. The Gospels, in other words, are not historical documents, at least as we understand this phrase today, and they are not biographies of Jesus. This does *not* mean that the Gospels are without value and it does *not* mean that they are not true, but it does mean that the question of the value and truth of the Gospels is not one that can be dealt with in a naive or simplistic way. It means that the Gospels can be true in the deep sense of bringing us into the truth about ourselves and about God, only if we know what the Gospel writers were attempting to say and only if we understand something about the resources of thought and expression which they had at their disposal. Those who insist that the Gospels provide a clearcut record of objective events, after the fashion of a video camera, never discover the truth of the Gospels, because they exclude in principle the one approach which makes that truth accessible.

1.22 What the Gospels Do Not Tell Us

The peculiar relationship of the Gospels to the life of Jesus has a number of consequences, some of them vigorously and even passionately resisted by conservative Christians, but no less inevitable or important for that reason. First, many of the Gospel narratives do not recount objective events; rather, they are stories, created by people whose imaginations and thought processes differed radically from our own. They intended, in writing these stories, to express their faith in a Jesus who really lived, and whose continued existence was vitally important to them at the time in which they lived. An example is provided in the infancy narratives of Matthew and Luke: these chapters do not provide us with a historical record of the strange events which preceded and followed the birth of Jesus. Rather, they are the highly symbolic expression of the faith of one or more Jewish-Christian communities, about forty or fifty years after his death. The truth of these infancy narratives does not consist in the fact that they recount objectively verifiable events, but in the fact that they give us *an objective account of the faith* of one important group within the early church.

Further, the fact that the Gospels are not historical documents in the modern sense of the word means that much of the miracle tradition cannot be taken literally, but is a way of speaking about Jesus and about the fact that, in him, God entered into the brokenness of the human condition, and conquered that brokenness radically and in principle. Similarly, many of the words and sayings of Jesus in the Gospels are not a word for word record of his actual remarks, but probably found their way into the Gospel texts as a result of attempts of communities of later times to apply their faith in Jesus to problems of their own day.

What all of this means is that the Gospels are excellent historical sources, not directly and immediately for the events of Jesus' life, but rather for events in the life of the church during the last four decades of the first century. As such, they are of enormous importance for our faith. However, to insist that the Gospels are verbatim accounts of eye-witnesses, written to inform us of the objectively verifiable words and actions of Jesus, is to identify faith with the denial of critical intelligence.

These judgments about the Gospels and their historical reliability seem rather negative, but actually they have great positive import for faith. The Gospels intend to say things which are vitally important for life and for death, for time and for eternity, and this is precisely what is missed by those who approach the Gospels with the wrong expectations. There is no need to apologize for the fact that it is the faith of the early community with which the Gospels bring us into immediate contact, because it was the faith of these early communities which has mediated faith in Jesus to all later communities, including our own. It is for this reason that the Gospels are priceless documents. The Gospels do not confront us directly and immediately with the historical Jesus, but they tacitly demand that we raise the question of who this man was, in whom these early communities believed, and in whom they found the meaning of life and death. The Gospels themselves force us to raise the question of how we can penetrate them, how we can move behind them, to discover the Jesus who really lived and whose words and actions have an impact which lasts to our own day and beyond.

1.23 The Jewish Background

Jesus was a Jew, as were all of his earliest followers. They all lived and acted out of a rich tradition which was already over a thousand years old by the time Jesus was born. Jesus' own preaching and the word which others preached about him are unintelligible without an understanding of what it meant to be a Jew during the middle years of the first century of our era.

First of all, to be a Jew meant to have a history which was intimately connected with the land of Israel. According to Jewish tradition, this history began with Abraham, a nomadic chieftain, who answered the call of God and traveled from a city in Mesopotamia near the Persian Gulf, to the land which would later become Israel. Abraham himself did not become a permanent settler in the land, but wandered about in it, pasturing his flocks, as did his son and grandson after him. According to the same ancient Jewish tradition, Abraham's great-grandson, Joseph, had been sold into slavery in Egypt by his own brothers. There, through a remarkable series of events, he won the favor of the Pharaoh, reached high position, and at a time of famine in Israel, brought his father and brothers to Egypt, where they lived as honored guests. Later, with the accession to power of a "Pharaoh who knew not Joseph," their position changed, and they became little better than slaves.

According to this tradition, hundreds of years later God appeared to Moses, an Israelite who had been given an Egyptian upbringing, and commissioned him to lead the Israelites out of Egypt and into freedom. After escaping from Pharaoh's forces through the direct intervention of God, Moses and the Israelites wandered in the desert and eventually came to the mountain of Sinai. Here God appeared again to Moses, and through him gave the Israelites the *Law*, a detailed list of the demands which God made on the people he had chosen to be his own. After further wandering, Moses died, and under Joshua, his successor, the Israelites moved into the land which had been promised them, and through a combination of conquest and infiltration claimed the land as their own. Here they lived in a loose confederation, occasionally uniting under charismatic leaders to defend themselves against hostile neighbors. By the middle of the eleventh century B.C. they found themselves subject to increasing pressure from the Philistines, a people recently arrived on the western coast of Palestine. Faced with the Philistine threat they united, somewhat hesitantly, under a king named Saul. This first experiment in monarchy was a failure, but in the year 1000 B.C., David became king of the united monarchy of Israel (in the north) and Judah (in the south) and he, followed by his son, Solomon, ruled the united monarchy, each for about forty years.

After Solomon's death, the kingdom was divided, and the Old Testament tells the story of the next four hundred years as a tale of internal strife within the kingdoms and of their attempts to retain or regain their independence from foreign powers. These attempts finally failed. The northern kingdom lost its independence and its population was dispersed in 721 B.C. Judah fell to Babylon in 597 B.C. and this marked the end of Israelite independence. These developments led, not to despair, but to an ever more intense longing for the restoration of the kingdom of David—a restoration which would be effected by one who, like David and the kings of Judah after him, would be an *Anointed One*, called by God and endowed with the power to fulfill God's will in history. The Hebrew word for "Anointed One" has given us the word *Messiah*.

From the time of David on, it is possible to reconstruct much of Israel's history on the basis of the Old Testament. However, what the Old Testament presents as the history of pre-Davidic times is largely the construction of writers of David's own day, who created an "historical" framework for events which had come down to them in the form of legend and folklore. Of course, some of these legendary and folkloric elements originally had a basis in fact. Moses was, without doubt, an historical figure (probably an Egyptian), although in later times many legendary details were attracted to his story. But before Moses' time, events recede into the mists of legend and folklore, and it was a creative religious genius of great ability and daring at the time of David and Solomon who fashioned the story of Abraham and his family, of the events of the Exodus, of the theophany on Sinai, and of the conquest of the land of Canaan. He did not simply invent this story, but used the mixture of myth, legend, folklore, and historical reminiscence, which was circulating in oral form in his time.

Jewish faith in Jesus' day (and this includes the faith of all of Jesus' earliest followers) can be understood only against the background of the history of Israel, which has been sketched in the briefest possible compass here. There are a number of elements in this Jewish faith which are extremely important for an understanding of Jesus. *First*, unlike all of the other nations and ethnic groups of their day, the Jews had room for only one God—a God who was absolutely transcendent and therefore infinitely holy, his reality separated from ours by an unbridgeable chasm.

But there is a *second* affirmation of Jewish faith which stands in a paradoxical relationship with the first: this absolutely transcendent God has intervened directly and immediately in history, and has revealed himself in his total control of the historical process, both within Israel and in the world at large. For Israel it was the Exodus from Egypt which was the great revelation of this God who is the lord of history, for it was at that time that "with a mighty hand and outstretched arm" he led a mixed band of slaves out of Egypt, toward the land which he had promised to their forefathers. And although perhaps only a small percentage of the Israelites in David's day actually had ancestors who had been in Egypt, all later Israelites adopted the story of the Exodus as their story and as the revelation of their God. Israel understood itself as the people of this God, on whose behalf he had acted on the stage of world history. For God did not address the Jew solely as an individual, but as a member of a *people*, God's people, who had a past, a present, and a future, precisely because God had definitively intervened in history in their favor.

A *third* element of Jewish faith is the conviction that after leading their ancestors out of Egypt, God made a *covenant* with them (that is, an agreement or contract) in which he formally stated that he would be their God and they would be his people, and in which he laid down the conditions which were binding on them because of this agreement. These conditions were summed up in the *Law*—the clear and detailed statement of God's will for his people. Israel understood this Law, not as a burden to be borne grudgingly, but as God's greatest gift, and as a source of peace and of joy.

A *fourth* element in Jewish faith appeared in many variant forms. In the Jewish view, God's plan embraced the entire human race and Israel was destined to play a special role in asserting God's lordship over the whole world. This vision could be narrowly nationalized, and this happened frequently enough, whenever Israel identified its own political or military success with the triumph of the cause of God. But the vision could be broadened, and at least at certain times Israel was conscious of playing a special part in God's plan for the entire human race. This element of Jewish faith was an important part of the belief in a *Messiah*—an individual chosen and commissioned by God to liberate Israel and to lead it to the fulfillment of its vocation.

There were certain features of Jewish life in Jesus' day which were not unconnected with the major themes of Jewish faith, but which were not simply derived from them and were rather the result of historical developments within Judaism for centuries before Jesus' time. *First,* in the four centuries before the birth of Jesus, Jewish views of the Law had changed in a way which reflects the enduring danger of religion: it becomes, almost inevitably, a way of saving oneself by determining exactly what must be done to please God in all areas of life. This leads to the concept of the "just" man or woman as one who has done what is required in a number of narrowly defined religious areas and who, in virtue of this, has a claim on God. Although it would be unfair to characterize Judaism in Jesus' day as merely a religion of law in this sense, Jesus' own obvious desire to relativize the claims of the Law, as well as Paul's rejection of justification by doing the works of the Law, make it clear that the danger was real.

A *second* feature of Jewish life in Jesus' day was its great diversity, not only in religious practice, but in terms of what was believed as well. A group known as *Pharisees* viewed the Law as the sum and substance of Israel's faith. They spent their time discussing the Law, striving to determine its exact demands, and developing techniques to insure that even the most insignificant prescription of the Law would not be violated. The Pharisees believed firmly in the resurrection of the dead, in eternal joy for the just and, probably, in eternal punishment for the wicked. Many of the Pharisees must have been sincerely religious men, and there is good evidence that some of them became Christians in the decades after the death of Jesus. The *Sadducees* on the other hand were members of the priestly families of Jerusalem. They were concerned primarily with the formalities of cultic sacrifice and nothing that we know of them suggests that there was much religious substance in either their faith or their practice. Like priestly bureaucracies in all times and places, they were probably most interested in securing that political stability on which their own prosperity depended. There was another group in Jesus' day, whom we do not meet in the New Testament but whom we know from other sources—the *Qumran* community, or the community of the *Dead Sea Scrolls*. This community was made up of Jews who despised the lack of religious substance in the Jerusalem priesthood and set up their own monastic-like community in the Judean wilderness above the western shore of the Dead Sea. There they hoped, by their exact observance of ritual and dietary law, to bring about the final intervention of God in history. The last group, and one occasionally mentioned in the New Testament, was that of the *Zealots*. Although more of a political party than a religious group, it was their reading of the Old Testament which inspired them to hope for the intervention of God when they rose violently against their oppressors and sought to restore the independence of Israel by military means. The Jewish War of 65–70 A.D. and the final uprising of 135 A.D. were the direct result of such convictions. Attempts are occasionally made to link Jesus with the Zealots, but they are exercises in fantasy, not fact.

A *third* characteristic of Jewish life in Jesus' day probably did not affect his ministry to any significant degree, but was extremely important for the early church. For many centuries, large numbers of Jews had been living outside the Holy Land. Not all of those who had been taken to captivity in Babylon returned, and many decided to remain and make their fortunes in that land. About the same time, others had gone to Egypt, and over the course of centuries a large Jewish community had grown up in Alexandria. About two centuries before Jesus' time, small Jewish communities could be found in Syria and along the Cilician coast in southeastern Asia Minor. By Jesus' time there were Jewish settlements in most of the cities of Asia Minor, in the larger cities of Greece, and in Rome itself.

These Jews of the *Diaspora*, as it is called, remained loyal to their faith. Jerusalem was their holy city and they kept in contact with the religious leadership there. But even though these Jews usually lived apart from their pagan fellow countrymen, they were more open to cultural influences coming from the non-Jewish milieu, and were, in general, more broad-minded and progressive than their fellow Jews of Palestine. Some groups of these Diaspora Jews were extremely important in the early church.

This summary of Jewish faith and life in Jesus' day is minimal, but it is indispensable for the understanding of Jesus. This is true, not because Jesus was totally conditioned by his world and its values, but precisely because he distanced himself from that world and questioned its values, and, above all, its picture of God. But Jesus did this, not by rejecting the God of the Old Testament or the faith for which that God called; he did it by claiming to reveal the one who had been the God of Israel from the beginning, and he did it by reaffirming the faith for which that God had called, but which had been obscured and sometimes lost under a suffocating layer of human religiosity.

Israel's history is important for another reason: the early church saw itself as the new Israel, as the fulfillment of the hope and longing of Israel's prophets and holy men, and as the new and definitive people of God. For this reason, the church's image of itself and the picture which it strove to present to the world are both unintelligible without an understanding of Jewish faith and hope in Jesus' time.

1.24 The Life of Jesus

We have no detailed chronology of Jesus' life. We do not even know the year of his birth. The story of the Wise Men is legendary, but even if it were not, we would have no idea of the space of time which separated his birth from the first appearance of the star (or the conjunction of planets) which probably took place in 7 B.C. The census of Quirinius, which was the supposed occasion of Mary and Joseph's journey to Bethlehem, is of no help either. Luke has probably confused the dates, and we know from other sources that the census of Quirinius actually took place in 6 A.D.—a very unlikely date for the birth of Jesus.

We do not really know where Jesus was born. The infancy narratives of Matthew and Luke are not reliable sources here, and from the Gospels of Mark and John it might be supposed that he was born in Galilee, most probably in Nazareth. The year in which Jesus' public ministry began is uncertain. Luke's attempt to date the beginning of the ministry of John the Baptist would seem to be helpful, but, apart from other difficulties, we have no idea of how long John was preaching before Jesus appeared. We do not know whether Jesus' public ministry lasted for one year, as Matthew, Mark, and Luke would seem to suggest, or for three years, as John implies. We do not even know the exact year of Jesus' death, although it is moderately probable that it occurred in either 30 or 31 A.D.

However, apart from detailed chronology, we know a great deal about Jesus. About the year 29 he appeared among those who were being baptized by John the Baptist. John was preaching about the imminent end of the world and the coming wrath of God, and he demanded of his hearers a radical change in their lives. He was in many ways the last of the prophets and a successor of those great prophetic voices of Israel who called for unswerving loyalty to Yahweh and demanded justice toward one's fellow human beings. It is possible that through the encounter with John, Jesus came to understand the meaning of his own vocation in a final and definitive way.

Shortly after the encounter with John, Jesus appeared in Galilee. The message that he preached was very different from that of John the Baptist, and the radical newness of his preaching set him apart from the entire prophetic tradition of Israel. He asserted that God is present, with all of his power, in the ordinary and secular events of life. When the world fails us, God will not, and he is especially near to those who do not dispose of themselves and their world and who have no control over their destiny. God is with us as a loving father, and all we are called upon to do is to accept his love. Jesus insisted that there are no preconditions: God's presence among us is not limited to the religious realm, and he seems to have gone out of his way to show that God is with those who have no religious credentials and who are rather careless about their observance of the Law of Moses. Jesus certainly relativized the importance of observing the Sabbath, and in Mark's version of another story (Mk. 2:18–20) he came close to mocking the religious practice of fasting. Finally, Jesus affirmed that the man or woman who accepts this unmerited love of God will be totally transformed by it.

Jesus himself cannot be separated from the call of God which he voiced. Preaching was the most important thing that he did, and on more than one occasion he suggested that it was his purpose in life. In a peculiar way, he himself incarnated and embodied God's call: his preaching was always the offer and the demand, not to accept some teaching, but to follow him and to let him be *Lord*—the one who determines the meaning of the word "God" and the meaning of the word "human being." Jesus was indifferent to titles, and his mystery was evident above all in the fact that no title could adequately describe him or hold him. To follow him is to be completely *free*—so free that one can be unrestrictedly there for the neighbor, for every human being one meets. To follow him is to receive one's identity, one's very selfhood, from him.

The peculiar thing about Jesus' preaching is that it was not really *about* God at all; rather, Jesus spoke and acted in God's name and with God's own power, and he brought people into the presence of God, and made God real for them in a wholly new way. He himself called God "Father" in a unique sense, and through him people encountered God in such a way that they were healed in both mind and body. These healings constituted the core of a miracle tradition which, in its later stages, certainly acquired many legendary and folkloric elements, but the core of the tradition is historical.

Jesus' preaching often consisted in telling stories in which his hearers suddenly found themselves confronted with the offer and the claim of God himself—a God who accepted them without condition, but who demanded that they accept precisely that. The actions of Jesus were in harmony with his words: he sat at table with sinners and he interpreted this as God's invitation to them. As we have seen, his attitude toward religion was at least distanced, and it is a thorough misunderstanding to make him into the founder of the Christian religion.

Jesus knew that in him and in his word something absolutely new had happened, and because of this he was totally confident, but without the slightest touch of arrogance. And yet there is a dark side to this: he was a stranger in the world, and he was a stranger even to his own family and followers, who frequently misunderstood him.

Jesus' preaching initially drew great crowds, but he sensed that they did not understand him. They were eager for the healing power which emanated from him and they had a dim awareness that they needed him, but most of them seem to have looked on him as a political messiah, and this he could not accept. As time went on, he turned his attention to a smaller group, his disciples or followers, but they also had great difficulty in understanding him. They were drawn to him and in their own way they loved him, but he remained a stranger in their midst.

After about a year of this, Jesus seems to have felt the need to confront the religious leadership of his people with his message, and he went to Jerusalem. The reasons behind the events which followed his appearance there are very obscure, as are the motives of the persons involved. The Jewish authorities took him into custody and then handed him over to the Romans to be executed. It seems clear that these Jewish authorities objected to Jesus, not because he preached political revolution, but because he preached religious revolution, and in this they may have understood him more deeply than most of his own followers. But it is probable that the authorities used the charge of political revolution as a pretext to win the support of the Roman procurator for their plans. Jesus'

career ended with dramatic suddenness and appalling brutality; and yet, in a deep sense, his death was the appropriate
reaction of the world to the concept of God and the concept
of human being which he preached and made real.

1.25 Did Jesus Found a Church?

The Greek word *ekklesia* which we translate as "church"
occurs rarely in the Gospels: we find it only in Matthew, and
there in only two places. But much of what we mean by the
word "church" today is present in the New Testament and included there under terms such as "kingdom," "way," "followers" and "word."

The question of whether Jesus actually founded a church
is one which has divided his followers up to the present day.
One of the more interesting answers (and the one most often
misunderstood) is that of the French scholar, Alfred Loisy,
who summarized his views in the early years of this century by
saying that what Jesus preached was the kingdom, but what
actually came into existence was the church. Loisy did not intend, in making this apparently cynical statement, to say that
the church came into existence as the result of a misunderstanding of Jesus' intentions. What he meant, surprisingly
enough, was that the kingdom which Jesus preached could
never become a reality without the church. When people took
Jesus' preaching seriously, they began of necessity to reflect
on the institutions which were indispensable if that preaching
was to continue. For Loisy, the church was the sum total of
these institutions.

Since the Reformation, both Protestants and Catholics
have tried to show that Jesus did indeed found a church: precisely, of course, the church to which they themselves belonged. Catholics affirmed that Jesus had founded a
hierarchical church, with a clearcut distinction between clergy
and laity, and, within the clergy, a clearcut distinction between bishops and priests, priests and deacons. Catholics further argued that the church which Jesus founded was the
papal church, in which supreme power was possessed, at least
in church matters, by the Bishop of Rome, Peter's successor.

It was affirmed that the Pope not only enjoyed moral authority, but that he had true *jurisdiction*—the right to make laws which bind in conscience. Finally, it was argued that a number of other points of doctrine—especially the existence of seven distinct sacraments—can be traced directly to Jesus' words and actions.

Protestants tended to argue that Jesus founded the church in the sense of a spiritual community. They tended to find in the organizational trappings merely human arrangements which might be useful for a time, but which, if the situation demanded it, might be set aside with impunity because they did not originate with Jesus himself. Furthermore, Protestants have often argued that at various periods of church history, beginning with the second century, the church strayed, through human error, from Jesus' original intentions, and that it was only at the time of the Reformation that all of these errors were rectified. In the Protestant view, these departures from Jesus' original plan included such things as the development of the jurisdictional power of the papacy, the belief in the objective efficacy of sacramental actions, and the use of philosophical terms of relatively late origin ("transubstantiation" is a good example) as necessary ways of expressing Christian faith.

Both Protestant and Catholic thinking ("polemic" would be more accurate) on these questions was little more than wishful thinking, and a new climate of ecumenical respect should make it possible to raise the question of what Jesus really did and intended, without fearing an honest answer. Briefly, the answer would look something like this: During the one or two years of his public life, Jesus was surrounded by followers who were captivated by his word and by his person. Some of them shared all of the conditions of his life; others followed at a greater distance or more sporadically. What Jesus preached was not an esoteric doctrine, which an individual might choose after cool examination. Instead, his words and actions were *community-forming*, and they kept this peculiar power when they were repeated after his death and when the word of what God had done for him began to spread. This community, which had been formed by the word of Jesus, was made up of sinners who had been accepted by him in the name of God. During Jesus' public life, he often ate meals with sinners as an *effective sign* of the acceptance of God which he offered them; after his death the community continued to celebrate these meals, in the belief that the risen Lord was now there again with them. The community came to understand that in dying, Jesus had shared in the brokenness of human existence, and in doing so made God's acceptance of human beings historically real. And they came to understand that in celebrating Eucharist, in "breaking the bread and passing the cup," they were celebrating the real presence in their midst of their crucified and risen Lord.

If "church" is the community of those who see in Jesus the very word and act of God, and who, for this reason, continue to preach his word and the word his followers preached about him, then *in this sense* Jesus undoubtedly founded a church. And if "church" is the community of those who continue to celebrate his meals with sinners, because they know that when they share in his death they will also share in his life in eternity, then *in this sense* Jesus also undoubtedly founded a church. But he founded this church, not because he brought it into existence, fully formed, during his lifetime, but because "church," as described here, is a necessary consequence of his words and deeds.

On the other hand, if "church" means essentially the apparatus or the organization, with all of its structures, either of the first century or of today, then Jesus neither founded a church nor did he directly and immediately intend one. This does not necessarily mean that church structures and apparatus result from a misunderstanding of Jesus' intentions or from treason to his message. Human communities *need* organization and structure, and the history of the church in the first century (particularly the history of Paul's communities) shows this conclusively. If preaching and the celebration of the Lord's supper were to continue, the community had to arrange for the orderly handing on of the various competences required, and the community had to develop adequate ways of testing the preaching of its ministers at any given moment, to make sure that the original message was being preached in its purity, and that Christian faith did not lose more and more of its substance as time went on.

1.26 The Resurrection

It seems clear that when Jesus died his followers did not expect his return. In fact, they thought that his death meant the end of all of their hopes, and this was a shattering realization for them. The predictions of the passion and resurrection which we find in the eighth, ninth and tenth chapters of Mark, and in the parallel synoptic passages, are not historical; they are constructions of the early community, "retrojections" from a later date. Jesus' followers were not prepared for his death, and when he died they did not know how to cope with it. And yet it is clear that just a short time after Jesus' death, a number of his former followers became convinced that he was alive and that they had met him. This encounter had not come about, as they saw it, because Jesus had returned to ordinary life, but rather because he had taken on a completely new kind of existence. In various ways, the resurrection narratives point to this completely new and different kind of existence: people who had known Jesus intimately did not recognize him; he would suddenly materialize in places where he had not been and he would just as suddenly disappear. But these appearances were not given for the private consolation of those who experienced them; they seem, instead, to have been a vocation, a call to action. And as a result of these experiences, the followers of Jesus came together to form a new group and to celebrate their awareness of the fact that through Jesus and his word they had been made whole in time and eternity.

Jesus' early followers did not yet see all of the implications of this. In the first days after the resurrection, they apparently had no inkling of the relationship between his death and the new wholeness which they experienced. For this reason, we might say that they had *begun to become church*, or that in them *church was coming into being*. It would take years of experience and of reflection on that experience before the church would exist in a full and final way (and there is a sense in which the church, even today, is always in the process of coming into being). The early community's reflection on its experience coincides almost perfectly with the coming into existence of the New Testament, and it is this fact which accounts for the permanent dependence of the church and the New Testament on each other.

1.3 FROM JESUS' DEATH TO THE CONVERSION OF PAUL

The period to be outlined here is a short one; it probably lasted for no more than three years, and yet it is extremely important for the history of the church and for the future of Christianity. At first sight, part of the New Testament itself would seem to be a valuable source for this period, because the first chapters of the book called *Acts of the Apostles* seem to mention all of the major actors and to recount their activities during this period. But, as we will see in the next section, the book of *Acts* is not a reliable historical source. Luke's theological interests led him to edit his material, and a careful reading reveals contradictions which lurk beneath the surface. *Acts* is a valuable historical source for the life of one community (that of Luke) in the late eighties or early nineties of the first century, but it is only when we read between the lines in a careful and critical way that we can make any use of the book as a source for our knowledge of events in the weeks and months after Jesus' death.

1.31 The Earliest Days

It is not at all certain where the followers of Jesus experienced the resurrection, or, more accurately, experienced him as the risen Lord. Mark's Gospel, although it has no accounts of the appearances of Jesus to his followers, assumes that these experiences took place in Galilee; this Gospel was probably written in and for a community which was convinced that this was the case. Luke, on the other hand, knows only of appearances of Jesus in Jerusalem or in the vicinity.

Matthew and John seem to know of appearances both in the region of Jerusalem and in Galilee. The earliest written witness we have of the resurrection—Paul, writing in *1 Corinthians* 15—talks of appearances which probably took place in the vicinity of Jerusalem. (Paul wrote *1 Corinthians* in the mid-fifties, but in that letter he included material which had been communicated to him at the time of his conversion, in the early thirties, just a few years after Jesus' death.) It is not really possible to reconcile or harmonize the accounts of the resurrection which we find in the Gospels and in Paul. They do not simply complement or supplement each other; in some cases they contradict each other. Another problem is that Paul, who is the first to write about the resurrection, does not seem to know about the empty tomb, and yet the Gospels either assert that the tomb was empty or hint at the fact.

We really do not know where the closest followers of Jesus went and what they were doing in the few days immediately after his death. It is possible that they stayed in hiding in Jerusalem, but it is just as possible that they left in small groups for Galilee. However, what does seem clear is that a short time after Jesus' death (and this would be a period to be reckoned in weeks and not in months) they were in Jerusalem, that they formed a community, and that within that community Peter played a leading role. It seems likely that Peter's leadership role was based partly on the community's acceptance of the fact that the risen Lord had appeared first to him.

In this earliest community there was a group known as "the Twelve." Note carefully that this group did not consist of "twelve apostles." The "twelve apostles" were not an historical group but were the creation of a later theology, which took two distinct groups in the early church—"the Twelve" and "the apostles"—made them into a single group, and then projected the founding of that group back into the public life of Jesus. It is possible that some of the Twelve may have been considered to be apostles in the early church, but the groups were formally distinct. The very fact that the institution of the Twelve was not the work of Jesus but of the earliest community gives us valuable information about what this community was and about how it viewed itself: it was a Jewish apocalyptic

group and it understood itself as a community of the end-
times, of the final days of the history of the world. The earliest
Christians thought that the end of the world was imminent,
and that it would be inaugurated by the even more imminent
second coming of the risen Lord on the clouds of heaven. The
first Christians understood their mission as that of converting
as many of the Jews as possible to their views. Such Jewish
apocalyptic groups were apparently quite common for as
much as a century before Jesus' time and a century after, and
there was ample room in contemporary Judaism for their
radicalism and their diversity.

The other Jews would have had no problem with these
Jewish Christians, because the latter continued to observe the
Law, took part in Temple worship, and took their Jewishness
just as seriously as their non-Christian coreligionists. Their
messianic hopes and expectations were probably just as na-
tionalistic as those of their contemporaries. In any case, their
mingled political and religious hopes were intense, and these
hopes stimulated a great outpouring of missionary zeal which
left its traces in the Pentecost narrative of the book of *Acts*. But
the story, as Luke tells it, is clearly a construction in which,
about sixty years after Jesus' death, Luke edits and reinter-
prets events in terms of his favorite theological themes.

We know very little about the liturgy and sacramental life
of this earliest community. It is possible that they already
practiced Baptism as an initiatory rite, but it is more likely that
Baptism came into the Christian community about a decade
or two later, when a number of former followers of John the
Baptist became Christian. The meals eaten by these early
Christians have been a source of interest up to the present
day, because they would seem to provide us with evidence of
what Jesus intended to do at the Last Supper. Some have attempted to make a clear distinction between meals which
community members ate merely to satisfy their hunger, and
other meals which they understood as ceremonial or liturgical
actions; but the evidence for this distinction is weak. It seems
probable that in the earliest days the community came together to eat just one kind of meal. They ate to satisfy their
hunger, as they had when Jesus was with them; but because

they were convinced that he now lived and *was with them again,* they celebrated these meals as the joyous experience of his presence, as they had during his earthly life. It seems clear that in these earliest days the community had not yet linked these meals with the death of their Lord, as Paul would later do, but it is just as clear that these meals were a specifically Christian event, and that they cannot be understood on the basis of either Jewish or Hellenistic models.

1.32 Organization

We know very little about the organization of the early church. It is probable that it was highly fluid, although it is clear that Peter was the leader of the community. As we have seen, these early Christians did not reckon with a lengthy stay on earth, but saw everything in the light of the imminent coming of their Lord. It does seem, however, that there were three groups which played an important role as the community began to realize that the end of the world was not quite as imminent as they had first thought. First there were the *apostles* (*not* the Twelve), who were sent by the Lord and commissioned by him to work in his name. The *prophets* formed a second group; they spoke the word of God or of his Risen One in situations which Jesus himself had not encountered. The *teachers* formed a third group. They provided instruction, probably by repeating the words of Jesus, and then elaborating them with questions, answers, and further examples. The *Twelve,* mentioned in the preceding section, were probably not involved in the governance of the community; their role was symbolic and they were the twelve spiritual fathers of the new community, as the twelve sons of Jacob were thought to be the twelve physical fathers (ancestors) of the old community.

1.33 The Hellenists

A critical reading of the New Testament indicates that there were certain features in the religious life of these early Jewish Christians which did not harmonize well with Jesus and his message. Furthermore, there were certain elements in Jesus' preaching which were quite absent from the religious life of these early Christians, although most of them were certainly unaware of this. But there was one group in the early church which was aware of these discrepancies, and they were extremely important for the history of the later church.

These Jewish Christians who saw some of the implications of Jesus' message which escaped their contemporaries belonged to a group known as the "Hellenists"—congregations composed of Diaspora Jews (those who had lived outside the Holy Land) who had returned to Jerusalem and taken up more or less permanent residence there. Perhaps they lived by themselves, somewhat apart from the other Jews—we don't know. But as we have seen, these Diaspora Jews were more open to new ideas and less rigid in regard to ritual law than their fellow Jews. These Hellenists, when they were converted to Christianity, seemed to sense that, although their new faith had come into existence entirely within the Jewish religious world, it could not be limited to those who were willing to undertake the strict observance of Jewish dietary and cultic law. They seem to have sensed the radical incompatibility between Christianity and legalistic Judaism as it was lived at the time, and they began to draw some practical consequences. (Paul would be the first to develop the theory and the theological justification for this, some years later.)

Because they came to these conclusions and probably stopped observing parts of the ritual and ceremonial law, these Hellenists were apparently despised and persecuted by the non-Christian Jews, and were eventually driven out of the city of Jerusalem. On the other hand, those members of the Jewish Christian church who remained law-abiding Jews got along very well with the Jerusalem Jews and evidently did nothing whatsoever to support the Hellenists; possibly they were glad to see them go and were happy to be rid of the embarrassment. We don't know how many of the Hellenists were driven out at the time, and we don't know where all of them went, but in view of later developments, it seems certain that the Christian communities in Damascus and Antioch owe their origin to them, and that their departure from Jerusalem was providential for the spread of the new faith. Perhaps surprisingly, these Hellenistic communities remained in contact with Jerusalem, and they seem to have accorded the Christian community of Jerusalem a normative role in matters of faith. The strict Jewish Christians of the old capital probably did not know quite what to make of this new breed, and there are tracks of these early tensions in Luke's *Acts of the Apostles*. How these tensions would have been resolved we do not know, because at this precise moment a man appeared who not only drew practical conclusions about the obligatory character of the Jewish Law, but developed a theory and a theology of the relation of Jesus and his message to the Mosaic Law, which rocked the church to its foundations and gave it a new direction which has determined its future up to the present day.

1.4 THE CONVERSION OF PAUL AND ITS AFTERMATH

Paul's importance for the early church is paralleled by his place in the New Testament: more of the New Testament is by or about Paul than is the case for anyone except Jesus himself. Paul began as an outsider who had persecuted the early Christians, but he brought about a radical reinterpretation of Christianity, as it was understood by the official leadership of his day. In a church which was, at least in appearance, a Jewish sect, he preached a radical liberation from Temple and Synagogue. This brought him into open conflict with the authorities of the Christian community, but it was the indispensable step which was needed to fit the church for the Gentile mission. Paul's conflict with the leadership of his own church was resolved in his favor (even though some of his opponents tried to renege on the agreement) and his victory represented not simply a tactical change, but rather a totally new self-understanding of the church.

1.41 The Second Founder?

Paul's role in the early church raises some serious questions. Paul has been called the second founder of Christianity, and it is not at all inappropriate to ask whether he remained true to the message of the first founder—Jesus—or whether he relativized the importance of Jesus and twisted the meaning of his message. Paul encountered embittered opposition in his own day, and in modern times the question has frequently been raised of whether Paul distorted the simple message of Jesus—the message of the fatherhood of God and the brotherhood of man—and warped it into the theory of the atonement of an angry and vengeful God by means of a bloody sacrifice. Paul has been accused of exaggerating man's guilt and despair beyond all bounds and of stripping the human being of all self-respect. His references to purity, to sexual sins, and his contrast of flesh and spirit, have led some theologians to find in him the source of that perverse hostility to the body which characterizes so much of what Augustine and the fathers of the eastern church wrote. All of these accusations have at least some foundation, and they force us to raise the question of whether Paul was a clever, if unbalanced, innovator, or, on the other hand, the privileged interpreter of Jesus.

Christians have tried to cope in a number of ways with the problems raised by Paul and his theology. The most common and successful way was that taken by Luke in his *Acts of the Apostles*: Paul is domesticated, integrated into the mainstream of church life, by ignoring his unique message—his theology of the cross and of God's gratuitous justification of the sinner. Luke and others did this, not from a deliberate attempt to silence Paul, but simply because they had developed a theology and a view of Christian faith which had no room for Paul's unique message. Others have written off Paul's Gospel of the justification of the sinner as his attempt to address the Jews of his day in terms which they could understand, and to show that the Christian faith could come to terms with the central problem of Judaism more successfully than the Jewish Law itself. Those who hold this view argue that once the Jewish Christian church ceased to exist, the term "justification" should yield to others, such as "love" and "salvific will."

But even more often, Paul's theology has been disarmed

and ignored by paying it lip service and not taking it seriously. Paul's own frequently overloaded style is to some degree at fault here, and it has led many to despair of understanding him. As a consequence, his epistles have often been used as a source of texts with which to prop up the theses of the dogmatic theology texts, or to score points in confessional debate.

1.42 Paul's Life: The Sources

Some of the difficulty we have in understanding Paul and the role he played in the early church comes from the fact that we appear to have two sources for Paul's life. On the one hand we have his own letters, and on the other we have Luke's *Acts of the Apostles*. It has been common practice up to the present day, particularly in Catholic circles, to construct a life of Paul by harmonizing these two sources; but this approach does not do justice to Paul. *Acts*, written by Luke (and remember that the name "Luke" means only "the author who also wrote the third Gospel") gives more space to Paul than to any other Apostle (although Luke never uses the term "Apostle," in speaking of Paul, in the same sense in which he uses it in speaking of the group he called "the Twelve"). A tradition dating from the second century identifies Luke as the traveling companion of Paul on some of his journeys, but this tradition is unreliable, and is a patent attempt to give apostolic or eye-witness "cover" to the third Gospel. Despite these attempts, and despite Paul's apparent importance for the author of *Acts*, there are very serious reasons for doubting the accuracy and the historicity of much of what this book has to say about Paul. First, as we will see later, it is really impossible to reconcile the account of the Council of Jerusalem which Paul gives in *Galatians* 1 and 2 with the account given by Luke in *Acts* 15. Second, *Acts* presents Paul as an *emissary* of the Apostles, in a way which Paul, as we know him from *Galatians*, would certainly not accept. Third, the author of *Acts* clearly knows nothing of the central theses of Paul's theology: both the theology of the cross and Paul's teaching on justification are virtually absent from his work. All of this means that it is only in the most indirect way that *Acts* gives us any usable information about Paul, and it means that when Luke's picture diverges from that which we find in Paul's letters, as is often the case, then we should rely only on Paul's own works.

But Paul's own letters are problematic as a source for his life, because they do not contain much biographical information. Paul's letters were a response to the concrete needs of communities which he founded and his letters reflect the difficulties which he had with these communities. Some of what Paul wrote is obscure or only partially intelligible, because we know so little about Paul's life and because we have so little historical information about these communities. This is frustrating, but we should not try to fill the gaps by writing an historical novel about Paul or by engaging in pious speculation. There is a further problem with Paul's letters, because competent scholars disagree about the number that he actually wrote. Most modern editions of the New Testament list fourteen letters as written by Paul, but modern scholarship rejects the Pauline authorship of up to seven of these. All responsible exegetes reject the Pauline authorship of *Hebrews*, of *1* and *2 Timothy*, and of *Titus*. *Ephesians*, *2 Thessalonians*, and *Colossians* are debatable, and some good scholars hold that Paul wrote them. This leaves seven letters and contemporary scholarship agrees that at least these are genuine: *1 Thessalonians*, *Galatians*, *1* and *2 Corinthians*, *Philippians*, *Philemon*, and *Romans*. In my view, attempts to reconstruct Paul's life and to understand his theology should limit themselves to these seven letters.

1.43 The Chronology of Paul's Life and Travels

We do not know when Paul was born: he could have been anywhere from about ten years younger to ten years older than Jesus. We are not even certain where Paul was born: Tarsus is mentioned as his home only in *Acts*, but since the point is not theologicially tendentious, it is possible that he did come from there. He himself had a strict Jewish upbringing, and it would seem that even though he came from the Diaspora, exact interpretation of the Law was highly prized in his family. According to *Acts*, he was a student of Rabbi Gamaliel in Jerusalem, but this is doubtful for several reasons. Gamaliel belonged to the liberal wing of rabbinic Judaism and Paul (or "Saul," as he was known at the time) certainly did not follow him in that respect. However, Paul's own writings indicate that he had received a good Jewish education and that he was thoroughly familiar with Jewish ways of interpreting the Old Testament. Paul obviously knew the popular Greek of the time and he wrote it well, and he made use of ideas which were current in the popular Greek philosophy of the day. But in his way of thinking and in his fundamental values he remained a Jew.

Paul had persecuted Christians—most probably the Hellenists mentioned above (Jews of the Diaspora who had settled in Jerusalem and become Christian). We do not know just what this persecution consisted in; the story of the men who stoned Stephen laying their garments at Saul's feet is probably apocryphal, and the story that he was on his way to Damascus to discharge a commission of the High Priest is quite improbable. We do not know what Saul's real motives were; perhaps he was going to Damascus as some kind of private vigilante. However, in about 34 A.D., as he was on his way to Damascus, something out of the ordinary happened to him, and he always interpreted it as an encounter with the risen Lord. The details of this encounter, as given in *Acts*, are probably legendary, but Paul himself leaves no doubt that it was Jesus whom he met, and he speaks of this encounter in the same way as that in which he speaks of the early appearances of Jesus to Peter, to the Twelve, to the Apostles, and to the five hundred, which he recounts in *1 Corinthians* 15. In this encounter Paul received his apostolic commission—the mission of preaching to the Gentiles the good news of Jesus Christ who saves us, apart from the works of the Law. For Paul, the revelation of Jesus on the road to Damascus meant the end of all barriers between Jewish and Gentile Christians. In that encounter, Paul was given to understand that the Lord had chosen him from his mother's womb, to make known a mystery which had been hidden from all eternity and which was now going to be revealed through him.

After this encounter, Paul presumably continued into Damascus. But apparently quite soon after that, he went off

into the area known as Arabia (not Saudi Arabia, as we know
it today, but rather the Roman province of Arabia, south and
east of Damascus, where there were both desolate regions and
some important cities). We know absolutely nothing of what
he did there. Perhaps he lived as a hermit, or perhaps he
preached in some of the cities; we have no information at all
about what he did during this period. In about the year 36,
Paul made a trip to Jerusalem; he stayed just about two weeks
and met Peter and a few of the other leaders of the community. He himself emphasizes the brevity of this stay and he insists that he did not derive the content of his preaching from
any of those who were Apostles before him—probably referring to Peter and the others whom he met on this occasion.
Paul will return again and again in our discussion of the history of the church in the first century, but it will be useful to
mention Paul's travels and achievements briefly now so that
we will have them in mind as we examine the history of the
next twenty-five years.

   After his trip to Jerusalem in the year 36, Paul probably
went to Antioch, and for the next thirteen years we have no
details whatsoever from Paul himself about his life. Obviously
he did some preaching and missionary work, because otherwise the confrontation at the Council of Jerusalem would be
inexplicable. It is possible that Paul traveled and preached in
various provinces along the southern coast of Asia Minor—
Cilicia, Lydia, Lycaonia, Pisidia—and the memory of this
might lie behind some of the events recounted in *Acts* and
later called the "First Missionary Journey." But it is more
probable that the stories and the geographical settings of this
"journey" are constructions of Luke, and that Paul preached
only in Syria and Cilicia.

   In the year 49, Paul came to Jerusalem to meet with the
other Apostles and to defend, in the presence of the Jewish
Christian church, his Gospel of freedom from the Law. This
is the event which is commonly referred to as the "Council of
Jerusalem"; there are many problems connected with it and
they will be discussed in the proper section below. But here it
is important to note that Paul always affirmed that the Law-
free Gospel which he was preaching to the Gentiles was ap-

proved at the Council. This approval was important to him, because he felt that without it, all of his apostolic work would have been in vain. Paul was deeply concerned about the unity of the church and he was pained when, in later years, some of those who had given their approval to his preaching went back on their bargain and demanded that the burden of the Law be imposed on the Gentile converts.

Later in the same year (49), Paul appeared in the city of Philippi, in northern Greece. It seems probable that he came through Asia Minor, but we are not certain of his route. He probably spent seven or eight months, working in Philippi and Thessalonica, and then came down, probably through Athens, to Corinth, where he arrived in the fall of the year 50. (This date seems quite certain and it is a pivotal one in Pauline chronology, because we can correlate it with an event of secular history—the arrival of the Roman proconsul Gallio in Corinth.) Incidentally, a much modified version of this trip appears in *Acts*, in the sections later referred to as the "Second Missionary Journey," but much of this material is undoubtedly a Lucan construction.

Paul probably remained in Corinth until the spring of 52, when he left and returned to Antioch. But his stay in this city was very brief, and we soon find him in Ephesus, on the west coast of Asia Minor, where he stayed from the middle of 52 until some time in 55. From there he wrote a number of letters: *Galatians* (probably early in his stay), and then *Philippians, Philemon, 1 Corinthians*, and part of *2 Corinthians*. From Ephesus he made at least one trip to Corinth.

In the year 55, Paul left Ephesus, probably in connection with some kind of disturbance or dispute, and he spent the next two years in Macedonia (northern Greece) and in Corinth. From Macedonia he wrote the rest of *2 Corinthians* and from Corinth, in late 57 or early 58, he wrote *Romans*. These travels, beginning with his return to Ephesus from Antioch, lie behind those sections of *Acts* which later came to be known as the "Third Missionary Journey." Perhaps early in 58 Paul went to Jerusalem, bringing with him the collection for the church there. The only account of the trip itself is in *Acts*, but in his own letters Paul does talk about preparing the collection, and he asks the various communities to appoint men to travel with him as he brings it to Jerusalem.

When Paul got to Jerusalem, apparently some kind of riot took place, and it may be that Paul was arrested and spent two years in prison in Caesarea, from 58 to 60. He may then have been transferred to Rome and have spent some time under house arrest there. We have no evidence from Paul himself about this period, and the account of the journey in *Acts* has been embroidered with a number of legendary features. Although it seems very likely for other reasons that Paul got to Rome, there is no evidence that he ever left that city. It is clear from *Romans* that Paul intended to go to Spain, but it is extremely unlikely that he ever got there. As we have seen, it is doubtful that Paul wrote *Colossians* and *Ephesians*, but if he did, they could be placed at the time of his Roman captivity. It seems likely that his stay in Rome ended in martyrdom sometime in the early sixties.

1.5 THE CHURCH FROM THE MID-THIRTIES TO THE COUNCIL OF JERUSALEM

1.51 The Role of Jerusalem

Jerusalem itself was the earliest center from which the Christian faith radiated. This may have begun when some Jews from the Diaspora, who were visiting Jerusalem on the occasion of one of the feasts, were won to the new faith and brought it back home with them. But far more important were the Hellenists, who, as we have seen, were driven out of the city and took up residence in Antioch and Damascus. From these two cities, the new faith spread into the Syrian hinterland and probably along the southeastern shore of Asia Minor. Antioch seems to have become a center of missionary activity among the Gentile population of the eastern Mediterranean basin at a very early date, and it is quite likely that it was a center of some of Paul's activity between the years 38 and 48. He probably preached at least in Cilicia, and perhaps even farther afield. It seems clear that the Christians in Antioch remained loyal to the Jerusalem leadership and that they prized their union with the mother church; but they were already embarked, without realizing it, on a collision course with the conservative Jewish Christians of the old capital.

In the thirties, the church spread in Palestine, and the communities in Galilee are probably as old as the Jerusalem church itself. The resurrection narratives in Matthew and John, and Mark's supposition that the Lord will appear in Galilee, make this virtually certain. Communities in Nazareth, Capharnaum, and Tiberias were the ones which preserved the memory of Jesus' activity there. Farther to the south, in Samaria, the communities may date from the late thirties.

The Christians of Jerusalem remained thoroughly Jewish. For them, Jesus was the Messiah, the Anointed One of Israel, and through their faith in him, they had become the loyal remnant and the authentic bearers of Israel's heritage. These Jewish Christians may have become even stricter in their observance of the Law after the departure of the Hellenists, and this undoubtedly improved their position with the non-Christian Jews of the city. And yet, for all of their overt and undoubtedly sincere loyalty to Jewish tradition, these Jewish Christians knew that God had acted definitively, once and for all, in Jesus, and that it was one's stance toward Jesus which determined one's relationship with God, in this world and in the next. Although they were not clear about this, this view of Jesus necessarily relativized the importance of Jewish Law and tradition. However, at least in the thirties and forties, there is no indication that any of the Jews in Jerusalem, Christian or non-Christian, were aware of the implicit contradiction.

It is very likely that during this entire period, Peter continued to be the recognized leader of the church in Jerusalem, even though he was to lose that position at a later date. It was probably Peter himself who constituted the group known as "the Twelve" after the resurrection, perhaps on the basis of a symbolic statement of Jesus about how his followers would judge the twelve tribes of Israel—a statement which Peter and the others interpreted literally. But "the Twelve" seem to have declined in importance very rapidly, and to have disappeared in just a few years—undoubtedly because the group was a product of the intense eschatological hope of the early days and did not long survive the demise of that hope. As early as the time of Paul's visit to Jerusalem in the year 36, they seem to have been replaced by those whom Paul calls the "pillars" of the church—probably Peter, James, and John.

1.52 Developments in Palestine in the Forties

After the departure of the Hellenists, the church in Jerusalem seems to have been left in peace by the Jewish authorities. Their observance of the Law was exemplary, but, as we have seen, there was an inner contradiction in the position of these Jewish Christians, and when this came to the surface unexpectedly, then the Jewish authorities could react swiftly and brutally. It was possibly such an episode which led to the martyrdom of James, the son of Zebedee, during the reign of Herod Agrippa (41 to 44), on the grounds that he was not a true observer of the Jewish Law.

We know very little about the liturgical life of the church during this period. There are some indirect hints in later writings, which indicate that Baptism may have been taken over from the followers of John the Baptist during this period, and its acceptance as an initiatory rite may have come about because a large number of John's disciples were entering the church. A number of Pharisees may have become Christian around the same time, and if this was the case, then we can understand that Paul's preaching of salvation without the works of the Law would have been an acute embarrassment to the Jerusalem community. It must have seemed to them that by his every move he was undermining the main apostolic task of the church—the mission to the Jews. As a matter of fact, it probably was true that Paul's preaching marked the beginning of the end for Jewish Christianity. But the tragedy of the situation was that it was only Paul's view of salvation which could prevent Jewish Christianity from falling back into sectarianism and from abandoning what was distinctively Christian in its faith. This seems, in point of fact, to be exactly what happened to Jewish Christianity even before the end of the first century.

1.53 The Church outside Palestine up to the Council of Jerusalem

We have no first-hand information about the churches outside Jerusalem and Galilee during this period, but there are a few inferences which we can draw from Paul's letters, and, with much greater caution, from *Acts*.

Even before Paul's time, Christian faith was being offered to non-Jews in Antioch and in the communities founded from Antioch, without imposing on them the burden of the Jewish Law. Paul continued this practice and, in addition, provided it with a theoretical and theological basis. It is probable that at the same time as this Law-free Gospel was being offered to pagans, *some* of the Jewish Christians outside Palestine began to draw the obvious conclusions and to give up the ceremonial and dietary laws. Paul's comment about Peter's behavior at Antioch, which may refer to this period, makes this very likely. However, there were some very strict Jewish Christians in the Diaspora communities who continued to oppose the preaching of salvation without the works of the Law, even for Gentiles. There was probably an even larger group which regarded such preaching as acceptable, as an interim measure for the Gentiles, but which insisted that the Law in its entirety was to be kept by the Jewish Christians. Obviously, in any community where there were both Jewish and Gentile Christians, this policy led to the splitting of the church into two groups, precisely at the Lord's Supper—a practice which ran counter to the very nature of the Eucharist (a sacrament the whole purpose of which is to foster unity in the church) and a practice which, for this reason, was forcefully opposed by Paul.

The Gentiles of Asia Minor, Greece, Egypt, and Rome, to whom the Gospel was now being preached, had not been living in a religious vacuum. Most of them had been devotees of the so-called mystery religions, in which they believed that through some kind of initiatory rite they shared in the power of the god, and that this showed itself in various kinds of "in-spired" behavior (ecstasies and incomprehensible speech were typical). In most of these mystery religions, the devotees also celebrated a sacred meal, and believed that through eating this meal they shared the very life of the divinity. To judge from Paul's comments about the way some of the people in his churches interpreted his preaching, Baptism must have been regarded as this kind of gift of the "Spirit"—that is, the manifest power of God—which was expected to show itself in ecstatic phenomena like those mentioned. Paul's rather strange reserve in regard to the sacrament of baptism (one might almost speak of his desire not to be associated with the sacrament as a minister) might be explained this way. He accepts the fact that Baptism is the normal way in which one enters into the Christian community, but it is possible that he wanted to distance himself from a view of baptism which had its origin in the mystery religions.

Paul also knew that there was great danger for the church in the tendency of the Gentile congregations to interpret the Eucharist or Lord's Supper as a sharing in the life of the risen Lord. This tendency led to a concentration on oneself and on the gifts one had received; it led to self-elevation and to contempt for the neighbor, and it divided the church into boastful little elites. For this reason, Paul corrected the contemporary Gentile notion of Eucharist, by insisting that it did not give a direct and immediate share in the *life* of the risen Lord, but rather a share in the cross, in his suffering and death.

This view of the sacraments as shares in divine power and divine life, which was apparently almost second nature to the Greek-speaking Christians of the eastern Mediterranean, was just as serious a danger for the early church as was Jewish sectarianism and legalistic self-salvation; and it was Paul who developed the theological insights to combat both of these dangers. In the face of the claims of the Law, he argued for the unique mediation of Jesus and the absolute sufficiency of faith for salvation. In the face of the distortions in the Gentile communities, Paul developed his theology of the cross, according to which the Christian is called to share in the suffering and death of the Lord and to find in service of the neighbor and in the building up of the community, the highest and noblest of the charisms.

Apparently from about the mid-forties, complaints began to pour into Jerusalem from Jewish and Jewish Christian communities in Syria and Asia Minor. These complaints centered on Paul and on his way of preaching the good news. As we have seen, Paul's *practice* may not have been very different from that which was common in the Antioch community as early as the mid- or late thirties. But Paul was not content to leave things on a pragmatic level, where they could be explained, or at least glossed over, on the grounds of temporary expediency. Instead, Paul developed a theology of the powerlessness of the Law to make human beings just in the sight of God. The fact that he was only drawing conclusions which were implicit in the view of even strict Jewish Christians in his day, and the fact that his conclusions were direct and immediate consequences of the life and preaching of Jesus, did not make Paul's theology any more palatable to his opponents. These Jewish Christians were apparently urging the leaders of the church in Jerusalem to use their authority and to discipline Paul. Matters were coming to a head, and the Jerusalem leadership could not avoid taking a position. This brings us to one of the most important events in the history of the church in the first century: the Apostolic Council or the Council of Jerusalem.

1.6 THE COUNCIL OF JERUSALEM

The term itself is misleading, because it implies that the meeting attended by Paul and a number of other Apostles about the year 49 was much like the later councils of the church—Nicaea, Chalcedon, Lateran IV, Trent, or Vatican II, to mention just a few. It suggests that the difference was that, although these later councils were attended by bishops who were the successors of the Apostles, the Council of Jerusalem was attended by the "original twelve Apostles" and a

few others, including Paul. But this view is simply an anachronism.

1.61 The Problem of the Council

It is very difficult to determine what kind of meeting took
place in the year 49, for a reason which is familiar to us now:
the meeting is discussed in two places in the New Testament—in *Acts* and in Paul's *Epistle to the Galatians*. These two
accounts are not only quite different in perspective and content; they are really irreconcilable, and the differences between them are important for evaluating the historical
reliability of *Acts*.

In their accounts of the Council, Luke and Paul differ in
important respects. *First*, they differ in the reasons they give
for Paul's attendance. *Second*, they differ on the nature and
character of the discussions. *Third*, they differ in their judgment about who actually made the decisions at the Council.
Fourth, they differ on the substance of the decision which was
reached and on the conditions which were imposed by the
agreement. *Fifth*, they differ on the question of the collection
of money which was to be taken up in Paul's churches and
given to the mother church in Jerusalem, and on the relationship of this collection to the later interpretation of the Council.

1.62 Why Paul Attended the Council

Was Paul summoned to Jerusalem, called on the carpet
by the Apostles, to explain what he was doing and to defend
his style of preaching? Luke's account in *Acts* does not go quite
this far, but it does seem to be the situation which he assumes.
What Luke actually says is that Paul was sent by the community in Antioch to lay a problem before the Apostles, so that
they might solve the problem and pass judgment on the question which was causing dissension in the community at Antioch—the question of whether the Jewish Law in whole or in
part was to be obligatory for the Gentile converts.

On the other hand, in *Galatians* Paul asserts that he went on his own initiative, in response to a revelation. Remarks that he makes in his letter to the *Romans*, about eight or nine years later, indicate that Paul went to Jerusalem because he was deeply concerned about the unity of the church, and because he wanted to make sure that the Gospel which he preached was the same Gospel as that which was held in the church at large. It is clear from all of Paul's letters that he had no doubt about the dogmatic correctness of his views on the Law, and he knew that his views were the only ones consistent with the faith professed by the Jewish Christians themselves. But Paul knew that the time had come for the Jerusalem church to draw the obvious conclusions and to make the definitive break with the Synagogue. This is probably what he had in mind when he spoke of going to Jerusalem in response to a revelation which he had received.

1.63 The Discussions at the Council

The pictures in *Acts* and *Galatians* are very different. In *Acts*, the Apostles (excluding, of course, Paul!) seemed to preside calmly and serenely over a meeting at which proponents of the two opposing schools presented their views and then waited obediently for a decision to be handed down by Peter and James (after they had conferred with the other Apostles). *Acts* seems to imply that Paul accepted this decision as one which had been made by the supreme authority in the church.

Paul's picture is very different. The discussions are lively and perhaps acrimonious. Paul speaks, not as a subordinate of the Apostles, ready to accept with due docility the decision handed down from on high; rather, he knows that he himself is an Apostle, inferior in no respect to those who were Apostles before him and with no less authority than they. When the decision is made, it is not handed down by Peter and James, but is a common agreement, hammered out by all of the participants.

1.64 The Decision

Superficially, *Acts* and *Galatians* would seem to be in agreement here. Both assert that the Council decided that the Jewish Law was not to be obligatory for the Gentile converts. But no sooner is this stated in *Acts* than a number of conditions, *derived directly from Jewish ritual and ceremonial Law*, are imposed on the Gentiles. They are not to eat meat which had been offered to idols; they are not to eat foods which had been prepared with blood; they are not to eat the meat of animals which had been strangled; and, finally, they were to abstain from what is sometimes called "fornication," but which certainly refers here to marriages within that degree of consanguinity which were forbidden by Jewish Law. In other words, according to *Acts*, the Gentile Christians were by no means entirely free of the Jewish Law; rather, a selection was made from elements of dietary, ritual, and marital law, and this selection was to be imposed on the Gentile congregations.

Paul's account is irreconcilable with this. He insists that the Gospel is simply the good news that we are saved without the works of the Law, and that nothing less than this was accepted by those who took part in the Council; and he insists that *absolutely no conditions* were imposed on the Gentile congregations. From other letters of Paul, it is clear that he himself is certain that this was the agreement, and it is clear that he acted on this conviction for the rest of his life. This is the most critical disagreement between Paul and Luke. It is obvious that if there *was* a written document (as Luke implies), circulated among the churches, and containing the conditions which Luke enumerates, then Paul's opponents in Galatia could have discredited him openly and publicly, simply by making that document known. Paul himself would certainly have been aware of that danger, and if such a document had ever existed, it is inconceivable that he would have written what he did in the first two chapters of *Galatians*.

There is only one way of explaining the discrepancy between these two accounts. Paul's description of the course of events at the original meeting in the year 49 must be the accurate one, although it is probable that the Jerusalem leadership at that meeting thought that they possessed an authority which Paul himself certainly did not recognize. However, at the meeting, as a result of Paul's forceful defense of his position and of the theological substance of that position, his view prevailed. But in the years that followed, some of the Jewish Christians, including perhaps important elements of the Jerusalem leadership, headed by James, may have felt that too many concessions had been made to Paul, and that at least some minimal conditions should be imposed on the Gentile Christians. These conditions would have been ignored (and would have been totally irrelevant) in the churches founded by Paul, since these were overwhelmingly *Gentile* churches. However, at least for a time, these conditions may have been imposed in those communities which were made up of both Jewish and Gentile Christians. They would have been imposed precisely in order to make it possible for the Jewish Christians to remain in one community with the Gentiles and to share the Eucharist with them. In other words, this may have been a practical arrangement, worked out for churches in Palestine and in parts of Syria, where there were a substantial number of mixed communities.

In Luke's time, it is certain that even this situation was a thing of the past. For Luke, the account of the Council of Jerusalem serves an entirely different purpose: it is a way of asserting his own theology of the church. For him, the church is an organization which is founded on the Twelve Apostles, who were the unquestioned leaders in the early period (which is, by Luke's time, a distant and almost epic past), and whose wise decisions were accepted and implemented by all of the members of the church in their time.

1.65 The Collection

Paul reports that, although no conditions were imposed on him or on his churches, the other Apostles requested that Paul's churches "remember the poor" of the Jerusalem church. Paul understood this as a request that he take up a collection in all of the churches which he had founded, and that he or others bring that money to Jerusalem and give it to the mother church there. For Paul, this collection was a matter of great importance. He was continually urging his churches to be generous, and he tried to motivate their generosity in a variety of ways. He pointed out that they were the beneficiaries of a faith which properly belonged to the Jews, but which, in the providence of God, was now being offered to them. In every respect, Paul played the part of a dedicated, clever, but very sincere fund raiser. Oddly enough, he never motivated his request by pointing to the true poverty or the real need of the Jerusalem community; rather, he saw the collection as something which would promote the unity of the church, and which would make manifest the fact that there is no longer any barrier to the presence of both Jew and Gentile in the church of Christ.

This may have been Paul's way of asserting that, whatever others had done in the years after the Council of Jerusalem, he had been scrupulously loyal to the agreements which had been made and accepted there. If this is true, then Paul's dedication to the collection was his sincere (and by no means subtle) way of affirming the validity of the agreements of the year 49.

1.7 FROM THE COUNCIL OF JERUSALEM TO THE JEWISH WAR

1.71 The Jewish Christians of Jerusalem

Some time during the fifties, Peter left Jerusalem, and the leadership of the community passed to James (not the son of Zebedee, but that other James who is known simply as "the brother of the Lord"). We do not know whether Peter left on his own initiative, or whether he was forced out of his role as leader by James and by other conservative and traditionalist elements in the community. Furthermore, we do not know where Peter went when he left. It is very likely that much later in his life he was in Rome, but it is probable that at this point, in the fifties, he went to Antioch. Paul mentions a confrontation with Peter which took place in this latter city, and it probably dates from this period. What happened was apparently this: in Antioch, Jewish and Gentile Christians had been living in harmony and celebrating the Eucharist together. When Peter arrived in Antioch, he adopted this practice; but then when (as Paul says in *Galatians*) "people from James" arrived, Peter allowed himself to be intimidated by them and reverted to the older Jewish Christian practice of refusing communion with those who did not observe the Law, and from that moment on he no longer took part with the Gentiles in the Eucharistic celebration. Paul saw the inconsistency in this practice, and he called Peter to task in the most forceful terms.

1.72 Peter's Position in the Church

Although Peter may have been forced out of his role as leader of the Jerusalem church, in the eyes of many Jewish Christians he did not lose his position of authority. The text of *Matthew* 16:18 probably does not go back to Jesus himself, but *precisely for this reason* the text is inexplicable unless, in Matthew's time (the mid-eighties), there was a church leader who claimed to be Peter's successor, and who was accepted as such by many in the church. The fact that this text appears only in Matthew's Gospel makes it likely that the group who recognized the authority of Peter's successor was made up of Jewish Christians who opposed the rigid traditionalism of James, and who, very probably, were living somewhere in Syria.

Incidentally, there are indications that there were other Jews, probably in Galilee, who belonged to neither party and who were inclined to reject the claims of both groups. There are some hints that Mark was the spokesman for such a group. Mark is quite harsh in his treatment of Peter; the crassness of Peter's denial of Jesus is presented in some detail, and Mark is quite pointed in telling how Peter failed to comprehend Jesus and his message. This would suggest that the quite worthless tradition which we find in the writings of Papias, the bishop of Hierapolis, about 130 A.D., according to which Mark was the "interpreter" of Peter, may originally have been intended to blunt the anti-Petrine bias of Mark's Gospel.

Paul's position in respect to Peter is complex. He was obviously not inclined to accept orders from Peter, and when he speaks about the Council of Jerusalem, it is clear that he met with Peter and the others as a perfect equal. Furthermore, Paul was uncompromising in his assertion that Peter had made a serious mistake (in what we would call today a matter of *dogma*) when Peter withdrew from communion with the Gentile Christians at Antioch. Finally, far from recognizing Peter as the head of the universal church, Paul affirms that Peter had been entrusted with the mission to the Jews in the same way in which he, Paul, had been entrusted with the mission to the Gentiles.

But at the same time, Paul's forceful opposition to Peter in Antioch shows that Peter was not just an ordinary Christian, but that he had a special position which was widely recognized; and it was this which made Paul's opposition so passionate and so necessary. This altercation in Antioch is a very important episode for understanding the origin and nature of papal power, even though hundreds of years would pass before anyone who could properly be called a "Pope" would appear in the church. A careful study of the background of this episode shows that neither the traditional Protestant nor the traditional Catholic polemic positions on the papacy can appeal to scripture on this point: Peter certainly enjoyed nothing like what would later be called "jurisdictional primacy" and his ignorance of the real issues involved in the question of intercommunion between Jewish and Gentile Christians does not say much in favor of his possessing infallible teaching authority. But at the same time, Peter's importance was recognized by friend and foe alike. From other events in the history of the first century, it is clear that his leadership role was based on his position among Jesus' followers during Jesus' life on earth and on the commonly accepted view that the risen Lord had first appeared to Peter.

1.73 Paul and the Jewish Christian Church

We have already seen that Paul was very active as a missionary during this period. He took seriously the agreement of the Council of Jerusalem which assigned to Peter the reponsibility for the Jews and to him, Paul, the task of preaching to the Gentiles. In attempting to fulfill this task, Paul was often opposed by groups called "Judaizers," who made trouble for him in the churches which he founded. (These were Jewish Christians, or those influenced by them, who asserted that observance of the Jewish Law, in whole or in part, was necessary for salvation.) We have no indication of whether these Judaizers were wandering Jewish Christian preachers who were acting on their own, or whether they were emissaries of the conservative Jewish Christian leadership in Jerusalem, which was in control there during all of Paul's apostolic life. Paul's reference to the "people from James," when he is speaking of the dispute in Antioch, makes this latter supposition somewhat likely, but this is very speculative. What is obvious, though, is that Paul insisted on maintaining union with the Jewish Christian church. And in this connection, it is good to note that the collection which he took up in the Gentile churches had another purpose besides the one we have mentioned. Perhaps even more, it was Paul's way of affirming that there was *one* church for Jew and Gentile alike, and that the confession of Jesus Christ as Lord means the end of this and of all other human barriers to unity.

1.74 The Jewish War

By the mid-sixties, Rome had been in control of the Holy Land for more than a century. The country was ruled by Roman military governors, known as *procurators*, and for years this position had been filled by men who were incompetent, insensitive, and brutal. The Jews were near the breaking point, and in the year 66, revolt flared in Judea. After some initial successes against the surprised Romans, the war began to go badly for the Jews, as was inevitable, and the Roman army started making preparations for the siege of Jerusalem. Shortly before the noose was drawn tight, almost all of the Jewish Christians left Jerusalem and escaped to the city of Pella, across the Jordan. In this way they avoided the suffering of the siege and the indiscriminate slaughter which followed the Roman triumph, but the break with non-Christian Judaism was final, and from that time on, they were regarded by the Jews as traitors. Although it was probably not obvious at the time, this also marked the beginning of the end for Jewish Christianity, which had tried to reconcile faith in Christ with the continued observance of the Jewish Law. As long as the Jewish Christians had been accepted by their non-Christian brethren, it was possible for them to dream of the day when all Jews would come to accept Jesus as the long-awaited Messiah. It was also possible to think that Jewish Christianity was far more important than Gentile Christianity, and that the latter was an experiment which would have to be evaluated, and that at some future date these Gentile Christians would be brought into the Jewish religious world. Perhaps the Gentile converts themselves could be allowed to conform to only minimal requirements of the Law, but their children could be raised as good, law-abiding Jews. The Jewish War of 65 to 70 put an end to these dreams and illusions. From this time on, Christianity and *religious* Judaism would have to go their separate ways, even though neither the Jews nor the Jewish Christians saw this with complete clarity until the early nineties.

Many of the Jewish Christians in Galilee and Syria, however, seem to have seen this at a relatively early period. They merged with the Gentile churches there, which were probably quite willing to observe those parts of the Jewish ritual law that would facilitate the coexistence of Jews and Gentiles in the same churches. As we have seen, this is probably the situation which Luke projected backward to the Council of Jerusalem, and which he asserted, quite anachronistically, to have been the condition imposed by the Council on all Gentile converts.

Other Jewish Christians chose to remain Jews, but to do so they had to abandon the very substance of their Christian faith: that Jesus alone is Lord, and that it is one's stance toward him and that alone which determines one's relationship to God. These Jewish Christians drifted back into Judaism, and many were probably absorbed in it, without leaving any trace of their passing allegiance to Jesus and to their belief that he was the Christ. Others (they are often called the "Ebionites") were able to continue a kind of splinter existence as sectarian groups which were neither Jewish nor Christian for several hundred years.

1.8 THE GOSPELS

Strangely enough, it was precisely in this period, beginning with the Jewish War, and extending for about twenty-five years, that Jewish Christianity produced some of the most strikingly original literature that the world has ever seen. We have already noted that the Gospels are not four lives of Jesus; rather, they are documents which reflect the hidden agenda of Jewish Christianity during the final thirty years of its existence. Parts of this hidden agenda are common to all of the Gospels, and others are found in only one or two of them. One common element, and perhaps the one which is of greatest importance in the hidden agenda, was the problem of how to cope with the delay in the second coming of the Lord.

As we have seen, the earliest Jewish Christians lived in an atmosphere of intense hope that the Lord would quickly come on the clouds of heaven. The institution of "the Twelve" was probably an expression of the intensity of this hope, and the disappearance of the Twelve as a recognizable group was probably one of the first effects of the fading of this hope. But although the hope faded, it was not abandoned; Christians merely projected its fulfillment farther and farther into the future. But such delays became more and more embarrassing, as the months lengthened into years and the years into decades. Even before the Jewish War began, Christians of the first generation were passing from the scene, and there was still no sign that the coming of Jesus was any nearer.

1.81 The Gospel of Mark

Sometime during the Jewish War (probably about the year 67), a Jewish Christian who belonged to one of the congregations in Galilee wrote a very remarkable document. It was without literary pretensions, but it was a theological achievement of enormous importance, because of its deep understanding of the death of Jesus and of the role which his death played in the salvation of all human beings. In simple stories and in an unpretentious style, Mark presents Jesus as savior, who made known a God who had been unknown—a God who takes his place in the brokenness of the world and in the emptiness of human existence, and, in so doing, destroys the barrier which human beings have erected by sin. In Mark's Gospel, Jesus is Lord, but he *is* Lord precisely as a weak human being, who is neither omnipotent nor omniscient, as these terms are usually understood. For Mark, the cross is the central event of the life of Jesus and it is not without reason that this Gospel has been called a passion narrative with a long introduction. Mark sees the cross not as the end of the life of a good man, but as the presence of God in the place and at the moment at which the world fails. And Mark sees that it is *this truth* which is confirmed by the resurrection. For Mark, as for Paul, the resurrection does not make the cross an event of the past, which has been expunged by the triumph of Easter. Rather, the resurrection makes the cross and its message the permanent rule of Christian discipleship.

Although Mark probably thought that the second coming of Jesus was imminent (perhaps in connection with the final events of the Jewish War), he really *relativizes* the second coming, so that it does not make any difference whether it happens immediately or after many years. The exact date is no longer important, because God has proclaimed his definitive "being for us" in Jesus; and Mark is convinced that this Jesus is present in and with the community when they proclaim God's word and when they celebrate the Eucharist. The very idea of a Gospel in the original sense of the word, that is, *the proclamation of the saving and transforming presence of God through Jesus, in such a way that God becomes present in and through the proclamation,* is an invention of Mark, and one of the greatest theological achievements of all time. In this sense of the word, Mark is the only one to write a Gospel. By convention, we refer to the three other documents which are printed together at the beginning of the New Testament as "Gospels," but their purpose is very different from his.

If Mark is typical, the Jewish Christians in Galilee had already drawn some conclusions about the possibility of the co-existence of the Law and the Gospel, and they had done this even before the Jewish War began. It is striking how thoroughly Pauline in substance the Gospel of Mark is—particularly so, because there is no evidence that Mark had ever read Paul (special Pauline terminology is almost entirely absent from Mark's Gospel). One of the most intriguing things about the New Testament is the fact that Paul, who asserts that he never knew Jesus before the latter's death, gives us a Christ who is no other than the Jesus of Mark's Gospel. In fact, it is in a critical reading of Mark's Gospel that we find the Jesus who anchors firmly in history Paul's Gospel of God's unconditional acceptance of the sinner—an acceptance which becomes real in the life of the sinner through faith alone.

1.82 The Gospel of Matthew

About seventeen years after Mark wrote his Gospel, another document began to circulate in the churches of Syria and Palestine. Although it is conventionally called a Gospel, it differs both in purpose and scope from Mark's Gospel.

It is often said that the author of this work was Levi, the tax collector whose conversion is recounted in the Gospel itself, and the claim has been made that Levi was another name for that "Matthew" who is mentioned in some of the lists of Apostles chosen by Jesus. But this tradition is not reliable, and critical study of the text shows that the Gospel was not written by an immediate follower of Jesus or by an eye-witness of the events of his life. It was written by a fairly conservative Jewish

Christian of the second or third generation, but apart from this, we know nothing about him except what we can conclude from the text of the Gospel itself.

Matthew (and the name means "the individual who wrote the text which is now printed at the beginning of the New Testament"—nothing more) used written sources. He made use of Mark's Gospel, and he made use of a collection of sayings of the Lord, which he also had in written form. (This collection no longer exists independently, and it is referred to in New Testament scholarship as "Q.") The Gospel was written, like the rest of the New Testament, in Greek, and it is possible that the author was a Jew of the Diaspora, who, unlike many of the others, was quite strict in his interpretation of the Law. The tradition that there was an Aramaic document which Matthew used, and which had been written by an Apostle of the Lord, is found as early as the writings of Papias, about the year 130, but, like Papias' other remarks, it has no historical value.

The author of the Gospel not only takes the Law very seriously; he is also well trained in the Jewish scriptures—that is, the Old Testament. Matthew and his community apparently read the Old Testament as a collection of predictions about Jesus, and it is more than likely that certain of the stories about Jesus which we find in the Gospel came into existence precisely to demonstrate that the ancient "prophecies" had been fulfilled. Parts of the infancy narratives probably reached their present form in this way, and although this procedure seems more than strange to us today, we have to remember that Matthew and his audience posed the question of historical factuality and reliability in an entirely different way. The question which they asked was this: "Is Jesus the fulfillment of all of the hopes and longings which we find in the Old Testament?" They wanted to answer that he *was* (as, presumably, *we also do today*), and for them (though *not* for us), the framework of prediction and fulfillment was a natural one to use.

Matthew "corrects" Mark in some subtle ways. He apparently found Mark's Jesus all too human, and certain features of Mark's picture of Jesus are played down. Jesus' strong emotional reaction to the leper's request, his family's lack of faith in him, his lack of omnipotence and omniscience—all of these features are either expunged or toned down. Matthew also shows some tendency to heighten the miraculous element in some of the miracle stories. Even more significantly, he tends to "judaize" Jesus. Although, in Mark, Jesus' attitude toward fasting, ritual ablution, and sabbath observance is quite negative, Matthew tempers Jesus' sharp attack on the Law and has Jesus make that strange statement about the binding character of even the smallest prescription of the Law, which we find in 5:17.

By Matthew's time, the estrangement between Jews and Jewish Christians had grown, and his attitude toward his non-Christian brethren is strange. It seems on the one hand as though he wants to make one last attempt to convert all of the Jews to faith in Jesus as the Messiah. But on the other hand, Matthew is embittered by the opposition of the Jews, and it is in his Gospel that we find that somber line which has been the source of so much "Christian" anti-semitism: "His blood be upon us and on our children."

Matthew organizes his material about Jesus into five great sermons, in which Jesus appears as the second Moses, who brings the new and more perfect Torah (teaching). But from one of Matthew's most important texts, it is clear that Jesus is not merely a second Moses, but that he has replaced Moses, and the text of the "antitheses" (Mt 5:21ff) shows that Matthew is aware of something about Jesus which actually conflicts with his (Matthew's) own explicit theology. Only the individual who replaces Moses *and the Mosaic Law* can possibly speak as Jesus does, and the Jesus of 5:21 cannot possibly be the Jesus of 5:17.

There is another interesting text in Matthew's Gospel, and it is important for our picture of church life and organization in the eighties of the first century. It is clear from the sixteenth chapter of the Gospel that Matthew is writing for a community which had taken Peter's role as leader of the early community very seriously. (Peter was certainly dead by Matthew's time and had probably died as many as twenty years before the writing of the Gospel.) But Matthew's statement about Jesus founding his church on Peter would be pointless, unless there was, somewhere in the church, an individual who claimed to be the legitimate successor of Peter, and who had a position something like that which Peter held in the earliest Jerusalem community. We do not know who this individual was and where he lived, and to call him a "Pope" would be an anachronism, but unless he existed, the sixteenth chapter of Matthew's Gospel is very difficult to explain.

1.83 The Gospel of Luke

At about the same time as Matthew's work, another document began to circulate among the communities in Syria and Palestine. It is conventionally known as a Gospel, but it also differed very much in purpose and scope from Mark's Gospel and these differences are underlined by the fact that the Gospel does not stand alone, but forms a two-part work, of which the second half is the book of the *Acts of the Apostles*, which we have already seen in connection with Paul's ministry. We do not know who the author of these documents was, and in this case we lack even the historically unreliable tradition of Papias. It is not until the year 180, in the writings of Irenaeus, and then in some early prefaces to the Gospels which we find about ten years later, that we find the Gospel attributed to a man named Luke, who was supposedly a Gentile convert, a doctor, and a traveling companion of Paul. This tradition is not only late; it is also very unlikely on internal grounds. "Luke" (the name means only "whoever wrote the third Gospel") never calls Paul an Apostle in the sense in which he uses that term of the others, and he evidently either does not understand or does not approve of Paul's theology, because the characteristic themes of this theology are absent from *Acts* and from the third Gospel. Finally, Luke's treatment of the Council of Jerusalem in *Acts* 15 makes any connection with Paul very improbable. Luke has equipped his Gospel with a short preface in which he makes some remarks about the careful use of written sources, and this has led some to insist that his Gospel is historically reliable and merits our full confidence. But this is a nervously defensive posture.

Luke was not an historian in the modern sense of the word. He was by no means incompetent or deliberately deceptive, but modern notions of historical method were unknown in his day, and it would be very unfair to demand that he write like a modern historian.

Luke was probably a Gentile, and it is quite likely that he was living in a church which was mixed—that is, made up of both Jewish and Gentile Christians. It is possible that before his conversion to Christianity, he belonged to the group known as the "God-fearing"—that is, those who, without taking upon themselves the full burden of the Law, had been drawn toward Judaism by its radical monotheism and its high moral code. It is certain that Luke was not a conservative Jew; like Mark he relativizes the Law, and, despite some ambiguities in his attitude toward Paul, he clearly sees in him the hero of the first generation.

Like Matthew, Luke makes use both of Mark and of "Q"—the collection of sayings of the Lord—and it is possible that he was acquainted with a variant form of the tradition which is found in John's Gospel just a few years later. Again, like Matthew, there is a sense in which he retouched Mark and "divinized" Jesus: he either softens or omits entirely those parts of Mark which show that Jesus was totally and unrestrictedly human, and that he was sometimes powerless and was not accepted by his own followers and family. But most important is another difference: although most of the narrative material in Mark appears in Luke, the stories play an entirely different role. For Mark, these stories are *proclamation*—the event in which the risen Lord is present and active in the community, and in which his call to discipleship is voiced at the moment the word about him is preached. But when Luke tells these same stories, he transforms them into "history"—the recounting of events which belong to a past which is already receding into the distance. For Luke, Jesus belongs to that past. Together with his twelve Apostles, he belongs to the heroic age of the Christian church, and this is an expression of Luke's theology. In relegating Jesus to the past, Luke has made time for the church as a religious institution; and what the church became in the decades after Luke, and in the centuries which reach from his day to the present, is to a great extent the fulfillment of his vision. Luke would be very much at home in an organized, hierarchical church.

Precisely because Jesus himself and his first followers belong to the past, and because the present is the time of the church, Luke pushes the second coming of Jesus into a future which is, if not remote, at least indefinite. In doing this, Luke made the first definitive break with early Christianity's belief in the imminent end of the world, and in doing so he offered a solution to the delay of the second coming which enabled the church to avoid this perpetual embarrassment and to get on with the business of living and of gaining converts.

In both the Gospel and in *Acts*, Luke's picture of Jesus and the early church is dictated in almost all of its details by his theology. For him, the new faith began in Galilee, but it moved resolutely and irresistibly to the centers of religious and of secular power—first to Jerusalem and then to Rome. In the Gospel, Luke concentrates on Jerusalem, and a major part of the material in his Gospel which is unique to him deals with Jesus' journey to that city. In Jerusalem, Jesus proclaims his message, and after the brief setback of the cross, all is set right again by the resurrection. (Luke never discerns any inner meaning in the cross, and never attributes to it any unique role in bringing salvation to all human beings.) According to Luke, the risen Lord appears only in and around Jerusalem, and it is there that the Apostles win their first converts (by the thousands!). It is in Jerusalem that the Apostles resolve the first great crisis of the young church—the problem of the relation of the Gentile converts to the Law.

But Jerusalem is not the ultimate goal, and about halfway through the book of *Acts*, Luke virtually abandons the other Apostles and concentrates on Paul, in and through whom the Christian message is brought, through the strange working of divine providence, to the capital of the Empire. Paul's arrival in Rome is so important an event for Luke that at that moment the book of *Acts* suddenly ends; once the Apostle of the Gentiles has arrived in Rome, Luke has no more interest in him or in his fate. But Luke has prepared for this moment even in his Gospel. His account of Jesus' suffering and death again and again shows his interest in absolving the Romans of all responsibility for the death of Jesus. From the beginning, Luke prepared Christianity for its acceptance by Rome, and thus he equipped it for its great task of converting the entire Empire.

1.84 The Gospel of John

In the early nineties, the last of the Gospels appeared. It was written after the definitive break between the Jews and the Jewish Christians—that is, after the meeting of the rabbis at Jamnia, in Palestine, in 91 or 92 A.D., at which they decided to expel the Jewish Christians from the synagogues. In many places, John's Gospel reflects this new hostility and the hardening of fronts which resulted from it.

For centuries it was supposed that the Gospel was the work of John, the son of Zebedee (and this is another part of the Papias tradition as we have seen); however, the Gospel as it stands is certainly not the work of an unschooled Galilean fisherman. It is not impossible that John, the son of Zebedee, might have been the source of some of the traditions in this Gospel, but there is no reason for assuming that this is the case.

This fourth Gospel is strikingly different from the other three. It has often been called "the spiritual Gospel," with the implication that the first three Gospels (the synoptics) give a more or less straightforward account of what Jesus said and did, while this fourth Gospel probes deeply into the meaning of his words and works. However this approach does not do justice, either to the first three Gospels or to that of John, and leaves us with the task of accounting for the striking differences. In John, for example, the public life of Jesus cannot be fitted into a period of less than two and a half years, while for Matthew, Mark, and Luke one year would be enough. Furthermore, John and the Synoptics differ on the date of the Last Supper and on the date of Jesus' death, and therefore in John the Last Supper cannot be a Passover meal. Finally, John's approach to the miracle tradition is very different. He does not use the Greek word which we usually translate as "miracle" (and which really means "a marvelous work which manifests the power of God"). Instead, he uses a word which is translated as "sign," but which really means "an event which points to the deep reality of things, far beneath surface appearances." Most of the miracle tradition, as we know it from the synoptics, is absent from John's Gospel; but on the other hand, John includes some of the most striking miracles which appear in the New Testament, and *he is the only one to include them.* Most prominent among these are the story of the changing of the water into wine at the marriage feast, and the story of the raising of Lazarus from the dead. But even the style of John's Gospel is very different. His Greek is often quite Semitic in tone, but the Gospel is beautifully written, and it is impossible to read it without being touched by its poetry and power.

In its present form, the Gospel seems to have gone through a number of stages or "editions," and it is the product of much editorial work. There are some subtle differences in theological views and emphases, and it seems that the Gospel received its final editorial retouching shortly before it became widely known in the church. In fact, this final editing may have been done in order to secure for the Gospel a wider and more sympathetic audience, by conforming its theology more closely to what was believed and expected in the church at the time.

We do not know where the Gospel was written. The tradition which asserts that it was written in Ephesus, on the west coast of Asia Minor, is not reliable. A point of origin somewhere in Syria would fit in well with the content of the Gospel and with the history of its rather slow acceptance in the church, but here we are on uncertain ground. It is sometimes asserted that the Gospel was the work of a "Johannine circle" or "Johannine community" which was responsible for the various early editions, and it is further suggested that this "circle" may have been something like a religious community or religious order. That some kind of "Johannine school" was involved in the production of the Gospel seems very likely, and it is *possible* that this group lived in something like a religious community in Syria at the time, but we have no evidence for the existence of such communities in Syria (or anywhere else) at that period, so the point remains interesting but purely speculative.

Another sign of John's originality is the solution which he gives to the problem of the delay of the second coming of Jesus—an even more radical solution than that which was offered by Luke. It seems very likely that the earlier stages or "editions" of the Gospel removed the second coming of Jesus entirely from the future and located it *within the faith experience of the individual.* In other words, for the Gospel at this stage, the second coming was not an event of either the near or the distant future. It was rather an event which had *already* taken place, as often as Jesus came to take up his abode with those who believed in him; and it will continue to happen, as men and women throughout the ages come to believe in him. The last edition of the Gospel retouched this view slightly by inserting a few passages which speak of the second coming as a future event, but the original, more radical solution is still visible.

John's picture of Jesus is strikingly original. He is an exalted, divine figure, whose speech is enigmatic, poetic, mystical, powerful. John's Jesus often begins a conversation with a man or woman in a concrete situation, but then, almost imperceptibly, Jesus begins to leave that situation and to move to a place above and beyond time, where he speaks in veiled language of the mysteries of God. John's Jesus is undoubtedly divine; in fact, he is the eternal divine person, who strides as sovereign Lord through all of the vicissitudes of life, and goes to his death, untouched at the center of his being by all that the world has tried to do to him. He is immune to the world and to its threats, because he came from beyond the world and he is returning there in his own good time. John's portrait of Jesus is certainly very far from the actual history of the man from Nazareth, but it has had a greater influence on Christian piety and on the development of christological dogma than the portrait of Jesus which we find in any of the other Gospels.

In fact, John's portrait of Jesus has been problematic, precisely because it threatens the authentic humanity of Jesus. But the fault is not that of John. It is very probable that in writing his Gospel he intended to give us a highly dramatic and symbolic meditation on the meaning of Jesus, and it is probable that he was aware of the non-historical character of the great sermons which he preached. But problems arose when these symbolic meditations and homilies were misread as history, and when it was assumed that the Gospel intended to tell exactly what Jesus had said and done. John was, in this sense, "historicized" by the later church, in a way not unlike that in which Mark's Gospel was historicized by Luke. Those who did this were quite unaware of what they were doing, because as the Gospel moved into the Greek-speaking world of the second century, there were few around who understood the literary forms in which Jewish Christians had articulated their faith.

1.9 THE CHURCH IN THE YEAR 100

The church of the year 100 was no longer that small group of men and women whose hopes had been shattered on a spring afternoon of the year 30 or 31. And the church of the year 100 was no longer that same group, as they came to share their experiences of their Lord who now lived, and who was the basis of their new-found hope. The church of the year 100 was no longer the Jewish sect, with headquarters in Jerusalem, which Jesus' followers had organized in the first year or two after his death, and which was to remain within the framework of contemporary Judaism for almost forty years. The church of the year 100 was no longer the charismatic community, living solely out of the power of the preached word about the cross and resurrection—that is, it was no longer the community which Paul had striven to build through his preaching from the late forties to the late fifties. But the church of the year 100 differed from each of its predecessors, not because it had lost the pristine purity of its faith, and not because it had undergone essential change. Rather, it differed from each of its predecessors *because it was still in the process of coming to be.* And although that process was not complete by the year 100, it was well under way, and now is the time to enumerate the different aspects of that development.

1.91 The Growth of the Church

It is impossible to come up with any reliable numbers, but in less than a decade the church had spread to Damascus and Antioch, and it seems likely that Paul had already preached in Cilicia, along the far southeastern shore of Asia Minor, before the year 49. In the course of the fifties, Paul brought the good news to the western coast of Asia Minor and down into mainland Greece. From Corinth, in the year 58, he wrote a letter to the church in Rome, and it is probable that the community there had been founded as much as a decade before that time.

1.92 A Church for Jews and Gentiles

The church was no longer a Jewish sect; in fact, by the year 100, distinctively Jewish Christianity had already left the mainstream and had taken a course which the later church would stamp as heretical. But the church had emerged from the Jewish cocoon, not because it had departed radically from Jesus' teaching. Its emergence was due to Paul, who reflected on his life as a Pharisee and on certain experiments in the Jewish Christian Diaspora communities of Antioch and Damascus, and discovered something which was implicit in Jesus' message but which had apparently escaped Jesus' earlier followers who were the founders of the Jerusalem community. This "something" was the fact that Jesus was the sole mediator between God and human beings, and that it was faith in him alone which saved, and not adherence to the Jewish Law. The success of Paul's interpretation in the years before and after 70 A.D. may have led to the increasing isolation of those Jewish Christians who wanted to have it both ways, and it may have been instrumental in pushing that group out of the mainstream. In any case, by the year 100 it was clear that the future of the church lay with the Greek-speaking world. Paul had given Christianity the theological equipment it needed if it was to become a worldwide faith. Paradoxically, the method which he used to achieve that goal virtually guaranteed that the characteristic themes of his theology would be forgotten. We can see this happening before the year 100, and it is very clear in three letters, written shortly after the turn of the century, which claimed to be the work of Paul, but which were really written by others who came long after him. These later followers revered him as a great figure of the past, even though they did not understand the central themes of his theology. The letters referred to here are the so-called *Pastoral Epistles*: *1* and *2 Timothy* and *Titus*.

1.93 Church Organization

The church of the year 100 faced an enormous missionary task and it could not have coped with such a task without becoming more tightly organized. The charismatic communities founded by Paul, in which real authority belonged to the Spirit and was verified by tangible manifestations of his power, were clearly on the wane. In these Pauline communities there had been no clear distinction between clergy and laity, although there were (particularly in Philippi) some members of the laity who clearly exercised a leadership role and who took greater responsibility for the community. But really all of the members of these churches seem to belong to what we would call today a *lay priesthood*. However, Paul's own experience of the confusion and disorder in such communities led him to search for criteria which might be used to judge supposed manifestations of the Spirit. His preaching of the cross was partially motivated by his desire to find such a criterion; and it was in the light of this preaching that he argued that the most convincing manifestation of the Spirit was the desire to build up the community of believers in an orderly and therefore effective way. As Paul's apostolic life drew to a close, he began to see that his churches needed some members who would take responsibility for the community as a whole, and who would therefore be given special authority to lead and to guide. To refer to this group, he chose a word with purely secular overtones—a word which meant something like "manager" or "director"—and it seems probable that he deliberately avoided the word which we translate to-day as "priest." It is possible that these "directors" and the institution as such might have been derived from Hellenistic religious models, and in some of Paul's communities this is even probable. In other communities the authority structure of the local synagogue may have provided the model, although it is worth noting that the synagogues were presided over by "elders" and this word does not appear, in the technical sense, in those seven letters which are undoubtedly Pauline.

Although Paul's communities moved from an initial charismatic period toward greater organization, this does not seem to have been the case with the Jerusalem community. Here they probably followed contemporary Jewish models, and authority and organization seem to have developed in the earliest days. It seems clear that Peter exercised a position of authority in the mother church until the Council of Jerusalem, and that shortly thereafter he was replaced by James. The fact that the Jerusalem church had a single head from the beginning, and not merely a collective leadership, may have provided a model for those churches in its sphere of influence, which would have included the churches of Palestine as well as some of the non-Pauline churches of the Diaspora, including Rome, if Peter was ever there. In any case, as the first century drew to a close, an institution with the somewhat pretentious title of "monarchical episcopacy" was developing. This meant that in each local church there was one individual who had final authority and responsibility. This form of "office" in the church was by no means universal, even by the year 120, but it was spreading, and it was obviously the institution which would prevail.

1.94 A Church for the Future

The church of the year 100 was equipped theologically and sociologically for the enormous task which faced it. It had a clear sense of its own identity, and this sense of identity had already found its way into the written word—in the letters of Paul and in the four Gospels. About the year 1900, Protestant historians in Germany coined the phrase "early Catholic" to describe the church of this period. Those who coined it implied that the church of the year 100 had already moved quite far from its golden age and in the direction of the organized juridicism of the later Catholic church. In this sense it has recurred in Catholic/Protestant controversy up to the present, and Catholics have often rejected it because of its connotations. But if it is stripped of its pejorative overtones, it can be a useful term to describe the church of this period. By the year 100 the church had been in the process of discovering its identity for about seventy years, and by the year 100 it had assumed many of the features which would characterize it during the more than fourteen hundred years which would pass before the Protestant Reformation.

It is not certain to what degree the monarchical episcopacy had developed in Rome itself by this time, and to refer to that Clement, whose name is traditionally associated with a letter from Rome to the church in Corinth about the year 96, as the third Pope is certainly an anachronism. But it is clear that the church of Rome, basing itself on the commonly accepted tradition that Peter and Paul had died there, claimed to exercise an authoritative role in regard to at least one church in the east, before the end of the first century. This was by no means a claim to exercise jurisdiction in the proper sense (the power to make laws binding in conscience), but it was still a kind of primacy, and we can say that the first steps had already been taken toward the institution of a supreme bishop in the church, who bears special responsibility for the whole church, and with whom each local church should be in communion.

By the year 100 the church was no longer grappling with the problem of Jewish versus Gentile Christianity; that problem had been solved, in theory about fifty years before, and in practice during the last thirty years of the century. The church had chosen (as it would at other privileged moments in the future) the way of *Exodus*—away from the old and the secure, toward a new world full of uncertainty and risk. At its deepest level, this decision was motivated by the insight of those early Jewish Christians, who saw that the universal claim and offer and demand of Jesus Christ, could not be encompassed by the religious vision of Judaism, and who made (as is clear in the case of Paul) a very painful break with the past.

The rule then, and ever since, has always been the same (and has often been forgotten): the church is never nearer to its Lord than when it abandons the pseudo-religious security of its past, and the support of secular or political power in the present, so that it may turn to the future, relying solely on the promise of God, the presence of the Lord, and the power of the Spirit. In those parts of the New Testament which were written by the year 100, the church had received a priceless gift: the critical norm which would enable it to reform and to judge itself for as long as its sojourn on earth was to last. When the New Testament is read and understood, the church is called again and again to its task of being the wandering people of God, who confidently face both life and death, strengthened solely by the power of his word.

2

The Church in the
Second and Third Centuries

2.1 INTRODUCTION

By the year 100, the church had developed most of the institutional forms which would equip it to fulfill its task in a world very different from that in which it came into being. During the second and third centuries, converts swelled the ranks of the Christians, but no changes occurred which were even remotely as radical as those which had taken place during the first century. However, during this period, the church experienced intermittent attacks by the Empire, and had to cope with even more serious problems, posed by a quasi-religious movement called Gnosticism, which threatened it from within.

2.2 THE BEGINNING OF PERSECUTION

It was by no means obvious that the Roman government should persecute Christians. Jesus himself was not a political revolutionary, and Paul, certainly the most profiled Christian of the first century, had urged his readers in Rome to be obedient to civil authority in a way which is very embarrassing to modern proponents of a "theology" of revolution. About twenty years after Paul died, Luke tried, in his Gospel, to exonerate the Romans and to absolve them of guilt in the matter of Jesus' death, evidently in the attempt to make the new faith acceptable to the citizens and rulers of the Empire.

Furthermore, Christianity was not the only faith to compete with Roman civil religion. There were scores of other religions practiced throughout the Empire, and yet Christianity was virtually the only one to be persecuted. The various pagan faiths were welcomed into the Roman pantheon, and Judaism, which wanted no such welcome, was protected and even accorded some privileges. What was it about Christianity which led to the violent persecution of its adherents?

There were a number of factors. First, and most important in the long run, was the *exclusivity*, the absoluteness of Christianity's claim. Christians were unwilling to have their God take his place with other gods in the pantheon. And because there was only one God and Father, there was only one Lord, his Son, Jesus Christ. No hero, and above all, no Emperor, could take his place, and he was the one way of salvation. There could be no divided loyalties.

In a state where the official gods served to guarantee peace, prosperity and public order, to choose the Christian God was not simply an act of religious allegiance; it was a political statement as well and was so interpreted by the Roman authorities. From our point of view it may seem strange that these authorities were unable to make a clearcut distinction between loyalty to the state and religious allegiance, but in their day no one had ever dreamt of the distinction between church and state, between religion and civic duty. In fact, the notion that one's belief in God is independent of one's willingness to assume the duties and obligations of a citizen is distinctly modern and would probably have surprised most of the founding fathers of the American republic. In this connection it would be interesting to ask if even today, when the concept of the totally secular state seems to be in peaceful possession of the field, civic virtue is really its own reward. Is it possible that the only enduringly valid motive for civic virtue, as well as for all other morally good activity, public or private, is the belief in God? Such questions are not popular today, but precisely for that reason they should be asked.

2.21 Early Persecutions

The first persecution of Christians in Rome took place under the Emperor Nero, who ruled from 54 to 68. But what happened under Nero was less a persecution than a single brutal act on the part of one of the more degenerate Emperors of the first century. The background of the events was this: In the year 64, fire swept through large parts of the city of Rome and the rumor spread that Nero himself had had the fire set in order to make room for his grandiose building plans. Nero desperately needed a scapegoat—an individual or group who could be blamed for the fire—and he found that scapegoat in the Christian community of the city of Rome.

It has often been pointed out that the Christians were an obvious choice because the populace despised them and was ready to blame them for any and every disaster which struck the city. Christians had done nothing to incur this hatred; they were hated because of a very basic, though most unattractive fact of human nature: their faith was new and they themselves were different. They professed a high and demanding ethical code, and, even worse, many of them lived their lives in accordance with it. Furthermore, in a world where pagan religious practice, no matter how devoid it might be of religious substance, still touched every facet of public life, Christians were easily identifiable, and despised for being different.

Life was harsh and brutal in mid-first century Rome. Hopes had been high two generations before, when Augustus had assumed supreme power as first Emperor, and had promised to restore the ancient glory of Rome. But the dream was short-lived, and the line of Emperors from Augustus to Nero had more than its share of perverts and homicidal maniacs. The whole world seemed to be in the grip of an implacable destiny, and individuals felt powerless to alter their fate. As always, this led to a growing sense of frustration and hopelessness. When masses of people are held in the grip of growing despair, they look for someone to blame, and they find that person or persons among those who are different, and, preferably, weak and defenseless. Nero capitalized on this sentiment, and this was to be the pattern for over two hundred years.

After Nero, Roman Christians were apparently left in peace for about thirty years. In the year 95, a brief persecution flared up under Domitian, but this again was not systematic and the reasons for it are not at all clear. It was not until early in the next century, during the reign of Trajan (98 to 117), that we find the first persecution of Christians decreed, or at least approved by a Roman Emperor.

2.22 Trajan's Letter

At some point between the years 110 and 115, the Roman writer Pliny, who was at the time governor of Bithynia, a Roman province in Asia Minor, wrote to the Emperor Trajan, and asked his advice about appropriate legal action to be taken against Christians. It seems clear, both from Pliny's letter and from Trajan's response, that punitive action was already being taken against Christians in many parts of the Empire, but Pliny apparently wondered about the legal justification of the punishment being imposed on them. He asked the Emperor if the very fact that one was a Christian merited punishment, or whether charges could be brought only if there were some overt action on the part of Christians which threatened public order.

Trajan's answer was in the form of a private letter, in which he made a number of points that would be very important in coming years. He told Pliny that the very fact of being Christian merited punishment, but he added that there was no need to hunt Christians down and that, above all, no one should be punished on the basis of anonymous denunciations. Pliny mentioned that if those who were brought before him as Christians were willing to give up their faith, he pardoned them, and Trajan agreed with this practice. Pliny further noted that when Christians refused to give up their faith, he threatened them with death, and if they persevered in the faith, then he had them executed. He defended this conduct by saying that, regardless of what else they might be guilty of, their stubbornness in the face of authority should be punished; Trajan approved this practice as well.

The exchange of letters between Pliny and Trajan was private, but the content of the letters soon became widely known, and Trajan's approval of Pliny's practice took on the character of law. As a result, for almost two hundred years, even in periods when the Roman state took no active role in the persecution of Christians, the legal position of the latter was insecure. In the eyes of authority, the very fact of being Christian made one's loyalty to Rome questionable.

This was the situation which prevailed during most of the remaining years of the second century. There were no organized persecutions throughout the Empire. Mobs could easily be incited almost everywhere to attack Christians and to denounce them to the public authorities, and famous martyrs like Ignatius of Antioch (killed in 109) and Polycarp (killed in 165) were victims of the anti-Christian hatred of such mobs. Roman officials, either for personal reasons, or to curry favor with the populace, often staged their own persecutions in the areas they controlled, confiscating the property of Christians and subjecting them to torture and death. Apparently the persecutions we know of in some detail from Lyon in Gaul in 177 and from Numidia in Africa in 180 come under this heading. But in much of the Empire, throughout the second century, Christians were able to lead more or less normal lives. They had no legal security and they were always vulnerable to outbreaks of hatred on the part of fanatical mobs, but they did not have to face a unified and organized assault on the part of the state as such.

2.3 CHRISTIAN INTELLECTUAL LIFE IN THE SECOND CENTURY

As we have already seen, much of the New Testament had been written before the year 100, including the four Gospels, the letters of Paul, and a few of those letters attributed to him but actually the work of later followers. During the second century there was a vast increase in the literary output of Christians. Although Christianity had originated within Judaism, in this respect the two faiths differed. The Jews had the Old Testament, but this document had come into existence over a period of about eight hundred years, and apart from commentaries on and paraphrases of the Old Testament, and the writings of Philo and Josephus, Israel produced little other literature. However, Christians took to writing early in their history, and in this fact something essential about Christian faith comes to light.

Christianity was an essentially missionary faith. It was not content to remain accessible, open to those who might be drawn to it because of the high moral code of those who professed it. Rather, it sought converts aggressively and tried from the beginning to adapt its message to those who came from cultural backgrounds very different from that of the world in which Christianity was born. Furthermore, and even more important, Christians could not be content with preserving tradition, in the sense of the memory of miraculous events of the past. The resurrection is central to Christian faith, not because it is a remarkable past event, but because it is the basis of our knowing and proclaiming that Jesus *lives* and cannot be relegated to the past. The New Testament was written, not out of the need to cultivate religious nostalgia, but out of the need to relate Jesus Christ to the contemporary concerns of Christians during (in the main) the latter half of the first century. As Christians turned to new and different audiences, they *had to write*. There was no single cultural or ethnic group which could serve as the bearer of their tradition, and they had to engage in the struggle for the minds and hearts of men and women of other traditions who had very different ways of thinking and of posing and answering the fundamental questions of life.

2.31 The Apostolic Fathers

The earliest Christian writings which did not gain entry into the New Testament were actually written before the New

Testament itself was completed, and it is interesting to raise the question of why some works got into the New Testament and others did not. Earlier ages had a ready answer: some were the work of Apostles or their immediate followers, and they became part of the New Testament; others were the work of good and holy men who were not Apostles, and they did not. The problem, of course, is that we know now that, with the exception of the authentic writings of Paul, there is probably nothing in the New Testament which was written by anyone who could be called an Apostle in the accepted sense of the word. The decision on which books were to gain entry into the canon, the officially accepted list of New Testament books, was made by the church in the course of the first four centuries, apparently on the basis of erroneous views about the authorship of the works in question.

The earliest non-New Testament Christian writings are, like many of the New Testament writings, *epistles*, that is, more or less public or open letters to groups of Christians, urging them to maintain unity or to be steadfast in the face of persecution. The so-called *First Epistle of Clement to the Corinthians*, dating from about the year 96, is a letter from the church in Rome to the church in Corinth, urging the members of the latter church to be of one mind and spirit, as Paul had exhorted them forty years earlier. Some traditions identify the author as Clement, supposedly the third successor of Peter as Bishop of Rome, but this tradition comes from about the middle of the second century and may have apologetic motives. Furthermore, it is not at all certain that the institution of monarchical episcopacy had been adopted in Rome at this early date, and it is certainly an anachronism to refer to Clement as the third Pope. On the other hand, this letter does show that the church in Rome claimed and was accorded a kind of authority in overseeing the other churches and in calling them to task when they failed.

Another specimen of early Christian literature dates from about fifteen years later. During the reign of Trajan (98 to 117), Ignatius, the bishop of Antioch, was sent to Rome to face martyrdom. On his way he wrote seven letters to the leading churches of Asia Minor, and these letters are most remarkable in their expression of the deep joy which he felt at being allowed to face martyrdom for Christ. At the same time they give us a valuable insight into the organization of the church in at least some of the congregations in Asia Minor about the year 110. It is obvious from these letters that the institution known as "monarchical episcopacy" had taken over everywhere in the area with which Ignatius was familiar, and Ignatius clearly sees the bishop as the one with whom all members of the congregation must be in agreement, and as the one who guarantees unity and harmony in the congregation. The fifty years which separate the death of Paul from the death of Ignatius saw developments more far-reaching than any which occurred during the remaining nineteen hundred years.

From a period shortly after this time, we have a long letter from Polycarp, bishop of Smyrna, to the Philippians. The letter has always attracted much interest, because, according to a later tradition, the author had known John, "the Apostle," when he, Polycarp, was a young man. But a careful comparison of the relevant writings and traditions shows that it is very difficult to know for certain who this "John" was—that is, whether he was John, the son of Zebedee, or another John who was a leading figure in one of the churches in Asia Minor, possibly Ephesus. Polycarp himself died as a martyr in the arena at Rome, probably not far from the year 155.

From about the same period, or possibly a decade or two earlier, comes the *Didache* or the *Teaching of the Twelve Apostles*. We know nothing whatsoever about the author, but the work is interesting because of what it reveals of liturgical practice and church organization toward the middle of the second century. From about the same period we have a strange work, called *The Shepherd*, by a certain Hermas. It is a highly allegorical account of the meaning of baptism, and it raises the question of the possibility of reconciling to the church those who have sinned seriously after baptism. The document is very important for understanding the early history of the sacrament of reconciliation (penance).

2.32 The Apologists

About the year 150, a new type of writing appeared in the work of the *Apologists*. This was a very important development, because for the first time Christians did not confine themselves to exhorting each other to union and steadfastness in faith. Rather, the Apologists undertook to defend and explain the faith to the cultivated classes in the Empire. The most famous among them, Justin, who died at Rome as a martyr about 165, was obviously well-trained in the Greek philosophy of the day, and used it in his attempt to show that Christianity was the best and the truest of all philosophies.

2.33 Heresy in the Second Century

At about the same time, other Christians turned to the task of defending the faith against distortions from within—that is, against heresy. It is clear that as early as New Testament times, some Christians abandoned the common faith of the church and developed strange and esoteric doctrines. They were frequently able to attract great numbers of followers because of the strict asceticism which they practiced—something which appealed greatly to Christians at the time.

One of the more famous of these heretics in the second century was Marcion, who came to Rome about the year 140. Marcion taught a peculiar doctrine which distinguished between the God of the Old Testament, who created the world, but who was a God of hatred and revenge, and the God of the New Testament, the God of love, and the Father of Jesus Christ. As a consequence of this view, Marcion rejected the Old Testament in its entirety, and he carefully pruned the writings of the New Testament, in order to excise what he regarded as Jewish additions and distortions. He was left with the writings of Paul and with part of the Gospel of Luke. According to Marcion, Jesus was not truly human, but only *seemed* to have taken a human body, and it was this very fact which made it possible for him to triumph over death. Marcion's theology is typical of Greek thought at the time, in its contempt for matter, flesh, and the human body, and in this it resembled almost all of the early Christian heresies. At times this way of thinking made serious inroads even among Christians, even though, in the formal sense, they remained orthodox believers all of their lives. Just how dangerous the Greek philosophy of the day could be for Christian faith was evident in a movement called *gnosticism,* which involved the church of the second century in a life and death struggle.

2.4 THE GNOSTIC CRISIS

Gnosticism was not a religion, but rather a movement, or, even better, a tendency or style of thinking about God and about the human condition. But it was precisely this fact which made it dangerous: it was not a competing religion from which Christianity could distance itself, but rather a way of thinking which could infect Christianity from within.

The gnostic movement was never systematically organized and the leaders of the movement never agreed on one set of teachings which were binding on or common to all gnostics. In general, gnosticism, the origins of which go back to pre-Christian times, was a synthesis of some classic themes of Greek thought, which can be found even in some of Plato's writings. There are five characteristic themes which recur in the works of almost all of the gnostics. *First,* God is not only immutable, but he is remote, infinitely separated from the world and without immediate contact with it. This must be the case, because otherwise God would be contaminated by the world, and would share in its weakness and limitations. *Second,* since God cannot touch the world directly, the only contact that the world has with him is through intermediate beings who are, in some way, a reflection of him or emanate from him, pour out of him, without affecting him or diminishing his reality in any way. Some of the gnostic teachers posited great hierarchies of intermediate beings who mediated between God and man and who merited our attention and even worship. *Third,* the souls or spirits of men and women are sparks which emanate from or reflect the divine being. They are the last and least of all the emanations and they have been imprisoned in the dark and confining world of matter and flesh. The human body is ignoble and is the source of ignorance and sin; it conspires ceaselessly against soul and spirit and does all in its power to drag them down to its own level. *Fourth,* true salvation consists in the liberation of the soul from matter, flesh, and the body so that the soul can return to God. *Fifth,* this liberation consists essentially in, and is effected by, an esoteric knowledge of hidden mysteries, which are revealed only to an elite (the gnostic teachers themselves!). This knowledge (*gnosis* in Greek) is what gave the movement its name.

2.41 An Unchristian Philosophy

The problem with gnosticism consisted precisely in the fact that it was not a competing faith. When, in the early years of the second century, the church began to turn to those with intellectual pretensions, people with gnostic tendencies joined the church in considerable numbers, and a kind of half-baptized gnosticism constituted a mortal danger for the church through much of the second century. Particularly insidious was the fact that gnosticism used much of the same terminology as Christian faith, even though these words were given entirely different meanings. But gnostic doctrine was totally unchristian. It effectively denied the humanity of Christ, because the very symbol of that humanity, the body of Christ, was, according to gnostic doctrine, a sign of alienation from God. Further, the gnostics rejected the Old Testament, finding in it the story of the evil god, who had created the world and matter, flesh and the body, and who was responsible for imprisoning the spirits of human beings in the body. This evil god of the Old Testament was conquered by the true God, who was manifest in Jesus Christ. Gnostic teaching was evidently dualistic—it was a belief in two divine beings—and it argued that Christ's essential work was the conquest of the vengeful and evil god of the Old Testament.

Perhaps the most serious problem with gnostic teaching and practice was one which was not always noticed at the time: it propagated a false other-worldliness which effectively exempted the real material world of human existence from the offer and the claim of God. The asceticism which it proposed, and which won it so many adherents, was essentially a flight from the world and a rejection of the world. As was clear from the lives of many of the so-called gnostic elite, such an ascetical rejection of the world can easily turn into a life of unbridled sexual excess, precisely because the world and the body are without inner meaning, and what one does with one's body has no effect on the life of the spirit.

The danger presented by gnosticism was not immediately perceived, and at times good Christians made harmful compromises with gnostic doctrine. It was not until shortly before the middle of the second century that the church mobilized to fight on all fronts. The church in Rome took a leading role in identifying those gnostic teachers who came to that city and in expelling them from the church if they persisted in their teaching. In Irenaeus, bishop of Lyon, the church found a worthy defender of Christian orthodoxy, and his work *Against the Heresies* was probably the single factor which contributed most to the collapse of "Christian" gnosticism before the end of the second century. Irenaeus had read the works of all the gnostics who were known in the West, and he refuted them in detail.

2.42 Tradition and the Scriptural Canon

The conflict with gnosticism was important, not simply because the integrity of Christian faith was at stake, but also because the battle against gnosticism forced the Christians to raise two questions about the relationship of the church of the first generation to the church of all later periods in history. The first question was that of *tradition:* how and from whom is the authentic faith handed down, and how do Christians in every age distinguish this authentic faith from heresy? The second question was that of scripture: what writings belong to the official list of those which record the revelation of God and which are therefore normative for Christian life at all times? To the first question, Irenaeus and others answered that only that teaching which Christ had entrusted to his Apostles and which had been handed down through their

successors could be considered authentic. This teaching constituted a *rule of faith,* and it was the common possession of
those bishops who remained united with that church which
traced its origins back to Peter—the church of the city of
Rome. As would so often be the case during its long history,
those periods in which the church had to face serious threats
from within and without were the very periods which contributed most to the development of the primacy of the Bishop of
Rome.

The second question was that of which books really belong to the Old and New Testament scripture, and it was one
which was answered gradually, over the course of the three
hundred years after the death of Paul. This obviously does
not mean that the church was without the New Testament for
the first three centuries of its existence. The Gospels of Matthew, Mark, and Luke were known and regarded as normative in most Christian communities by the end of the first
century, about the same time as the letters of Paul were being
collected, copied, edited and distributed. It took John's Gospel longer to win acceptance, but probably by the year 150 it
was known and regarded as canonical in most areas of the
church. In the early years of the second century, a number of
the so-called "catholic" epistles—prominent among them
were *1 Peter* and *James*—had won acceptance, probably on the
grounds that they were the work of Apostles.

However, it is true that during much of the second century, some works were included in scripture which later lost
this status and are not recognized as canonical today. Furthermore, a few books which we count as scriptural today
were not recognized as such then—notable here, of course, is
2 Peter, which was probably not written until after the year
130; but even *Hebrews,* which, although not Pauline, was written at a much earlier date than *2 Peter,* did not win recognition
until the latter half of the century, and its entry into the canon
was not universally acknowledged. In fact, it was not until the
year 367 that the list of scriptural works which was published
by Athanasius, bishop of Alexandria, was generally accepted,
and this is the list which is still recognized by almost all Christians today.

What is significant in the church's reaction to the gnostic crisis is that it was then, in the last half of the second century, that the question of the canon was first raised and the first attempt was made to give an answer. As we have already noted, Christian writers of the second century (and long after) attributed apostolic authorship to some works which modern critical scholarship locates in the early years of the second century, and to other works which, though written in the first century, dated from a period long after the death of the last immediate followers of Jesus. All we can say today is that the canon which took form toward the end of the second century was not only based on criteria which we today would regard as suspect; it was also somewhat indistinct around the edges. At its core were works which were essential for the self-understanding of the church in the last half of the first century, but it also contained works which represented the views, not of the church at large, but of smaller communities within it, and which later won acceptance only because of the legend of apostolic origin. It was this legend which made it possible to strip them of their particularism and to interpret them in a way acceptable to the church at large.

The problem of the canon is not an easy one to resolve. The church and the canon of scripture always stand in a relationship of mutual dependence. The church is the community which discovered itself and came to full awareness of its nature and destiny in the act of writing these books, and which, for this reason, regards these books as normative throughout its history. At the same time, these books were written in the church, and, in a certain sense, by the church, and the decision to regard them as normative is an act of the church and an event of church history. Church and scripture are correlative concepts: each includes the other in its definition.

2.43 Hellenizing the Gospel

The lines against gnosticism were most clearly drawn in the western half of the Empire, simply because anyone who wished to make a name for himself and secure a following in any walk of life, including religion, arrived in the capital sooner or later. But there was another reason for which the lines were drawn more clearly in the West. Like all successful heresies, gnosticism filled certain important needs, and apparently the orthodox (that is, *accepted*) theology of the East had already gone far in the direction of filling these same needs. The great eastern theologians lived under the spell of Plato, and philosophically they were close to the contemporary form of his thought which was known as Middle Platonism. Most of them shared with this philosophy at least a strong suspicion of and contempt for spatial and temporal reality, for matter and for the body, and they were predisposed to find salvation in an esoteric knowledge which would be accessible to an elite. Some of them, for example Clement of Alexandria, went so far as to speak of a "Christian gnosis." It would not be fair to accuse Clement of compromise with gnosticism, but it would be accurate to speak of a form of Christianity which shared many of the concerns and interests and desires that made gnosticism popular at the same period. Obviously this could lead to serious difficulties, and nowhere is this clearer than in a statement of the same Clement of Alexandria, an orthodox Christian teacher who had founded a theological school in Alexandria toward the end of the second century. Clement affirmed that the human nature of Jesus enjoyed a perfect *apatheia,* a perfect immunity against all of the ills and limitations of ordinary human existence. This not only comes dangerously close to denying the authentic humanity of Jesus; it has really gone over the edge. Clement, like so many of the theologians of the eastern church after him, had difficulty coping with the authentic humanity of Jesus. These theologians are formally orthodox, because they always affirmed the reality of Jesus' humanity, but their orthodoxy was endangered because they were never able to find any function for that humanity to fulfill.

It is developments like these which raise the question of the so-called *hellenization* of the Gospel, and it is appropriate to discuss this problem briefly here, at the end of the section on the gnostic crisis. When the term was coined at the end of the last century, it was used in a negative and pejorative sense.

The implication was that when the Gospel was preached to the educated classes of the eastern Empire, from the second century on, use was made of ways of thinking and speaking which were essentially alien to the Christian message and which led to fundamental changes in the content of Christian faith. It was implied that the Christian message was not only adapted, but that it was distorted in the process.

The problem, of course, is that the Gospel cannot be preached to people without using a language which they understand; it is inevitable that in this process, the preaching of the Gospel will be influenced by that language, and the question of where the line is to be drawn is not an easy one to answer. There is one extremely important, though often neglected fact about the theology of the East from the end of the first century, which indicates that the line was not always drawn in the right place: the central themes and the characteristic theses of Paul's theology seem to have gone underground, if not to have been entirely lost, during virtually the entire Greek patristic period. Paul's notion of God's utterly gratuitous acceptance of the sinner, and his notion of faith as our acceptance of precisely that—these key elements of Paul's thought are virtually absent from the works of the Greek fathers. Characteristically, a deep understanding of and sympathy with Mark's Gospel and with the theology of the cross which it contains are absent as well. Mark's Gospel had already been written off as a summary of Matthew, and one which lacked the literary grandeur of the original. For the Greek mind, God, as he is presented by both Mark and Paul, is far too involved and engaged in the negativity of human existence, to the point of sharing in it and being implicated in it on the cross of Christ. And according to Paul, man is too alienated from God, not simply or even mainly in the realm of matter and body, but above all in the domain of mind, thought and intention as well. Platonic thought was not at ease with either of these views, and it seems that at least in these two respects Platonic thought triumphed. These problems were far less serious in the western half of the Empire, and western theology was always more able to cope with the real humanity of Jesus. The sharp western reaction against gnosticism was typical of this, as was the fact that Irenaeus, although he spoke and wrote in Greek, was bishop of a Gallo-Roman city, and obviously shared these distinctively western concerns.

2.5 CHURCH LIFE TOWARD THE END OF THE SECOND CENTURY

This would be a good place to summarize some changes in church organization, in doctrinal development, in sacramental theology, and in popular piety, which occurred during the second century.

2.51 Church Organization

First, during the second century, the church became more tightly and more hierarchically organized as a result of the gnostic crisis. Before the middle of the century, the institution of monarchical episcopacy had already become universal. The problem of dealing with gnosticism and with other heretical movements on the basis of a uniform understanding of apostolic tradition led bishops, above all in the western half of the Empire, to assert that that tradition had been preserved in its purity in the church of Rome. The authority of the Roman church increased during the second century. Undoubtedly, the fact that the Empire was ruled from Rome made it seem appropriate that the Roman bishop should be, if not precisely a ruler, at least the one to whom one looked for leadership. Furthermore, although the church still lived a very insecure existence, churchmen themselves were beginning to have a picture of the church in their minds which made it analogous in some respects to civil society. The word "Pope" has a somewhat technical meaning which should be respected; it refers not simply to the Bishop of Rome, but to the latter precisely as one who possesses *jurisdiction* in the strict sense—that is, the power to make laws which are binding in conscience. In that sense of the word, it is an anachronism to speak of "Popes" during this period. The position of the Bishop of Rome was unique at the end of the second century, not because he possessed either jurisdiction or actual control over the churches in either part of the Empire; the Roman bishops did not presume to appoint bishops in other dioceses, and such pretensions would undoubtedly have been rejected. But, in the view of very many Christians, Rome was the one diocese, the one episcopal see, with the head of which it was important to remain in union; this seems to have been accepted almost universally in the West and to have been accepted tacitly, with a bit of grumbling, in the East.

2.52 Rigorism

Second, toward the end of the second century, Christianity in many parts of the Empire seems to have been characterized by a certain moral rigorism and a strong emphasis on ethics which went far beyond what is found in the New Testament. Some of those who were drawn to this ethical rigorism went to extremes and left the church; we have already seen that Marcion was expelled from the church, and he took many followers along with him, who were attracted by the severity of his ethical demands. In the years after 170, a sect known as *Montanism* arose in Phrygia, in the northwest part of Asia Minor. This sect emphasized a very strict ethical code and bitterly criticized the humane and merciful elements in the penitential practice of the church. The great North African theologian Tertullian fell into this heresy in the early years of the next century. But many more who believed in this ethical rigorism remained within the church, and there they developed certain views and imposed moral demands which went far beyond the New Testament evidence, and which did some real harm to the church. These people put an inordinate emphasis on fasting and, in general, they esteemed ascetical practices very highly. They rejected second marriages for those whose spouses had died, and regarded those who did marry a second time as little better than adulterers. Renunciation of the world was their ideal and they regarded martyrdom as the proper and appropriate end of Christian existence. They felt that Baptism was so deep and total a commitment to a new life in Christ, that any sins committed after Baptism should be treated with the utmost severity. They seemed quite unaware of Jesus' teaching about God's acceptance of the sinner and ignorant of the parable of forgiveness which should be granted "seventy times seven"; and they insisted that, at the very outside, reconciliation could be offered only once to the Christian who had sinned seriously after Baptism. This seems to be the teaching in *The Shepherd* of Hermas, the work of the mid-second century which was mentioned earlier; and toward the end of the second century there were wide areas in the church where it was taught that there were some sins which were in principle unforgivable. The list of these sins varied, but murder, apostasy and adultery figured prominently on most of them. In all of this, those who insisted on such ethical rigorism were not only being unrealistic; much more serious was the fact that they had wandered far from the spirit of the New Testament and from what was evidently practiced in New Testament times.

There was, of course, a positive side to this rigorism. Baptism was taken very seriously as the source of a totally new and wonderful life to which one had been called and for which one had been empowered by this sacrament. The Christian was seen as one who is called to be in the world but not of it, and who can be summoned to sacrifice even life itself if the integrity of faith is at stake.

Christianity had faced massive external and internal problems during the second century. In general, it had coped successfully with the frequent, if somewhat unorganized persecutions, but its record in regard to internal problems was mixed. By the end of the century, gnosticism, insofar as it was a fifth column within Christianity, had been defeated, and this was, to a significant degree, the work of Irenaeus. On the other hand, the problem posed by those heretical movements which had ascetical and rigoristic roots had not really been seen, and they were to cause much difficulty in the first half of the next century.

2.53 The Spread of Christianity

Christians had become much more numerous during the second century, although it is very difficult to provide accurate figures. The following can be called an educated guess: By the year 200 there were somewhere between forty and seventy-five thousand Christians in the western half of the Empire, most of them in the cities of Italy, North Africa and Gaul. At the same period in the East there were perhaps two to three hundred thousand Christians. Many of these were in the cities, although by this time the Christian faith had begun to penetrate the rural areas as well, particularly in central Asia Minor.

2.6 CHRISTIANITY IN THE EARLY THIRD CENTURY

2.61 New Apostolic Methods

As the third century dawned, Christians could be found in almost all parts of the Empire—almost everywhere in the minority, although, as noted above, more numerous in the East than in the West. However, by this time, Christianity had become an attractive faith for all classes of society and it showed great inner vitality. Converts were numerous and strict standards were laid down to govern the testing of potential converts. The institution known as the *catechumenate* developed—a period of instruction in Christian faith and in the moral demands of Christian life. Candidates for the catechumenate had to be recommended by Christians of proved integrity, and during the period of instruction they were allowed to attend only the first part of the liturgy, the liturgy of the word, where the readings from scripture and the chanting of the psalms would be a part of their instruction in the faith. They were then dismissed and could take no part in the celebration of the mysteries themselves. During this time of testing their conduct was closely observed by the leaders of the Christian community. This, at least, was the ideal, although events in the later years of the century were to show how far practice fell short of this ideal in many parts of the Empire.

2.62 Christian Writers of the Third Century

During much of the second century, Christian writers had employed their skills in defending the church against heretics from within and in trying to secure a sympathetic hearing for the faith on the part of those outside it. In the third century, some highly prolific Christian writers went on the offensive, engaging paganism on its own ground, and confidently asserting the superiority of Christian faith over both the popular paganism of the masses and the philosophy of the elite.

We have already mentioned Tertullian, who lived from about 160 to 220, and was the most important theologian of the western church before Augustine. He had been trained as a lawyer and was careful to define his words carefully and use them accurately; important elements of the Latin theological vocabulary go back to him. Tertullian defended the Catholic faith eloquently and forcefully for about the first half of his active career, although even in these writings there are traces of a certain rigidity in moral questions. In about the year 207, he turned away from the Catholic faith which he had defended so well and embraced *Montanism,* a highly ascetical and rigoristic distortion of the faith, which had originated in northwestern Asia Minor about thirty-five years earlier. Sadly, Tertullian now attacked his former Catholic faith with the same zeal and skill with which he had defended it, and did so until his death in the year 220.

Another Christian whose works have been preserved in part from this period is Hippolytus. He was not a noteworthy writer, but his works provide us with an interesting picture of the way the liturgy was being celebrated in Rome in the early years of the third century. Hippolytus had come to Rome about the year 205, and not long after that he had become embroiled in a dispute with Callistus, the Bishop of Rome at that time. Hippolytus, like so many of the Christian elite in his day, seems to have had strong rigoristic tendencies, and he apparently accused Callistus of moral laxity in administering the sacrament of reconciliation, and of leniency toward those who had weakened during persecution. His dispute with Callistus, which took place about 220, led to his being chosen as bishop in competition with Callistus by a group of like-minded, ascetically oriented Christians, and because of this he is often referred to as an "anti-Pope." However, Hippolytus was an heroic Christian, and he died as a martyr in the year 235.

2.63 Origen

The most profiled and brilliant theologian of the third century was an Egyptian, named Origen. He was born about 185 in Alexandria, and had studied, as a young man, in the catechetical school which had been founded in that city by Clement. After Clement's departure, he took over the leadership of the catechetical school. While on a trip to Palestine in 230, he was ordained to the priesthood by some bishops who were much impressed by his ability, but this led to a break with Demetrios, the bishop of Alexandria, who objected that the ordination had taken place without his permission. As a result, Origen did not remain in Alexandria, but settled in Caesarea, in Palestine, and continued his scholarly work there. He was imprisoned and tortured in the persecution of Decius in 250, and he died in 254 as a result of his sufferings while in prison.

One of Origen's works for which he was most famous in his own time was a book with the title *Against Celsus*. Celsus was a learned pagan who had undertaken, about the year 170, to write a comprehensive refutation of Christianity. He had taken some pains to acquaint himself with the main teachings of the Christian faith, but his view seems to have been somewhat jaundiced by the aristocratic contempt which he had for the Christians, who, in his day, still belonged mainly to the lower classes. His work was important enough for Origen to undertake a refutation seventy years later, and Origen's defense, using the resources of both philosophy and scripture, was celebrated in its day.

Origen's main field of work was scripture and he was a leading proponent of what is called *allegorical exegesis,* that is, the interpretation of scripture which finds in every detail of the text a hidden meaning and a symbolic reference to one of the truths of the faith. Such exegesis is dangerous, because under cover of a quite sincere piety, it strips scripture of the power to be a source of faith and a critic of dogma and of theology. The problem was particularly severe in Origen's case, because he was eager to use all of the resources which Greek philosophy put at his disposal, in order to penetrate the mysteries of the Christian faith; and although he was a man of great learning, high intelligence, and deep Christian commitment, there is no doubt that what he gives us is a strongly hellenized version of the Gospel. Certain ambiguities in his teaching about the nature of Christ, which were a consequence of this hellenization, were to cause great difficulties for the church in the early years of the fourth century; but the discussion of these problems belongs to the next chapter.

2.64 Cyprian

Another prominent churchman of the century was Cyprian, the bishop of Carthage. He had been baptized in the year 246, and was already consecrated bishop just three years later. About the year 250 he wrote a book on the unity of the church and he suffered martyrdom in the year 258. We still have the text of the court acts which ordered his execution, and this interesting document gives a rare insight into the motives the Roman government had for persecuting Christians.

Cyprian's views about the role of the Bishop of Rome in the church universal are very important. He saw Peter as the leader of the Apostles and as the first Bishop of Rome and he argued that union with Peter's successor is the guarantee of the unity of the universal church. Cyprian certainly did not believe that the Bishop of Rome had jurisdictional power, and the argument which he had with the Roman Bishop, Stephan I in 255, would indicate that he was not prepared to find in the Bishop of Rome an authentic, much less infallible, source of doctrine. It is clear that for Cyprian, each bishop was supreme in his own diocese, and yet it is equally clear that for him, each local church is the realization, in one place, of the universal church, and that it is the Bishop of Rome who presides over the universal church and who is the sign and symbol of its unity.

2.7 THE ROMAN GOVERNMENT AND THE ADVANCE OF CHRISTIANITY: THE PERSECUTIONS OF THE THIRD CENTURY

Early in the third century there were sporadic persecutions, much like those which we saw in the second century, and they began under Septimius Severus, who was Emperor from 193 to 211. Christians were persecuted particularly after the year 202, but it is possible that this persecution came about because they were being confused with Montanists, who were propagating a version of the faith which was hostile in almost all respects to the Roman government. Members of this sect refused military service and seem to have despised all involvement in civic life and every exercise of civic duty. With the death of Severus, a forty year period set in, during which the Christians were left in peace. As always, in one city or another, fanatical mobs could be whipped into anti-Christian sentiment, and they occasionally found a Roman official willing to curry favor with them, probably to distract their attention from more pressing problems which he could do nothing about.

2.71 The Decian Persecution

In the year 250, Christians faced a persecution which sprang from entirely different motives and which employed methods more sophisticated than any which had been tried before. Decius, the Emperor, decided that the time had come to eradicate Christianity from the face of the earth and he planned his program carefully. He issued an edict, in accordance with which all citizens of the Empire were to offer sacrifice to the gods. This edict was not overtly directed against Christians; however, it seems clear that Decius had decided that Christians were the main obstacle which had to be removed, if he was to bring about the moral and spiritual regeneration of Rome. And Christians were, in fact, the only group which would really find it impossible to obey such a decree.

There was nothing informal about the act of offering sacrifice to the gods: it was watched closely by imperial officials, who recorded the names of those who sacrificed, and who issued a document, called a *libellus*, to those who had conformed to the decree. Those who, after a certain period of time, could not produce such a *libellus* were hit with the full fury of the state: confiscation of goods, imprisonment, torture and death. The number of Christians who conformed, and to some degree denied their faith, was enormous. Some had actually offered sacrifice, while others had collaborated in more devious ways, either by bribing officials in order to secure a *libellus* or by having pagan friends offer sacrifice in their name and secure the document for them. The church as a whole was confronted by the shocking experience of its own weakness and vulnerability.

Decius died in battle against the Goths, only a few months after issuing this decree, and his successor, Valerian, did not immediately renew the persecution. But in 257 the persecution was renewed with full vigor, and it lasted until the death of Valerian. Persecution now was directed particularly at the clergy and the Christians of the upper classes, apparently in the hope that if the community could be deprived of its leaders, those left would meekly obey the imperial edict. In this second phase the number of defectors was far smaller—a sign that the church had had a few years to reflect on the effect of forty years of peace and the weakness of faith and laxity of conduct which had been the result of it. Valerian died in 260, and his successor, Gallienus, put an end to the persecution— probably because he saw that it was not working and was consuming too much of the energy of the state.

But it was now that the inevitable question was raised

openly in the church: what was to be done about reconciling those who had offered sacrifice or who had procured *libelli* in more devious ways? In an age when rigorism was so widespread among serious Christians, this was a question which could seriously endanger the unity of the church, and it did just that for decades. It was widely held that those who had actually offered sacrifice to the gods had committed so terrible a sin, that unless they had begun to do penance immediately after their denial of the faith, they could not be reconciled even at the point of death. The others who had procured the *libelli* in indirect ways could be reconciled to the church, but only after a lengthy period of penance.

When Gallienus cancelled the edicts which demanded sacrifice to the gods and which imposed severe penalties on those who refused, he inaugurated another period of forty years of peace, during which persecution was virtually absent from the Empire. Few could foresee that this period of peace would be followed by the most brutal of all the persecutions, and one which, at least in the East, once again committed all of the resources of the Empire to wiping Christianity from the face of the earth.

2.8 THE FINAL ASSAULT

Diocletian became Emperor in the year 284, and for almost twenty years he seemed more than tolerant of Christianity—it was even rumored that his wife and daughters were Christians. Diocletian was a man of great ability, and he had a better understanding of the problems which faced the Empire than any Emperor of the century. He devised political and social programs which would bring about inner stability within the Empire, and make it more effective in dealing with threats from without. And he understood that in the world of the fourth century, political and social renewal could rest only on the foundation of religious renewal. His one error in judgment was to think that this religious renewal was possible through a return to civil religion and to the ancient gods of Rome.

In 303 Diocletian ordered the destruction of the churches and the burning of the holy books. In the same year, he stripped all Christians of the Empire of their civil rights (effectively denying them the protection of Roman citizenship). In the same year he ordered the imprisonment of the clergy, with torture and death for those who refused to sacrifice to idols. One year later he extended this decree to all Christians.

In the year 305 Diocletian abdicated (a sign of his political genius was the fact that for the first time in three hundred years provision had been made for the orderly transfer of power to a successor), and in the West persecution stopped almost immediately, although it continued unabated in the East, under Galerius. But five years later, in 310, Galerius' health failed, and when he was near death, he issued a most remarkable decree, the substance of which is found in four Latin words: *ut denuo sint Christiani*—"that Christians might exist (!) again." The edict of Galerius is a fascinating one to read. The reasons for the persecution are given in detail and the reasons for its failure are duly recorded. Christians are now asked to pray to their God for the Emperor and the Empire. This really marked the end of persecution, although it flared up briefly again in the East under his successor.

2.9 CONSTANTINE AND THE BEGINNING OF A NEW ERA

While persecution continued in the East under Galerius (in the years after Diocletian's abdication), it had stopped in the West, where Constantius Chlorus was one of two co-rulers. In the year 311, Constantine, his son, was proclaimed Emperor by his troops and returned to Italy from Britain, in order to vindicate his claim over a rival, named Maxentius. It is hard to separate fact from later legend and to discover what Constantine really thought of Christians and their God at this point. Apparently he had some kind of vision before the final struggle with Maxentius, and, as a result of this, he adopted the Christian God as his protector and had the cross in some form imprinted on the standards which his legions carried into battle at the Milvian Bridge the following day. Needless to say, Constantine won the battle and at that moment a new era for the church began.

Although Constantine was not baptized until many years later, he soon took action in accord with his new convictions. In 312 he wrote to Maximinus in the East and demanded an end to the persecution there, and in the same year he wrote to the prefect of North Africa and ordered him to return church property which had been confiscated, and to free the clergy of the area from the obligation of public service so that they might devote themselves to worship. In the following year these steps were formalized throughout the western Empire in the *Rescript of Milan,* which affirmed as imperial law that *licet Christianos esse*—"it is permissible for Christians to exist." This marked the formal and final end of two hundred and fifty years of intermittent and sometimes violent persecution and for the first time it made the position of Christians legally secure.

There were a number of incidental measures enacted into law at this time which are significant because they indicate the penetration of the new faith into public life. In 315 the practice of branding criminals on the face was prohibited on the grounds that the face of man is the image of God. In the same year, the bishops of the Christian church were granted the powers of civil judges if the parties requested it. In 321 Sunday became a state holiday, and in 323 the pagan religion was characterized as *superstitio*—false worship.

Almost overnight the church became the favored religion of the Empire. (Before the century was over, in 395 under the Emperor Theodosius, paganism was outlawed and pagans were persecuted.) The church had been a persecuted minority; now it not only grew in size, but it was on the way to becoming the state religion. The church took over the political divisions and structures of the Empire (dioceses, for example) and converted the pagan temples to Christian worship; the Pantheon, temple of all of the gods, became the Church of All Saints—a change certainly not without danger! Bishops were given the rank of high civil officials and in the

East the church became "the kingdom of God on earth," no longer distinguishing its earthly or secular dimension from secular political structures. The biblical notion of the *people of God* gave way to a far more political concept—*the Christian people*—who were identified more and more with the population of the Empire. More dangerous still, those who were outside the Empire were outside the church. The cross, which had first been used as a military symbol at the battle of the Milvian Bridge, became a political monogram and the church became the imperial church.

Constantine's motives for all of this were not entirely clear—probably not even to him. He probably thought of the Christian God as some kind of tutelary deity whose cause and worship he furthered, and who, in turn, gave him protection and success. Like Diocletian before him, Constantine had a political vision of a restored Empire, and he knew that religious unity was the only basis on which such a restoration could rest. Unlike Diocletian, he knew, consciously or unconsciously, that the heart had gone out of pagan religion and that it no longer had enough religious substance to provide a basis for political and social renewal. Perhaps instinctively, Constantine realized that the Christian faith did.

But it was precisely this which constituted a mortal danger for the church. Faith has God for its origin and its ground, its motive and its object, and it is blasphemy to employ it as a means to achieve any merely secular purpose or worldly goal. But it was precisely this that churchmen in Constantine's time did not see, and perhaps could not see. They had just emerged from a decade of the most brutal persecution, and it must have seemed to them, in the years after 312, that the resources of the Empire were being put at the disposal of the church, and that heaven had dawned on earth. But the benevolent state was a far greater danger to the church than the hostile state had ever been, and in the second decade of the fourth century policies were made and precedents set which have haunted the church to the present day.

3

From the Arian Crisis
to the Council of Chalcedon

3.1 INTRODUCTION

For more than one hundred and fifty years after the peace inaugurated by Constantine, the church in the eastern half of the Empire was torn by strife—a strife which was not political or social in origin, but religious and, perhaps even more, theological. It almost seemed that, once the persecutions had passed, the church now had the leisure to devote itself to metaphysical problems of the kind which had always delighted the Greek mind. But the ensuing struggles were divisive in the extreme, and the formulas of faith which eventually prevailed not only drove whole areas of the church in the East to separate themselves from the main body of believers, but they often proved to be just as dangerous to Christian faith and life as their formerly heretical opposites had been.

3.2 THE ARIAN HERESY

To understand the Arian crisis, we have to return for a moment to Origen, the greatest theologian of the third century. This speculative genius had been fascinated by the question of the relationship of the Word (the divine principle in Jesus Christ) to God the Father, and he had described the Word in a Greek term which, unfortunately, can be translated in two ways (and which, incidentally, was just as ambiguous in Greek): it could mean either *second God* or *secondary God*. Inevitably, Origen's legacy would move in either of these directions. If one underlined the word *God*, then the unity of Jesus and the Father was affirmed; but if one underlined the other word of the pair, then the meaning was clearly "secondary"; and since God is unique, then the Word is not God, but is merely the highest and greatest of creatures.

The bishops and theologians of the eastern church were all Origenists in the closing years of the third century, and they seemed unaware of the dangerous ambiguities in Origen's thought. (The persecutions under Decius and Valerian, and then, forty years later, under Diocletian, confronted them with much more immediate problems of survival.) But the Constantinian Settlement provided the leisure for that theological speculation which was the glory and the bane of the East, and in 318, only five years after the Rescript of Toleration, Arius, a priest of the diocese of Alexandria, began to preach and teach that the Word was not God, but was rather a creature—the first and the highest of the creatures, to be sure—and therefore not eternal.

Heretical movements in the church up to this time had almost always been either rigoristic, appealing to those with an ascetical bent, or they had been charismatic—enthusiastic, appealing to those with a great need for an emotional involvement which bordered on irrationality. Arius' teaching, on the other hand, appealed to those who prized their ability to think clearly and reason accurately (and what Greek did not?). To cater to such an audience, Arius was able to sum up his theology concerning the Word in a simple syllogism (in itself not a very good sign of the depth of his thought!) as follows: God has no origin; but the Word has an origin (precisely in God); therefore, the Word is not God. If there had been bumper stickers in Arius' day, the essence of his theology would have appeared in a single sentence: *there was a time when he (the Word) was not*—in other words, the Word was not eternal, although God is.

Arius was disciplined by his bishop, but he found other bishops ready to support him, and his teaching caught on quickly with the rationalistically inclined, as well as with those who, true to the Neo-Platonic tradition, were concerned, above all, to safeguard the absolute unity and transcendence of God. Constantine had clearly hoped that the Christian faith would bring religious unity to his Empire, but only a few years after the Rescript of Toleration had been issued, his policy now faced a serious setback.

Earlier disputes about theological questions had sometimes been settled at meetings of the bishops of the region where the dispute had arisen. This had been customary in the East for almost a century, and the custom had spread to the West by the early fourth century; but by the early 320's the Arian question had gripped the theological imagination of much of the Empire, and no merely local synod could cope with the problem. Constantine saw his dream of an Empire united on a religious basis evaporating into thin air, and he pressed for a meeting of the bishops of the whole Christian world (that is, the Empire, the civilized world, the *oikoumene*). He hoped that at this meeting a dogmatic formula could be found, to which all could subscribe, and which would restore unity to the church. Constantine's origins had been in the western part of the Empire and he probably had little taste for theological subtlety, but he had been briefed by his theological adviser, Ossius, the bishop of Cordova, who had not only pushed the idea of a council, but probably proposed the formula to which all would be ordered to subscribe. Ossius had probably also convinced Constantine of the need to condemn Arius, and if it had not been for the Emperor's resolute stance, it is quite likely that Arianism would have prevailed, at least in the eastern half of the Empire.

3.3 THE COUNCIL OF NICAEA

This *ecumenical* council of bishops was composed almost entirely of bishops from the eastern part of the Empire (only a handful of westerners were there) and it met in the small town of Nicaea, in northwestern Asia Minor, not too far from the imperial capital. Here, under some pressure from the

Emperor to agree on a formula acceptable to all, the bishops affirmed that Jesus Christ was "true God from true God, begotten, not made" and that the Word, the divine principle in Jesus Christ, was *of the same substance* as the Father—the Greek word for this sameness of substance was *homoousion*—and after a great celebration of the newly regained unity, they left for home.

When the bishops returned home from the Council of Nicaea, they and their theologians had an opportunity to discuss what had happened, and many of them came to believe that they had been prodded into accepting a formula which went far beyond what they really believed. It was not that they objected to what we today would call the divinity of Christ, but rather that to speak of "unity of substance" between Jesus and the Father seemed to obliterate all distinction, and both their Neo-Platonic philosophy as well as their (in this case correct) understanding of the New Testament rebelled at this. Most of them probably did not realize that Nicaea had taken an important step in redefining the meaning of the word "God," but they were very ill at ease with what had happened there.

Nicaea's formula was a clearcut rejection of Arianism, but many in the East were not satisfied with the new formula, and they did all in their power to reverse the decisions of Nicaea. In this attempt, they were often aided by powerful bishops and by one of the sons of Constantine who succeeded him and who was a follower of Arianism. The overwhelming majority of the bishops who were dissatisfied with the Nicene formula were not themselves Arians, but they disliked the *homoousion* formula which departed from New Testament usage in two respects. First, the council had employed for the first time a non-scriptural term and insisted that accepting this term was necessary for faith. The history of the next fifty years would indicate just how troubled many of the bishops were by this fact. The second departure from scriptural usage was more significant, because many at the time were only vaguely aware of it. In the New Testament, the word *God* refers to the one whom Jesus calls "Father"—that is, to the one whom he knows and loves in a unique way, but at Nicaea the word *God* was for the first time given a much larger area of meaning, and it began to refer, not to that person with whom Jesus is in dialogue, but rather to that which Jesus and that person (the Father) *have in common.*

The Council had met at Constantine's initiative and during his lifetime no one dared call the Nicene formula into question. Opposition to the Council had to use more devious methods, and these consisted largely in attacks directed at those bishops who supported Nicaea, and in the attempt to discredit them with the Emperor. Constantine died in 337 and he was succeeded in the East by his son, Constantius, who was Arian in sympathy, and who encouraged the arianizing bishops of the East, especially Eusebius of Caesarea and Eusebius of Nicomedia. In the beginning of his reign, Constantius shared power with his brothers, but by the year 351 he alone ruled the entire Empire, and his Arian sympathies came into the open; in the next ten years the Nicene doctrine was rejected and Arian teaching affirmed at a number of local synods or councils in both parts of the Empire. It looked, about the year 360, as though Arianism had won and would become the faith of the Empire.

That it did not was the work, above all, of one man, Athanasius, bishop of Alexandria, who spent many years of his life in exile because of his firm support of the Nicene teaching. Athanasius recognized that only a small percentage of the opponents of Nicaea were truly Arian in sympathy, and that they had supported the Arian position at the local councils and synods because of what they regarded as the danger of the *homoousion* formula. But the very success of rather blatant Arianism after 351 made it possible for Athanasius to convince these more moderate opponents of Nicaea that the term *homoousion* could be given an acceptable definition, and that if defined this way, it was a formula without which the church could not live. Between the death of Constantius in 361, and 381 when the second ecumenical council met in Constantinople, Athanasius won his victory. There were three other theologians of this period, who, although less prominent in the battle on behalf of Nicaea, provided much of the theological foundation for the Council of Constantinople in 381, as well as for later theorizing about the mystery of the Trinity. All three were from central Asia Minor—a territory which had been Christian for some time and which did more than its share in providing the eastern church with intellectual leadership. The three were Basil the Great, Gregory of Nyssa and Gregory of Nazianzus. Perhaps their deepest insight appeared in their view that the Trinity was best thought of as *three ways in which God possesses his existence.*

Athanasius' victory was a necessary one for the church, but it was the tragedy of Nicaea that this victory was necessary, and that questions had to be raised and answered in a language so entirely different from that of the New Testament. The struggle against Arianism made the church cautious of, and even embarrassed by, all of those New Testament texts which speak of the genuine humanity of Jesus Christ. As has so often happened in the history of the church, victory over one heresy made the church vulnerable to what might be called the polar opposite of the same heresy.

3.4 WHO AND WHAT IS JESUS CHRIST?

No sooner was the question of the divinity of the Word settled than a new problem surfaced. If the Word was God, then what was to be said about the humanity of Jesus Christ? Does he have a human nature, fundamentally like ours, or does he have only one nature, that of the divine Word? And if he does have two natures, what is it which holds them together, unifies them, and makes him just one person? Different solutions to these three questions divided the two leading cities of Alexandria and Antioch, and the theological struggle was compounded by questions of church politics.

The first attempt to solve the problem of how Jesus Christ could be at one and the same time God and man was made in Alexandria, and it is often called the *Word-flesh* christology. Those who held this view argued that, in Jesus, the Word (that is, the divine principle in him) took upon himself not a complete human being, but rather a human body, and that the Word discharged for this body all of the functions which are usually taken care of by the human soul. The radical members of this group actually denied that Jesus had a human soul, and they used to speak of *the one incarnate nature of the divine Word.*

Now even in Alexandria this went too far. It was not that theologians there saw such a teaching as an assault on the genuine humanity of Jesus (which it was!). Their objection was based on their teaching about how human beings were saved by Christ. They argued that unless the word had taken to himself a complete human nature, body and soul, then human beings would not be saved, since it was by the union of human nature with divine nature that the saving power of God becomes accessible to us. This very Platonic view of salvation was expressed in a famous slogan or catchword: *what has not been assumed has not been saved.*

This slogan saved the formal orthodoxy of Alexandria, but even though the main line of Alexandrian theologians did not deny the humanity of Jesus, they were never able to take it very seriously, or, in the terms in which they thought about the human condition, they were never able to find anything for the human soul of Jesus Christ to do. This was a problem for almost all theologians who came from that city, and we saw it earlier in Clement of Alexandria, who, writing about the year 180, spoke of the perfect immunity of Jesus from all of the limitations of human existence. Later, Athanasius would speak of how Jesus "pretended" weakness and ignorance, apparently in order to give us good example (although one might wonder in just what respect such example is good!). Nothing could indicate more clearly the dangers involved in the victory of Nicaea. Alexandria had developed a clever way of explaining the *unity* of Jesus Christ, but theologians there based that unity solely on the controlling and directing power of the Word. As a result, they passed on to later ages a Jesus who was divine but dehumanized.

In the city of Antioch, theologians approached the problem of relating the humanity and divinity of Jesus in an entirely different way. Here, they started with the fact of Jesus' humanity and divinity, and they asked how these two realities could be *joined* so as to constitute the one God—man Jesus Christ. Their great strength was that they took the humanity of Jesus seriously and they accepted the fact that he was a vulnerable, and eventually broken man. Their theology was weak in explaining the unity of Jesus Christ, and even the best exponents of Antiochene thought tended to speak vaguely about how one person "resulted" from the coming together of the two realities, the divine and the human.

The theological rivalry of the two cities might have gone on unabated for centuries, untroubled by anything more damaging than an occasional anathema, but in the year 428 the question ceased to be merely theological and became political and personal. Nestorius, a not overly bright representative of the school of Antioch, became bishop of Constantinople, and therefore titular head of the eastern church. At this very moment, the church of Alexandria was ruled by a bishop named Cyril—a man who was proud and ruthless, but also dedicated to the church and to the preservation of pure doctrine. Of course, he identified pure doctrine with the typical Alexandrian teaching about the unity of Christ through the power of the divine Word.

No sooner had Nestorius assumed his position as Patriarch of Constantinople than he began to teach a rather carelessly worded version of the Antiochene theory concerning Jesus Christ's humanity and divinity. What he really held was that the Word had been united with a complete man (this was called a *Word-man* christology, to distinguish it from Alexandria's *Word-flesh* christology), and that both of these natures, the human and the divine, had their own concrete reality. Unfortunately, he used language which made it seem as though these natures were merely joined together, and he said nothing about the role of the Word in providing the unity which made Jesus one person. This made it seem to Cyril and the other Alexandrians that he was teaching that there were two persons in Christ. More unfortunate still, for Nestorius, was the fact that he decided to express his teaching about Jesus by asserting that Mary was not the mother of God, but the mother of Christ. This touched the issue of the growing devotion to Mary in the eastern provinces, and brought strong emotions into play, above all on the part of the monastic communities in Constantinople.

In 430, Cyril, who had written to Pope Celestine about Nestorius' teaching, was commissioned by the Pope to resolve the problem. Cyril undertook to do this by sending to Nestorius a list of teachings about the unity of the divine and human in Jesus, with orders to accept them by condemning the opposing positions. (It is for this reason that they are often referred to as the *anathemas.*) Needless to say, the list was a summary of the most extreme Alexandrian position, and it appeared to Nestorius (and other more intelligent Antiochene theologians) to be nothing more than blatant heresy. Nestorius, as Cyril must have foreseen, refused to accept Cyril's *anathemas.* The bishops of two of the major dioceses in the church were now accusing each other of heresy, and for the good of the church and the Empire, peace had to be restored. By this time, an ecumenical council was accepted as the ordinary way of handling such problems, and the Emperor summoned one to meet in Ephesus in 431. Cyril and his friends arrived early, before the Antiochene bishops, and promptly excommunicated Nestorius. The Emperor's commissioners objected, but the legates of the Pope approved, and this is the council which has gone down in history as the Third Ecumenical Council of Ephesus. Just a few days later, Nestorius met with his fellow bishops and excommunicated Cyril and his supporters.

There were no precedents for such a situation. The very step which had been taken to solve the problem had now resulted in the mutual excommunication of two of the major sees of Christendom and it seemed as though nothing could get the church out of the impasse. There were two major obstacles; the first was the excommunication of Nestorius at the Council of Ephesus (which almost all of the bishops from Antioch had taken as a personal insult) and the second was the list of "anathemas"—the propositions summing up Alexandrian theology which Cyril had ordered Nestorius to sign. It was a time which called for a spirit of compromise that was motivated by a deep love of the church, and, perhaps surprisingly, the major disputants acted in precisely such a spirit, and a compromise was achieved just two years after the Council of Ephesus, in 433.

The compromise was the joint work of the leading theologian of the Antiochene party, John, bishop of Antioch, and of Cyril of Alexandria. Cyril explained what he had really meant by his anathemas, and the theologians of Antioch were willing to admit that he had interpreted them in an orthodox sense. (Cyril may, on this occasion, have realized how dangerous some of his formulations were, since he apparently never made use of them again.) For their part, the Antiochenes agreed to the excommunication of Nestorius.

3.5 THE COUNCIL OF CHALCEDON

If Cyril had lived longer, his agreement with John might have settled matters for good, and the history of the eastern church might have been very different. But Cyril died in 444, and he was succeeded as bishop of Alexandria by Dioscuros, a ruthless opponent of his compromise with John. Dioscuros made himself the leader of a group which wanted to disavow the *Symbol of Union,* as the agreement between John and Cyril was called, and were looking for a pretext to do it.

They found this pretext in a dispute which broke out in Constantinople in 448. There, an apparently pious but very confused monk by the name of Eutyches became the spokesman for a group which rejected the *Symbol of Union* and asserted a particularly radical form of the old Alexandrian theology, affirming that Jesus' humanity had been *absorbed* in his divinity, so that one could speak properly only of the *divine* nature of Jesus. Many in Constantinople felt that this was not traditional doctrine (it was not!), and reported the matter to the Pope, Leo I. In the following year (449), Leo wrote a letter to Flavian, Patriarch of Constantinople, pointing out that Eutyches' teaching was heresy. In his letter, Leo outlined the theory of the two natures of Christ, divine and human, which had been held in the church of the West since the middle of the fourth century. In that same year, the Emperor, Theodosius II, ordered the calling of a council which was to meet in the city of Ephesus. In the summer of 449, Dioscuros and his cronies arrived in Ephesus, took complete control, refused to allow Leo's letter to Flavian to be read, and rehabilitated Eutyches. The Pope's legates protested, but the Emperor's commissioners accepted the "council" and approved its decrees. The problem had now become more serious: not only were Antioch and Alexandria locked in hostile confrontation, but the Pope and the Emperor were now on different sides.

Providentially perhaps, the Emperor died in July of the year 450, and his successor, Marcion, summoned a council to meet in the small town of Chalcedon, near Constantinople, in the following year. This *Council of Chalcedon* met in October, and the Emperor's representatives insisted from the very beginning that the assembled bishops find a formula on which all could agree. They found this in Leo's letter to Flavian, and they reaffirmed that Jesus Christ is true God and true man, and that in him there are two principles of operation which remain distinct, but that there is only one acting subject, and that this subject is the divine Word.

Actually, what Leo had asserted in his letter was the same doctrine as that of the *Symbol of Union* (although Leo had used the characteristic language of western theology), and it was clear that Dioscuros and those who viewed the agreement between Cyril and John as a sell-out to Antioch were not prepared to accept the decrees of the Council of Chalcedon. For almost two hundred years the Emperors of the East tried to tamper with the decrees of Chalcedon, in order to make them more palatable to the Alexandrians and those who agreed with them. This was done, of course, for purely political reasons, to secure Egypt's loyalty to the Empire, but it did not work. The Egyptian church drifted off into the heresy known as *monophysitism*—the theory that in Jesus Christ there is only one nature, the divine nature—and when the Moslems appeared on the frontier little more than two hundred years later, they were regarded by the leadership of the monophysite church as an improvement over rule from Constantinople.

Chalcedon brought to an end a century and a half of christological dispute—argument about who and what Jesus Christ was and is—within the church. Tragically, the disputants had often talked, not with each other or even to each other, but past each other. Antioch and Alexandria conceived of the problems in entirely different ways, and they often used *the same terminology* but meant something very different by it. Another unfortunate result of the Council could hardly have been foreseen. The highly technical language of Leo's letter and of the conciliar decrees has been translated over the years into other languages used by Christians, so that we find ourselves today speaking, at least in the creeds, of the *one person in two natures* in Jesus Christ, without asking whether these words really translate what was in the minds of the council fathers. As a matter of fact, they probably do not, and the result has been that Christians often feel obligated to speak of Jesus in a language which is as alien to their world as it would have been to the world of the New Testament. The attempt to distill the scriptural message into more or less philosophical terminology, which had begun at Nicaea, was probably unavoidable, but the results of this attempt were unfortunate.

3.6 AUGUSTINE AND HIS TIMES

3.61 Introduction

Unlike their eastern counterparts, the theologians of the western church were not overly concerned with metaphysics; their real interests were practical, and they raised questions about ethics and about the use of freedom. At the period which interests us here (the fourth century), the church in North Africa occupied a leading position, numerically and intellectually, in the West, and it was in many ways the heir of Tertullian, the great African theologian who had fallen into the Montanist heresy in the early third century. This inheritance was apparent also in a certain rigorism with which Africa's ethical concerns were always tainted. The church was also the heir of Cyprian's thought, in a respect which would cause serious difficulties throughout the fourth century and into the fifth. Cyprian, like most other African theologians at the time, rejected the validity of baptism by heretics or by those who had failed to confess their faith during the time of persecution. It was this position which would split the church in North Africa right at the time of Constantine's accession to power, and which created the schismatic and very powerful Donatist movement and Donatist church. Augustine played a fateful role in the intellectual defeat of Donatism, as well as in the suppression of the schismatic church by Roman civil authority.

3.62 Augustine's Early Life and Conversion

Augustine was born in Tagaste, North Africa, in 354, the son of a pagan father and a Christian mother—a woman of very forceful character, named Monica. In his *Confessions* Augustine has left us a vivid picture of his childhood and youth. In accordance with the custom of the time, he had not been baptized, and as a young man he would have nothing to do with the Christian faith. In the *Confessions* he describes his life at the time as one of great sexual license, but this was written when he was an elderly ascetic. Even as a young man he was interested in basic problems of life and conduct, and in the year 374 he joined the religious sect of the Manichees—a group of Persian origin, who held that there were two supreme beings, one responsible for good and the other for evil. Possibly Augustine was drawn to this theory as a way of coping with the fact that his body and his spirit seemed to be pulling him in opposite directions. He had been trained as a teacher of rhetoric, and in the year 384 he settled in the north Italian city of Milan, a move which was to bring him into contact with one of the most profiled Christian churchmen of the time—Ambrose.

3.63 Ambrose

Ambrose was fifteen years older than Augustine, and, at the age of thirty-five and still unbaptized (!), he had been chosen bishop of Milan by popular acclamation. From that moment on he dedicated himself entirely to the church, and became one of the most zealous churchmen of the time. Ambrose was a gifted organizer, and he had a clear idea of the proper relation of church and state, which led him to reject any subordination to imperial power (on one occasion he called the Emperor Theodosius to task and made him do public penance). Ambrose was also a talented preacher and he spoke regularly in his church at Milan. It was there that Augustine came to hear him, and was won over to the Christian faith.

3.64 Augustine's Life after his Conversion

After his baptism in 387, Augustine returned to North Africa, where he lived with some like-minded friends in a kind of monastic community in his home city of Tagaste. But a man of his ability would not be allowed the leisure of such a life, and on a visit to Hippo in 391 he was ordained by the bishop there. From this moment on, Augustine devoted all of his enormous energies to the church. He became bishop of Hippo in 395. For all but the last ten years of his life, Augustine was involved in combatting the Donatist schism, and these battles led to important developments in his theology. Because this schism was an important fact of church life for more than a century, this will be an appropriate place to look at the history of the movement.

3.65 Donatism

North African theology had always been peculiar in emphasizing the importance of the holiness of the priest or bishop who administered the sacraments, going so far as to call the validity of the sacrament into question if it had been administered by one guilty of serious sin. Shortly after the last persecution, a dispute arose in the church at Carthage over the validity of the consecration of their new bishop, because he had been consecrated by a man suspected of abandoning the faith during persecution. Those who objected consecrated a bishop of their own choosing. A few years later, in 313, this bishop died and was succeeded by a certain Donatus, who gave his name to the movement.

Constantine was the new Emperor at this time, and he was not pleased at developments in North Africa. He ordered the Donatists to settle their dispute with the Catholics and restore unity to the African church, but the Donatists appealed his decision and the Emperor ordered that the dispute be settled at a council in Arles, in Gaul, in the year 314. Although the decision of the bishops there went against them, the Donatists were able, by incessant delays and repeated appeals, to avoid the reunion with the Catholics which Constantine wanted. Finally, in the year 320, Constantine gave up and accepted the existence of two Christian churches in North Africa.

From this moment on and for much of the century, the Donatists constituted the larger of the two groups, and as the years passed, the Catholics often seemed to be a rather pitiful and powerless minority. By the year 345 the Donatists were so strong that they appealed to the Emperor of the West, Constans, for official recognition as the one church in North Africa. This request was to have fatal results for them and for their church.

In that very year, Constans sent two legates, Paulus and Macarius, to North Africa, to check on the situation and to report to him. Donatus suspected that the two were pro-Catholic, and he began to stir up the members of his sect against them; so great was the threat of violence that the two legates felt that they could continue their tour of inspection only if they were accompanied by detachments of Roman troops. In a number of towns there were riots, and even armed resistance against the imperial forces, and from this moment on, the Roman authorities began to regard the Donatists as responsible for religious and civil disunity in Africa. As a result of these events of the year 346, Constans issued an edict which ordered the reunion of the church in North Africa under Catholic direction.

This "reunion" lasted from 347 to 361, but it remained largely without effect. The Catholic side lacked strong episcopal direction and no attempt was made to win the minds and hearts of the Donatists. In 361 when Julian became Emperor and made an attempt to restore paganism as the official Roman religion, he was pleased to have two squabbling groups of Christians in the North African church and he ordered a return to the situation which had prevailed before 347. The Donatist bishops returned from exile, and among them was a man of great intellectual ability and spiritual stature, Parmenian, who became Donatist bishop of Carthage. He was a man of moderation and a fine speaker, and under his direction the Donatist church in Carthage became by far the stronger of the two confessions, so that the Catholics there looked more and more insignificant.

Parmenian seemed not only intellectually but even spiritually superior to his rather colorless Catholic counterparts. In many ways, he looked like a worthy successor of Cyprian, but there was one fatal flaw in his teaching which set him apart from his great predecessor, and which, more than anything else, led to the downfall of Donatism. Parmenian, like all other Donatist bishops, insisted that the North African church *alone* was the true church and accused all who were in communion with the North African Catholics of heresy. This led to the increasing isolation of their church and made them appear to the church in other parts of the Empire as fanatic sectarians. Furthermore, outside Carthage itself, especially along the northern coast and in Numidia, the Donatist church became increasingly involved in anti-government action, with the result that Roman authorities tried to forbid Donatist religious services, although this was difficult to enforce.

In 389 Parmenian died and was succeeded by Primian. The choice was a disaster for the Donatists. Primian held a particularly radical version of Donatist theology and was brutal and fanatical. He put himself at the head of some equally unbalanced cohorts in the outlying districts, and became involved in armed insurrection against the Roman authorities, with the result that from this moment on, Rome used its power in favor of the Catholics in North Africa.

This brings us to the year 391. Augustine had just been ordained a priest for the church in Hippo, and from this moment on, for almost thirty years, he dedicated himself to the restoration of church unity in North Africa. He began by doing everything possible to foster personal contact with the Donatist leadership. He was more than conciliatory, but the Donatist hierarchy spurned his efforts. Augustine saw that the Catholics would have to unite under strong leadership, and he urged his fellow bishops to meet each year to discuss the situation and plan action. He was always on the side of a peaceful solution of the schism.

At the Synod of Carthage in 403, the assembled Catholic bishops proposed that there should be a religious discussion between the two groups. As was to be expected, Primian, the Donatist bishop, rejected this proposal, and began to incite his followers to violence against Donatist bishops who were leaning toward the Catholic side, as well as against the Catholic bishops themselves. Violence against Catholics was so prevalent that in 404 the Synod of Bishops in Carthage asked for the protection of imperial forces against Donatist excesses, and the government obliged. At first, Augustine did not want to forbid Donatism, but the violence was so great that he finally came to believe that force was the only way that Catholics could be protected and that Donatist Christians themselves could be freed from the threat of brutal reprisals on the part of Primian and other fanatics. Augustine himself always rejected the death penalty for recalcitrant Donatists, but he gave a scriptural justification of the use of force on the side of the state which was cited by Christians of other days and ages and which has left a tragic legacy in the Crusades, the Inquisition, and innumerable religious wars.

In 405, Honorius, the western Emperor, responded to the request of Augustine and the Catholic bishops of North Africa and issued the Edict of Union, in accordance with which the Donatists were to be treated as heretics, their churches were to be given to the Catholics, and those Donatist bishops who refused to become Catholic were to be banished from North Africa. However, the use of force simply provided the Donatists with martyrs, and in the year 410, the Emperor ordered another religious discussion, which was to take place in Carthage in the following year.

This time the Donatist bishops could not avoid the confrontation, since the civil authorities ordered them to attend. For their part, the Catholics did all in their power to create a favorable climate for the discussion. When the two groups finally met, the Donatists tried to delay discussion with procedural questions, but Augustine insisted that the discussion should center on the real theological issues which separated the two churches and he adroitly brought the assembly back to these questions. Once he had done this, he spoke so convincingly that on the third day of the meeting he carried the day for the Catholic side, and Marcellinus, the imperial commissioner, gave his judgment in favor of the Catholics. This decision was confirmed by a rescript of Honorius in January, 412. From that time on, it became clear, even to sincere Donatist Christians, that the Catholic position was theologically sound, and many of the laity, together with their priests and a few of the bishops, entered the Catholic church, and unity was restored to the church in North Africa. Donatism declined, although it continued to exist, especially in the rural areas, until the Vandal invasion in 429.

The Donatist episode took up slightly more than a century of the history of the church in North Africa, and it did incalculable harm, fueled as it was by the always corrosive mixture of theology and politics. For its members, the Donatist church was not only the one place in which the true faith was to be found; it was also, often unconsciously, a way of asserting a North African ethnic and political identity against Roman authority which was being exercised from Ravenna, in North Italy, and against the economic exploitation of their land. It would be false to reduce the Donatist schism to economic or political terms, but it was precisely the presence of these elements which fueled passions and which led to such enormous suffering on both sides during the hundred years of religious conflict. Augustine's interests were naturally theological, and in terms of Christian tradition as it was understood in his time, his judgments were theologically correct. But Augustine had no understanding of the social and political factors which played a role in the religious wars. If he had understood them, he might have been much more reserved in calling upon the Roman state to suppress Donatism.

Theologically there were two important results of Augustine's victory. First, Augustine asserted that the sacraments do not depend for their efficacy on the holiness of the one who administers them, but rather on the holiness of

Christ, who is always the real minister who works through the human instrument. Second, Augustine distinguished between the church as it is—that is, the existing church, in which saints and sinners live—and the church which is to come—the holy church, which will be found only at the end of time. This distinction was not only realistic but also theologically important, because it put an end to the arrogance and false elitism which had done so much harm in the Donatist church of North Africa. For Augustine, it is not human holiness which is the bond of union in the church, but the holiness of God himself, that is, the Holy Spirit.

3.66 Pelagianism

Even before the Donatist question had been settled, Augustine had to turn to another theological issue. A British monk named Pelagius had come to Rome about the year 390, where he lived an ascetical life and began to preach a stern ethical code which he asserted to be binding on all who wished to be true Christians. Pelagius had great confidence in the power of the human will to achieve whatever the human being really wanted, and his preaching had great appeal to those who prized strength of will and who longed to be ethical over-achievers. The great motive which he proposed for strenuous ethical exertion was the thought of merit accrued and a reward earned in heaven.

Pelagius' moral preaching colored his view of sin and salvation. According to him, original sin consisted merely in the bad example of Adam's sin, and the integrity of free will remained untouched. In the same way, *grace,* which Paul had thought of as the effective love of God which completely transforms the conditions of human activity, was interpreted by Pelagius as merely the good example given by Christ.

Pelagius' teaching spread throughout much of southern Italy, Sicily, Spain, North Africa, Gaul and Ireland, but as it spread, some theologians began to have serious doubts about its orthodoxy. Many found that Pelagius' teaching about original sin called into question the widely accepted practice of infant baptism (and, in fact, Pelagius did seem to question the need of baptism for children). Others were annoyed by his constant harping on poverty and the evils of riches. Augustine, however, had far more serious objections. He saw that Pelagius' teaching cheapened the grace of Christ by suggesting that human beings were able to be *justified*, that is, to come to have the right relationship with God, on their own power and through their own merits, thus making salvation by Jesus Christ unnecessary.

In 415 Pelagius went to Palestine, and his presence there caused much disturbance. The bishops of the area were urged to hold hearings to determine whether he was orthodox in faith, but Pelagius succeeded in interpreting his teaching in a way which met with their approval. Augustine asked for the official records of these hearings and he was able to point out that there were discrepancies between Pelagius' writings and things that he had said at the hearings.

In 416 the bishops of North Africa, at their annual meeting in Carthage, asked the Pope to condemn the Pelagian errors, and Innocent I did so in the following year. But Pelagius then returned, and was able to convince the new Pope, Zosimus, that his teaching was genuinely Christian and that he had been condemned unjustly. Shortly after this, the Emperor, Honorius, had Pelagius expelled from Rome, and finally Zosimus, too, saw the light and condemned Pelagius.

With the departure of Pelagius from the scene, leadership of the movement passed to a younger man who was bishop in the town of Eclanum, in southern Italy. His name was Julian, and his father had been a bishop before him. Well educated, and fluent even in Greek, he was clever, if crude, in argument, and pressed the case for Pelagius' doctrine against Augustine. Julian's view of human nature was optimistic, typical of the enlightened humanism of his day, and perhaps every other day, and he seems to have had little grasp of the destructive tendencies which lurk just beneath the surface in human nature. His writings deserve a much wider reading, because, although in his dispute with Augustine the latter certainly had by far the greater religious substance, it is Julian's point of view that probably corresponds more closely in fact, if not in theory, to the feelings of Christians today, Catholic and Protestant, clergy and laity. As a result of his dispute with Augustine, Julian was deprived of his office of bishop and went to live in the East. Between 420 and 430 the Pelagian movement came to an end as an identifiable heretical movement, although it has lived on as a permanent temptation for those who seek ethical perfection through observance of what they understand as the clearly defined law of God. It was a serious danger in many of the religious orders of the post-Tridentine church, and not a few of the "spiritual classics" of the period owe more to Pelagius than to Paul.

Augustine's later years were occupied with problems which had developed out of his debate with the Pelagians, and he busied himself more and more with the question of grace and free will. For him, the freely given love and acceptance of God were the beginning of salvation and the ground of all the good works of which the human being was capable. Far from interfering with free will, Augustine argued that it is grace which creates it and empowers it. This view of Augustine's, which has often been misunderstood, is a deep one, because he saw that freedom does not consist essentially in *indifference* but rather in *the power to act rightly and well*. Unfortunately, Augustine's theology of grace was flawed by his philosophy, and he spoke at times of grace as a *thing* which could be possessed, gained and lost, and this conflicted with the deepest intent of his own thought, which equated grace with the freely given love of God.

As the years went by, Augustine became more and more obsessed with the problem of *predestination,* and this somber concept began to weigh more heavily than that of God's loving acceptance. In later times, theologians and teachers who were disposed to emphasize the divine justice at the expense of the divine love found a rich source for their theses in Augustine's writings. The church never accepted Augustine's teaching in this matter.

Augustine was not only the most important theologian of his time; he was also the most influential on later ages, and it is not without reason that he is called the father of medieval theology. He had something profound to say on almost every issue, philosophical or theological. To these universal interests he joined a rare gift of introspection and psychological insight. He applied these insights to the theology of the Trinity, that is, the "three-fold-ness" of God, and his work here was never surpassed by later theology. Especially worthy of note in this respect is his great reserve in regard to the use of the word *persona* (which in his day was coming to mean something very much like the modern word *person*) to speak of the Father, Son, and Spirit.

The Neo-Platonic philosophy to which Augustine had given his allegiance even before his baptism, together with his experience of the imperious nature of his own sexual drives, conspired to give him a more than jaundiced view of human sexuality and conjugal love. Ironically, his opponent, Julian of Eclanum, would probably be a much sounder guide here. Augustine regarded sexual activity even in marriage as basically shameful, and argued that it could be excused only if both partners had the intention of procreating a child. In this respect, Augustine was not much worse than many of the Greek fathers of his day, and statements even more appalling can be culled from the works of Gregory of Nyssa, Gregory of Nazianzen, John Chrysostom and many others. What is unfortunate is that Augustine's teaching was followed by almost all of the medieval schoolmen, as well as in the instruction booklets which were used to guide priests in the administration of the sacrament of penance, and that it was regarded as normative, at least for Catholic Christians, until the recent past.

In Augustine's reflections on faith and grace, the heart of Paul's theology came close to being rediscovered—probably for the only time during the entire patristic period. But genuine rediscovery faced two insurmountable obstacles, and in the face of them it failed. The first was Neo-Platonic philosophy, and the second was a scriptural exegesis which was fundamentalistic, allegorical and fanciful. This was, of course, not Augustine's fault. He was a man of his time, and with the exception of Antioch, the entire Christian world was the victim of this most destructive consequence of that hostility to history which had characterized Greek thought since Plato.

3.7 OTHER PERSONS AND EVENTS IN THE FOURTH AND EARLY FIFTH CENTURIES

3.71 Jerome

Jerome was an earlier contemporary of Augustine. He had come to Rome as a young man, and, like so many of the more serious Christians of his day, he became fascinated by the ascetical life. He encountered some monks on a trip to Gaul, and decided to embrace monastic life himself. In 379 he went to Antioch, probably with the idea of experiencing the monastic movement in those areas in which it had been born, and, while there, he was ordained to the priesthood. In the year 382 he returned to Rome at the request of the Pope, Damasus, to revise the Latin translation of the bible which was then in current use. Actually this translation, known as the *Vetus Latina*, existed in a number of various forms, and during Jerome's three year stay in the old capital, he completed his revision, using the Greek (for the New Testament) and Hebrew (for the Old Testament) texts which were available in his day.

When Damasus died, it seems likely that Jerome thought that he would be elected Pope, but his irascible nature and the stern asceticism which he preached had won him too many enemies among the clergy and laity of the city of Rome. Disappointed in his hopes, he returned to the East and settled in Bethlehem, where, with the support of a rich Christian woman named Paula, he established a monastery for men and another for women, the latter under the direction of Paula. He continued to take an active part in church life, and was one of the first to raise questions about the orthodoxy of Origen's theology. When Pelagius and some of his followers came to the East, Jerome brought to the attention of the bishops there the fundamentally unchristian basis of pelagian asceticism. Jerome died in 420, and the *Vulgata*, his revision of the Latin bible, was his monument. It was in this form that the scriptures were known to the Latin West throughout the medieval period, and it was the *Vulgata* which was the basis of

Catholic translations of the scriptures up to quite recent times.

3.72 Caesaropapism

The word is derived from two Latin words: the word for "Emperor"—*Caesar*—and the word for "Pope"—*papa*—and it refers to the tendency of the Roman Emperors, once the Empire had become nominally Christian, to act not only as head of the state but as head of the church as well. Caesaropapism was a particular problem in the East, as we have seen, because Constantinople was the principal capital of the Empire, and, in general, the Emperors of the East were stronger characters and had more political power at their disposal than did their counterparts in the West.

In the fourth and early fifth centuries, the church in the West was beginning to unite around Rome, in the sense that the Roman bishop was increasingly seen as the symbol and bond of unity. To be in communion with Rome was to be in communion with all the other churches, and those who were in communion with Rome felt that their national churches were the local incarnation of the universal church. In the East this was not possible, because the Emperors, time and time again, tried to act as Popes, but of course their goals were political and not religious. However, their very presence tended to isolate the eastern church from developments in the West, and to make the eastern church more and more a national church for ethnic Greeks, and this was an important fact in the eventual dissolution of the Empire and in the fragmenting of the eastern church into a number of mutually hostile national churches.

It is more than possible that developments in the West would have taken the same course. The ease with which Honorius issued edicts dealing with religious questions in North Africa, and with which both Catholics and Donatists requested state intervention in their favor, make it quite probable. But two things prevented this from happening. First, the Emperors in the West ruled from Ravenna, a city on the Adriatic some distance from Rome, and this gave the Bishop of Rome some autonomy in his own city. And, second, the attention of the western Emperors was concentrated on the Germanic invaders who were pouring across the northern frontiers in the years after 400. After Honorius there were no other strong and profiled Emperors in the West, and in 476 the Roman Empire of the West formally came to an end, when the Germanic chieftain who was ruling Italy at the time sent the insignia of Empire back to Constantinople.

3.73 Converting the Masses

When the persecutions came to an end, the church found itself in the minority in all but a few cities of the East, and it was now confronted with an enormous task—nothing less than the conversion of the population of the entire Empire. It actually accomplished much of this task in the fourth and fifth centuries, although it was not until the sixth and early seventh centuries that the new faith penetrated some of the more remote areas. Naturally the process of christianization proceeded with different speed in the different areas. Egypt, for example, was mostly Christian by the year 400, whereas very little progress was made in Palestine. In Syria, the cities had a Christian majority by the end of the fourth century and great advances had been made into the countryside by the middle of the fifth. In Asia Minor, both the cities and the countryside were largely Christian by the end of the fifth century, and one area, Cappadocia, had been thoroughly christianized by the end of the fourth century, and had provided the church with some of its most prominent theologians at the time of the Nicene crisis. Surprisingly, progress in Greece was slow, and conversions did not really begin to pick up until after the year 400. It was not until the early fifth century that some of the temples in Athens were turned into churches.

In the West, in general, progress was slower, and except for cities like Ravenna and Milan in the north, which had a flourishing church life in the early fourth century, much of Italy waited until the fifth and even sixth centuries to become Christian. Rome itself was a largely pagan city through the fourth century. In North Africa the church had a very firm

footing by the year 300, but then, with the end of the persecutions, came the Donatist schism which absorbed almost all
the energies of both parties and which made conversion to
Christianity a problem for pagans, since they had to choose
one of two competing forms of the new faith. In Gaul, the cities were largely Christian in the fourth century, and the country districts were christianized in the fifth and sixth centuries.
In Spain, the cities on the southeast coast were Christian as
early as the beginning of the fifth century, but the Vandal invasions in the early fifth century brought all progress to a halt.
In Roman Britain, there were Christian communities in the
larger towns in the early 400's, but the invasion of the Angles
and the Saxons before the middle of the century virtually
eradicated Christianity from all but the far western parts of
the country.

3.74 Problems with the Sacrament of Baptism

As we have seen, the institution of the *catechumenate* had
been introduced in the second century to deal with the increasing number of pagans who sought entry into the church.
The idea had been to provide the future Christians with a
solid foundation in faith and a basis for the stern ethical demands of their new religious commitment. However, the
widespread rigorism of the second and third centuries, together with the extremely strict approach to the forgiveness
of sins which were committed after baptism, led many to de-
fer baptism as long as possible, so that all their sins might be
forgiven, and they would go safely to heaven, without having
had to pass through the savage penitential discipline of the
church. Logically, this could lead to delaying baptism until
one was on the point of death, and this is precisely what happened in many cases. Surprisingly, even leading churchmen,
like Basil, Gregory Nazianzen, John Chrysostom, Ambrose,
and Augustine, were not baptized until their mature years.

Apparently many would enroll in the catechumenate,
since then they could be considered Christian, but would delay baptism indefinitely. Toward the end of the fourth century, bishops in many areas began to realize how destructive

(not to say superstitious) this practice was, and they took steps to try to determine which of the catechumens were really serious and which intended to play the waiting game. One sign of their success is that by the early fifth century, infant baptism was becoming very common throughout the church.

3.75 Developments in Christian Piety

Martyrs had always been highly regarded in the church, and during the times of persecution those who had compromised their faith under pressure often turned to those who had suffered and asked them to make intercession with God and with the leadership of the church on their behalf. When the persecutions were over, Christians began to look back on the martyrs as heroes of the past and they venerated them. It was also a common wish to be buried near the martyrs, in the cemeteries which, by law, were located outside of the cities. In time, it was felt that the remains of the martyrs should be nearby when liturgy was celebrated, and so the custom of bringing the bones of the martyrs into the churches and interring them under the altar developed. This preoccupation with the remains or relics of the martyrs led at times to almost a mania, and each church was eager to have at least part of the body of a well-known martyr under its altar. In time, of course, the bones ran out, and then people had to make do with cloths which had been brought in contact with the bones or at least with the cases in which they were preserved, and miraculous powers were attributed to these "once removed" relics. The possibilities for superstition and magic were almost unlimited, and the foundations of all later medieval abuses in this direction were laid in the fourth and fifth centuries.

The sermons of famous churchmen of the period show that there must have been much superficial Christianity at the time, and that pagan customs and usages were slow to die. Churchmen often tried to cope with this residual paganism by "baptizing" one or another pagan feast or place or practice, but this was dangerous, because the old paganism often lived on under a thin Christian veneer.

Asceticism was highly prized among the elite of the fourth and fifth centuries, and it was an asceticism which emphasized distance from the world. Fasting was esteemed and the practice of virginity was urged on the laity, even if they lived at home and not in religious communities. The popularized versions of Neo-Platonism which were current, as well as the prevalence of sexual perversion in the late ancient world and in paganism in general, led to this emphasis on virginity and celibacy, but for the wrong reasons. No real understanding of the sanctity proper to the married state, including a truly Christian evaluation of sexuality, was ever reached in the early church.

3.8 THE YEARS 311 TO 451 IN RETROSPECT

In the period of one hundred and forty years which we have been examining in this chapter, the church faced great challenges. Each of these challenges confronted the church with possibilities of success as well as failure, and the record of the church at the end of the period was very mixed.

When the persecutions ended, Christians found themselves free to practice their faith and to preach it openly, and they turned with great confidence to the task of converting the Empire. But at the same time, it became politically advantageous to join the Christian church, and therefore the motives of many of those who thronged the churches in the early fourth century were more than questionable. Unfortunately, the religiously neutral state was not a possibility at the time, and so the leveling of Christian faith and practice to a least common denominator, at least in many places, was probably inevitable.

During this period, the teaching of the church on the identity of Jesus Christ and on his relationship to God underwent great development, and a serious attempt was made to appropriate the mysteries of the faith, using all of the resources of Greek thought. But in some respects, the Christian mysteries were recalcitrant and they did not yield to the methods of Greek thought. There were even more serious consequences for the future: the theologians of the time thought and expressed themselves in terms alien to the New Testament and foreign to us and our world, but these are the same terms which Christians today feel obliged to recite in their creeds. If only the church of later times had been able to see the achievement of theologians of the fourth and fifth centuries as one which was valuable and made sense *then,* and had not felt the need to impose their terminology on later generations as a condition of faith, little harm would have been done. But in practice, the dogmatic formulas of Nicaea, Ephesus and Chalcedon were taken more seriously than the text of the New Testament itself, and this was very harmful for the faith of later ages.

The church of the early fifth century overcame the Donatist schism in North Africa, and this restored unity to a local church which had suffered enormously for over a century. However union was achieved at the price of asking the Roman government to intervene and use force on behalf of the Catholic church, and this established a precedent which would do untold harm to the church right into modern times. The church in this period never had any conception of how to separate the competences of Caesar from those of God, and later ages learned this lesson slowly, if at all.

During the fourth and early fifth century, the faith was preached throughout what was thought to be the civilized world, and by the end of this period it had become the faith of the majority of the citizens of the Empire. But the apparent success of the church was purchased at a high price; Christianity was now the official religion of the Empire and this set a fatal precedent. European colonial churches until the recent past identified Christian faith with western values and culture and this made the faith seem profoundly alien in Asia and in large parts of Africa up to the present day. Tragically, the universalism of Christian faith was absorbed in the universal political claims of the Empire, and of its various political and cultural descendants.

It is, of course, the task of the church, not to abandon the world but to transform it, but it is called to do this without becoming worldly in the process. The church must respect the autonomy of the world in its sphere and it must affirm its own autonomy in its own sphere, while keeping a critical distance between itself and the world. This was the challenge faced by the church in the fourth century, and on the basis of the record we would have to say that the church yielded to the temptation of political power and did not keep its critical distance. The real tragedy was *theological* in nature. Allegorical exegesis of the scripture was the rule at that time, and therefore the one factor, scripture, which was capable of judging and criticizing the appropriation of worldly values and standards was effectively neutralized.

4

From the Germanic Invasions to the Dark Age

4.1 INTRODUCTION

The year 313 is of epoch-making importance in church history, not because it marked the victory of the church over the Empire, but because it is the year in which Constantine made the politically astute judgment that the Christian church and it alone was capable of providing the spiritual substance and the religious unity without which the Empire itself would not endure. The year 313 marked the beginning of an alliance between the church and the Empire. It was an alliance fraught with enormous risk for the church, particularly in the eastern provinces, and it was an alliance which, even in the West, raised questions about the relationship of church and state which have not been answered up to the present day.

4.2 THE END OF THE ANCIENT WORLD

When the persecutions ended with the Edict of Galerius in 311 and the Rescript of Constantine in 313, the Empire which had finally been compelled to grant to Christians the right to exist was itself moribund, and its days were numbered. Whatever spiritual energies the Empire had ever had were now exhausted, and economic stagnation had brought large areas to the brink of ruin; and yet, at this precise moment, vast sums of money were needed to support the armies

125

on the frontiers of the Empire. Diocletian's administrative and economic reforms of the 280's, shrewd as they were, had been unable to stop the slide toward ruin, and in the year 313, although no one realized it, the Empire was poorly prepared to meet the onslaught from the north and the east. The church had made its peace with the Empire rather too quickly and easily, at the very moment at which the foundations of the Empire began to crumble, and an astute observer of the time might have wondered what the collapse of the Empire would mean to that organization which had, in the course of the fourth century, become the imperial church. Would a church which associated its destinies with those of the Empire be able to survive the fall of that same Empire?

4.21 The Germanic Tribes

The German tribes which were poised on the frontier from the middle of the fourth century on were not a nation and the political unification of all of the Germanic peoples was not achieved at any time in the period under discussion in this chapter. The only unity the Germans possessed was ethnic and linguistic. They spoke languages which were, except for those at the extreme ends of the territory, mutually comprehensible at the end of the fourth century, but they themselves were divided into a large number of independent tribes, whose original homelands had stretched from the Black Sea to the Baltic.

The Germans crossed the frontiers of the Empire not because they sought the material or cultural wealth of old Rome (although they were quite willing to appropriate whatever remained of each, once they got there). Rather, they moved to the south and west because they, in turn, felt the pressure of Slavic and Turco-Tartar tribes farther to the east. The Germans served, in a way, as buffers for the old Empire, against the still more savage peoples who were erupting from the steppes of central Asia.

It was undoubtedly an awareness of this valuable function which led the eastern Emperors and the prefects of some of the former provinces of the West to allow bands of Germans to settle permanently within the frontiers. This policy had led to increasing contact between Constantinople and the Goths, and there was one consequence of this which was fateful in the extreme for the church in the West and for the history of western Europe. A young Goth named Wulfila (311 to 382) had been converted to Christianity while in Constantinople, either as a guest or as a hostage. His conversion took place during that period, after the death of Constantine, when Arianism was supreme. In the year 341 he was consecrated bishop by the Arian extremist, Eusebius of Nicomedia, and sent to take care of the Christians in Gothic territory, and to win the pagan Goths to the Christian faith (in the Arian form in which he had learned it). Wulfila took his mission seriously and did his work well. The new faith spread rapidly among the eastern and western Goths, helped by Wulfila's translation of the New Testament into Gothic. Arian Christianity spread with equal rapidity among the other Germanic peoples with whom the Goths were in contact. The new faith, though heretical, had enough Christian substance left in it to secure a hearing among the serious, and it had those trappings of fourth century orthodox Christianity which guaranteed that it would secure the adherence of the superstitious. Furthermore, Arian Christianity became a kind of trademark of the Germanic peoples. It gave them a sense of unity and identity and a way of distinguishing themselves from the Catholic population of the Empire. Arianism was *the German faith,* and in an age when the separation of religion from political and social existence was unthinkable, the Arian faith of the Germanic tribes effectively blocked their assimilation of the older culture. In doing this, it delayed for more than a century the beginning of Christian Europe.

Although in the view of Latin and Greek writers of the day, the Germanic tribesmen were simply *the barbarians,* they were scarcely cavemen or primitive savages. They were an agrarian people who developed no real cities within their domains, but they had an elaborate code of customary law which was handed down orally within each tribe. Their law strongly emphasized property rights, and included a carefully worked out system of compensation for injuries inflicted—probably developed in order to prevent the extinction of entire clans as a result of feuds. The Germanic tribes were warlike, and their gods were, by and large, a savage lot, and death in battle was the most noble fulfillment of a warrior's life. This attitude toward war and battle was probably an important factor in the development of the crusading ideal and in the rise of the military orders during the medieval period.

4.22　Initial Contacts with the Empire

The Emperors of the East were quite adroit in deflecting the German menace from their capital and from the choicer hinterlands, but a number of western Goths were settled within the imperial frontier in 376. This led to inevitable friction with the imperial forces, and, just two years later, to the defeat of the Emperor Valens and his army by the Goths at Adrianople in 378; but Valens' successors were able, by treaty and tribute, to send the victors to Italy. Gothic war bands ravaged that unfortunate peninsula for decades, and finally Alaric, the chief of another tribe, captured and sacked the city of Rome in 410. This event had a symbolic importance all out of proportion to its immediate political effect. It sent shock waves through the West and led Augustine to write his great work, *The City of God,* in which he tried to give a Christian interpretation of the great calamity.

By far the larger group of Germans penetrated the western Empire, not by way of Constantinople, but directly across the northern frontiers. Small groups had been allowed in as allies, and then, from about the year 400, large groups moved in without the formality of invitation. Frankish tribes had bridged the Rhine near Mainz at the very end of 399. The Vandals crossed over in 406, and by 425 they were in Spain. From there they moved on to North Africa, and they were besieging the city of Hippo at the moment of Augustine's death. Western Goths set up a kingdom in France which lasted from 418 to 507. The Lombard kingdom in Italy dates from 568 to shortly after 750.

The Germans did not arrive precisely as enemies in the former lands of the Empire and many of them were more than willing to serve in Rome's armies. In the year 451, when the troops of Attila, the Hun, were defeated at the battle of the Catalaunian Fields in Gaul, the Roman army was largely Teutonic, and their general, Aetius, was half-German.

As we have seen, the so-called fall of Rome had no real political significance. Roman power in the West had declined sharply since the death of Theodosius in 395, and the first attempt to fill the power vacuum was made by the Gothic chieftain, Theoderic, at the very end of the fifth century. He tried to unite all of the Germanic peoples on both an ethnic and religious basis, but Arian Christianity lacked both the religious substance and the link with ancient culture which would have made such an attempt successful. For a short period after the death of Theoderic in 526, Justinian, the eastern Emperor, was able to assert Roman power in the West again.

4.23 A New Task for the Church

The Roman Empire in the West was dead, and forces beyond Justinian's control made his brief reconquest an exercise in nostalgia. As the Empire declined, Catholic churchmen— bishops and Popes—assumed more and more of the functions of civil authority. This happened, perhaps surprisingly, not because they sought that power, but because it was thrust on them by various groups in society, and not least by the Germans themselves, who came to realize that churchmen were the only ones able to guarantee a stable civil order.

During this period, the church in Rome became particularly important, not for strictly theological reasons, but because a number of bishops of the city at this time were men of outstanding ability, who accepted civil power, and asserted, at the same time, their religious authority and primacy in the church. As we have seen on occasion, since the end of the first century the church in Rome had claimed a special position in the universal church. Victor (Pope from 189 to 199) had intervened successfully in a dispute that was going on in the East about the date of Easter, and Stephen (Pope from 254 to 257) had strongly asserted Rome's doctrinal primacy against

Cyprian, himself a strong-willed and dedicated churchman in North Africa.

It was always difficult to determine whether Rome's primacy was based more on its position as capital of the Empire, or more on strictly religious grounds—the fact that it was commonly believed that Peter and Paul had been martyred there. When Constantinople became the capital and grew in political importance, this question became much more serious. At the Council of Chalcedon in 451, Constantinople was accorded equality with Rome, and Leo the Great, the Pope at the time, entered a strong protest against this decision. At the end of the same century, Gelasius (Pope from 492 to 496) was responsible for further development of the theory of papal primacy. He asserted that civil and religious powers had to be distinguished, but he further asserted that in important respects civil power was subject to religious power, and of course he claimed supreme religious power for himself and his office.

It was above all the Bishops of Rome—and from this time on they can correctly be called *Popes*—who began to see that the future of the western world, including, of course, the church, lay with the Germanic tribes. The Popes who saw this were actually wielding a good deal of civil power, but they did so neither as Emperors nor as vassals of the eastern Emperors, and they had no real emotional investment in the old Empire. Their immediate task was that of converting the Germans, either from Arian Christianity or directly from paganism.

4.24 The Church in the East

The separation of orthodox (eastern) Christianity from Roman (western) Christianity is often dated to the year 1054, when the Pope and the Patriarch of Constantinople excommunicated each other. But these excommunications were short-lived and without much importance. What was important was the fact that they were symbolic of a situation which had been festering for hundreds of years. The two churches had taken very different directions and their estrangement was inevitable. From the early fifth century, the West was effectively without an Emperor. In many cases, the clergy took over administrative duties and became the custodians of the traditions of Roman law. (And this emphasis on law has been a characteristic of Catholic Christianity up to the present day.) The imperial tradition, on the other hand, was maintained in the East, and the church there was effectively under imperial control from the time of Constantine. The Emperors functioned very much like priest-kings.

Within the eastern Empire itself, theological and doctrinal disagreements had produced lasting divisions. The Council of Chalcedon worked out a formula which might have made doctrinal coexistence possible, but the eastern Emperors insisted on tampering with the Chalcedonian settlement for political reasons. But none of their measures worked, and dissident groups who rejected either the Council of Ephesus or the Council of Chalcedon separated themselves from the main body of believers. After 460, the Nestorian church transferred its headquarters to Nisibis in Mesopotamia, where they would be effectively outside imperial control, and from there that church engaged in wide-ranging missionary activity which would bring Nestorian priests to China in 635. Egypt's rejection of the Chalcedonian settlement and the creation of a Monophysite church there was probably a major factor in the success of the Moslem conquest of Egypt in 641.

4.3 MONASTICISM

Attempts to explain the origins of Christian monasticism on the basis of either Jewish or pagan models have not been successful. The monastic movement resulted from the desire of some Christians to follow their Lord in an unrestricted way and to imitate him totally. They took very seriously the dialectic of winning and losing life, temporal and eternal, as we find it in the eighth chapter of Mark's Gospel. But there is one fact about monastic life which is often not seen; although the monks saw the need of distancing themselves from the world, and of refusing to accept uncritically the world's scale of values, genuine monasticism was never really a flight from the world. In the period under discussion in this chapter, there was probably no group in either the East or the West which was as totally involved with the world and as creative of the future as were the monks.

4.31 The Origins of Monasticism

The beginnings of monasticism can be traced to Anthony, an Egyptian hermit who lived from 251 to 356. He was something of a prophet in the Old Testament mold, who spoke the demanding word of God to the world of his time. Anthony experienced and voiced the uncompromising character of the call of Christ, and this call was heard by many in his day, who went into the deserts of Egypt to find God far from the comforts and temptations of civilization. Some of the followers and successors of Anthony went in for ascetical feats which strike us as strange today, but all were motivated by the desire to keep a critical distance from the world's values. Under Pachomius, who lived from 287 to 347, the emphasis shifted from the solitary hermit toward the monk who lived in community with others, and great monasteries were established on the fringe of the Egyptian desert near Thebes.

It is possible that the rather long period of peace before the Decian persecution in 251, and, later, the Constantinian Settlement itself, stimulated the development of religious life. Martyrdom had been regarded as the ideal consummation of Christian life, and as long as the state was willing to oblige, Christians knew that the total gift of self might be demanded at any moment. However, when the state itself became Christian (whatever that meant, precisely!), then the faithful had to turn elsewhere in search of a new ideal.

4.32 The Spread of Monasticism

Athanasius, who had done so much to insure the triumph of Nicene theology, wrote a life of Anthony, which brought the monastic ideal to the attention of thousands; and when, on one of his many trips into exile, he came to Trier in the mid-fourth century, he was accompanied by two monks, and this made the monastic life known in the West for the first time. Basil the Great, who died in 379, wrote a rule which gave important direction to eastern monasticism. In accordance with this rule, monks for the first time became involved with works of charity, and monasteries began to appear in the towns and cities. In the East, these monks, who were close to the people and were admired and loved by them, exercised considerable power in the church. On many occasions they resisted the meddling of the Emperors in religious questions, and opposed even the higher clergy and the Patriarch in the name of traditional and conservative religious values.

In the West, a monastery appears to have been founded at Lerins, off the southern coast of France, about 405. Even before this, Augustine had thought highly of the monastic ideal from the time of his conversion, and he organized the life of his clergy in North Africa in accordance with this ideal. In the West, the monks were responsible for bringing the faith to the rural areas, and this was very important for the future of the church, because outside Italy the old Roman cities had gone into decline, and the Germanic peoples themselves never developed an urban civilization during this period. If Christianity put down strong roots in the West and in northern Europe between the fifth and the ninth centuries, this was due in the main to the work of the monks.

4.33 Ireland

The church in Ireland is an interesting case here; it was almost entirely the creation of a man named Patrick (ca 385 to 461). Probably of Roman-British origin, he had been captured and taken as a slave to Ireland. After escaping, he may have been a monk for some time at the monastery of Lerins. In 432, answering what he was convinced was a call from the Irish people, begging for one who would lead them to Christ, he returned as bishop, and spent the final twenty-nine years of his life directing the successful conversion of almost the entire population, and creating an ecclesiastical organization to serve the new church.

The organization which Patrick created was unique. Instead of dividing the country into dioceses, headed by the bishops of the principal cities of the region, Patrick divided Ireland into areas presided over by individual monasteries. Each monastery served a *clan*—a large group of distantly related people, together with their slaves and dependents, who were settled in a single area. Religious services were provided by monks who were ordained as priests, and, when necessary, consecrated as bishops. This was a departure from previous practice—the first monks had been laymen—and it linked the two vocations of religious life and priesthood in a manner which still determines the way we think about them today. More immediately, it provided a model for the monasticizing of the priesthood, which was zealously promoted by Rome from the end of the eleventh century on.

4.34 Private Confession

In Ireland, Patrick's death was followed by almost three hundred years of impressive development in culture and spirituality. As early as the sixth century, Irish monks were leaving their homeland and traveling to the continent. Here they preached an essentially monastic spirituality which was a major influence on the development of medieval piety. This was most evident in the changes they introduced in the practice of confession. The confession of sins and the subsequent granting of reconciliation by the bishop in the name of the church had been a rather public matter since the early days of the church. Those who had committed publicly verifiable sins and crimes performed public penance for a considerable period of time and then were publicly reconciled in a ceremony which brought them back into full communion with the church. In the sixth and seventh centuries, the monks privatized the practice of confession, and in this process much more emphasis was placed on hidden sins, of which one might be aware only after a careful examination of conscience. Confession of these sins was made in private, and the sins were remitted privately. In the hands of the monks, confession became an important tool of spiritual direction, and some laypeople undertook to follow the direction of a monk, even while continuing to live their lives in the world.

4.35 The Irish Monks in Europe

The Irish monks traveled widely in Europe, mostly in what is now France and Germany. It is true that they often did not remain in an area long enough to touch the faith of the inhabitants in more than a superficial way, but they did one very important thing. They founded monasteries which lasted for centuries after their deaths, and which were instrumental in making genuine Christians out of the descendants of tribesmen who had entered the church at the time of the mass conversions, when an entire tribe would be baptized because the chieftain thought it was a politically wise move. The work of one of these Irish monks was especially important. Columban lived from 530 to 615 and traveled in Gaul, Burgundy (east central France), Switzerland and North Italy. He founded monasteries and organized the lives of the monks and of the laypeople who depended on them for religious instruction, and because of this his work was more enduring than that of the other wandering monks.

4.4 THE CHURCH TAKES THE INITIATIVE

The tribes that swarmed into the territories of the old Empire in the fifth and sixth centuries were a challenge for the church in every sense of the word. It was a challenge of which the church became aware only gradually, and a challenge which the church met in stages.

4.41 Troubled Coexistence

In the beginning, the Arian German newcomers and the Catholic native population regarded each other with suspicion and contempt. Ethnic distinctions were compounded by religious differences, but there was one factor which kept violence to a minimum, because it limited contact between the two groups. This was the fact that most of the Catholic Christians lived in the cities and towns of the former empire, while the invading Germans settled in the countryside. The town and the countryside needed each other, of course, but in many respects they were complementary and not competitive, and commercial contacts between the older population and the invaders provided the first opportunity for peaceful encounters. It was in the old province of Gaul (roughly, modern France) that the German percentage in the population was the highest, although with the exception of the eastern provinces it seems clear that the Gallo-Roman element always constituted the majority. In the fourth and fifth centuries it was often the bishops in these old Gallo-Roman towns who provided for public order and did all in their power to make contact between the two ethnic groups as peaceful as possible. Martin of Tours, who died in 397, was one of the earliest of these "prefect-bishops"; Remigius of Rheims, who died in 533, and Caesar of Arles, who died in 542, continued the tradition, and were directly involved in a decision which, more than any other, created the medieval world as we have come to know it.

4.42 Chlodwech and the Gallo-Roman Bishops

It was the Arian faith of the Germans which prevented their religious and cultural assimilation. As the fifth century drew to a close, Remigius of Rheims and a number of other Gallo-Roman bishops were quite aware of this fact and they also realized that there was no possibility of converting the Arian Germans to Catholic Christianity in the near future. But they were also aware of another possibility: for almost a century, the Franks, another Germanic tribe, had been moving across the Rhine into lands which now form part of Holland, Belgium, and northern France. These Franks had come from a part of Europe too far to the north and west to be influenced by the Goths and their Arian Christianity, and therefore they were still pagans when they arrived in Gaul. If they could be converted directly to Catholic Christianity, there would be no barrier to their mixing with the native population, and they might even succeed in winning their Arian kinsmen to the true faith.

Remigius and his fellow bishops must have been dimly aware that the future of the church and the future of Europe lay with these new arrivals from beyond the Rhine. The course of events is not entirely clear, but we do know this: in 486 the young Frankish chieftain, Chlodwech, defeated a Gallo-Roman army in northern Gaul. A few years later, some Gallo-Roman bishops, led by Remigius, persuaded Chlodwech to accept baptism, and Chlodwech and thousands of his troops were baptized in Rheims on Christmas day of the year 496.

No one will ever know exactly what Chlodwech thought of his new faith, but he does appear to be the first of the Germans to realize how much could be gained from an alliance with the Catholic bishops, and how helpful it might be to face a populace which regarded him not as an alien heretic but as a brother in the faith. From this moment the two populations could begin to merge, and although national unity was still centuries away, from this time on we speak of *France* instead of *Gaul*. (And Chlodwech is often referred to as *Clovis*, the French form of his name.) Supported by the Gallo-Roman bishops of the region, Chlodwech consolidated his hold on the north and turned to the east, where he conquered the Alemannic tribes, to the south, where he conquered the Burgundians who had been settled there for nearly a century, and then finally to the far south, Provence, where he incorporated the kingdom of the eastern Goths into his growing Empire. After each of these conquests, Chlodwech's new faith was imposed on the defeated population. In this way, much of France became at least nominally Catholic in the early years of the sixth century.

4.43 A Problematic Decision

The baptism of Chlodwech and his army was certainly not without problems. The Gallo-Roman bishops themselves probably had little idea of what a proper *catechumenate* was (that is, the lengthy period of preparation and instruction which had been demanded of potential converts in the third century, and which was designed to insure the depth and the genuinity of the conversion). Chlodwech and his soldiers probably regarded Jesus Christ as a new and more powerful tribal god, whose main purpose in life was to give the Franks victory in battle. (An important law code of the period, the *Lex Salica*, speaks of God precisely in this vein—as one who loves the Franks and will guarantee victory for Frankish arms.)

There was a second problem, of which no one at the time was aware. It never seems to have occurred to the Gallo-Roman bishops to offer the Franks a liturgy in their own language, or to give them a vernacular translation of scripture, nor did it occur to Chlodwech and his followers to demand this of the guardians of their new faith. Liturgy was celebrated in a language unintelligible to the newly converted masses, and mystifying pomp replaced the genuine mystery and dignified clarity of a text which was still quite well understood by the Romance-speaking populace. There is no doubt that the newly converted tribesmen were awed by the magnificence of the ceremonies which they witnessed, but awe without understanding breeds superstition, and a Christianity which believes that it can dispense with a vernacular version of scripture deprives itself of the one means of effectively criticizing that superstition.

The third problem presented by the mass conversion of the Franks was a direct result of the breakdown of communications throughout the former Western Empire during the sixth and seventh centuries. The new Frankish church lost contact with the churches in the other lands of the West and became an isolated and inbred body, directed by unworthy prelates and, ultimately, under the control of a degenerate monarchy. This situation lasted for over two hundred years after the death of Chlodwech, and it is just one of a great number of historical facts which force the serious observer to raise some questions about the unity of the church and about ways of fostering and preserving that unity. Whatever one holds about the jurisdictional primacy of the Pope and however much one may justly criticize the abuses of papal power, it remains true that local and national churches have been able to keep their integrity and their freedom to the degree to which they affirmed their link with Rome, and through it, to other local churches throughout the world.

4.44 The Conversion of the Franks and the Future of the Church

Catholic church historians have tended to be optimistic in their view of the conversion of Chlodwech and his army, and they have traced to the ceremony at the cathedral in Rheims in 496 the birth of that France which would later be called the eldest daughter of the church, and they have found there the first step in the creation of the medieval world which they regard as the highest achievement of Catholic culture. But the real picture is more complex and it is a far more subtle blend of light and shadow.

Genuine faith is always a gift of God, but it is a gift which respects our humanity and all that is distinctive about it. Precisely for this reason, genuine faith is always a free and intelligent act. Faith cannot be conveyed simply by the performance of a ceremony or a rite, nor can it be the automatic result of one's membership in an ethnic group, or in a civil or military body. Furthermore, Jesus Christ, who is the ground and object of our faith, did not come to conform to our all too human expectations about God and about ourselves. Rather, he came to proclaim the good news of a God whom we had never known and whom we could never invent, and he came to tell us that we are closest to the real God precisely at the moment that our all too human expectations come to nought. Christian faith is not hostile to wisdom, to culture, to authority, or even to power; but it does tell us that all of these and all other human values can be safe only when they are criticized by the scriptural word, which is always the *word of the cross*. Churchmen in the Eastern Empire had forgotten this at the time of the Constantinian Settlement, and the Gallo-Roman bishops who baptized Chlodwech seem to have been quite unaware of it in 496.

It is quite correct to point out that, given their background and their training, and the world in which they lived, they probably could not have acted in any other way, but this is really beside the point. It is usually not the task of church history to assess the guilt or innocence of churchmen of the past; but any church historian who wishes to be more than a mere chronicler of ecclesiastical events must attempt to make correct objective judgments about the policies adopted by churchmen, and about the appropriateness of these policies in the light of the New Testament message. Medieval churchmen never seem to have grasped the ambiguity of power, any more than they understood the depths of superstition in which the great mass of common people lived. More tragically still, they failed to see that the very reform of the church in head and members which many of them sincerely desired was an impossibility unless parish priests were thoroughly familiar with scripture, and unless they could read it and preach it to their congregations in a language which all understood. These multiple tragedies were the direct result of decisions made and opportunities missed in the year 496.

4.5 THE SECOND INITIATIVE OF THE CHURCH IN THE CREATION OF THE MEDIEVAL WORLD

The church met the challenge posed by the invasions of the Germanic peoples and did so in three different stages. The first stage culminated in the baptism of Chlodwech and his army and in the establishment, through that move, of an at least nominally Christian Frankish kingdom which covered much of the territory of modern France. The first stage ended rather ingloriously with the decline and decay of the Frankish kingdom and the Frankish church, which began in the sixth century and lasted well into the eighth. By the early seventh century, it was clearly time for the church to take the second step in the creation of medieval Europe.

4.51 Gregory the Great

This step was taken by a remarkable individual who was Pope from 590 to 604. Gregory had been born into a wealthy

Roman family about the year 540. By the standards of the day, he was well educated, and he had been prepared for a career in civil life; but when his parents died, he converted the family estate into a monastery, where he and a group under his direction lived a strict monastic life. But Gregory was able to remain a monk for only four years, and even during that time he was continually called on by the reigning Pope for advice in religious and secular matters. On the death of the Pope, he was the obvious choice, and much against his will he was elected Pope.

The accession of a man of Gregory's ability to the papacy at this precise moment made him something like the *de facto* ruler of the lands of the former western Empire, and although the turmoil of the Germanic invasions limited his ability to reestablish order throughout the West, he acted quickly and effectively to remedy that situation, and he did so both as Bishop of Rome and as the civil protector of Rome and of Italy. Gregory saw clearly that it was futile to look to the East for protection against the Germanic tribes which had been streaming into the old Empire for more than two hundred years. He saw that the future of the church lay not in defending itself against the invaders, but in winning them to the Christian faith and in creating, with them, a new world. He cultivated good relations with the Franks, but he had no illusions about either the Frankish kingdom or the Frankish church. Instead, Gregory turned to other Germanic tribes who were either still pagan, or who had continued in their Arian Christianity, and he looked for peaceful ways to win them to the faith. In the very first year of his reign he sent the Roman monk Augustine to England, and this move was of epoch-making importance for both England and the continent. Closer to home, he was able to effect the conversion to Catholic Christianity of the royal house of the Western Gothic kingdom in Spain, and of the Lombards, a Germanic tribe who had established a kingdom in northern Italy some thirty years earlier. Both of these steps greatly facilitated the blending of the Germanic and Romance elements of the population and, at least in the case of the Western Goths, it resulted in the forging of a strong link between the local church and the papacy. Both of these features are distinctive elements of the medieval period, and even though they would come into full vigor only after half a millennium, Gregory had taken the all-important first step.

Gregory realized the importance of a competent and dedicated clergy, and he took steps to reform the clergy and to improve their training. He wrote two books which were much read and which were influential for centuries: the *Liber Regulae Pastoralis,* which was a handbook for parish priests in the performance of their duties, and the *Moralia in Job,* which was a practical guide to moral theology. Both books were used for the training of priests throughout the entire medieval period. In addition, Gregory wrote a life of Benedict of Nursia, which insured that the rule which Benedict had written in the early fifth century would give western monasticism its distinctive shape and form for more than a thousand years. In addition, Gregory reformed the liturgy, and in some way that we are not entirely clear about, he made some important changes in liturgical chant. It was this which led to the association of his name with various collections of liturgical music that originated before his time and whose careful codification and purification was the work of monks for hundreds of years after his death.

4.52 The Anglo-Saxon Mission

Gregory's initiative in sending Augustine to England was crowned with success even before Gregory's death. In the year 597, the West Saxon king, Ethelbert, and ten thousand of his warriors were baptized at Kent, in another one of those mass conversions which seem so strange to us today (and which would have been equally shocking to Christians of the second century). In the 620's and 630's the Christian faith made great progress in Wessex and Northumbria. Much of the work here seems to have been done by monks, and although the situation is not clear, it seems that much of the preaching and subsequent instruction was done by Celtic monks, who had been pushed to the far west of Britain at the time of the Anglo-Saxon invasions, and who now took advantage of the friendlier climate to preach the faith to their former enemies. In any case, we know that by 660 there was some friction between the "Roman" Christians who were the followers of Augustine of Canterbury, and the Celtic Christians who had come back from the west or had come over from Ireland.

The two churches were organized along very different lines. Augustine himself had been sent by the Pope, and his followers had maintained the Roman connection. The Celtic church, on the other hand, was more independent, and the monks who controlled it had only the most tenuous connection with Rome. In addition, the churches were divided by a dispute over the dating of certain liturgical feasts—something which does not seem important today, but which loomed large at the time. In 664 a Synod, or gathering of bishops, at Whitby, brought peace to the two churches. Some small concessions were made to the Celtic church, but it was tacitly recognized that the Anglo-Saxon church, with its strong link to Rome, was to be firmly in control. It is true that the initial conversion was quite superficial, and after the middle of the century there was a resurgence of paganism, but by 690 virtually the entire island was nominally Christian.

4.53 Anglo-Saxon Missionaries on the Continent

Given the conditions of the day, there is nothing surprising about the fact that many of the conversions in England were superficial. What *is* surprising is that there were some Englishmen, born less than one hundred years after the conversion of Ethelbert and his ten thousand, who played a major role in bringing the Christian faith to those parts of France and Germany which were still largely pagan. These Anglo-Saxon monks were more effective than the Irish monks of a century before for two reasons. First, the Anglo-Saxons maintained a close link with Rome, since this had been their tradition from the very beginning, and they were aware that a national church, isolated and separated from the universal church, could easily fall under the control of secular authority. Second (and to some degree counterbalancing what was just said), these Anglo-Saxon monks were careful to secure the support of local and regional political authority for their work. Both of these factors made their work more enduring.

Even more than their predecessors, these monks founded monasteries in the lands through which they traveled. These monasteries were a source of spiritual power and they kept the spark of learning alive during the dark age which was about to break over the continent. Two names stand out among these Anglo-Saxon monks: the first was Wilfried of York, who began the mission to the Frisians, a tribe who lived in what is now northwest Germany and who were closely related to the Anglo-Saxons. The second was Winfried, his successor in this mission, and the most successful of all of the Anglo-Saxon monks.

Winfried, later known as Boniface, was born in 672. Before beginning his missionary work, he asked and received permission from Charles Martel, the actual ruler of the Frankish kingdom, and then he turned to the Pope for religious authorization. In the year 722 he went to Rome and was consecrated bishop by the Pope, and on that occasion he took a special oath of loyalty to the Pope. After successfully beginning his reforming work in the Frankish church, he felt that an even closer link with Rome would be helpful, and he returned to Rome in 732, to be consecrated archbishop by Gregory III. This gave him greater authority to pursue his life work, which was the reform of the Frankish church—a reform which he carried out between 738 and 747. During this period he organized a number of synods which dealt with the training of candidates for the priesthood and with methods of pastoral practice. More than anyone else outside of the palace, Winfried prepared the way for the Carolingian Empire and for its revival in the form of the Holy Roman Empire of medieval times. Even as an old man, Winfried did not abandon active missionary work, and it was while engaging in this activity that he and a number of his companions were slaughtered by some pagan Frisians in 754.

4.6 THE THIRD INITIATIVE OF THE CHURCH IN THE CREATION OF THE MEDIEVAL WORLD

This third initiative looks very much like the first. At the very end of the fifth century, the Gallo-Roman bishops had turned to Chlodwech, the Frankish chieftain. And now, in the middle of the eighth century, they turned to a family of talented soldiers who were administering the affairs of the almost defunct Frankish royal house.

4.61 The Decline of the Eastern Empire

For the medieval world to begin, the papacy had to break definitively and formally with what remained of the Roman Empire—that is, with the Emperors who ruled from Constantinople, and with their claims to the territory of the old western Empire, which had come to an end in 476. When, in that year, Odovaker had sent the insignia of the Empire back to Constantinople, this was tacit recognition that the eastern Emperor now ruled the West as well, at least nominally. But as we have seen, except for a short period under Justinian, the eastern Emperors were never able to assert their authority in the West. Despite this, their claim remained and was recognized in principle by all; even though there had been a *de facto* political vacuum in the West since before 476, nothing could be done to fill that vacuum until some way could be found to legitimate the transfer of authority from Constantinople to a new center in the West.

After the year 600, the Empire of the East became more and more occupied with its own problems. Slavic, Bulgar, and Avar tribes were poised on the borders, and were making tentative forays into the Empire. In about 605 the Persians began to move against the Empire, and they had conquered Egypt by 619. They were not finally defeated until 627, outside the ancient city of Nineveh.

But no sooner were the Persians beaten than a more formidable threat appeared, that of Islam. The Islamic religion was founded by Mohammad, a merchant who lived in the region which we now call Saudi Arabia, where he had been born in 571. On his journeys he became acquainted with Judaism and Christianity, and he was impressed by certain aspects of both—above all with their monotheistic faith and their consequent conviction of the absolute power and transcendence of God. When Mohammad was in his forties, he had a religious experience in the form of a revelation of the power and presence of God, which moved him to fashion a faith that was based on total submission to this God. For this faith he fashioned a simple set of teachings. He selected elements from both Judaism and Christianity, and he strongly emphasized fatalism and God's will that all submit to him, even if convinced only by force of arms. This clear and simple faith appealed to the wild Arabian tribesmen, and as early as the year 630 the tribes were converted and welded into a powerful military force, which understood its mission as that of bringing the entire world to faith in the one true God, whose prophet was Mohammad. This blending of religion with military conquest was powerful medicine, and in a short time the Moslems swept through the Near East. They conquered Damascus in 635, Jerusalem in 637, and Egypt in 641.

The eastern Empire saw itself stripped of much of its territory by the Moslem drive, and finally the Moslems turned against Constantinople itself, which was hit with wave after wave of assault between 674 and 678, but which threw back the attacks with great heroism. Meanwhile, the march across North Africa continued, and in 711 the Moslems crossed the Straits of Gibraltar and landed in Spain. Within twenty years, they had swept through the Iberian peninsula and crossed the Pyrenees. Here they were finally stopped at Tours, in France, by Charles Martel, and they returned over the mountains to Spain, where they were to remain for seven hundred years.

The Moslem conquest left the city of Constantinople a capital without an Empire, and the message of Charles' victory at Tours in 732 was certainly not lost on the papacy. If the church needed protection, it could no longer turn to the East; rather, it would turn west, to Charles Martel and his sons, who were trying their best to preserve the Frankish kingdom from total collapse. And it was precisely at this moment that the papacy found itself in need of political and military support.

4.62 The Papacy Seeks Help

The Popes of the time soon needed help—this time against another Germanic tribe which had moved into north Italy about the middle of the sixth century. The Lombards had been Arians when they founded their kingdom there in 568, but they had been won to the Catholic faith by Pope Gregory the Great, with the cooperation of their Catholic queen, Theodelinda. However, in the years after 712, the Lombards cast covetous eyes on the center and south of the Italian peninsula, and although the Lombards were now Catholics, the Popes were not inclined to tolerate such ambitions. For almost three hundred years, the Popes had played the role of defenders of Rome and of all central Italy, and they were not about to relinquish a position which, although it seems to us to be purely political, provided them with a base for independent action, without which their claim, even to religious primacy, would have been very weak.

In the year 739 Pope Gregory III asked Charles Martel for help against the Lombards, but Charles had to refuse, because of an alliance which he had concluded with the Lombard ruling house shortly before this time. As a result, Gregory III had to conclude peace with the Lombards on rather unfavorable terms. However, developments were under way which insured that the papacy's next request for help would receive a more favorable answer.

Charles Martel's son, Pippin, began his career as administrator for the decadent Frankish royal house in 741, and he soon decided that he should have the power and office which were commensurate with his ability and responsibility. However, among the Franks, as among the other Germanic tribes, there was a strong sacral and religious component in royal office. The king was a representative of God and could not simply be overthrown by a revolt of the palace guard. Pippin could become king only if his assumption of office could be legitimated, and for this he turned to the one man in western Europe who was capable of providing that legitimation— Pope Zachary, who ruled from 741 to 752. Zachary agreed that the last of the Merovingian kings should be deposed, and he arranged for Pippin to be anointed king of the Franks in 751. This event marks the definitive turning of the papacy from the Emperors in the East to the royal family of the new Frankish monarchy.

Zachary died in 752, and his successor did not delay long in asking Pippin for help. The Lombards were on the move again, threatening to take over Rome and much of central Italy, and in 753 Pope Stephen II asked Pippin for help and received it. In 754 Pippin arrived in Italy, at the head of a Frankish army, and defeated the Lombards. On that occasion, Stephen repeated in Rome the anointing which Pippin had received in France three years before. After defeating the Lombards, Pippin promised almost all of central Italy to the Pope as the permanent possession of the Bishop of Rome, and although some of the promised territory was never handed over to the Pope, Pippin's gift marks the beginning of the *Papal States,* that is, those territories in central Italy which were under the direct political control of the papacy. At that time and for a thousand years after it, it was felt that this political power base was necessary to secure the freedom and independence of the Pope. When the age of revolution dawned in Europe at the end of the eighteenth century, Italian patriots began to think of the Papal States as an obstacle to national unity, but in the middle of the eighth century this was far from anyone's mind.

The real problem for both Pippin and the Pope was the fact that Constantinople still claimed jurisdiction throughout the entire territory of the old Roman Empire, and this included, of course, Rome and central Italy. The problem was not unlike the one which Pippin had faced in deposing the Merovingian kings, and a way had to be found to legitimate Pippin's gift and Stephen's acceptance of that gift. The problem was solved by means of a clever forgery which was produced somewhere in the papal bureaucracy between 750 and 760, and which is known as the *Donation of Constantine.* According to this interesting document, Pope Sylvester, who reigned from 314 to 335, was given sovereignty over the whole western Empire by Constantine, when the latter transferred the seat of power from Rome to the new capital on the Bosporus in 330. Incidentally, it seems certain that Pope Stephen had nothing to do with the forgery, even though it did provide cover for the control which he and his successors exercised over central Italy. However, from Stephen's time on, the document was accepted as genuine. From the eleventh to the fifteenth centuries, it was the basis of repeated papal claims to supreme political power in the West, and it was of enormous importance because of the support it gave to claims of papal omnipotence in matters both temporal and spiritual.

Paradoxically, although it was a forgery, the document legitimated a situation which corresponded quite closely to the political realities of the mid-eighth century. Although it is true that the Pope lacked military forces to defend himself and his lands, he was the one man who could anoint kings and depose them; the general acceptance of his deposition of the last of the Merovingian kings and of his anointing of Pippin made this clear.

4.63 Charlemagne

Pippin's son Karl had received the anointing at Rheims in 751, when he was only twelve years old. He became king of the Franks in 768 and ruled until his death in 814, and it was during his reign that the turning of the papacy and the church to the Franks and their kingdom became definitive. Here again, it was the Lombards who were responsible for bringing the papacy and the Franks together. About 770 they again began to move toward central and southern Italy, and when the Pope appealed to him, Karl and his army came south and defeated the Lombards once and for all in 774. After this victory, Karl himself assumed control in northern Italy and repeated and extended Pippin's gift of much of the center and the south to the Pope.

Karl was a gifted military leader, and he conquered much of central Europe in the name of the church and the

Frankish kingdom. His campaigns took him to all corners of the continent. In 795 he was in northern Spain; between 772 and 804 he was involved in a series of brutal campaigns against the Saxons, who lived mainly in the north German plain, and in 777, after an impressive victory, he ordered the defeated Saxons to become Christian. A few of the noble families did, but most of the Saxons made Karl's order into an occasion of repeated revolts, which were repeatedly suppressed, usually with great brutality. It was not until 804 that revolt was definitively crushed, largely by the deportation of large numbers of Saxons to the old Frankish territories to the west. Between 789 and 805, Karl campaigned against the Slavs on the eastern frontier of his Empire, and in 808 against the Danes in the north.

The conversion of the Saxons was effected with a degree of brutality unusual even in that brutal age. And yet, once converted, the Saxons became remarkably effective defenders of the Christian faith. Monasteries were established throughout the Saxon lands, and one of the first works of Christian German literature was written there—the Heliandlied, a poem which presents the story of Jesus as though it took place in Saxon lands in the ninth century. And when, in the tenth century, the Empire rose from the ashes, the new Emperors were Saxon kings, the sincerity of whose concern for the faith could not be doubted, although their ways of showing it were sometimes questionable.

Karl (conventionally known in England since Norman times as "Charlemagne") brought about the political union of much of Europe and brought the Christian faith to many previously pagan areas. He resurrected the imperial ideal which had been effectively dead in the West for four centuries, and he prepared the way, not only for the medieval Empire, but for the modern concept of a united Europe. The fact that his own Empire was in total disarray less than fifty years after his death does not make either of these facts less certain.

Just as important as Charlemagne's political and religious unification of Europe was his dedication to culture, which led to the founding of schools in connection with the monasteries and the larger urban churches. It was these schools which preserved much of the literary patrimony of Rome for the medieval world. The city of Aachen, in Germany, was the working capital of the Frankish Empire from about 790, and it was there that Charlemagne founded what we would call today a "court academy"—a gathering of the best scholars of Europe and of the British Isles. These scholars were invited by Charlemagne and were supported by him; many of them were monks who were well acquainted with Latin literature, and some of them wrote Latin of a style and quality which had not been seen since the early days of the Roman Empire. Alcuin, the Anglo-Saxon monk, presided over the academy, and Charlemagne himself enjoyed taking part in the discussions. According to Einhard, his first biographer, he learned Latin so well that he was able to speak it as fluently as his native German.

Charlemagne seemed to sense instinctively that the Frankish church would remain strong and authentically Christian to the degree to which it preserved its bond of union with Rome. To this end, he modeled the Frankish liturgy closely on that of Rome and he insisted on the reform of religious and clerical life according to Roman directives. As a result of this policy, even when the appalling decline of the church and the Empire set in less than a century after his death, the Frankish church never reverted to the state of inbred isolation which had done so much harm during the Merovingian period. And it was from a monastery which had been founded on the territory of Charlemagne's Empire (Cluny) that the spiritual impetus for the restoration of papal power at the end of the eleventh century was to come.

Charlemagne had no conception of what we refer to today as the separation of church and state. As the years passed, he took more and more control of state affairs, and in this he was probably inspired by the Byzantine model. He took the sacral or religious side of his royal office very seriously, and he joined it to the Old Testament idea of the king as the anointed son of God. He expected the bishops in his Empire to render political service when called upon to do so, and he did not hesitate to intervene directly in the affairs of the church. He regarded his military ventures as holy wars, waged for the benefit of both the Frankish kingdom and the church, and with the passage of years he had more and more difficulty distinguishing the two. There is no doubt that the medieval phenomenon of the *crusade* was derived largely from Charlemagne's concept of the holy war, directed against those who were outside the faith.

4.64 Troubled Relations with Byzantium

As the Frankish kingdom extended its control not only over northern Europe, but, directly or indirectly, over all of Italy, relations with Byzantium (Constantinople) were bound to become a problem. However, to understand the events which later caused so much havoc in the relations between the eastern and western churches, we have to move back in time to a crisis which wracked the eastern church, and which started shortly after the year 700. This was the so-called *iconoclastic controversy,* which centered on the question of whether it was proper to honor the images of Christ, of Mary, and of the saints.

There were two main theological issues involved in the controversy. First, as we have seen in chapter three, after the Council of Chalcedon, Alexandrian theology began to prevail in the East, aided and abetted by imperial meddlers who used it as a tool to secure the loyalty of Egypt and the eastern provinces. This theology was never really at ease with the humanity of Jesus, and it was precisely for this reason that the pictures of Christ presented a problem. In the nature of the case, these images could depict only the humanity of Jesus and not his divinity, and for this reason, in the Alexandrian view, they could not do justice to the real Jesus Christ. In the eyes of many eastern theologians, these pictures were heretical, in fact if not in intent. The second theological issue involved was that of superstition. People who were poorly educated in the faith, or in whom a thinly veiled paganism lived on, could easily begin to pray to the picture, thus making it into an object which had supernatural power, and in this they would be very near idolatry.

Both of these factors—danger of superstition and a theology which neglected the humanity of Christ—contributed to a certain distaste for sacred images which had grown among many of the educated classes in the East for hundreds of years. The monks, on the other hand, were zealous defenders of the sacred images, and argued that they played an important role in the faith of the masses. The problem turned into a crisis in the year 730, when Leo the Isaurian became Emperor of the East. In that year he issued an edict which forbade the veneration of sacred images, and the disturbances which wracked the eastern Empire for the next fifty-seven years are difficult for us to comprehend today. Imperial officials enforced the law with a brutality worthy of the pagan Emperors, and the monks responded with stubborn and resolute resistance. The result was that in certain parts of the Empire monastic communities were virtually wiped out, since Leo did not hesitate to put to death those who refused to obey his edict.

It was not until the year 787 that the Empress mother, Irene, agreed to the restoration of the images, and had this formally approved in the same year at what has come to be called the Second Ecumenical Council of Nicaea. There the tragic tale would end, except for the fact that Charlemagne was furious when he found out that an ecumenical council had taken place without anyone notifying him of the event, and was therefore inclined to resist in principle any decree which came from such a council. In the year 790, Theodulf and several other Frankish bishops, at the instigation of Charlemagne, wrote a work known as the *Libri Carolini,* which attacked the theology of the Second Council of Nicaea, and categorically rejected the veneration of sacred images. The problem was that neither Charlemagne nor the Frankish bishops who produced the work really understood the Greek terminology in which the council decrees were framed. The Latin translation made it appear as though the council had authorized the *adoration* of the images, whereas the Greek word simply meant *veneration* or *reverencing.* Like so many other tragic misunderstandings between East and West, this one rested not on honest disagreement but rather on ignorance.

As a consequence of these incidents, from about the year 795, Charlemagne began to act very much like an Emperor in the western part of the old Empire. His actions here were favored by the fact that in the year 797, Irene, who had been Empress mother, formally assumed power as Empress of the East. By western standards of the time, this was so unthinkable an act that Pope Leo III had her name struck from the liturgy, and so, for the first time since Constantine, no Roman Emperor was remembered in the liturgy of the western church.

What steps Charlemagne would have taken to fill the power vacuum in the West we do not know, because on the occasion of his visit to Rome in December of the year 800, on Christmas day and in the presence of an enthusiastic crowd, the Pope crowned Charlemagne Emperor. According to Einhard, the monk who was his first biographer, Charlemagne was not pleased by this gesture, and he did not use the imperial title for over two years. The reasons for his hesitation are not clear, but we can probably surmise that he was not pleased to accept supreme political power as a gift from the hands of the Pope, because to do so would imply that this power was the Pope's to give and the Pope's to take away. In time he grew accustomed to the title, and used it up to his death in 814. As the years passed, he imitated more and more the caesaropapism of the East.

4.65 The Collapse of the Frankish Empire

Charlemagne's son, Louis the Pious, reigned from 814 to 840, but he was not a strong ruler. He continued the reform of the Frankish church, and he promoted culture, much as his father had done, and in the monasteries of his Empire there were monks who were well educated by the standards of the day. Louis also sent missionaries to Scandinavia in 826, but almost three hundred years would pass before these northern lands could be said to form part of western Christendom.

Louis had three sons, and he had already divided the Empire among them in 817. Lothar was to be Emperor, and he received the central portion of the Empire. Pippin received the western portion, with its capital in Aquitaine, and Ludwig the German received the eastern portion, including Bavaria. However, after Louis' first wife died, he married again, and the son of this second union, Charles the Bald, was to be given that part of Charlemagne's Empire which corresponded more or less to southwest Germany and Switzerland as his inheritance. But the other sons objected, and war ensued. The four sons fought against each other and against their father. Finally, in 843, Charles the Bald, ruler of the Romance-speaking part of the former Empire, and Ludwig, ruler of the eastern part of the former Empire (which had remained German-speaking), agreed to make their domains into separate and independent kingdoms. Although in subsequent years the descendants of one or the other managed to reunite the Empire of Charlemagne for brief periods, practically speaking the Treaty of Verdun in 843 meant the end of the Empire which had seemed so strong in the year 800. By 889 the imperial title had passed into the hands of Italian noble families, but by that time it had lost all real meaning.

With the collapse of the Frankish Empire, Saracens moved into southern Italy and Norsemen began to sack the cities along the coasts of the North and Baltic Seas. As the years passed, they moved far inland, along the rivers that flowed into these two seas, and England became a favorite object of their attacks. They brought devastation wherever they went, and the brutality of their assaults and the vandalism which accompanied them led many in western Europe to think that the end of the world must be near. Caesar Baronius, a church historian of the sixteenth century, coined the term *saeculum obscurum,* the Dark Age, for this period. Baronius was typically Latin, in asserting that this Dark Age lasted until 1076, with the accession of Gregory VII to the papal throne. But it had really ended more than a century before, with the restoration of the Holy Roman Empire, under Otto I, and with the accession to the papacy of a number of serious and talented men who were, to all intents and purposes, appointed to their office by Otto and his successors. However, Baronius' term certainly did apply from about 850 to 950. Most of the events of this period belong to European political and social history, and are not the proper subject of church history, but the period does underline one important fact: when the social fabric is rent, and life is stripped of all security, it takes heroic commitment to remain Christian in anything more than name.

4.7 EUROPE RISES FROM THE ASHES

In some ways, nations and peoples are very much like individuals; they seem able to go through periods of sleep, from which they awaken, without having forgotten their former experiences, ideas and ideals. In fact, they often seem to return to them with new freshness and vigor. The history of the Dark Age seems to bear this out. The imperial ideal and the orderly reform of the Frankish church must have seemed to thoughtful men of that day like sad memories of a lost golden age. And yet, the Dark Age came to an end because the descendants of those Saxons, who had been forcibly converted or slaughtered about a hundred and fifty years before, revived the imperial ideal and consciously restored the Holy Roman Empire of Charlemagne. And the papacy emerged from the most appalling degradation, because German Emperors, acting in the spirit of caesaropapism, but also convinced of the divine origin of the Petrine office, appointed far-seeing men of great ability to be successors of Peter. But this brings us to the next chapter.

5

From 900 to 1300

5.1 INTRODUCTION

When the tenth century dawned, Europe was almost precisely at the mid-point of its darkest age. The tide of civilization had receded and was now at low ebb. Charlemagne's Empire lay in ruins and there was no central civil or religious authority to unite the peoples of the continent. The cities had declined and the overwhelming majority of the population dwelt in the rural areas, where they lived in grinding poverty. Most of the land belonged to members of the nobility, who were little better than robber barons. They had private armies at their disposal and their principal occupation was that of maintaining a state of perpetual war with others like themselves. Amid all of this, the peasantry, who were little better than slaves, bore the brunt of the suffering.

The faith of most people during this epoch seems to have been even more superficial than at other periods of history. In Western Europe, most people were descended from tribesmen who had been baptized en masse at the time of the great "conversions." Neither their faith nor the faith of their descendants had ever been deepened to any significant degree, because the Carolingian renaissance had lasted for all too short a time.

The clergy, who should have been devoting themselves to this task, were often ignorant and incompetent. In theory, the priests who served the parishes were trained at the school associated with the principal church of the diocese, but in this period most of the cathedral parishes did not maintain schools. Most priests picked up what little training they received from those who had been priests before them in the village—often their fathers, since the law of celibacy was frequently not observed. The knowledge of Latin was not widespread among these priests; many of them knew barely enough to mumble the words of the Mass with little or no comprehension. The bible was not even read, much less understood. These priests received part of their support from fees charged for the administration of the sacraments, and this opened the way to multiple abuses. In other cases, noble families had set aside property, and arranged that the rents from this property should be used to support the priest who served the area. However these *benefices*, as they were called, were often given to younger sons or other dependents of the nobility, who had no interest in serving the church and who used the money for purely worldly and often quite disreputable purposes. (In such cases it was usual to hire a substitute who would perform the religious duties for a fraction of the sum which had originally been set aside, and the quality of the religious services given suffered proportionately.)

Higher offices in the church often had huge benefices attached to them and this led to the practice of *simony*—the buying and selling of church offices. The initial investment might be high, but then one was assured of a regular income for life. Needless to say, this practice inflicted a number of bishops on the church who had no interest in preaching the Gospel and whose lives were indistinguishable from those of other members of the nobility. Most of the Popes of the period were members of noble Roman families, for whom the papacy was a prize sought only for the prestige and wealth attached to it. These men lacked all concern for the universal church and they had no understanding of the role of the Bishop of Rome in promoting the unity of this church and in striving to spread and to deepen the faith.

5.2 LAYING THE FOUNDATION FOR REFORM

And yet, in Europe's darkest hour, just nine years after the new century had begun, a monastery was founded in the province of Burgundy in France, which had as its goal the revival of the monastic spirit of Benedict of Nursia. This monastery was one of the two sources of a spiritual renewal which revitalized church life in less than one hundred and fifty years; and this same monastery, Cluny, was a major factor in the creation of the High Middle Ages, which ran from shortly after 1150 almost to the end of the thirteenth century.

5.21 The Effects of the Revival of Monasticism at Cluny

When the monastery of Cluny was founded in the year 909, the French nobleman who financed the venture insisted that the monks should be free of interference, both on the part of meddling noblemen and on the part of the local bishop. The monks were to be free to choose their own abbots and to devote themselves to the fulfillment of the ideals of Benedictine monasticism—quiet prayer and the exact and dignified performance of the liturgy.

This reform, which seemed to be nothing more than a matter of private religious devotion for some monks who lived far from the centers of secular and religious power, was to become one of the two great forces which created the medieval church. Cluny grew quietly for about a century, but even before the tenth century had ended, other monasteries had associated themselves with the Cluniac reform. By the middle of the eleventh century, more than two thousand communities belonged to Cluny's monastic reform movement. The abbot of Cluny was something like a religious superior over monks who lived in France, Spain, Italy, and England. Other monasteries which did not actually associate themselves with Cluny were nevertheless influenced by its example, so that monastic life throughout Western Europe experienced a profound and lasting reform. As has always been the case since the origin of religious life in the church in the third century, when this life is lived with great intensity by those who love the world and yet feel called to relativize the absolute claims of worldly values, the whole church begins to live more fully and more deeply. This is precisely what happened to the church in the late tenth and through the eleventh and twelfth centuries as a result of the attempt of the monks of Cluny and its daughter foundations to incarnate the Christian ideal.

5.22 The Empire and the Reform of the Church

The second and perhaps surprising source of spiritual renewal was the East Frankish kingdom. Shortly after the foundation of Cluny, the kingdom of the East Franks, which included most of the German speaking areas that had belonged to Charlemagne's Empire, came into the hands of a family of strong and talented rulers. Almost by accident they created one of the institutions that gave medieval Europe its distinctive stamp.

When Otto (later to be called "the Great") became king of the East Franks in 936, much of the territory which he nominally ruled was actually under the control of quarrelsome nobles who had no use for any central authority. Initially he tried to regain control by installing his relatives in key positions which had become open through his victories in battle, but his relatives then plotted against him and he came to realize how unreliable they were.

At this juncture he decided to try something new. He turned to the bishops who headed the dioceses in his kingdom and he made them civil officials who were endowed with all of the privileges of office. The move was brilliant for a number of reasons. First, since bishops had no (legitimate!) heirs, there was no danger that they would become the founders of princely houses which would later threaten the monarchy. And second, although the bishops were hardly learned men, they were among the best trained and talented that one could find during this period of general decline and decay. In fact, these *prince bishops* served Otto well, and during the following centuries they were firm in their support of the Empire.

Of course from the standpoint of the Christian faith

there were serious problems with Otto's solution. Bishops who are servants of the state are not in a position to maintain that distance from worldly power and secular authority which the prophetic side of the Christian vocation demands. In the years after Otto's restoration of the Holy Roman Empire in 962, the state and the church entered into a kind of symbiosis which had within it the seeds of bitter conflict. The conflict which resulted ultimately led to the dissolution of the specifically medieval unity and paved the way for the break-up of both the church and the Empire which was the signature of the Reformation period in the sixteenth century.

Otto was crowned Emperor in 962, and for the remaining eleven years of his life he dedicated himself and his Empire to the reform and restoration of the church. He assumed responsibility for the papacy itself, and in 963 he began a tradition which lasted for almost a thousand years: from that time on, no Pope could be elected without the consent of the Emperor. His policies were continued by his successors, Otto II, Henry II, Konrad II, and Henry III. These Emperors had their hands full in trying to control centrifugal tendencies in the Empire, but insofar as they could turn their attention to Italian affairs, they appointed or urged the election of worthy and reform-minded Popes, while keeping full control of the church in all parts of the Empire. This union of church and state did not mean that the state was *using* the church; rather, the Emperor put all of the resources of the Empire at the disposal of a church which, quite appropriately as he thought, was under his exclusive control.

When Henry III became Emperor in 1039, the political situation in Germany was so stable that he could turn his attention to the papacy, which had again become the political plaything of two of the more disreputable noble Roman families. In the year 1046 he was invited to Rome by the reform party. On his arrival, he found three contenders, all claiming to be Pope, and in December of the same year he held two synods, in Sutri and Rome, at which he deposed all three pretenders and appointed the bishop of Bamberg, in Germany, as the new Pope. This Pope, Clement III, lived for only a year, as did his successor, another German bishop. In 1049 Henry appointed an Alsatian, Bruno of Egisheim, to the papacy. Bruno took the name Leo IX, and in his short reign of only five years he took the first step to redress the balance of power between the church and the Empire. By his time it had tipped so sharply in the direction of the Empire that the church seemed about to abdicate its authority in favor of the secular powers. Leo and his successors realized that the relationship between church and state would have to be put on an entirely new basis, and it was the monastic reform, begun at Cluny, which was to provide the drive and the spiritual substance for this new kind of reform.

5.3 REFORM: INSIDE AND OUTSIDE OF THE CHURCH

5.31 The Cistercians

The reform which had its origins in Cluny spread far beyond the monasteries which were directly dependent on the mother house, and in the late tenth and early eleventh centuries a number of monastic and eremitical communities were started in France and Italy. One of the most remarkable of the new foundations had its origin in the desire of some monks to return to a stricter form of Benedictine monasticism than that which they found practiced in Cluny and its dependent monasteries. In the year 1098, Robert of Molesme founded just such a community at Cîteaux in France. (The name by which they are known even today—Cistercians—is derived from the Latin form of Cîteaux.) In the twelfth century, they found in Bernard of Clairvaux a gifted organizer, who at the time of his death in 1153 was something like the general superior of a congregation made up of three hundred and fifty monasteries.

Bernard's purpose was the reform and renewal of monastic life through the full realization of the Benedictine ideal, by undertaking to live the harsh and demanding life of the "desert" and finding God in the denial of self. Paradoxically, Bernard, whose congregation was dedicated to finding God in silence, mortification and hard physical labor, became one of the most political figures of his age. It was he who preached the second Crusade at Vezelay in 1146, and leading figures in church and state in the twelfth century sought his advice on all matters.

5.32 The Regular Canons

It was inevitable that the reform of monastic life would sooner or later affect the lives of those priests who were not monks but who lived in the world and served the laity in the parish churches. The general high esteem of monastic life led many people to believe that these *secular* priests (Latin *saeculum* = world) should be something like monks who lived in the world—living in poverty, not marrying, and giving obedience to their bishops. During most of the eleventh and twelfth centuries (and actually until the sixteenth) this remained an unattainable ideal for the majority of the priests who served in the parishes. But one group was affected: those priests who were attached to the main or cathedral parishes of the diocese, and whose principal function was to provide for the dignified performance of the liturgical services in the cathedral. During the eleventh century, these "canons," as they were called, were exhorted again and again by Popes and bishops to live in accordance with the rule that Augustine had written for the priests who shared his home when he was bishop of the city of Hippo. Sometimes groups of these canons joined together in something very much like a religious order. In 1120, Norbert of Xanten founded such a religious order for the secular clergy. These *Premonstratensians*, as they were called, became one of the great missionary associations of the Middle Ages.

5.33 The Mendicant Orders

The renewal of religious life in the thirteenth century owes very much to two other religious orders which were founded in the early years of that century. The first was the work of Francis, who had been born in Assisi, in Italy, in 1181.

When Francis was about twenty-five, he had a religious experience which led him to embrace the ideal of absolute poverty for the sake of Christ. Although Francis wanted to follow Jesus by sharing the same privations which had characterized Jesus' own life, there was nothing somber about his piety, because in those very privations he found joy and peace.

Francis' way of life proved very attractive to many people in his age, and by the year 1210 he had a number of followers who traveled with him through the countryside, preaching of the joy to be found in being poor for Christ. In that year he went to Rome to request papal approval for this way of life, and, after receiving it, he traveled widely through Italy, Spain, and southern France. At the time, the Catharist heresy was strong in southern France, and Francis wanted to bring people to abandon it, not by violence, but by instructing them and preaching the love of Christ. Unfortunately his solution was not adopted, and church leaders of the time dealt with the Cathari with appalling brutality.

In the year 1221, Francis attempted to give his new order a *rule*—that is, a constitution which would outline the character of Franciscan life; but organizational ability was not Francis' strong suit. A few years later, this rule was expanded and considerably changed by one of the cardinals who was later to become Pope. Francis died in 1226, and after his death the order was torn by many disputes about which of these rules really embodied the Franciscan spirit, about the kind of poverty which should be practiced in the order, and about how much organization should be welcomed.

Francis was a charismatic figure, and in many ways his order outgrew him. But it was in this latter form that the Franciscans became the great popular missionaries of the medieval period and the great foreign missionaries of the age of discovery in the sixteenth century. The Franciscan ideal of poverty was the perfect answer to the obsession with money and property which had led to so much corruption in the church during the two centuries preceding Francis' time.

A few years before Francis, a Spaniard named Dominic founded the second of the two great medieval orders which embraced the life of poverty—the Dominicans. Dominic was a priest and had served as a cathedral canon, but on a trip to southern France he was deeply impressed by the spiritual need of the people of the region and he conceived the ideal of winning the Cathari back to the faith. Like the Franciscans, Dominic's men were dedicated to poverty and to preaching, but, unlike Francis, Dominic was convinced that solid intellectual training, particularly in theology, was an absolute necessity. Like Francis, he went to Rome to request papal approval for his order and he received it in the year 1216. Of all of the orders of this period of church history, it was the Dominicans who did the most for the intellectual life of the church; from their ranks came Albert the Great, and his even more brilliant pupil, Thomas Aquinas, whose *Summary of Theology* is one of the most profound theological (and philosophical) works ever written.

5.34 Religious Movements among the Laity

The reform of monastic life which had begun with the revival of the Benedictine ideal at Cluny in the very early tenth century, and had continued with the founding of the Cistercians in the early twelfth century, eventually affected the laity, especially in the Romance-speaking lands of the West. The meditative reading of scripture was an important part of monastic life, and some laypeople benefited from this, either because they came to the monastery for liturgical services or because the monks occasionally left the monastery to preach to people in the surrounding areas. In this way, people were brought into contact with the preaching of Jesus, and with the picture of the poor and sometimes persecuted church of the earliest days. As lay piety was nourished by these pictures of the pure faith and of the integrity and simplicity of church life in those distant days, it was inevitable that people would compare that period with the church in their own days, disfigured as it was by corruption and by the lust for pomp and power which they saw at all levels of the hierarchy in the early medieval church. It was inevitable that the call for reform would, at least at times, take on a distinctly anti-clerical character.

In the middle of the twelfth century, Arnold of Brescia,

an Italian preacher, called on the church to renounce its possessions, and was particularly critical of the papacy's quest for wealth and power. Still more important was a religious movement which began with a prosperous business man who lived in the city of Lyon in France. About the year 1175, Pierre Waldes rediscovered, through his reading of the Gospels, the ideal of evangelical poverty. He distributed his goods to the poor and became a wandering preacher. His preaching on the necessity of poverty for individual Christians and for the church as a whole, and his open and blunt criticism of the church of his day, did not sit well either with his local bishop or with the Pope. Waldes and his followers were excommunicated in 1184, and following this, Waldes became more and more radical, railing not only at the corruption of Rome, but also attacking practices of long standing, such as Masses and prayers for the dead, and the necessity of confessing one's sins to a priest. Waldes demanded that the Bible be translated into the modern languages and put at the disposal of the laity. In his view, the Bible, taken in a very literal sense, was the sole guide of Christian life. Waldes died in 1217, but the movement he founded lived on after him. The Waldensian faith was in many ways a precursor of Lutheranism, which appeared just three centuries after Waldes' death, and the Waldenses, as they were called, were eventually absorbed into various Protestant sects in the sixteenth century.

The *Catharist* movement, which was mentioned briefly in connection with the Franciscans and Dominicans, was a strange phenomenon, very difficult for us to understand today. It was strong in the early part of the thirteenth century, in the region around the city of Albi, in southern France, and the members of the sect were for this reason sometimes called the *Albigenses*. This particular heretical movement seems to have prospered because the clergy in southern France were, if possible, even more corrupt and more obsessed with wealth than the clergy of other areas, and because the level of religious instruction of the laity was abysmally low.

The Cathari were not in any real sense of the word Christian; actually they were dualists, who believed that the world is the stage on which a battle is waged between the supreme principle of good and the supreme principle of evil. Some historians have thought that these dualistic ideas may have lived an underground existence from very ancient times in southern France and may have been disguised by a thin Christian veneer at the time of the mass conversions. But it seems more probable that various forms of Manichaeism and other kinds of dualistic thought were brought back to Western Europe by Crusaders returning from the Holy Land.

These ideas spread rapidly, and as is always the case when church and state are linked inextricably, religious differences became a way of making a political statement. At this very time, the feudal lords in the region of Albi were ready to make a stand against the demand of the French king that his sovereignty over the south of France be recognized, and the Albigensian faith became a rallying point for Provencal opposition to the expansionist drive from the north.

In 1209 Innocent III called for a Crusade against the Albigenses, thus making an essentially political struggle into a holy war. For twenty years, until 1229, the French kings Louis VIII and Louis IX battled the Albigenses, ostensibly to crush a despicable heresy, but in reality to consolidate the hold of the French monarchy on the south. Tragic for the church forever after was the development at this time of the institution known as the *Inquisition*. The Inquisition was a bureau or commission which had branches in most of the larger dioceses in Spain, France, and Italy, and which was empowered to call on the civil authorities to help them detect heretical movements. Once heretics had been detected, the church authorities conducted a kind of judicial process to determine the guilt of the accused; the peculiarity of the process was that guilt was assumed and the burden of proving innocence rested on the accused parties. When it was determined that the accused party was guilty, he was then handed over to the civil authorities for appropriate punishment. This whole process led to appalling suffering, particularly after Pope Innocent IV, in the year 1252, authorized the inquisitors to secure confessions by the use of torture.

Certainly no more conclusive evidence could be found for the estrangement of the church of the thirteenth century from its Lord. The Inquisition is beyond doubt the greatest scandal that has ever disfigured the life of the church, and attempts to explain it by pointing out that men of the day could not make a clear distinction between heresy and revolution really miss the point. It is, of course, a fact that no such distinction was made, but the Inquisition originated, not with princes or Emperors who wanted to use the power of the church to crush revolution, but with churchmen who wanted to use the power of the state in its most brutal form in order to crush those whose picture of Jesus differed from their own, or whom they perceived as a threat to their power or privilege.

In 1229, the Council of Toulouse imposed a religious settlement on the Albigenses, and in accord with this the laity were to be deprived of all direct access to the bible and no vernacular translations were to be allowed. The medieval church could maintain its position of wealth and power only by denying to the laity the word of God. Probably no harsher judgment could ever be made on the church than the one which is implied by the decrees of this council.

5.4 REFORMING POPES AND REFORM OF THE PAPACY

A great change came over the papacy with the accession of Leo IX to the chair of Peter in 1049. Leo and his successors to the end of the century had rediscovered a conception of the papal office very much like that which had guided Gregory the Great at the very end of the sixth century: the Pope was the supreme bishop of all Christendom, and had the responsibility and the authority for the spread and deepening of the faith throughout the world.

The rediscovery of the universal meaning of the papacy rescued it from the quagmire of Roman city politics, but the problem was that the reforming Popes from the time of Gregory VII (who became Pope in 1073) had a notion of the reform in the church which was quite different from that which was envisaged by most of those who were calling for change.

For these Popes, it was not the papacy itself which needed reform, but rather those civil and ecclesiastical institutions which limited the freedom of the Popes to act as they wanted and which made the Pope subservient to the Emperor. Reforming Popes of this period, no matter how simple and austere their personal lives might have been, never understood how great a scandal the worldliness of the papal court was for sincere Christians of the day.

To these Popes, *reform* meant the securing of what they referred to as the *freedom of the church*, but they really meant by this term the reassertion of papal power at the expense of the Holy Roman Emperor. These Popes directed their reforming zeal above all at that institution which had been invented by Otto I about a century before: that is, the institution of the prince-bishop, who, as an imperial vassal, firmly supported the Empire, and who received all of the insignia of his office directly from the Emperor. This practice of being invested with the insignia and symbols of civil and church office clearly implied that it was the Emperor who was supreme in both domains. In the view of the reforming Popes from Gregory VII on, the Emperor, despite his high office, was still a layman, and therefore not competent to determine who would receive offices in the church. They combatted what they called *lay investiture* because it symbolized that very relationship of church and state which they abhorred. More and more, these Popes began to equate the freedom of the church with the power of the papacy, and, tragically, they were blind to the ambiguity of the power which they coveted and ultimately gained.

5.41 The Gregorian Reform

It was during the pontificate of Gregory VII (1073-1085) that the struggle between Pope and Emperor came to a head. Hildebrand (Gregory's name before becoming Pope) was born not far from Rome in the year 1025 and he had been, for a time, a monk in Cluny. As early as 1060 we find him in Rome, a zealous member of the reform party, intent on eliminating simony (the practice of buying and selling church offices), and on enforcing clerical celibacy. But absolutely central to Hildebrand's view of reform was the elimination of lay investiture, because he saw that if this battle could be won, then real power over the church in western Europe would be put firmly back in the hands of the Pope.

Two years after his election to the papacy, Gregory issued one of the most important documents of medieval church history—the so-called *Dictatus Papae* or *Dictates of the Pope*. In this document he claimed that papal power, both spiritual and temporal, was absolute, and that the Pope was, in all spheres, the supreme head of Christendom. We can better appreciate the thrust of this document and the scope of its claims by citing several of the points which Gregory made. He asserted that the Roman church was founded by the Lord alone, and that the Roman bishop is the only one who can rightly be called universal. He alone has the right to make new laws, to found new congregations and to depose bishops without the approval of a synod. He alone has the right to wear imperial insignia, and he can depose Emperors. No general council can take place without his approval, and he can be judged by no one. The Roman church has never been in error and never will be in error, and no one who is not in agreement with the Roman church is to be thought of as Catholic. Finally, and most significant, the Pope can free subjects from the oath of loyalty which they have sworn to their superiors (and, by implication, from the oath of loyalty they have sworn to the Emperor!).

According to the *Dictatus Papae*, it was absolutely forbidden to laymen, including the Emperor, to interfere in the election of bishops and Popes, or to give to bishops the symbols of their sacred office. When the Emperor, Henry IV, who ruled from 1056 to 1106, crossed the Pope in this matter, Gregory VII threatened to excommunicate him. In the year 1076, Henry reacted to the Pope's threat by declaring Gregory deposed. Gregory responded by declaring that Henry was now deposed as Emperor, and by freeing all of his subjects from their oath of allegiance to him.

Excommunication was so fearful a penalty (entailing, as all believed, eternal punishment if one died without absolution) that the princes of the Empire could not find the courage to support Henry IV. In fact, they informed him later that same year that unless he secured absolution from the Pope, they would declare the throne vacant and elect a new Emperor. In the face of this threat, Henry went to Italy and stood as a penitent for three days in the winter snow outside the castle at Canossa in northern Italy, where the Pope was staying at the time.

The Pope granted Henry his absolution, but the agreement did not last. For seven years Henry had his hands full, trying to crush revolt in various parts of his Empire, but he was firmly in control by 1084 and in that year he moved on Rome, declared Gregory deposed, and installed an anti-Pope, who called himself Clement III. Gregory left the city and died in exile in 1085, apparently the loser in his struggle with Henry for the freedom of the church.

But appearances were deceptive. Gregory's assault on lay investiture had rocked the Empire to its foundations, and so weakened it politically that only an *imperial papacy*, that is, a papal authority which arrogated to itself the claims and prerogatives of the Emperor, could fill the resulting power vacuum. Gregory's victory led directly to the medieval papacy, which, in the name of the church, claimed absolute power in all areas of public and private life, and did so in a way which was a tragic mockery of Jesus, who had spoken of how the meek and the poor in spirit are the ones who are near to God. In the world of the late eleventh century, separation of church and state was inconceivable. The Gregorian Reform pitted the church against the Empire across a broad front, and the fact that, by and large, the church (or, *much more accurately*, the papacy) emerged victorious was a tragedy, not primarily for the Empire, but for the church itself.

Gregory's reform of the church went far beyond his rejection of lay investiture (that is, the civil control of ecclesiastical offices). Not only did he oppose simony, but he decreed that those who had received their ecclesiastical offices in return for money were to be deposed. Not only did he renew the prohibition of marriage for priests, but he enforced this by forbidding the laity to take part in a Mass which was celebrated by a married priest. Clerical marriage was declared to be not only *illicit*, that is, against the law, but *invalid*, that is, not a real marriage at all. In other words, married priests were declared to be living in sin. All of this legislation gave the church a distinctly monastic stamp. As Yves Congar puts it, "The church became a kind of large abbey, in which the laity were something like married lay brothers and sisters, who busied themselves with the earthly needs of the servants of God."

Gregory's successor ruled for only a year, but then another zealous reformer, Urban II, became Pope in 1088, and ruled for eleven years. It was he who, in the year 1095, on the occasion of a council in the city of Clermont in France, called for a united effort on the part of all Christendom to recover the Holy Land from the Moslems into whose hands it had fallen hundreds of years earlier.

During the twelfth century there were a number of good and talented Popes, but they continued to see their task as that of affirming papal power against the Emperor. Adrian IV (1154-1159) did this against Friedrich I (Barbarossa). Alexander III was Pope from 1159 to 1181 and he continued the struggle against Barbarossa, and won out after twenty years. In doing so, he drove another nail into the coffin of the medieval Empire, and made the way clear for the imperial church which was to appear at the very end of the twelfth century. It was this Alexander III who was able to assert papal power over Henry II of England at this time, when the latter was commonly believed to have been responsible for the death of Thomas Becket.

5.5 THE SUMMIT OF PAPAL POWER

The medieval world was a field of force, constituted by the two powers which were supreme in their respective realms—that is, the Pope and the Emperor. The medieval world grappled with an essentially insoluble problem—that of reconciling these two powers and of assigning them their proper competences. In the name of the freedom of the church, Gregory VII struck a blow at imperial power from which it never recovered, and in the year 1140 a very important summary and compilation of church law was issued, which made the principles of the Gregorian Reform into the official law of the church. This *Decree of Gratian* strongly emphasized the power and prerogatives of the papacy, and it provided the legal and juridical weapons for the papacy in its struggle with the Empire throughout the latter part of the twelfth century.

5.51 Innocent III

In the year 1198, a man was elected to the papacy who was destined to bring the office to the summit of its political power and, perhaps in virtue of that fact, to prepare for its decline as a spiritual and moral force. In doing this, he paved the way for rise of the Renaissance papacy in the fifteenth and early sixteenth centuries.

Lothar of Segni, the future Innocent III, was born in 1160. He had an exalted view of the papal office which he assumed in 1198 and held until 1216. In his view, Christ had left to Peter the governance of the entire world, and Innocent had no hesitation in exercising this power in the most direct and immediate way. As Pope he intended to be both the spiritual leader of Christendom, and its political master as well; and it was from his hand that the Emperor and the kings of the various Christian states were to accept office as his vassals.

Innocent III exercised this political power throughout Christendom, and in all places the evil effects of this politicizing of the Christian faith made themselves felt, some sooner, some later. It was during the pontificate of Innocent III that the city of Constantinople was conquered and sacked by an army of Crusaders in 1204—an event which the eastern church (and above all the laity of that church) have never forgiven or forgotten and which has resulted in the tragic separation of the eastern and western branches of Catholic Christianity up to the present day. Innocent and most of those in his papal court undoubtedly felt that the establishment of a Latin hierarchy in Constantinople represented the triumph of the true faith against the schismatic and slightly heretical trends of the Greek-speaking East, but this tragic event did more to alienate the oriental churches from Rome than the excommunication of Michael Cerularius had done in 1054. The control over the oriental churches exercised by this Latin hierarchy was ephemeral, and the Latins were driven out of the city of Constantinople in 1261.

Innocent III, of course, did not confine his political ventures to the East. He meddled directly in the election of the German Emperor in 1198 and devoted all of his energy to frustrating the Emperor's plans to strengthen his hold on Sicily. In England, he forced King John to accept Stephen Langton as Archbishop of Canterbury. When John later tried to go back on his agreement and depose Stephen, Innocent excommunicated him, forced him to do penance, and then accepted John as his vassal, with the implication that he, Innocent, possessed supreme political power in England, and that the kings of England were merely exercising power in his name.

5.52 The Crusades

It is impossible to talk about the political power of the papacy in the Early and High Middle Ages without discussing the Crusades. They were called into existence by a Pope and they were supported by his successors for the two hundred years of their duration. Whatever abuses were associated with the Crusades, and they were frightful enough, there is no doubt that religious and spiritual factors played an important, though by no means exclusive, role in motivating the Popes of the period to support these campaigns. The Seljuk Turks had conquered Jerusalem in the year 1071 and they had made it increasingly difficult for Christians to visit their holy places in safety. At the same time the Turks were streaming into Asia Minor, and it was clear that they would soon be menacing the city of Constantinople. In the face of this threat, the Byzantine Emperor appealed to the Pope for help in defending both the church and the Empire. It was to this request that Pope Urban II responded at Clermont in 1095, when he issued a call to the knights of Western Europe to undertake a holy war to free from Moslem control the Holy Land in which Jesus had lived and died.

In economic and cultural terms, the Crusades contributed much to the development of modern Europe. In political, and, above all, in religious terms, they were an unmitigated disaster. As the crusading armies gathered in Europe they often engaged in sporadic attacks on the Jewish communities who lived there, apparently in the conviction that before facing the foreign unbelievers it was acceptable to practice on the domestic version of the same. When the city of Jerusalem was captured in 1099, the conquest was accompanied by the indiscriminate slaughter of the inhabitants.

The first Crusade enjoyed some initial success. After the capture of the city, the Kingdom of Jerusalem was founded, and by the year 1140 the Holy Land itself and a considerable amount of territory outside it were under the control of western knights, who set up principalities and kingdoms after the western feudal model.

The apparent success of this first Crusade led to a second, which was preached at Vézelay in 1146 by Bernard of Clairvaux. This Crusade was a military disaster, and ended with the slaughter by the Turks of an army made up mainly of French and German knights. Forty years after this second Crusade had begun, the city of Jerusalem was lost to the Turks.

The third Crusade, of 1189 to 1192, was organized in order to recoup the losses of the second. It attracted some of the more famous names of the period—Philip II of France, Friedrich Barbarossa of Germany, and Richard the Lionhearted of England. Their military efforts remained inconclusive, but in 1192 they were able to negotiate a treaty with the Sultan, in accordance with which Christian pilgrims were given the right to freely visit the holy places in Jerusalem.

The fourth Crusade was proclaimed by Innocent III, and it lasted from 1202 to 1204. It was on the occasion of this "holy war" that the Crusaders conquered and sacked Constantinople and set up a Latin hierarchy in the East. The tragedy of the fourth Crusade consisted above all in the fact that Innocent III regarded it as a great success—another indication of the state of the church at the beginning of the thirteenth century. The fourth Crusade was followed by the tragic interlude of the so-called Children's Crusade of 1212, which resulted in the death or enslavement of thousands of French and German children long before they got to the Holy Land. Groups of pre-teenage children had been gripped by a kind of crusading mania, and under the leadership of a pair of ten year olds, they set out for the Near East on foot. Most died on the way, and most of those who survived ended their days as slaves in the Moslem countries of the Near East and North Africa.

The fifth Crusade lasted for only about a year (1228/1229) and was a private venture of the Emperor, Friedrich II. He was successful enough to negotiate the return of the city of Jerusalem to the Christians, but fifteen years later the city was lost and never regained.

The sixth and last Crusade was that of 1248 to 1254. King Louis IX of France conceived the idea of conquering Egypt and using it as a base for the reconquest of the Holy Land, but the French army was handed a devastating defeat outside Cairo in 1250 and the king was taken prisoner. Louis bought his way out of captivity and tried to organize another Crusade in 1270, but the crusading spirit was dead, and Louis' attempts met with no success. In 1291 the last of the Crusader kingdoms in the Holy Land fell to the Turks.

The Crusades stimulated trade and they introduced important new ideas to the West, which prepared the way for the Christian appropriation of the riches of Greek philosophy in the thirteenth century. But from the standpoint of the religious ideals which had ostensibly motivated the Popes who summoned the knighthood of Europe to heroic feats on behalf of the cross of Christ, they were a monumental failure. They poisoned relations between Christianity and Islam up to the present day, and they hardened the estrangement of the Christian churches of East and West. They made the use of force and violence as means of Christian missionary activity quite acceptable in the eyes of western Europeans, and from the crusading armies issued the knightly religious orders which caused so much suffering among the Slavic peoples of central Europe and of Russia.

The final failure of the Crusades with the fall of Acco in 1291 was symbolic of the decline of the power of the papacy and it marked the end of the Middle Ages. When the first Crusade was proclaimed by Urban II in 1095, the star of papal power was rising; when the last Crusade ended, its star had set, although few in Europe were aware of it at the time. Three years after the fall of Acco, Boniface VIII became Pope, and he reigned until 1303. Boniface had mastered the rhetoric of papal supremacy, and in a famous document, *Unam Sanctam*, which was published in 1299, he claimed that the "two swords" of religious and civil power both belonged to the church (by which he understood, of course, the papacy). But by 1299, such claims were without substance, and when Boniface tried to force his claim against the French king, Philip the Fair, it was the Pope who lost. The European unity of the High Middle Ages was breaking up. The Popes themselves had so weakened the Empire that it was unable to restore that unity, and in the struggle with the Empire, the papacy had lost moral stature and spiritual substance. As the thirteenth century ended, the papacy was rapidly becoming a well-organized bureaucracy, which was dedicated not to playing the great game of power politics but to securing the steady flow of money into the papal coffers.

5.6 THE INTELLECTUAL LIFE

5.61 The Universities

In the years after 1100, schools were founded in many of the larger cities of Western Europe. Many of these schools came into existence in order to train those priests who would serve in the cathedral (that is, the bishop's church) of the diocese. Others were founded in connection with the monasteries, because by this time an important work of many monks was the copying of scripture and of the religious and secular texts of antiquity. For this, the monks had to be trained in the reading and writing of Latin, because the vernacular languages of Romance-speaking Europe had diverged so far from Latin that the latter had become virtually a foreign language.

These monastic and cathedral schools developed through the twelfth century, and their growth was fostered by more stable political and social conditions and by the consequent increase in population, which had begun shortly after the year 1000 and was to last until the early fourteenth century. As the twelfth century drew to a close, these schools began to serve the needs of the growing cities. Just as the papal court had grown during this century, so also did the office staffs of the bishops in many of the larger cities. Furthermore, in these cities, something like a middle class was beginning to emerge, and new (and more democratic) forms of municipal government were taking shape, which were needed if men were to cope with the greater complexity of urban life. Both church and state needed competent office staffs to fill the positions opened by this burgeoning bureaucracy, and the schools which had originally been founded to train monks and priests for the work of their calling now found themselves faced with much more complex tasks. To cope with this, the schools specialized—some concentrating on civil law, others on canon (that is, *church*) law, still others on medicine or arts (Latin grammar and composition) or scripture. Students and teachers in these schools shared many interests and concerns and felt that they should band together in order to promote those common interests by means which would be suitable in the new and more democratic climate.

In the early thirteenth century, a group of these schools in Paris came together to form a corporation; at about the same time, similar developments took place in Bologna, Naples, and Padua. These corporations were not specialized institutions; they included students and professors who were dedicated to very different fields of study. For this reason they came to be known as *universities*—from the Latin word *universum*, which has given us the word "universal" in the sense of "general, not limited to one sphere". In some places these universities quickly rose to importance and became famous throughout Europe. They were given special privileges by the Popes, including freedom from interference by the local bishop. Paris grew so quickly to a position of overwhelming importance among the universities that in the year 1284 a clever contemporary writer was able to sum up the contributions of Italy, Germany, and France to medieval society by listing the three institutions which, in his mind, were of equal importance: Italy had the papacy, Germany had the Empire, but France had the University of Paris.

5.62 Scholasticism

Medieval life, if not profoundly religious, was at least permeated by religion at every level, and it was obvious that as intellectual life developed, those who were committed to this life would try to understand the mysteries of their faith. They began to ask about the relationship between the truth which faith knows and the truth which we seek in other areas of life—medicine, law, literature, philosophy. The problem of the relation of faith to reason is not a distinctively modern one, and, more than any other, it was this problem which led to a way of thinking, a way of posing questions and finding answers, which we call *scholasticism* and which was the great intellectual achievement of the twelfth and thirteenth centuries.

About the year 1100, the language of learning and culture in western Europe, even in the German-speaking lands, was Latin. The growing estrangement of eastern and western Christendom was partly the cause and partly the effect of the fact that, aside from parts of southern Italy and much of Sicily, Greek was no longer read or understood in the West. As a result, the great Greek philosophers, of whom the best of the Romans were only a pale reflection, had no direct influence on intellectual life in the West at the time.

But in the twelfth century, ancient Greek thought began to make its way into the West by two routes. After the Turkish conquest of Asia Minor in the eleventh century, and before the sack of Constantinople in 1204, renewed contacts between East and West led to the permanent settlement of a number of Greek theologians and other scholars in some of the cities of the West. But the second route was more important. When Mesopotamia had fallen to the Moslems in the seventh century, the invaders were brought into contact with Greek thought in the city of Nisibis—that same intellectual center which became the headquarters of the Nestorian church from the sixth century on. In time the Moslem conquerors developed their own intellectual elite, and they had the works of Plato and Aristotle translated into Arabic. On the basis of these translations, a flourishing revival of Greek thought took place in the great centers of learning in the Arab world, from Bagdad in the East to Cordova in Spain, from the beginning of the eleventh century on.

Two of the most famous of these thinkers were known in the West as Avicenna and Averrhoes. The first (Ibn Sina was his Arabic name) had died in Bagdad in 1037, and the second (Ibn Roshd in Arabic) died in Cordova in 1198. Avicenna's works were translated into Latin some time after his death, and those of Averrhoes even during his lifetime; and through these Latin translations, the works of Aristotle (who had died in 322 B.C.) and of Plato, his teacher, became known in the West and had a profound effect on the way men thought about God and the world.

The depth and the brilliance of Greek thought led men to ask what role faith might play in such a structure, and how such a structure might serve faith. One of the earliest attempts to answer these questions was that of Anselm, an Italian who had been a monk at the monastery of Bec in Normandy, and who later became Archbishop of Canterbury, where he died in 1109.

Anselm raised the question of whether the existence of God can be known only by faith, or whether it can also be known by reason, by the power of native intelligence. The answer he gave was profound, though often misunderstood. He pointed out that human beings can form the concept of a being which is infinite, without any bound or limit, and that they do this even though nothing in their experience is, in any proper sense of the word, unlimited. Anselm then went on to ask how we can form such a concept of a thing which so transcends all of our experience, and he asserted that only the *reality* of such a being could possibly explain our ability to fashion such a concept.

After Anselm's time, and to a great extent stimulated by his work, the attempt to penetrate the mysteries of the faith with the help of Greek thought occupied the best minds in western Europe. Hugh of St. Victor, who died in 1141, wrote an ordered summary of the theology of his day, with the title: *Concerning the Sacraments of the Christian Faith.* Peter Abelard, who died in 1142, applied logic and dialectic to questions of faith, and developed a method of discussion and debate which was designed to clarify theological questions and lead to deeper understanding. Peter Lombard, who died in 1160, published a book called the *Sentences*, in which he had assembled quotations from the fathers of the church and other famous theologians concerning all of the theological questions which interested men of the twelfth century. Peter's book was the principal theological text of the late twelfth century and throughout the thirteenth. Bonaventure, a Franciscan who lived from 1221 to 1274, was particularly influenced by the Latin translations of Plato, and of a Christian writer of the sixth century who bears the impressive scholarly nickname of Pseudo-Dionysius the Areopagite.

However it was Aristotle who had the most enduring influence on medieval Christian thought, and it was the religious order founded by Dominic in the early years of the thirteenth century which devoted itself most successfully to understanding the thought of the Greek philosopher, and to adapting it so that it would be of use to Christians. This dedication to Aristotelian thought was not without danger. Aristotle was obviously not a Christian, and there were some elements of his thought which were simply irreconcilable with Christian faith. But the Dominicans accepted the challenge, and the result was one of the greatest intellectual achievements of human history. The first of these Dominican theologians to write a summary of theology on an Aristotelian basis was Albert the Great, a man of universal interests, who, if born in a later age might have been one of the great natural scientists. However, in philosophy and theology, he was outshone by his brilliant pupil and friend, Thomas Aquinas, who lived from 1224 to 1272, and who proposed an intriguing solution to the fundamental problem of scholastic thought.

Down through the centuries, Christian thinkers had offered various solutions to the problem of the relationship of faith and reason. Some, like Tertullian, argued that faith was the higher knowledge and must always prevail over reason. In virtue of this, Tertullian was proud to believe what would, by rational criteria, be pure absurdity. ("Credo quia absurdum—I believe because it is absurd.") Others argued that faith and reason each has its own proper sphere of activity. In the early medieval period, some who were impressed by Greek thought, but who wished, at the same time, to remain Christian, argued that there were two kinds of truth, and that something could be true in theology, from the standpoint of faith, but false in philosophy, from the standpoint of reason.

Thomas Aquinas had a different and deeper vision. In his view it is the longing for ultimate and infinite reality, the reality of God, which constitutes us as human beings and therefore as rational beings. For Thomas, faith is not the power which demands the mortification of intelligence, but is rather a light which aids human intelligence and helps it reach its proper object. Faith and reason do not simply coexist; they imply and demand each other. This vision and insight stands behind the enormous body of work which this prolific writer produced in a lifetime of less than fifty years. His great work, which is the systematic application of this vision to all areas of medieval theology, is his monumental *Summa Theologiae* or *Summary of Theology*, which was incomplete at the time of his death. Thomas' work was not well understood in his lifetime; his conception of the relationship of faith and intelligence was both too profound and too radical, and by the end of the century in which he died, men in the theological faculties of the universities were beginning to lose confidence in the power of human intelligence to understand God and his works. As is always the case, loss of confidence in the power of human intelligence marked the beginning of the decline of a great culture.

5.7 THE CHURCH IN THE EAST

The power and influence of Byzantium—the Empire of which Constantinople was the capital—grew in the tenth and eleventh centuries. The capital had defended itself heroically and successfully against the Moslem onslaughts of 674 to 678 and against subsequent attacks in 717 and 718, when Moslem forces were crushed at the very walls of the city. After that, the Islamic East settled down and lost much of its momentum. The power of Byzantium grew, and by the year 1050 it had reached a peak, and the rulers of the eastern Empire could begin to think of regaining some of the territories lost to Islam four centuries before that time.

But even before the eleventh century ended, hordes of Asiatic tribesmen, who had just recently been converted to the Mohammedan faith, began to move into Asia Minor. From then on, all of the resources of Byzantium were devoted to this life and death struggle against these Seljuk Turks which continued through the next four centuries, until the fall of Constantinople in 1453. It was in seeking help against the Turks that the Emperor had turned to the Pope at the end of the eleventh century, and it was his request which led, in part, to the multiple tragedies of the Crusades. It was the need to concentrate all efforts on the defense against Islam which absorbed the creative energies of the East, and possibly prevented the emergence of new forms of monasticism and new styles of thinking which would have resembled those which were so characteristic of the West through the twelfth and thirteenth centuries.

5.71 The Separation of the Churches in East and West

The passage of time, the geographical separation, and a series of tragic misunderstandings had gradually driven a wedge between the church in the East and the church in the West. Disputes arose over purely disciplinary questions, such as whether the Eucharist should be celebrated with leavened or unleavened bread, or whether the clergy should be married (or wear beards!) or not, and such questions weighed heavily in those days. Theological differences were not really important. What was important was that the leaders of the two churches had a tendency to absolutize their own ways of thinking and to refuse to admit that the Christian message could be preached in other "languages" than those with which they were familiar. (The word "language" here is used both in its ordinary sense—a system of communication which uses its own vocabulary and grammar—and in an extended sense— all of the resources of thought and expression which are available to people because of the time at which and the place in which they live.)

As usual for the period, political and religious questions were inextricably intertwined. In virtue both of the spurious *Donation of Constantine* and of Pippin's gift of lands in southern Italy in the eighth century, from that time on the Popes laid claim to that part of the peninsula. However, parts of southern Italy and much of Sicily had remained Greek speaking from early times, and were claimed by the eastern Emperor and the eastern church. In 1049 the reforming Pope, Leo IX, campaigned against the married Byzantine clergy in southern Italy, probably out of a mixture of political and religious motives. After an initial hostile reaction, Michael Cerularius, the Patriarch of Constantinople, wrote a conciliatory letter to Leo, but Leo rejected the letter and sent two papal legates to Constantinople to resolve the dispute in a way acceptable to himself. One of the legates, Cardinal Humbert, was one of the more narrow-minded and arrogant representatives of Latin Christianity, and when negotiations stalled, he entered the cathedral of Santa Sophia just before the Patriarch was to celebrate the solemn liturgy, and laid on the high altar the document which excommunicated Michael Cerularius. Although this excommunication was not of long duration, the Crusades, as we have seen, resulted in the definitive separation of the churches, which has lasted to the present day.

5.72 The Conversion of Russia

The first important political center in Russia was the old Ukrainian city of Kiev, where the Prince, Vladimir, was converted to the orthodox Christianity of the East in 988. The progress of Christianity was very slow: a number of the nobles had accepted Christianity, but the new faith remained a thin veneer. Among the common people it initially made almost no headway against superstition and the belief in magic which were the substance of the old paganism, but in time monasteries were founded, and they became centers from which the faith spread.

The fact that Kiev accepted orthodox Christianity already implied that developments in church life there would take a course very different from that in western Europe; but in the early thirteenth century an event occurred which sealed most of Russia hermetically from the West for almost two hundred years. The Mongols conquered the Russian principalities at this time and put an end to Russian political independence for the whole period of their occupation.

The Mongol occupation was in some ways a blessing in disguise for the Russian Orthodox Church. At the beginning of the Mongol domination, the monks, who lived in the partially christianized southern part of the country, fled to the forested regions of the north, where there were no cities and which were only sparsely populated. There, as in the West, the monasteries exerted a civilizing influence on the primitive rural society and they became centers from which the faith radiated among the pagan population. The liturgy was celebrated with impressive dignity and beauty in a slightly older form of Slavonic which was still readily understood. The scriptures were read publicly in the same language, and people became familiar with the biblical text in a way which was not true at that time in the West.

As the monasteries spread throughout old Russia, strong mystical tendencies made themselves felt. Men sought an immediate and deeply felt contact with God, and this was to be a characteristic of Russian Christianity throughout all later periods.

As the years passed, it became clear that there would be no organized persecution of Christians on the part of the Mongols. The conquerors were few in number and they never settled permanently on the land. As long as tribute flowed regularly back to the Khan's capital in Central Asia, they were quite content to leave the native inhabitants in peace. During the period of Mongol control, it looked for a while as though Western European influence might penetrate the country from the northwest, where Mongol control was only nominal. In the 1230's a Swedish army crossed the Baltic, and in 1240 the Teutonic Knights, one of the military religious orders which had issued from the Crusades, turned from its northeastward march through the Baltic lands and moved on the Russian city of Novgorod. In true crusading spirit, these Teutonic knights were engaged in a program of plunder, of land-grabbing, and of the forced conversion of the populace to western, Latin Christianity. But the Russian leader, Alexander Nevsky, was able to unite the northern tribes for a brief period. He defeated the Swedes in 1240, and destroyed the army of the Teutonic Knights in 1242, driving them back to the Baltic lands, and insuring that Russian Christianity would remain resolutely Orthodox (and, to a significant degree, anti-western).

5.8 DEVELOPMENTS IN THEOLOGY AND IN CHURCH LIFE

5.81 Theology

Canon or church law underwent great development in the western church during this period. After 1200 the papal court was increasingly involved in the game of power politics, and needed a code of church law, both to justify what it was doing and to insure that the wheels of the growing bureaucracy turned more smoothly. The Decree of Gratian, that collection of church law which strongly emphasized papal power and was published in 1140, was a landmark in this process.

From the eleventh century on, thinking about the sacraments (symbolic actions which give to the believer a share in the life of God) changed in some important respects. It would be almost the middle of the fifteenth century before general agreement was reached on the number of the sacraments, although theology was moving in that direction long before the thirteenth century was over. It was commonly accepted that these sacraments did not depend for their efficacy on the holiness of the one who administered them, but that they were effective in and of themselves, because this had been the intention of Jesus in instituting them. This theory of sacramental efficacy was sometimes interpreted by poorly instructed people to mean that the sacraments were independent of the dispositions and good will of those who received them, and this brought the sacraments dangerously close to the sphere of superstition and magic.

The theology of indulgences also underwent development during this period, in a direction which was to cause much difficulty later on. The theory commonly accepted was that Christ, through his death, won a great surplus of merit (a title to a reward which he obviously did not need for himself) and that through this same death he had offered more than abundant satisfaction or compensation to God to make up for the glory of which he had been deprived by sin. In doing this, Christ had set up a kind of treasury or bank account of merit and satisfaction and entrusted that to the church, so that the church would be able to put portions of this merit and satisfaction at the disposal of its members who did good works. The original idea was that Christians, by doing some good work, could be given a share in this merit and satisfaction, and that the time of punishment in purgatory, after death, would be proportionately shortened. For example, when Urban II proclaimed the first Crusade in 1095, he offered what was called a *plenary* indulgence—a remission of all the punishments of purgatory for those who undertook to fight in the holy war. In the thirteenth century, the belief spread that one could get this kind of indulgence not only for oneself but also for others who were already suffering in purgatory, and around this time church authorities began to offer indulgences not only for good works but for the financing of good works. This led to the shocking abuses which we know of during the late medieval period and which had reached scandalous proportions just before the Reformation.

Eucharistic theology took two directions which were to cause problems later on. Christians had always been convinced of the reality of the presence of Jesus at the eucharistic meal, but in the early medieval period, this belief often took on a strong superstitious coloring. Stories were told about how the eucharistic bread would bleed, if pricked with a pin, and priests were deeply troubled that the eucharistic wine tasted like wine and not like blood. The eucharistic theology of the early scholastics concentrated on the question of how the elements of bread and wine were related to the presence of Jesus and how he could be really present in and under the bread and the wine, and the question of what happened to these elements when the priest spoke the words of consecration. The attempt to answer this last question led to the formulating of the doctrine of *transubstantiation*, that is, the teaching that after the consecration of the Mass, the bread and wine only appeared to be there; what was really there was the body and the blood of Jesus, and therefore his whole reality, human and divine. This teaching led to a great fear that fragments of the bread or drops of wine might fall and be trampled underfoot. As a result, the chalice was no longer passed to the laity.

This concentration on the eucharistic elements led to a piety which did not emphasize the reception of the Eucharist and the sharing of the eucharistic meal, but rather the act of reverently looking at the "host" (the eucharistic bread) and adoring it when it was raised by the priest during Mass or encased in a holder and shown to the people at other times.

During this period, the theology of marriage underwent important changes. It came to be commonly acknowledged that marriage was one of the sacraments which had been instituted by Jesus, and because of this, divorce was absolutely forbidden. Further, canon lawyers argued that marriage was essentially a contract, and that for that reason free consent was of the essence of marriage. In time, the direct criticism of forced marriages and the indirect criticism of dynastic marriages which this implied had some effect on improving the generally poor position of women in both the church and in the larger society.

5.82 Church Life

Devotion to the saints grew in popularity throughout the High Middle Ages, and the saints came to be seen, not as Christian heroes worthy of emulation, but rather as powerful beings who would intercede with God on behalf of those who petitioned their help. Marian piety developed and for the first time the prayer known as the "Hail Mary" appeared, made up of elements partly scriptural, partly traditional. Repetitive saying of this new prayer and of the Lord's Prayer, while one meditated on the mysteries of Jesus' life and death, was popularized as the *Rosary*. The practice of going on pilgrimages, which had begun in the fourth and fifth centuries, spread widely; Vézelay in France and Compostela in Spain were the favorite places to visit. Some of these manifestations of piety were quite superficial, but at the same time, many in the church longed for mystical experience and yearned for immediate contact with God, in which they might feel his presence and power. Another and more broadly based piety found expression in the *confraternities*—associations for the laity which tried to adapt some of the features of monastic life for those who remained in the world. These confraternities were, not surprisingly, associated with the great religious orders, and as they spread, they began to satisfy some of the needs of the laity for authentic piety.

During this period, the Christian message penetrated more deeply into society, and the church attempted to curb the pervasive violence of life in western Europe by institutions such as the *peace of God*, which sought to exempt whole classes in society from attack by bands of robber barons and their retinues; the clergy, women and children, merchants, and sometimes others were among the exempt. Another institution known as the *truce of God* attempted to limit the vicious feuds among the nobles by declaring certain days of the week off limits for fighting—Sunday, the Lord's day, Friday, the day he died, and eventually other days of the week as well.

Shortly after the year 1000 a virtual mania of building swept over much of southwestern Europe. It began in the south of France and spread from there into Spain, into the north of France and then, a century later, into northern Germany. Even relatively small towns had to have their great cathedrals, which were built in a new and magnificent style— the Romanesque—which expressed the steadfastness and eternity of God by allowing the very massiveness of stone to be a symbol of him.

A more refined notion of Christian charity and love of neighbor led to the founding of hospitals in the years after 1100. These were understood not primarily as medical institutions, but rather as places of refuge to which the old, the poor, the sick, and even travelers might come to find a roof over their heads and some food on their table.

5.9 A BACKWARD LOOK

In all respects, the involvement of the church with civil power and worldly concerns had led to fundamental changes in the church's understanding of itself. The *laity* who were originally the *people of God* and therefore the whole Christian people, now came to be thought of as those who did not belong to the clergy and who therefore formed a group of lower rank in the church, and were, in a sense, second class Christians. The church became identified with the clergy and the hierarchy, and the laity became their subjects.

From the time of Gregory VII and throughout the thirteenth century, the church became more and more the *papal church*, and in the eyes of many Popes of the time came almost to be identified with the papal states of central Italy. The Popes of the time insisted that all offices in the church were simply delegations of papal power. *Romanness* or Romanità became the distinctive element of the church, as the papal court or *curia* grew in power and assumed control over liturgy, the granting of dispensations, and the appointment of bishops. Papal administration became highly centralized, and uniformity in all things was highly prized. Churchmen during this period spontaneously spoke of the church in *juridical* categories and canon law became the privileged place in which the church reflected on its own nature.

This church of the thirteenth century can properly be called the *imperial church*. It waged war with the help of Christian knights, and the Crusades were the perfect example of this mentality; thousands of Orthodox, Moslems, and Jews died, but the slaughter was justified by the slogan "Dios lo vult" (God wills it), which was the cry, in the Romance speech of the day, that greeted Urban's call in 1095. From the Crusades issued the knightly religious orders and the slaughter of infidels in the name of Christ was transferred from Palestine to Prussia and the Slavonic lands. This violence directed against the infidels could easily turn against the Jews and then against Christian heretics—the Cathari and the followers of Peter Waldes of Lyon were victims of such violence.

At the same time, counter movements surfaced in the church and strong mystical tendencies began to take shape. The call for reform in the church, from the Pope down to the parish priest, was voiced repeatedly during the Middle Ages, but by the year 1300 the Popes and their courts had become skilled in resisting such calls for reform. More than anything else, it was this skill in resisting reform which led to the decline and decay of the church in the fourteenth and fifteenth centuries, and to the Reformation of the sixteenth century.

The Gregorian Reform had begun with the attempt to free the church from secular control, but it had led ultimately to worldliness and to the obsession of churchmen with money and power. The church was ripe for reform, but unfortunately this reform was delayed for over two hundred years, and when it finally came it took place outside the Catholic church and against it. The events which led to this Protestant Reformation will occupy our attention in the next chapter.

6

From 1300 to 1500

6.1 INTRODUCTION

The word *Christendom* well describes the world of the Middle Ages. By birth, one was a member of highly structured society, in which supreme political power belonged to the Emperor and supreme spiritual power belonged to the Pope. In a sense, even the existence of these two highest lords, one spiritual and one temporal, was an offense against medieval man's quest for unity, and we have seen how the Popes, after affirming their spiritual supremacy, went on to win political power as well. The medieval world had a center—Rome—and the power which radiated from that city held all of medieval Europe in its sway.

Between the years 1300 and 1500, European unity came to an end. In the political sphere, the Empire lost whatever power it still had, after its disastrous encounters with the medieval papacy, for in the long struggle which had begun even before the time of Gregory VII in 1076 and lasted until the papacy of Innocent III in the early thirteenth century, the Popes were unquestionably the victors. The idea of a supreme authority in the secular realm, which would take the place of the old Roman Empire and govern the entire civilized world, had lost its hold on the minds of men. The *political* mystique of Rome, which had inspired Charlemagne and the medieval Emperors, was dead. Dante's *De Monarchia* in the early fourteenth century was an eloquent defense of imperial power and its rights against the imperial papacy, but it was a document which looked to the past and not to the future.

The medieval papacy had succeeded in wresting secular power from the Emperors, but its very triumph called into existence counter-forces which were purely secular and often hostile. At the time of the Gregorian Reform, church authorities were struggling against Emperors who saw the propagation of the faith as their highest task and most serious responsibility, and who naturally claimed the rights which were consequent on these obligations. But when the church became, to all appearances, one secular power among others, its victory led to the emergence of political powers which struggled with it for control, and which could not have cared less about the spiritual mission of the church. The emerging nation states in England, France, and Spain were far more successful in controlling the church than the Empire had ever been.

The period from 1300 to 1500 was a time of often conscious and deliberate rebellion against the old order and against the foundations of its social and intellectual life. The medieval world had been an *ordered* world. In feudal society, everyone had his assigned and allotted place, from the Pope, the supreme lord who granted entire kingdoms to his vassals, down to the serf who tilled the soil and was little better than a slave. Furthermore, everyone knew his place and was either content with it or fatalistic about it, and therefore feudal society was stable.

But even before medieval civilization had reached its highest point in the thirteenth century, institutions had arisen within it (and were, of course, created by it), which would eventually bring the feudal order to an end, and with it, the entire value system on which medieval European life rested. In the twelfth and thirteenth centuries, cities grew rapidly, a middle class began to emerge, and several of the great universities were founded. The feudal order was essentially rural and agrarian, and these new groups did not fit into such an order. The emerging middle class and the university graduates were upwardly mobile; they constituted a new kind of aristocracy, and they were not inclined to recognize the privileges of the old aristocracy which were based on inherited land and wealth.

Intellectual life in the Middle Ages was vigorous and it was characterized by a great trust in reason and profound confidence in the ability of human intelligence to discover the truth about God and the world, and to find values to live by and to die by. Scholasticism (the philosophy and theology of the writers of the medieval *summae*—summaries of theology) was a triumph of human intelligence and reason. But, as is always the case in history, the triumph of reason in one epoch leads to the distrust of reason in the next. Life is ambiguous and death is final, and the ultimate solution to the ambiguity of life and the finality of death always eludes our grasp and leads to frustration with, and distrust of, reason. At the very beginning of the fourteenth century, the emphasis shifted from intelligence to will, and men began to reflect on the arbitrary power of God and his human vicars, rather than on intelligible order in matters divine and human.

These political, spiritual, and intellectual developments which heralded the end of the medieval world might have been assimilated, and new forms of social and intellectual life might have emerged which were in greater continuity with the old, had it not been for an event which plunged fourteenth century Europe into the deepest despair, and which made the achievements of the thirteenth century look like sad and even arrogant illusions. The Black Death—a particularly virulent strain of the bubonic plague—had passed from the Near East to Constantinople, where it broke out in 1337, and it had been carried to Western Europe, probably by returning Crusaders. It broke out in Europe in 1347, and for more than twenty years a series of epidemics devastated England and the continent. Probably half of the population died in England, and on the continent the best estimates indicate that the death toll was near forty percent. The Black Death was particularly hard on the new religious orders; the orders themselves were decimated three times over by the plague, and the scarcity of vocations led to the acceptance of candidates who were not really suited to religious life.

The period between 1300 and 1500 saw the breakdown

of medieval unity and the gradual evolution of those institutions and systems of values which marked Western European life until the early twentieth century. As is the case with all periods of transition, it is very difficult to get a unified overview of these two centuries. In religion, politics, and culture, the tendencies were all centrifugal, and every facet and sector of life sought its own autonomy, and rejected subordination to any law or norm outside of itself. However, during this period there was a kind of oscillation between movements of decline and decay, on one hand, and movements of revival and reform on the other. And both of these movements were played out against the background of a newly independent secular culture, which was in some ways dangerous for the faith, but which could also lead to new forms of Christian piety and life.

6.2 THE AVIGNON PAPACY

Innocent III was the last Pope whose claim to supreme religious and political power in Western Europe was generally recognized. When Boniface VIII tried to renew these same claims at the very beginning of the fourteenth century, the French king, Philip the Fair, reacted by clapping the Pope in prison. Boniface VIII died soon after this, and as Philip stepped in to fill the power vacuum created by the papacy's victory over the medieval Empire, his policy was clearly motivated by his desire to make the papacy a French national institution. He almost succeeded, and the consequences, both for the papacy and for the unity of Christian Europe, were disastrous. After the death of Boniface, the number of French cardinals increased rapidly, as a result of pressure from the king, and the nine Popes who succeeded Boniface were all Frenchmen.

The first two Popes of this line already made it clear that they were not inclined to live for any length of time in Rome—a city which by now had become an unimportant backwater, noted mostly for its undisciplined and wild mobs and its appalling summer climate. When Clement V was elected Pope in 1305, he did not even bother to go to Rome, and in 1309 he selected the southern French city of Avignon as his residence.

This transfer of the papal residence was a highly symbolic move, and it marked the end of the universal, supra-national claims of the medieval papacy. When the Popes were in Rome there was no danger that the papacy would become an Italian national institution. For one thing, there was as yet no emerging Italian nation state, and the Pope's position as temporal lord of the papal states made him far more of a competitor of the noble families who ruled the far south and of the independent city states which were beginning to appear in the north. It was precisely this political situation of the Italian peninsula at the time which made it possible for the majority of Popes to be Italian and to reside in Italy, without seeming to favor the cause of any national group.

In addition, as we have seen, the Popes from the time of Leo IX, in the middle of the eleventh century, were the heirs of a political mystique which saw in Rome the city from which the entire civilized world might appropriately be ruled. (And Leo IX and his successors had simply taken up and developed that view of the Pope as heir to the prerogatives of the western Emperor, which had motivated Gregory the Great at the very end of the sixth century, and which had been legitimated by the spurious *Donation of Constantine* in the middle of the eighth century.) Rome had been the capital of the old Empire, and in the same way it became the capital of the imperial papacy of the High Middle Ages. There could be no clearer sign that the Middle Ages had abruptly ended than the transfer of the papacy to Avignon in 1309. It was obvious that these French Popes were Frenchmen first and Popes second, and they were pliable and willing tools in the hands of the French monarchy. At the beginning of the Avignon papacy, this meant that they were willing to serve the interests of Philip the Fair, without doubt one of the most unattractive figures ever to occupy the throne of France.

The domination of the church by Philip the Fair is evident from the affair of the suppression of the Knights Templar—certainly one of the saddest chapters in the entire history of the papacy. The Templars were a military order which had originated at the time of the Crusades. Many of them were French, and when the Crusades were over, most of them returned to France and lived there as feudal lords. Over the years they had acquired a great deal of wealth, and Philip the Fair was willing to use any means to get his hands on their money and their land.

In the year 1307 he had two thousand members of the order of the Knights Templar arrested on a single day, claiming that the members of the order were guilty of heresy and of all kinds of sexual crimes. Confessions were extracted under torture, and Philip pressured the Pope, Clement V, to suppress the order. The Pope meekly agreed, and at a council held at Vienne in 1312, and against the advice of a majority of bishops assembled there, Clement decreed the suppression of the Knights Templar. As soon as the Knights had been stripped of all security, Philip seized their property, and to make sure that former Templars would make no attempt to regain it, he had hundreds of them burned at the stake in 1314 and 1315.

Marsilius of Padua had been teaching at the University of Paris, but he had to leave the city for political reasons, and he sought refuge at the court of Ludwig in Bavaria. In 1326 in Regensburg he published a book, entitled *Defender of the Peace*, which was a direct attack on the institution of the papacy, as this had developed throughout the Middle Ages. Marsilius denied the divine origin of the papacy and rejected the entire hierarchical order of the church. He claimed that, according to the will of its founder, the church was an essentially democratic institution, and that supreme power belonged to all of the members of the church because the church is the community of all believers. Popes and bishops had not received divine authority from Christ, but were merely officials, whose duty it was to serve the church (and this word meant, for Marsilius, *the people of God*). Most important for the future was Marsilius' insistence that the church council was above the Pope and possessed supreme power in the church. Consequently, councils have the power to depose Popes, because the Pope is merely the servant of the council and continues in office at its pleasure.

It is clear that the antipapal sentiment which was pro-

voked by the Avignon Popes was quickly turning into a theoretical and theological questioning of the very foundations of
the papal church. But the French Popes seemed quite unaware of the storm which was brewing, above all in Germany,
as a result of Avignon's servile conformity to the wishes of the
French crown, and at this very time the Popes redoubled their
efforts to increase the revenues of their court.

The Avignon Popes and the bureaucracy which served
them were gifted fund raisers. It had been over a century
since the last of the Crusades had ended, but the tax to support these Crusades was still being levied on all of Christendom. During the Middle Ages, the papacy had reserved to
itself the right to grant dispensations (exemptions) from a
large number of church laws, and Avignon turned a hand-
some profit from this practice. Huge fees were charged for
the granting of important dispensations, and it was hard to
avoid the impression that these exceptions to the law of the
church were being bought and sold. Archbishops were required to pay heavy fees in order to receive the insignia of office, and for each and every administrative act of the papal
court, money changed hands.

The sorry scandal of Avignon continued for almost seventy years, until, in 1377, the Italian mystic, Catherine of
Siena, finally persuaded Pope Gregory IX to return to Rome.
The seven Popes who had made Avignon their residence
were, by and large, men of considerable administrative ability, and some of them were even men of personal piety, but
their ability showed itself in the skill with which they managed
the growing wealth of the papal court, and their piety was so
personal that it blinded them to the fact that their fiscal policies were alienating much of northern Europe. Politically, the
Avignon Popes were servile lackeys of the French crown, and
it was this which made the citizens of the Empire come to look
on the papacy as a hostile foreign institution. The Avignon
papacy prepared the way for the rebellion of northern Europe against the papacy and the papal church in the sixteenth
century and it ranks high on the list of causes of the Reformation.

6.3 THE GREAT WESTERN SCHISM

Although Gregory IX had returned to Rome in 1377, the prospect of living in the impoverished backwater which Rome had become so dismayed the Pope and the cardinals (a majority of them were French) that they were preparing to leave the city again, when Gregory died in 1378. In accordance with the very strict law governing papal elections, the new Pope had to be elected where his predecessor died, and the cardinals gathered in Rome for the conclave (the secret electoral meeting).

At this juncture, the cardinals' worst fears about the violence of the Roman populace were confirmed. On the day before the election, an armed mob broke into the palace where the conclave was being held, and informed the cardinals that if they wanted to live beyond the next day, it would be wise to choose a Roman Pope. Faced with an offer which they could not refuse, the cardinals obliged by choosing, not a Roman, but at least an Italian, the bishop of Bari, who took the name of Urban VI.

As soon as the election was over, the cardinals left Rome as quickly as they could. They returned ten days later for the coronation of the new Pope, and swore their loyalty to him, as ancient custom demanded. But three months later, the French cardinals left Rome again, returned to Avignon, and declared that the election of Urban had been invalid, because the Roman mob had deprived them of true freedom of choice. They proceeded to elect a new, French Pope, who took the name of Clement VII, and reigned from 1378 to 1394, most of the time in Avignon. Surprisingly, even the Italian cardinals went over to the new Pope.

It seems clear that the cardinals had not been free in choosing Urban VI, but had acted simply out of the desire to save their own skins. But if Urban had shown the least bit of tact, he might well have been accepted by the cardinals, so that, despite the questionable character of his election, we might at least speak of a retroactive approval on the part of those who were responsible for electing the Pope. But Urban proceeded to act, not just tactlessly, but in so fanatical a manner that many people felt that election to high office had driven him over the edge into insanity. The official Catholic position has always been that the true Popes were Urban VI and those who followed him in the Roman line, but it is really impossible today to reach any certitude about which election was valid. If a judgment had to be made, it would probably favor the Avignon Pope and his successor.

This new situation threw all of Christendom into utter confusion. There were now two Popes (who had excommunicated each other) and two papal courts. To some degree all of Europe divided by nations, with France and Spain supporting the Popes in Avignon, while Italy, England, Germany, and the other northern European countries supported the Popes of the Roman line. But the dispute about who was really Pope divided each country, each diocese, and each parish. Men and women who would later be canonized as saints could be found on each side. Vincent Ferrer, the most famous preacher of the day, was a fervent supporter of the Avignon Pope, and Catherine of Siena was an equally convinced partisan of the Roman line. This *Great Western Schism* was to last for forty years, and during that time there were four Popes, including Urban, in the Roman line. Two Popes, Clement VII (1378 to 1394) and Benedict XIII (1394 to 1417), claimed to exercise papal power from Avignon.

Since the Emperor was no longer regarded as competent in such matters, and the papacy itself was in dispute, it remained for that third great institution which had been inherited from the medieval world—the University of Paris—to propose a solution to the dilemma. In 1394 the theologians of that university suggested three possibilities. The first proposal was that both Popes abdicate and leave the field free for the election of a new Pope. The second proposal was that both Popes submit their dispute to binding arbitration. The third possibility was to call a general or ecumenical council of all of the bishops of the western church, and to entrust the decision to that council. Eventually it was this final solution which was chosen, and this led to the third great crisis of the church in the fourteenth and fifteenth centuries.

6.4 CONCILIARISM

If we reflect on the development of papal power from the year 1076 on, it would seem that an ecumenical council was not at all suited to bring the Great Western Schism to an end. Gregory VII had affirmed, in his *Dictatus Papae*, not only that the Pope was above the council, but that, in addition, only the Pope had the authority to summon the bishops to meet in council. In the century and a half since Gregory's time, councils were simply instruments of papal policy—summoned, given their orders, and terminated by the Popes of the period.

Nevertheless, it was acknowledged by virtually everyone, including the most rabid supporters of the imperial papacy, that it was possible that a Pope might become incapacitated and incapable of discharging his duty. It was even acknowledged by most that it was possible for the Pope, as an individual, to fall into heresy. And it was commonly admitted that if either of these possibilities became fact, then it was an ecumenical council and it alone which could declare the papal throne vacant and arrange for a new election. But the situation had never arisen up to that time, and there was some uncertainty about who had the authority to summon the bishops to meet in council; some argued that it was the right and duty of the cardinals, while others claimed that only the Emperor would be competent in such a case.

Of course, long before Marsilius of Padua published his *Defender of the Peace* in 1326, voices had been raised, suggesting that the evolution of the imperial papacy, from the time of Gregory VII on, was not legitimated by the New Testament and represented a total misunderstanding of Christ's words to Peter. Later in the century, the pro-French political stance of the Avignon Popes, as well as their scandalous fiscal policies, united the opponents of papal power in a movement called *conciliarism*. The conciliar movement brought together men who were acting out of the most diverse motives and whose attitudes toward the papacy covered a broad spectrum of opinion. Some questioned the very foundations of papal primacy, while others wanted to reform the institution so as to restore to the Pope the respect and authority which was due to him as the supreme spiritual leader of the Christian world. But there was one thing on which all the partisans of the conciliar movement agreed: no matter how frequently or how rarely it might be exercised, ultimate legislative power in the church belonged to the ecumenical council—the gathering of the territorial bishops of the Christian world.

Despite all of the uncertainty about when a Pope might be deposed and about who had the authority to call a council, and despite all of the differences among the members of that loose coalition known as the conciliar movement, it was becoming clear, as the fifteenth century dawned, that an ecumenical council was the only way of ending the schism. By 1408, thirteen cardinals, some of them from Avignon and others from Rome, had been won to the view that they, the cardinals, must summon the bishops to a council. They did precisely this, and in 1409 the council met in the north Italian city of Pisa. One hundred bishops were present, and an equal number sent representatives with full authorization to act in their name. The monasteries were represented, as were the universities.

The bishops assembled at Pisa decided to depose the two competing Popes, and then they elected a new Pope, who took the name Alexander V; he died later that year and was succeeded by a man known as John XXIII. But neither the Pope in Rome nor the Pope in Avignon accepted the decisions of the Council of Pisa, and neither resigned. Instead of solving the problem of two Popes, the Council of Pisa had created the problem of three.

If everyone could have been patient, it is possible that John XXIII would have prevailed. Support for the other two was waning, and it was widely agreed that the bishops at the Council of Pisa had acted not only conscientiously but in a legally correct way. However, at this juncture, the Emperor Siegmund, who supported John XXIII, decided that it would be useful to hold yet another council, to provide his candidate with broader support than that which had been generated at Pisa. Siegmund persuaded John XXIII to summon a council to meet in the city of Constance in 1414. (The Council of

Constance is probably best remembered, not for the theological debate about the powers of the Pope and the council, but for its tragic and tragically stupid arrest, trial, and execution of the Czech priest and reformer, John Hus. Hus and his reform movement will be discussed later in this chapter.)

When John XXIII opened the first session of the Council of Constance in that same year, he was convinced that he would be quickly confirmed as the sole legitimate Pope, and that the bishops would be able to return home without further ado. But John did not count on the persuasiveness of the French cardinal, Pierre d'Ailly, and of the Chancellor of the University of Paris, John Gerson. At the early sessions of the Council, these men won the majority of the bishops over to their view that the only real hope for unity consisted in deposing all three contenders and then holding a new election.

As soon as John XXIII saw that the Council was turning against him, he and his retinue left Constance, and took up residence in the small town of Schaffhausen, not many miles down the Rhine. His intention in leaving was to bring the Council to an end, and he was convinced that the bishops would not dare continue their meetings, once he had withdrawn papal approval. He almost got away with this, because many of the bishops were clearly uneasy about taking part in a council which continued to meet without the Pope. But the Emperor moved quickly and decisively, and ordered the bishops to remain in Constance until they had settled the question of who the real Pope was.

Just two days after the departure of John XXIII, John Gerson, the Chancellor of the University of Paris, spoke to the assembled bishops and argued persuasively that the Pope had no right to dissolve the Council; three days later the bishops voted to continue their work in the absence of the Pope. John XXIII did all in his power to cripple the Council, but on April 6, 1415, the bishops approved a decree, entitled *Haec Sancta*, in which they affirmed that their assembly was a true ecumenical council and that, as such, it had power directly from God. They further asserted that no one, not even a Pope, had the right to interfere before the assembled bishops had fulfilled their twofold task of bringing the Great Western Schism to an end and of initiating a fundamental reform of the church.

The meaning of this decree is often debated. Did the bishops at Constance intend to attack the very foundations of papal power by subordinating the Pope to the ecumenical council *in principle*, or did they regard their decree simply as a practical solution in an intolerable situation? There is no single answer to this question, because the bishops and theologians who voted for this decree were not of one mind. There were some there, and as far as we can judge they were definitely in the minority, who shared the views which Marsilius of Padua had expressed in his *Defender of the Peace* in 1326, and who intended to launch an attack, not only on the abuses of papal power, but on every independent use of papal power. But most of those who voted for the decree were more than a little uneasy about it; they probably felt that the ambiguity of the decree was at least matched by the uncertainty of whether John XXIII was actually Pope.

John XXIII continued his efforts to undermine the work of the Council, and when it appeared that he was going to move to France in order to have a secure base from which to continue his struggle, the Emperor had him arrested. At the end of May, 1415, he was deposed by the Council. Gregory XII, the Roman Pope, voluntarily abdicated on the fourth of July of that same year, and that left only the contender in Avignon, Benedict XIII. The Emperor himself tried to convince him to resign and got nowhere, but he did manage to persuade the Avignon cardinals to abandon their Pope and to come to the Council of Constance. Once they were there, the Council deposed the last of the Avignon Popes on July 26, 1417.

Now the way was clear for the election of a new Pope, but an interesting and very troubling question had to be answered first. The Council had met, not simply to bring the Great Western Schism to an end, but also for the purpose of effecting the reform of the church in head and members. Now if a Pope were to be elected first, he would be the undisputed leader of the church, and reform, if it ever came about, would be his work and his responsibility. On the other hand, if the Council decided on a program of reform before electing a new Pope, it would clearly be claiming responsibility for reform in the church, including reform of the papacy. If it did this, it would have gone far in the direction of affirming, in principle, the superiority of the Council over the Pope.

The bishops of England and Germany strongly favored the second solution and they pressed for a discussion of reform measures before the election of the new Pope, but the bishops from the Latin lands wanted no part of this. (And this disagreement between north and south foreshadowed events of the Reformation period, little more than a century later.) Finally the bishops agreed on a compromise: the Council agreed that in the future the Pope would be obliged to call a council every ten years, but this was the sole reform measure to be approved. This compromise cleared the agenda of everything but the most pressing question of all, and now the Council could turn its attention to the election of a new Pope.

On November 6, 1417, the twenty-six cardinals, their number augmented by six representatives each from England, Germany, France, Spain, and Italy, entered the conclave. Three days later they agreed on a new Pope—an Italian cardinal who took the name of Martin V. Forty years of division and uncertainty were over, and the new Pope immediately took full control of the Council. With his approval, some reforms were decided on, and he confirmed the decrees which the Council had approved before his election. This last move has again and again prompted the question of how he could accept a decree which apparently put the Council above the Pope. The answer is probably that, like a majority of bishops at Constance, he understood that decree (*Haec Sancta*) not as a statement of principle, but as an emergency solution. And when Martin V decided that the Council had done what it should, he brought the meeting to an end on April 22, 1418. The crisis of the papacy was by no means over, but Martin had maneuvered it safely through its most difficult period.

The Council which should have met in 1428 at the latest (according to the decree approved at Constance), was finally summoned by Martin's successor, Eugene IV, to meet at

Basel, in Switzerland, in 1431. The radical conciliarists immediately tried to take control and to win acceptance of the Council as the supreme legislative body of the church. They were fairly successful in pressing their views, and as the meetings dragged on (for years!), the Council began to act as though it had the power to judge the Pope and to call him to task for failing to implement its ideas of reform. Finally Pope Eugene IV had had enough of this, and in 1437 he transferred the Council from Basel to Ferrara, in northern Italy, where he felt more confident of being able to assert his authority. The radical conciliarists stayed in Basel for another twelve years, and even went so far as to elect their own Pope, but by this time Christendom had had enough of schism. The dissident remnant which continued to meet in Basel finally abandoned their efforts in 1449, and their anti-pope resigned in the same year.

The conciliar movement seemed to have gone down to defeat, but in the next century it would be a major factor in the success of the Reformation—both directly, in the anti-papal sentiment which it had nurtured in Germany, and indirectly, in the abiding fear of councils as such, which was a virtual obsession of the Renaissance Popes, and which led the Popes of the early sixteenth century to delay for so long the calling of the Council of Trent. In the fifteenth century, the papacy skillfully resisted both the attempts of the radical conciliarists to strip it of power and the attempts of the moderates to bring about reform. The unfortunate confusion between the two in the minds of the Renaissance Popes exacted a heavy penalty in coming years.

6.5 FROM 1300 TO 1370

6.51 Problems in Piety

We are already familiar with a major phenomenon of decline and decay during this period—the Avignon papacy. Nepotism, the practice of installing members of the Pope's family in high administrative positions in the church, was the order of the day, and the incessant demand for more money, enforced by threats of interdict and excommunication, was a scandal, above all to the Christians of northern Europe. The Popes themselves, and, increasingly, the papal office, became objects of derision and contempt.

But if religious values were neglected by the high and mighty of the age, things were no better at the opposite end of the social spectrum. There was an appalling lack of depth in the piety of the common people. Superstition was widespread, and the sacraments were often treated as a particularly effective form of magic. Saints had multiplied, and the popular canonization of reputed local wonder-workers was common. It looked as though much of the old pagan polytheism had lived on since the time of the mass conversions, simply donning a new guise so that it might outwardly conform to Christian theory. There was at least one saint specialized for every function or crisis in life, and this army of intercessors had replaced the one mediator, Jesus Christ. People treated these saints much as their ancestors had treated the gods. It was possible to make deals with them, and if one made the appropriate offering, one could feel sure that the saint would be won over by the petitioner's generosity and would grant the favor requested. In fact, it was precisely this *quid pro quo* piety which led to the multiplication of saints and shrines. Furthermore, the piety of the age was much given to crediting pictures and statues of the saints with miraculous power, and this kind of superstitious magic infected many of the pilgrimages which were still a popular manifestation of piety.

Probably as a result of the terror which permeated society in the wake of the Black Death, people became obsessed with thoughts of death and of the tortures of purgatory and hell. Religious practice concentrated on the gaining of *merit*, which was thought of as a kind of bank account made up of good works, and which could be cashed in at the point of death in order to guarantee a blissful existence in the future life. Masses for the dead were multiplied, and the rich established huge foundations to insure that Masses beyond counting would be said for them after their deaths. In this way, despite the sins which they had committed during life, they would be quickly freed from the tortures of purgatory.

Large numbers of priests were needed to say all of these Masses, but they were often poorly instructed, and knew barely enough Latin to mumble their way through the ritual. (Most of these Masses were private—that is, recited by priests without the presence of a congregation.) These "Mass priests" constituted a large clerical proletariat, quite unproductive in society, and usually living on the edge of poverty, either because no provision had been made for their support, or because they were filling in for absentee clerical lords, who skimmed most of the money off the top of the benefices (funds set aside for the support of priests) and left only a pittance for their hired substitutes.

6.52 Currents of Reform

And yet, at this very period there were movements of revival and reform in the church. As is often the case in times of political and social disintegration, men and women longed for the felt presence of God, and they strove to develop techniques to turn their minds from the transient pleasures and the all-too-real pains of the world, and to experience the infinite joy of knowing God and basking in his presence. Ludolf of Saxony, whose life coincided with the dates which outline our period, was the most famous of these mystics, and his works were still being read two centuries later, when they influenced the religious development of Ignatius Loyola, the founder of the Jesuits. The Flemish mystic, Jan Ruysbroeck, who lived from 1293 to 1381, founded a contemplative community in a forest near Brussels. Gerhard Groote, who was influenced by Ruysbroeck, founded a religious community called the Brethren of the Common Life. The men who belonged to this community (later there were houses for women, too) began by gathering in private homes for scriptural reading and meditation. This led them to take on apostolic tasks, and in time they established schools for the training of young people. Groote himself may actually have written the very influential little book called *The Imitation of Christ*, although it was later attributed to another individual on whom the piety of the Brethren had made a great impression—Thomas of Kempen.

6.53 Intellectual Life

In the early fourteenth century, many people with spiritual interests reacted against the confidence of thirteenth century theologians in intelligence and reason, and there is more than a touch of anti-intellectualism in *The Imitation of Christ*. At this very time, intellectual life was freeing itself from the tutelage of the church and was becoming distinctly secular, frequently anticlerical, and at times anti-Christian. The Italian Renaissance had begun in the early years of the fourteenth century, and many of its early protagonists affected a rather studied and self-conscious contempt for the learning of the medieval period. They rediscovered the old Latin classics, and they held the literary style of these works in high esteem. They were fond of contrasting the frank love of the world and of life which they found there with the deliberate other-worldliness and contempt for this life which they claimed to find in medieval times. These men of the early Renaissance were all nominal Christians, but in many of them a thinly disguised paganism lived on under a Christian veneer, and some of the Popes of the time were uncritical enough to invite these essentially pagan humanists to the papal court and to award them with high positions there. Other and more significant figures of the Italian Renaissance, such as Dante (who really bridged the gap between the Middle Ages and the new period), and Petrarch, were genuinely Christian, although quite aware of the abuses of clericalism which were all around them. Toward the end of this period, the new learning began to make its way northward, first to Paris, and then to centers in England and Germany. On northern terrain it remained skeptical of much in the institutional church, but it showed more genuinely religious concerns.

6.6 FROM 1370 TO 1415

6.61 Further Problems: Indulgences and Benefices

This second period coincides almost exactly with the Great Western Schism. Neither of the contending Popes was in a position to act quite as independently and arrogantly as their predecessors had (with the exception, of course, of Urban VI, whose fanatical arrogance had done more than anything else to cause the schism). However, the love of pomp and luxurious living, and the unabashed nepotism of the earlier period, continued unabated. Neither of the two papal courts could draw on the financial support of all of Christendom, and each was chronically short of money, and as a result, the old practice of selling church offices continued and the peddling of indulgences became even more common. This latter abuse had developed from the practice of offering to those who had performed some good work a remission in whole or in part of the pains of purgatory which remained to be paid after death. Little by little, the specific good work demanded for the indulgence came to be a financial contribution—the payment of a sum of money. This was already dangerously close to buying a remission of the punishments of purgatory, and in the popular mind it certainly crossed over the line.

During this period it became common for sons of the well-to-do and for relatives of high churchmen to be given the disposition of *benefices*—funds which had originally been set aside for the continuing support of priests who served in the parishes. Often these benefices would be *cumulated*—and many of them would be given to one favored individual—and the result was that funds originally set aside for spiritual purposes were now used for the private whims and pleasures of the sons of the nobility. This *absentee pluralism*, as it was called, was one of the great curses of the church from the late fourteenth century to the time of the Reformation.

6.62 Reform in the Latin Lands

And yet, at this very time there were stirrings of renewal and reform. The most famous preacher in the Latin lands at this time was Vincent Ferrer, a Spanish Dominican, who lived from 1350 to 1419. Vincent traveled through Spain, France, and Italy, and he drew enormous crowds with a kind of revivalist preaching which stressed the need of repentance and the awful punishments which awaited those who failed to reform their lives. In many respects, the preaching of Vincent was more like that of John the Baptist than that of Jesus. He was very effective in terms of the goals which he set for himself, but one wonders if the somewhat feverish and overwrought concentration on the four last things (death, judgment, heaven, and hell) and the unhealthy emphasis on fear of hell as a motive for Christian living might have been responsible for the fact that reform in the Latin lands during this period remained quite superficial and short-lived.

6.63 Wyclif

In northern Europe at this time, reforming preachers based their sermons directly on scripture, and for this reason their reforms had more religious substance and were, at the same time, more radical. John Wyclif, the first of these radical reformers, was born shortly after 1320; as a young man he studied philosophy and theology at Oxford, and stayed on to enjoy a brilliant career as a lecturer. During most of his career, he was rather conservative, preferring the thought of Thomas Aquinas to the newer philosophical ideas which were spreading in the universities in his day. But then, surprisingly, in the last eight years of his life, Wyclif began to preach and write in a new vein. It was his work during this period which was to make him famous and which was to prepare much of southern England for the English Reformation that took place about a hundred and fifty years later.

Wyclif began his writing and preaching in this new style in 1376. He protested against the wealth of the church and against the incessant demands for money on the part of

Popes, bishops, priests, and monks, and he argued that when churchmen did not make good use of their lands and benefices, the secular powers should intervene and give them to others who would make proper use of them. This was welcome news in England, at the very time the Avignon Popes were draining great sums from the country through ever increasing taxes and fees, and it insured that Wyclif had friends in high places who would shield him from the bishops and abbots who were disturbed at his preaching and who wanted him disciplined and silenced. Wyclif's preaching rapidly became more radical, and he turned from the abuses of wealth and power to what he regarded as the source of those abuses. He argued that the true church was not the visible organization which was such a scandal in his day, but rather the invisible community of believers, and he affirmed that each believer was a true priest and had all the power needed to celebrate the Eucharist. Wyclif attacked the cult of the saints, the obsession with relics, the multiplication of Masses for the dead, and the granting of indulgences, because he saw the deeply unchristian character of the contractual dealing with God which all of these practices promoted.

In a few years, Wyclif's enemies at the university got the upper hand, with the result that he was forced out and retired to a parish which he had been given. There he directed the translation of the whole bible into English, and he began to train and send out wandering preachers whose task it was to instruct the simple people of the countryside. Wyclif's own preaching and writing, as well as the sermons of his preachers, won many people to the reformed version of the faith. But the bishops were upset with Wyclif for attacking the basis of their wealth and power, and they were convinced that he was a heretic, because of his views on the church, on priesthood, and on indulgences. As is often the case with religious movements which appeal to the underprivileged, Wyclif's movement became a haven for those who longed for radical change in the economic and social order, and the Lollards (as his followers were called) were blamed for the peasant uprising of 1381. As a consequence, the government began to persecute them in 1401, and repressive efforts increased after

1415; in that year the Council of Constance condemned the teaching of Wyclif and ordered that his bones be removed from consecrated ground. Despite the persecution, the Lollards continued as an underground movement and they prepared many of the lower classes in England for the Elizabethan Reformation.

The movement begun by Wyclif is interesting because it shows how many of the tendencies which we think of as distinctively Protestant were in the air long before the Protestant Reformation began. It is also interesting because it shows the close connection between financial abuses and church discipline on the one hand, and doctrinal issues, such as the nature of the church, the existence of purgatory, and the legitimacy of indulgences, on the other. Catholic judgments on the reformers and their work have not always taken this into account because Catholics have often failed to see that some of these practices had very little support in the New Testament.

6.64 John Hus at the Council of Constance

Wyclif's writings influenced the other great reform preacher of the period—John Hus. Hus was born in the same decade as that in which Wyclif began his radical preaching and writing—between 1370 and 1380. He studied theology at the University of Prague, and when he was about thirty he was ordained to the priesthood. He was then given a parish in Prague and he quickly became one of the most famous preachers of his day. Even at this early date, his preaching showed some signs of that hostility to the papacy which Avignon had generated in northern Europe. Hus argued that Peter, although the prince of the Apostles, was not the rock on which the church was founded, and he affirmed that Popes were just as prone to error in dogmatic questions as was anyone else.

A political marriage had joined the royal families of England and Bohemia in 1382, and as a result of increased contact between the two countries, the writings of Wyclif became known in the Czech-speaking lands, and Hus read them during his student days in Prague. However, Hus was more conservative than Wyclif and avoided the latter's radical positions on the nature of the church and on the universal priesthood of the laity; but his criticism of the luxury in which the higher clergy lived earned him the enmity of the archbishop of Prague, who excommunicated him. Hus hoped that the Pope who had been elected by the Council of Pisa, John XXIII, would release him from this excommunication; but at this point he acted rather imprudently by condemning both the new Crusade which the Pope had proclaimed against the kingdom of Naples and the selling of indulgences to finance that enterprise. This move was too radical for the theological faculty of the University of Prague, and Hus lost their support at the precise moment at which he was put under formal excommunication by John XXIII.

Hus enjoyed great popular support in Bohemia, and the whole land was in an uproar. As a result of this, and in the hope of bringing peace to his eastern domains, Siegmund, who was effectively Emperor, though not yet invested with the insignia of office, urged Hus to present his case to the Council of Constance, which was then in session. Siegmund guaranteed his safety, and Hus arrived in Constance on November 3, 1414. The cardinals granted Hus a first hearing on November 28, and they were so disturbed by what they heard that they ordered him imprisoned as soon as the hearing was over (over the vigorous protests of Siegmund, who saw that the cardinals were making a mockery of his guarantee of safety).

The proceedings against Hus dragged on into the spring of 1415, and they were given a new turn when John XXIII left Constance and tried to destroy the work of the Council from his base in Schaffhausen. At this juncture the Council suddenly showed great interest in the Hus case, probably because some of the cardinals felt that if they could settle the dispute, this would show that it was the Council and not the Pope which had supreme authority in matters of faith. Under the leadership of the French cardinal, Pierre d'Ailly, and John Gerson, the Chancellor of the University of Paris, the Council condemned as heretical thirty statements which had been culled from Hus' writings. They called on Hus to retract and repent, but he refused.

Hus, of course, admitted that the writings were his, but he argued that if they were correctly understood they were not heretical. The cardinals then asked Hus if he would be willing to condemn at least that meaning which the statements had if they were *not* correctly understood, and he again refused. Finally, on the sixth of July, after repeated attempts to get him to recant, the Council declared that Hus was a heretic and condemned him to death. On that same day he was handed over to the civil authorities and burned at the stake. For the Council of Constance, the affair was obviously a minor matter, of little importance in comparison with the great crisis in church life which it was trying to resolve. This incredibly stupid judgment was just one more example of the total alienation of the high authorities of the church in that day from the New Testament message, as well as from the religious and political realities of Europe in their time.

6.7 FROM 1415 TO 1503

The Council of Basel had been called by Pope Eugene IV in 1431, but when that Council attempted to arrogate to itself supreme legislative and judicial power in the church, the Pope reacted by transferring it first to Ferrara, in 1438, and then to Florence, where it met from 1439 to 1442. It was here that a rather sad little episode, often referred to as the "reunion" of the Christian churches of the East and the West took place.

6.71 The Union of Ferrara-Florence

The eastern Empire had seen its dominions shrink ever since the Moslem conquest of the Holy Land and Egypt, at the end of the seventh century. In the following centuries, as new and warlike Turco-Tartar tribes moved west, they were converted to Islam, and they exerted increasing pressure on the holdings of Byzantium in Asia Minor. By 1300 they were in possession of almost all of the land which we now call, after them, Turkey, and in the years between 1350 and 1500 they conquered much of the Balkan Peninsula, bypassing Constantinople on the way.

The Emperor of the East, John VIII Palaeologos was desperate, and in his desperation he turned to the Pope for help. He was obviously not too well informed about conditions in the West, and he mistakenly thought that the Pope was still in a position to call a final crusade to save the eastern capital of Christianity, and perhaps to win back the territories of the Eastern Empire. But John did know that there was no hope of getting any help at all from Rome unless the religious questions in dispute between East and West were settled to the satisfaction of Rome.

With this in mind, John himself, together with a delegation of seven hundred churchmen, including the Patriarch of Constantinople and a number of other archbishops of the eastern church, appeared in Ferrara in March, 1439. The prelates of the eastern and western churches negotiated from March until July and they managed to reach at least verbal agreement on some of the old dogmatic differences and even on the more neuralgic point of the primacy of the Pope. All of the participants, with the exception of one eastern bishop, signed the Decree of Union on July 6, 1439.

But the union was not destined to last. The laity of the eastern church had never forgotten the sack of Constantinople by the Crusaders in 1204, and even the threat of the Turks at the gates of the city could not bring them to forgive those whom they regarded as heretics and barbarians. When the Greek bishops returned home after the Council, many of them were made to feel the wrath of their people, and some of them had to flee for their lives. The Patriarchs of Antioch, Alexandria, and Jerusalem rejected the Decree of Union, and in this they spoke for the overwhelming majority of the faithful of the East. In addition to all of these difficulties, the military support which the Pope had promised never really materialized; the small detachment of western troops which did arrive was a case of too little and too late, and they died in the futile defense of the capital. The city fell on May 29, 1453. In the year 1472 a meeting of Greek bishops in Constantinople (now the Turkish capital) formally abrogated the Decree of Union and excommunicated those who had signed it. A few of the eastern churches held to the union, and they formed the nucleus of those churches which are called *Uniate* in the present day—communities of eastern rite Christians who hold to their ancient ceremonies and customs, while recognizing the primacy of the Pope.

6.72 The Renaissance Papacy

Eugene IV died in 1447, and with few exceptions the Popes who followed him showed that they had learned nothing from the Avignon papacy and the schism which followed it. The loyalty of northern European Christians to the papacy had been severely shaken, and the Renaissance Popes who reigned from the middle of the fifteenth century until after the middle of the sixteenth lived in a style which was calculated to increase the estrangement of the north. The Popes of this period acted as though the Papal States were their personal property to be used to enrich their families (which included, in the case of many of these Popes, not only cousins and nephews, but also sons and daughters). That the papacy should be a supra-national institution, and that the Pope, as spiritual leader of Christendom, should be above party strife, never occurred to these men. They continued the fiscal policies of Avignon, and their revenues came more and more from northern Europe, where resentment was growing all the time. It is true that they spent much of their money in subsidizing the great works of Renaissance art and architecture for which Rome is famous to the present day, but they did this in the same spirit as the other Renaissance princes in Italy. They loved to be known as patrons of the arts, and they basked in the reflected glory of Michelangelo and Bernini.

With the accession of Innocent VIII (1484 to 1492), the papacy reached a new (though only temporary) low. He had probably bribed his way into papal office; and it goes without saying that Innocent and those like him had no intention of initiating reform in the church. It would have been more than comic if they had tried. Innocent VIII actually presided at the marriage of one of his illegitimate sons to the daughter of the Florentine prince, Lorenzo de' Medici. As a result of his involvement with these unscrupulous in-laws, he made one of Lorenzo's sons a cardinal at a tender age. The young cardinal made a very successful career for himself in the church, and went on to become Pope Leo X, who was reigning in great splendor at the time the Reformation began. Leo's motto could really stand for all of the Renaissance Popes: "Let us enjoy the papacy which God has given us!"

Innocent's successor, Alexander VI, who reigned from 1492 to 1503, was a legend in his own time. Having bought the papal office by bribing the cardinals, he dedicated himself to providing a secure future for the four illegitimate children who resulted from his union with a married woman of one of the noble families of Rome. The reign of Alexander is often referred to as the *pornocracy* of the papacy, and Alexander himself was so unworthy of his office that a number of people in his day actually wondered if he was even a Christian. His conduct in the Savonarola affair makes that a legitimate question.

6.73 Savonarola

Savonarola lived from 1452 to 1498. He was a Dominican who was deeply dedicated to the reform of his own order and to the moral reform of the city of Florence—the city where he lived as superior of a Dominican community after 1490. He was a powerful preacher, and in the years 1494 and 1495 he apparently persuaded almost the entire population of the city of Florence to turn away from what he regarded as their carefree and morally lax way of life, and to do penance, give alms to the poor, and live as much of a monastic life as could be managed outside the walls of a monastery. During these two years, he was the undisputed spiritual leader, and to some extent even the civil ruler, of the city state.

However, during his tenure in power, he got the strange idea that if Florence could be put under the protection of the

French monarchy, his reforms could be made permanent. This plan brought him into conflict with Pope Alexander VI, now also related by marriage to the Medici, who had been driven from Florence in 1494. Alexander solved the problem in a way typical for him: he excommunicated Savonarola in 1497. The Dominican responded by asserting that since Alexander had come to power through *simony*, the buying and selling of sacred offices, he could not be considered the legitimate Pope and had no power to impose excommunication on anyone. In fact, Savonarola suggested that a general council of bishops should meet to certify that Alexander was not the legitimate Pope and to elect a new one.

At this juncture, Alexander VI threatened the city of Florence with an *interdict*—the prohibition of all religious services, including the celebration of Mass, the administration of the other sacraments, and the ceremonies of Christian burial—unless immediate steps were taken to silence Savonarola. Suddenly support shifted away from the monk and he was put on trial for heresy. The proceedings were disgraced by the usual practices of torture, the calling of false witnesses, and the use of forged documents. Savonarola was condemned at the express order of Alexander VI, and he was burned at the stake on May 23, 1498.

Savonarola mixed religion and politics in a strange way, as did many in his day, but he was a good and holy man, and his execution was the blackest mark of all on the disgraceful reign of Alexander VI. Like Joan of Arc in the second and third decades of the same century, he was condemned because he felt immediately responsible to God, and he chose God's will over that of the corrupt church authorities of his day.

6.74 Reform of the Church in Spain

The reconquest of the Iberian Peninsula from the Moslems was virtually complete by the last quarter of the fifteenth century, but the clergy were poorly educated, and life in many of the religious orders had grown lax. Reform in Spain was the work of a brilliant organizer, named Ximenes de Cisneros. He had been trained in Rome and returned to Spain with an appointment to clerical office in Toledo. There, the archbishop would not recognize the appointment, but instead clapped Cisneros in prison for six years. When he was finally let out, Cisneros joined the strict branch of the Franciscan order, and lived for a few years as a hermit, until his election as provincial of his order in 1494.

As provincial, Cisneros began the reform of his own order, and despite opposition from within, the reform was a success. Queen Isabella, whose confessor he had been since 1492, had him appointed archbishop of Toledo, and in this position he managed the reform of the church in Spain. He knew that reform would last only if the educational level of the clergy could be raised, and to this end he founded the University of Alcala and made it a center of theology. Cisneros did not hesitate to make use of the Inquisition in his work of reforming the church, and this has, not without reason, cast a shadow on his name.

At the time of the reconquest, there were a great number of Moslems and Jews in Spain, but as Spanish control spread southward, there were some mass conversions, probably motivated mostly by fear of the persecution of non-Christians which followed on every Christian victory. In 1492, Ferdinand and Isabella, who through their marriage had joined Aragon and Castile, decided to solve the problem of the large Jewish community which remained, by ordering the Jews either to be baptized or to leave Spain. At the instigation of Cisneros, whose repressive policies had goaded the Moslems of Granada into an uprising, the latter were given the same choice in 1496, and in 1502 the Moslems who still remained in Castile were confronted with the same alternative.

Obviously a number of Jews and Moslems chose conversion over exile, and without doubt the faith of many of these new "converts" was superficial, or merely a facade. To solve this problem, a prominent Dominican superior named Torquemada pressed for the introduction of the Inquisition into Spain, and in 1480 the Pope agreed to the request, which had been submitted by the king and queen. The Spanish Inquisition brought torture and death to a number of former Moslems and Jews, and has become a symbol of the intolerance and fanaticism of which men are capable when pride and arrogance mask themselves as zeal for the faith. The Spanish church long suffered under the legacy of the rigidity and intransigence which it inherited from this period.

6.75 Intellectual Life

In the south, Macchiavelli (1469 to 1527) continued the essentially pagan traditions of the early Italian Renaissance. He was the theoretician of the new secular states which felt no need even to pay lip service to traditional Christian moral values. But even before Macchiavelli's time, there had been a shift toward a humanism of a more Christian type. In Florence the works of the early Christian mystic, Pseudo-Dionysius the Areopagite, were being read in the newly founded Platonic Academy. Pico della Mirandola, a member of this Academy, was typical of the humanism of this later Italian Renaissance. He studied eastern languages and Jewish mystical writings, and he tried to construct an apologetic, a defense of Christianity, from various strands of eastern thought. In the next two generations, this Christian humanism of the south expressed itself particularly in the great achievements of religious art which the Renaissance Popes used to beautify the city of Rome. Pope Julius II arranged for Michelangelo to design his mausoleum, and had Bramante design the new church of St. Peter's in 1506. Michelangelo did the ceiling of the Sistine Chapel at about the same time and Raphael painted the frescos in the Vatican apartments. They are brilliant works of religious art and they can be appreciated as such, even though the motives of the Popes who subsidized them were more than questionable, and even though they were funded through means which were very damaging to the church.

In northern Europe during this same period, the movement called *humanism* was in full swing. The leaders of this movement in Germany, England, and Holland were all convinced Christians, even though they were often quite skeptical of many practices in the institutional church and were blunt in their comments about abuses in the monastic orders. All of them kept a certain distance from the official church in their day, but they did this precisely in the name of Christian values. Nicholas of Cusa (1401 to 1464) had a fine classical education which was typical for the humanists, but in many ways he was more of a mystic. Deeply religious, he was an exponent of the so-called *negative* theology, which is based on the insight that God is separated from the world by an infinite chasm, and therefore we know far more about what God is *not* than about what he is.

Reuchlin (1455–1522) was the most famous humanist of his day. He had a good knowledge of both Greek and Hebrew, and he was one of the first to point out some of the errors of the Vulgate, Jerome's translation of the Bible. Erasmus, the "prince of humanists," lived from 1466 to 1536, and was very typical of Dutch and German humanism of the time. He had been ordained to the priesthood, but seems to have celebrated Mass only rarely, and the sacraments appear to have played no role in his personal piety. He was skeptical of the value of monastic vows and very critical of abuses in the church in his day. As is not uncommon in the case of those with calm temperament and scholarly interests, he seems to have viewed Christianity mostly as an ethical system. When the Reformation began, he did all in his power to mediate between the Catholics and the Reformers, but he could never understand or share Luther's deep religious passion. Thomas More, the English humanist, was a younger contemporary and friend of Erasmus, and, although a layman, he resembled him in many respects. We will meet him again at the time of the English Reformation.

6.8 RETROSPECT AND PROSPECT

In the fourteenth, and even more in the fifteenth century, the call for reform of the church in head and members had been raised again and again. But the one institution from which reform could have issued in the Catholic church of that period—the papacy—lacked the vision, the will, and the spiritual depth to effect that reform. In their own way the Latin lands of the south were as eager for reform as the Germanic lands of the north, but over the years the papacy had grown skillful in deflecting all efforts at reform, and the few Popes who were really interested in it were so preoccupied with other problems that they had no time for what was the really pressing problem of the day. Awe of the papacy remained so strong in the Latin lands that a program of church reform which might have been initiated by a council, acting on its own authority and not that of the Pope, did not stand a chance, and the conciliar movement failed. As a result, when reform came, it did not take place within the Catholic church, but outside it, and it would split the Christians of northern Europe from those of the south and divide Christians up to the present day.

7

The Reformation

7.1 INTRODUCTION

In the short space of less than four decades, from 1518 to 1555, a thousand years of Christian unity in Western Europe came to an end. The events in which this came to pass are grouped under the general term *Reformation*—a word which shares (unintentionally) in the ambiguity of the verb "reform": on the one hand it can mean "to eliminate abuses and to restore to a state of primitive simplicity and purity," and on the other hand it can mean "to regroup or to give a new shape or form." The sixteenth century reformers intended to eliminate abuses in the one church, but the movement they started gave European Christianity an entirely new shape and form which has left its impress to the present day on western Europe and on all of the lands which are culturally dependent on it. They wanted reform of the one church, but their work led inexorably to the hostile confrontation of many churches.

In one sense the Reformation had many causes, all of them so compelling that they make the split between the churches seem inevitable. Some of these causes were purely political and some were a mixture of the political and the religious. We have discussed most of them in the two preceding chapters: the development of the imperial papacy from Gregory VII to Innocent III; the victory of the papacy over the medieval Empire; the breakdown of medieval unity at the end of the thirteenth century; the French domination of the Popes of Avignon, and the obsession with money at that same

224

papal court; the Great Western Schism; the Conciliar Movement; the scandal of the Renaissance papacy.

7.2 LUTHER AND THE LUTHERAN REFORMATION

And yet, none of these "causes" made the Reformation inevitable. Like all of the great events of history, the Reformation resulted from the usually unconscious dialogue of an individual human being with the great historical forces which had been in motion for perhaps centuries before his birth. Like the other great men of history, Luther was an individual who felt the same hopes and fears as hundreds of thousands of men and women of his day, but he felt them far more deeply and he had an instinctive sense of how to give them voice.

The Reformation began and succeeded because a Catholic monk in Germany was able to articulate the religious longings of men and women of his day. As the Catholic priest and writer, Clemens Hofbauer, put it in the early years of the last century, "The Reformation came to pass because the Germans felt the need for authentic piety." It was Luther's profound need for such a piety, and it was the religious experience in which he found that very thing that he sought, which gave the Reformation its impetus and its characteristic stamp.

The church is always a church of saints and a church of sinners. It is always the ideal church, which Augustine called "the church of the future," and the existing church, which he called "the church of the present." It is always the community of those who hearken, listen attentively to the word of God, and welcome the offer and the demand which it embodies; and it is always the community of those who reject the word of God, refuse its offer and evade its demands. But there is no doubt that in the hierarchical church of Luther's day it was usually the second of each of these dichotomies which was particularly visible. In his day, that which most people called "church" was visibly and obviously corrupt and treason to the Gospel was manifest on every level. But although the cry for reform of the church in head and members had been on the lips of the faithful for centuries, the papal bureaucracy had developed effective techniques for resisting reform. Even those few Popes who were serious about it were unable to overcome the entrenched and intransigent inertia of the curial apparatus.

But in Luther, the entrenched resistance to reform which the hierarchy, the management sector of this church, had developed over the centuries finally met its match. A worldly church, with only a decadent scholasticism at its disposal to articulate its faith, met a man for whom the search for God was the one absolutely serious concern of his life. Religious superficiality met religious substance, and whatever other factors prepared for the Reformation or helped it succeed (and there were many), the Reformation remains essentially a religious and therefore a theological event.

Theology is serious thought about and reflection on who God is and on what the word *God* means, and, for Luther, theology was of prime importance in his life. But what Luther *thought* about God, grace, faith, forgiveness, and the justice of God never remained in the realm of theory; it reached into the core of his personality and from there it touched every facet of his being. His approach was what we would call today *existential*: he realized the uniqueness of every situation, the absolute character of every decision. He could never simply theorize about sin and forgiveness because his sense of alienation from God and of his radical powerlessness to heal that estrangement was so deep.

It was Luther's reading of the New Testament which convinced him that the church in his day was not true to the intentions of its founder and had lost all sense of its true mission, and it was for this reason that he called into question so many aspects of church life in his day. Some of these matters were purely disciplinary (by no means unimportant, but not matters of faith)—the demand for communion under both forms (bread and wine), and for a married clergy; rejection of church laws of fasting and abstinence, and of compulsory confession. Other criticisms touched more directly on at least the *terminology* which was thought to be essential to Catholic faith. For example, Luther objected to explaining the presence of Jesus in the Eucharist by means of the term *transubstantiation*. He was even more strongly opposed to the teaching that the sacraments work *ex opere operato*, that is, that they are effective in themselves, as long as they are received in faith and as long as the recipient puts no obstacle in their way. Furthermore, he did not accept the scriptural justification for papal primacy, and he found no basis in scripture for the Catholic teaching on indulgences, purgatory, and the propriety of private Masses.

On the one question which is arguably the central question of all theology and religious life, Luther's reading of the New Testament led him to take a position diametrically opposed to that of the church of his day. It was his position on this problem of the *justification of the sinner* (a very unfortunate translation) which gave the Lutheran Reformation its Christian substance and its religious dynamism. For Luther, the attainment of the right relationship with God is something which can only come about through *faith*, by which he means *our acceptance of this "right relationship" from God as a pure unmerited gift, which we have done nothing to deserve.*

Luther never touched on the major or minor questions of theology in a scatter-shot way, and his views on justification and faith led him to see Christian existence as determined by the three great alternatives. First, *either* one allowed the content of the word "Christian" to be determined by *both scripture and tradition* (with the latter word understood as "the practice of the church") *or* one took *scripture alone*, the word of God, as the sole norm which judges both the church and the individual Christian. Luther obviously chose scripture alone, and his motto was *sola scriptura*. Second, *either* God's grace is given to us in such a way that we can increase it by virtuous activity, so that God's grace and our good works are concurrent causes of his acceptance of us, *or* God's grace, his loving forgiveness and acceptance of sinners, is the only cause of salvation, which remains a pure gift which we can do nothing to merit. Luther chose grace alone, and his motto was *sola gratia*. Third, *either* faith and good works are both causes of salvation, *or* human beings are saved by faith alone (that is, by their acceptance of

the fact that God is *for* them unconditionally, without bound
or limit). Luther chose the second alternative, and his motto
was *sola fide*.

7.21 Luther's Early Life

Luther did not seem destined by fate for the role he was
to play. He was born in Eisleben (now in East Germany) on
November 10, 1483, the eldest child of what was to be a large
family. His father farmed his own land and through hard
work he had become moderately prosperous. But he wanted
something more for his son Martin, and the boy was sent to
schools in Mansfeld, Magdeburg, and Eisenach. Finally he entered the newly founded university at Erfurt and began to
prepare for a career in law.

In 1505, probably while on his way back to the university,
Luther was caught by a sudden storm, and a bolt of lightning
struck very near him. In his terror he uttered the promise that
if his life were spared, he would take the three vows of religious life and become a monk. His father was broken-hearted
over his decision, but in that same year Martin entered the
Augustinian Monastery in Erfurt. As a novice he devoted
himself with all seriousness to the search for perfection in religious life. He was ordained to the priesthood in 1507 (less
than two years after his entry into religious life!), and he began the study of theology in Erfurt in that same year.

The best medieval theology had emphasized that God
himself was knowable and that the order and symmetry of
creation was the worldly expression of the eternal truth of
God. God made sense; and reason, building on faith, could
discover much about God and his mystery. But by Luther's
time the philosophers had become pessimistic about the
power of reason to know God and had begun to doubt that
God was intelligible or that his plans and designs could be
understood. The theology of the English Franciscan, William
of Ockham, was in favor, and this theology emphasized the
unfathomable and arbitrary will of God.

This theology unfortunately conspired with Luther's
own fear of the judgment of God and with his anxiety about

whether or not he belonged to the predestined (to those cho-sen by God before creation to enjoy eternal life in heaven). Under the guidance of his sympathetic spiritual director, Staupitz, he tried to cope with his anxieties by devoting him-self with ever greater fervor to the various spiritual exercises of monastic life, especially to frequent confession; but noth-ing seemed able to bring him inner peace.

Luther continued his studies in Erfurt, and in 1512 he re-ceived his doctorate in theology. (He had made a short visit to Rome in 1510, in connection with business of his order, and was deeply scandalized by this contact with the Renaissance papacy.) In 1513 he was given the chair of biblical theology at the University of Wittenberg, where he began by lecturing on the Psalms, and then, between 1515 and 1517, turned to two major letters of Paul: Galatians and Romans. During this time, his anxiety about salvation and his fear of the all-con-suming justice of God continued, as he groped for the answer to his agonizing question: "How can I find a merciful God?"

7.22 Luther Becomes a Reformer

At some time in this period—possibly early in 1517—he found the answer as he was reading the text of Romans 1:17. In a sudden flash he realized that the *righteousness* or *justice* of God (neither translation is very good) which is alluded to there is not the vindictive justice in virtue of which God will pass harsh judgment on the sinner, but rather the "accepta-bility" which the sinner has, because of what God has done for him in Christ. Luther saw that the only task of the sinner is to accept, in faith, this great gift of God, and to trust in God's ac-ceptance of him, even though in himself he still remains a sin-ner. This insight brought him the peace which he sought and he was consumed by the desire to share his peace with others. His lectures during the summer semester of 1517 already show signs of his development.

Luther's understanding of faith had already moved some distance from what was being commonly taught at the time. (In conformity with the scholastic tradition, faith was gener-ally defined as an *intellectual* act, and consisted in affirming

those truths which had been revealed by God and entrusted
to the church.) However, Luther at this period was not teaching anything which could not be found in the works of a number of medieval theologians who had always been regarded as
orthodox. What was distinctive, although not easy to define,
was the *individualism* of Luther's approach. He had sought
peace in the traditional practices of monastic life (prayer,
mortification, examination of conscience) and in the reception of the sacraments which the church put at his disposal
(especially penance, the sacrament of reconciliation), and he
had not found it there. He found peace in his individual encounter with God, on the occasion of his personal appropriation of the scriptural word of God. This was bound to
relativize the role of the visible, institutional church in Luther's theology. Luther was well on the way to an understanding of *church* which was very different from that which was
current in his day. The fact that current views were hazy and
confused did not help matters and blinded both Luther and
his opponents to the essential originality of the Lutheran Reformation.

Luther was aware of the fact that human existence is not
simply a fact but is rather a predicament, and he sensed that
it was only in the *word of God* that he could find a way out of
that predicament. In scripture, Luther found the word of
God, addressed to him, in his situation, now, and all of the
theological positions which he took and all of the criticism
which he directed toward the institutional church of his day
were the immediate consequence of his reading of scripture.
It was there that he found grounds for condemning many of
the abuses of his day—the obsession with money, the selling
of indulgences, dispensations, and church offices, and the
whole fiscal organization of the Roman Curia. It was in his
reading of Paul that he found grounds for criticizing the *le-
galism* of the church, the emphasis on merit, and the bartering
with God, which was encouraged by so much of the popular
preaching of his day. It was in reading the Gospels that he
found grounds for condemning the frightful worldliness of
the church in his day: the spectacle of the papacy engaging in

war to safeguard its temporal power and making use of excommunication as a purely political tool.

Luther had always been critical of abuses in the church, and his trip to Rome in 1510 had increased his annoyance at the fiscal policy of the papacy, which was drawing more and more money from the industrious Germans to pay for the ostentation and moral laxity of Renaissance Rome. After his insight into the meaning of the "justice" of God, he began to suspect that many of the pious practices which made up the religious life of most Christians were no help, but rather an obstacle in the way of their coming to see that salvation comes through faith alone. At precisely this moment, Luther encountered one of the worst examples of the venality and corruption of Rome and of the decadence and degeneracy of theology and popular religion. The story reads like a bad soap opera, but it is unfortunately true.

In 1517 a young nobleman, Albrecht of Brandenburg, decided that he would like to be archbishop of Mainz—a position which would make him the most important prelate in the German church. According to church law at the time, he was too young to receive this honor, and therefore, in addition to the huge sum he was required to pay the papacy for the office itself, more money was needed to buy the dispensation. Albrecht took out a large loan with the banking house of Fugger, a leading financial institution in Augsburg, and began to look around for ways to repay the debt. Rome was gracious and understanding in his hour of need, and agreed to arrange for the preaching of an indulgence throughout Germany during the summer of 1517. For the gaining of the indulgence, various good works were prescribed, but a financial contribution was quite essential. The official line was that the money was going to finance the building of the new church of St. Peter's in Rome, but actually the papal court had agreed to split the money with Albrecht, to enable him to pay back the loan he had taken from the bank in Augsburg.

A Dominican monk, Johann Tetzel, was appointed to preach the indulgence in Wittenberg and other parts of Saxony, and a worse choice could hardly have been made. Tetzel's preaching was a parody of the faith, but unfortunately it corresponded to a view of indulgences which, if not that of academic theology, was very widespread among both laity and clergy at the time. In his sermons he actually stated that the indulgence (which could be gained in order to free from purgatory the soul of one who was suffering there) was gained immediately on deposit of the money in the collection box and that at that very moment the soul sprang out of the purgatorial fires.

This was too much for Luther, and on October 31, 1517, he sent his ninety-five "theses" (theological statements) on indulgences to the various bishops who had authority in the areas where the indulgence was being preached. Luther did not understand his action as one of revolt or rebellion; he wanted a serious theological discussion, which he hoped would remove the scandal. (It used to be affirmed that Luther nailed the theses to the door of the church in Wittenberg. He probably did not, but even if he had, it would not have been particularly significant: the church door served as something like an official bulletin board for such theological statements.) Without Luther's knowledge, the theses were translated into German, printed, and reached great numbers of people in Germany. They gripped the popular imagination, and, not entirely without reason, the date of their publication is regarded as day one of the Reformation era—though nothing was farther from Luther's mind at the moment.

Albrecht, whose plans for repaying his debt had just been torpedoed by Luther's theses, was not pleased, and he complained to Rome; in June of the following year (1518) the official process was opened in Rome to determine whether Luther was a heretic. He was summoned to Rome, but the prince who ruled Saxony, Friedrich the Wise, arranged for the hearing to take place in Augsburg, on the occasion of the Imperial Assembly (Reichstag) in October 1518. The most brilliant theologian of the day, Thomas de Vio (known to history as Cardinal Cajetan), conducted the hearing and demanded that Luther recant. Luther refused, and (probably recalling what had happened to Hus at Constance little more than a century earlier) left Augsburg in secret. On October 28 he appealed from the Pope to a general, or ecumenical council—a move which was calculated to make Rome exceedingly nervous because it raised the specter of conciliarism.

Neither Luther nor his opponents realized that Christendom was in the process of being divided. Luther wanted the issues to be brought out into the open, and to this end he agreed to a public debate in Leipzig, which took place in June and July of 1519. His opponent was Johannes Eck, professor of theology at the University of Ingolstadt. Under Eck's probing questioning, Luther probably came to realize more clearly the implications of his own theology. He admitted that he did not recognize the authority of the Pope and could not agree that the decisions of even church councils were divinely protected from error. Scripture was the only ultimate authority he could accept. Eck was sincere and a clever debater, but it is impossible to read the transcript of the debates without concluding that it was Luther who had real religious substance on his side (even though some of his views were dangerously one-sided) and that Eck was defending some practices and views of the late medieval church which were doubtfully Christian. In any case, the Leipzig Disputation gave Luther a valuable platform, and his views spread throughout Germany, helped by the new technology of the printing press.

The year 1520 was an important one for the spread of the Reformation. In May, Luther wrote his *Sermon on Good Works*, in which he pointed out that good works, while very important, are not the cause of salvation, but the *result* of God's acceptance of us, which becomes real in faith. In June, Luther wrote *On the Papacy in Rome* in which he questioned the divine origin of the papacy, and its claim to universal jurisdiction. In August he completed a major work, *To the Christian Nobility of the German Nation*, in which some of the teachings which were characteristic of the whole Lutheran Reformation were formulated for the first time. He affirmed the universal priesthood of all believers, and argued that each community should elect its own priest (whom he saw, not as an individual endowed by ordination with special powers not possessed by ordinary Christians, but rather as a servant [minister!], called and commissioned by the congregation to preach and celebrate the Lord's Supper). In this document, Luther reiterated his belief that Popes can make errors on matters of doctrine and that it is the council and not the Pope which has the highest legislative power in the church.

In October of the same year, Luther completed his work *On the Babylonian Captivity of the Church*, in which he developed his new theology of the Mass and denied that it was a sacrifice. He went on to point out that both baptism and Lord's Supper were sacraments, but he found no basis in scripture for the other five which were recognized in the church at the time and by Catholics up to now. Finally, in November he wrote an important work *On the Freedom of the Christian* in which he stated his views on the relation of faith and good works: works do not make a human being good, but a good person does good works. In other words, good works are not things which we do to achieve salvation; they are rather the manifestation and expression of a salvation which has already been received as a pure gift in faith.

Luther wrote in a clear, earthy, powerful German, and his books had nothing of the musty smell of academic theology about them. By the end of the year they were being read all over Germany and people began to realize that a movement was underway which would finally rectify the abuses that the Germans had been complaining about since the beginning of the Avignon papacy. Luther was very much the popular hero, and in a gesture symbolic of this, on the tenth of December, 1520, he publicly burned the papal document which threatened him with excommunication if he did not retract. On January 3, 1521 he was formally excommunicated in Rome.

7.23 The Reformation in Germany up to 1530

We now return to fall of the preceding year. On October 23, 1520, Charles V was crowned Emperor in Aachen, and everybody wondered how he would handle the increasingly unstable religious situation in Germany. In the election, Charles had triumphed over Francis I, the French king, who had been strongly favored by Pope Leo X, and people felt that

Charles might now take his vengeance by supporting Luther over the Pope. But he did not. He had a strong Spanish loyalty to the traditional faith, and he was always able to distinguish the papal *office*, which he believed to be divinely instituted, from the *individual Pope*, who might be inept, deceitful, or perverse. Charles felt so strongly about what Luther was doing that he intended to deprive him of the protection of law and to oblige all of the citizens of the Empire to hand Luther over to the civil authorities for the punishment which would be consequent on his excommunication.

However, Charles was not an absolute ruler and he could not risk alienating those princes of the Empire who were supporting Luther. For this reason he agreed to give Luther the chance to explain his position at the Imperial Assembly (Reichstag) in Worms, in April 1521, and he personally guaranteed safe passage for the monk. By this time, Luther's writings had won him a large and sympathetic audience, and his journey to Worms turned into something like a triumphal procession.

On April 16 Luther was confronted with his writings and ordered, in the name of the Emperor, to recant. He asked for time to think, and then on the following day he delivered an impressive talk in which he defended all of his positions and refused to retract unless and until it could be shown that the clear word of scripture was against him. He ended his speech with the words: "Hier stehe ich, ich kann nicht anders!" ("Here I stand; I can take no other course!")

On the following day Charles V spoke and his words left no doubt about where he stood. His final words were: "From this day on I will regard him (Luther) as a notorious heretic." True to his word, he allowed Luther to leave the Imperial Assembly, but he wanted him to be formally declared a public enemy (with all the consequences that implied: ultimately death by fire). On May 8 of the same year (1521) the Assembly acquiesced in the Emperor's wishes. But by this time most of the participants in the Assembly had left for home and the *Edict of Worms* which deprived Luther of the protection of law was of doubtful validity for that reason. Charles V might have been able to take decisive action later that year, but at precisely this moment political events forced him to leave Germany for nine years.

Luther's own prince, Friedrich of Saxony, feared for the monk's safety, and while Luther was on his way home to Wittenberg after the Imperial Assembly, Friedrich engineered a "friendly kidnaping" and Luther was brought to an abandoned castle (the Wartburg), disguised as a knight. He remained there for nine months, during which, in addition to other writing, he translated the entire New Testament into German. His translation was an outstanding literary and religious achievement and an event of epoch-making importance. He virtually created the modern German language: his influence on it was much like that of Shakespeare and the King James Bible together on modern English.

While Luther was in hiding in the Wartburg, events back in Wittenberg had taken a radical turn. His friend and colleague at the university, the priest Andreas Karlstadt, began to celebrate the Mass in German, and called for the removal of the statues and relics in the Wittenberg church as a means of putting an end to superstition. Soon thereafter he married, and this was a signal for many other priests to marry and for increasing numbers of monks and nuns to leave their monasteries. In January 1522 the General Chapter of the Augustinians, Luther's order, authorized any members who wished to leave the order to do so.

Luther approved in principle of a number of these moves—particularly the marriage of the priests and the termination of monastic vows—but he had no use for disorder and he feared the harm that imprudent radicals might do to the Reformation movement. In March 1522 cooler heads invited him back to Wittenberg and under his firm hand some degree of order was restored.

The Reformation showed from the very beginning a noteworthy power to unleash the spirit of change and revolt in almost all domains of life, and the next great milestone of the movement was an outstanding example of this. In 1524 the peasants in southern and southwestern Germany began to clamor for relief from the taxes imposed by their civil and ecclesiastical lords and for full ownership of the lands which they worked. Their leaders appealed to Luther for help, and he seems to have been favorable to their cause, although (in April 1525) he advised them to be cautious and to exercise restraint. But as the year drew on, some peasant mobs were responsible for violence, and Luther turned on them with a vengeance, advising the princes to suppress the revolt with the utmost violence, secure in the knowledge that when they slaughtered the rebellious peasants they were doing the work of God.

The princes, of course, hardly needed this encouragement and the uprising was brutally suppressed. Up to this time the Reformation had been a popular movement, but from now on things changed. Numbers of the peasants drifted back to the old faith, and the princes took a new interest in Luther's approach to the maintenance of civil order. In many ways the reformed faith was beginning to look more and more attractive to these princes. It gave them the opportunity to affirm their independence of the Emperor, to control church affairs in their own domains, and to use whatever measures were needed to insure the maintenance of law and order—and to do all of this with the approval of Luther and the backing of scripture itself. With the suppression of the Peasants' Revolt, Luther's reform movement had lost much of its popularity among the lower classes, but it had also gained important new allies. Paradoxically, the Lutheran Territorial Churches (Landeskirchen) which developed and prospered with the support of the princes were a far cry from what the Wittenberg monk had intended when he asked for a discussion of indulgences in 1517. And, strangely enough, although the Reformation was Luther's work and bore the stamp of his personality, control of the movement had already passed out of his hands by 1525.

The Lutheran problem was the principal question faced by the various Imperial Assemblies (Reichstage) during these years. One was held in Speyer in 1526, while the Emperor, Charles V, was still out of the country; in a move which foreshadowed later developments, it was decided that until matters had been definitively settled by a council, the princes could continue to regulate matters as they pleased. Three years later at the Assembly in the same city, Catholic delegates attempted, in the name of the Emperor, to demand enforcement of the Edict of Worms (1521: the declaration that Luther was an outlaw and was to be handed over to civil authorities for punishment). But the Lutheran delegates submitted a formal *protest*, and became known from this time on as the "protesters": Protestants.

In the year 1530 the Emperor was back in Germany for the first time in nine years, but he was no longer quite so eager for an immediate condemnation of Luther. He needed the political support of the princes who were leaning toward Protestantism, and he suggested that the religious differences might be resolved by negotiation at the Imperial Assembly which was to meet in Augsburg that same year. Luther's younger colleague and friend, Philip Melanchthon (1497 to 1560) worked out a statement of the Lutheran position, which was approved by Luther and which brought to a minimum the number of points of dispute with the Catholics. Melanchthon's document came to be known as the Confessio Augustana—the Augsburg Confession—and it was read to the Assembly on June 25, 1530. Melanchthon reduced the conditions for reunion to five points: the granting of communion under both forms (bread and wine), the abolition of private Masses and Mass stipends, the abolition of the laws of fasting and abstinence, dispensation from religious vows for those who wished, and an end to the exemption of clerics from civil law.

After a period of discussion at the Assembly, the positions were clarified, and the points of disagreement were reduced to another five: communion under both species for the laity, permission for priests to marry, abolition of monastic vows, the question of whether church property which had been confiscated was to be returned to its owners, and finally, the sacrificial character of the Mass. Surprisingly, on September 14 Charles V requested the Catholics to yield on all of these points in order to restore union, but the Pope's delegate refused. When the advice of Thomas de Vio (the same Cardinal Cajetan who was mentioned above) was sought, he said that in principle there was nothing against granting the Protestants the right to have a married priesthood and to receive communion under both species (at least until a council could make a final decision), but that the other points were non-negotiable. (This was a reasonable distinction, because the two points on which he yielded were merely disciplinary questions, whereas the others, at least in the view of the day, touched matters of dogma and faith.)

Reunion had seemed near, but it failed. Rome was not willing to compromise certain points, and if it had been, it is possible that Luther would not have been pleased. He seems to have grown increasingly restive and critical of Melanchthon's conciliatory spirit, and to have felt that his colleague was soft-pedaling some essential points of Reformation theology. This accusation has been picked up by others, who have asked why the Augsburg Confession does not mention such problems as freedom of will, transubstantiation, justification by faith alone, papal primacy, purgatory, and indulgences. What we have to remember is that on many of these questions there was no single "Catholic" position available in Melanchthon's day, and on others the dispute was more about the propriety of using philosophical terminology in dealing with matters of faith than about matters of faith itself. In terms of the ecumenical discussion today, papal primacy remains the only serious issue in dispute, and the Catholic position on this question hardened only in 1870. Melanchthon's effort has come to look more serious and sincere with the passing of the years.

The tragedies of the period were manifold, and they did not consist solely or even principally in the worldliness and corruption of the papacy and the hierarchy. They consisted partly in the appalling inertia of all human institutions, which go their own way and follow their own laws, as though they were living beings, with a perverse will of their own; and they consisted partly in the fact that even the sincere Catholics who opposed Luther did not have his religious depth and could not share his religious passion. Furthermore, the philosophical tools which they used to defend the faith as they understood it were those of a weakened and even decadent scholasticism which looked poor indeed in comparison with Luther's powerful invocation of the scriptural word.

But there were other tragedies too: Luther's own personality, linked with some factors which marked him as a man of his age, forced him inexorably to that break with the church which he never really wanted. Despite his natural, existential relation to scripture, and particularly to the writings of Paul, Luther's exegesis is tinged throughout with fundamentalism (as was true of everyone in that day). Furthermore, there was a peculiarly violent streak in Luther's character, and he tended toward extremes. He saw every question and every individual in terms of unrelieved black or blinding white, and he seemed totally incapable of any empathy whatsoever for those who disagreed with him. Finally, the church was so politicized in his day, so intertwined with the state, that the Lutheran Reformation soon became the concern of princes and kings, who meddled in church affairs with a self-assurance which would have embarrassed Constantine. Luther was unable to criticize this development (probably because of his fundamentalistic reading of Romans 13) and the resulting confusion of political and religious goals stripped his Reformation of much of its religious substance and power.

7.24 From the Augsburg Confession to the Peace of Augsburg

With the failure of the attempt at reunion, the Emperor insisted that the Assembly bring its meetings to an end with a decree which ordered the Protestants to abandon their position and return to the church. But the Protestants absented themselves from the final session and it should have been obvious to everyone that it was too late to enforce such a decree. Two years later in a document known as the *Religious Peace of Nürnberg*, it was agreed that there would be a truce in religious matters until all questions were settled by a council.

Discussions between Protestants and Catholics continued but results were inconclusive, and as the year 1540 came and went, Charles V came more and more to think of a twofold solution: a council to settle the purely religious questions and military victory over the Protestant princes to settle the civil issues. In 1545 the long-awaited Council was finally summoned to meet at the city of Trent, in the north of Italy but on the territory of the Empire. Events finally seemed to be going the Emperor's way. He won a great victory over his lifelong opponent Francis I of France, and in 1546 Luther died. The very next year saw the deaths of both Francis I, and Henry VIII of England. Later that same year Charles defeated the allied Protestant princes in battle.

The Emperor still hoped that the Protestants would come to the meetings of the Council of Trent, so that real union and religious peace would be the result of the deliberations, but at this very moment the Pope, Paul III, decided to move the meetings of the Council from Trent to Bologna, in north Italy. The Protestants had no intention of taking part in meetings on alien turf, where they were convinced that their concerns would not receive a sympathetic hearing, and from that moment on there was no hope of Protestant participation in what came to be called the Council of Trent. In disgust, Charles decided to arrange matters in Germany on his own, at the Imperial Assembly which met late in 1547 in Augsburg.

In May 1548 a document known as the "Augsburg Interim" was issued, which granted to the Protestants both a married clergy and communion under both species. But by this time Protestant positions had hardened, and concessions which might have made all the difference in 1520 were simply no longer enough.

In the years around 1550, the political situation in Germany became increasingly unstable, and Charles faced more than one revolt. He was saddened by his failure to bring about religious reunion and deeply hurt by the stupidity of the Popes who were more concerned about their Papal States than about the unity of the church. When the Imperial Assembly met in Augsburg again in 1555, the Emperor realized that without the support of the Pope he could not possibly restore unity to the church in Germany; but he also realized that Pope Paul III was a fanatic and would stop at nothing to weaken the Empire and to personally embarrass the Emperor. For these reasons, Charles V reluctantly approved the decree with which the Assembly ended: the so-called *Religious Peace of Augsburg*, of September 25, 1555. This decree allowed the kings and princes of the various states of the Empire to choose either the Catholic faith or the Lutheran form of Protestant faith. When they did, that religion became the official one of the state, and those subjects who were not happy with it could move to another state where their faith was the officially approved one. This was the famous principle *cujus regio, ejus religio*—one's religion was determined by the region in which one lived.

By 1570 more than two-thirds of Germany had accepted the Protestant faith in one form or another. The Council of Trent had ended only five years earlier, and the Catholic reform which it heralded had only just begun. In fifty years the religious map of Germany (and of much of Europe) had been permanently changed, in a way that Luther had certainly never intended. The Catholic church had sustained losses which it has never recouped. The tragedy was that all of this had happened largely because of, at first, the timidity, then the intransigence, and finally the fanaticism of a series of Popes, who were first of all Italian princes and whose responsibility for the universal church was far down on their scale of values.

7.3 THE REFORMATION IN SWITZERLAND

7.31 Zwingli and the Beginnings of Swiss Protestantism

Huldrych Zwingli, the first Swiss reformer, was a year younger than Luther. He had been ordained to the priesthood in 1506 and served both as a military chaplain and as a parish priest. He had been trained as a humanist and was a great admirer of Erasmus, sharing the latter's concern for the New Testament and for preaching which should be scriptural in inspiration.

Zwingli was appointed preacher at the Zürich cathedral

in 1519 and he immediately became popular. He was aware of what was going on in Germany at the time, but he seems to have limited his radicalism at the time to questioning the laws of fasting and abstinence and the law of clerical celibacy. (He had already been living for some time with a wealthy widow!) Church authorities finally decided to move against him, but Zwingli had powerful friends on the city council in Zürich, and they reacted by staging two public debates in 1523. In the course of these debates, Zwingli's position became more radical and he began to reject all traditional practices for which scripture provided no clear justification. He wanted to do away with the financial abuses in church life and, in fact, he wanted to deprive the bishops of all jurisdiction. Over and above that, he was an iconoclast and wanted to get rid of all elements of church life which appealed to the senses and which could lend themselves to superstitious misuse—splendid ceremonies, statues, pictures. By 1525 Zwingli had persuaded the city council of Zürich to ban the celebration of the Mass.

Outside of Zürich, opposition to Zwingli grew, and eventually in 1531 Catholics and Protestants fought it out on the battlefield. Zwingli himself was killed in battle in 1531, but by that time the leadership of Swiss Protestantism was about to pass to John Calvin. Zwingli's version of Protestantism was quite influential in southern Germany during the late twenties, and differences with the Lutherans were felt to be serious. A religious discussion was held in Marburg in 1529 to try to resolve differences, especially in the matter of the Lord's Supper, but nothing came of it. Luther held to the real presence of Christ at the Eucharist, while for Zwingli the Eucharist was merely a memorial. Melanchthon blocked the agreement because he was afraid that it would prevent the reunion of Lutherans and Catholics.

The early stages of reform in Zürich showed the same strange and even fanatical radicalism as we have noted in Wittenberg. There were those who wanted to abolish infant baptism, on the grounds that it was irreconcilable with the doctrine of salvation by faith alone. For it they substituted an adult baptism, which, of course, was a *re*baptism for those who had already received the sacrament as infants. They were called *Anabaptists* (from the Greek form) and we will encounter them later.

7.32 Calvinism

John Calvin was born in France in 1509 and grew up in a pious Catholic family. His mother died when he was still quite young, and his father, though not harsh by the standards of the day, ran a tight ship and demanded unquestioning obedience from his children. A number of historians have suggested that the absence of his mother during his formative years and his father's demand for unquestioning obedience may have had important consequences for Calvin's theology.

When he was little more than fourteen, Calvin began a course of studies in philosophy and theology which would normally have led to the priesthood; he had an older brother who was already a priest, and his father had an important position in the administration of the diocese. However, when Calvin was twenty, he suddenly interrupted his theological studies and transferred to law school. He himself does not give any reasons for the change, but, strangely enough, right at this time both his father and his elder brother who was a priest got into serious disputes with church authorities (the father was actually excommunicated and his brother refused to say Mass).

Calvin was obviously aware of developments in Germany, but, oddly enough, up to the year 1532 he showed no sympathy for the Reformation as it was unfolding in that country. He continued his law studies that year, and then in the year 1533 he had what he referred to later as a "sudden conversion" to the characteristic Protestant doctrines of salvation by faith alone and of the absolute primacy of scripture as a source of faith and Christian life. At the time he was living in Paris and studying liberal arts at the University there. But Paris was not then (or later, as would be tragically demonstrated before the end of the century) a healthy city for those with Protestant leanings, and Calvin left the city and went to Basel in Switzerland. It was in this latter city that he wrote his famous *Institutiones Religionis Christianae* or *Foundations of Christian Religion* (usually referred to simply as the *Institutes*).

Later that same year Calvin appeared in Geneva, just in time to capitalize on one of those strange situations so common in the sixteenth century, in which political disputes dictated the solution of religious problems. The city of Geneva was trying to achieve a measure of independence from the House of Savoy, to which both its bishop and the local prince belonged, and John Calvin was able to persuade the members of the municipal council that they could achieve the desired independence if they adopted the reformed faith and thereby rejected the authority of the Catholic bishop. The municipal council undoubtedly had no idea of what it was letting itself in for.

During his first stay in Geneva, Calvin wrote a new Christian creed which embodied his version of the reformed faith, as well as a catechism for children. In April 1537 he demanded that all adult males in the city appear at city hall and bind themselves by oath to support his new creed; those who refused were stripped of their civil rights and ordered to leave the city. He then turned his attention to the task of making Geneva into his own version of the city of God, or what later Calvinists would call a "Godly" city, in which every feature of public and private life would reflect the influence of the Calvinist gospel.

Needless to say, opposition to this type of tyranny formed quickly, and in 1538 a newly elected municipal council removed Calvin from his office as preacher and showed him the gates of the city. But unfortunately for Geneva this interlude of good sense did not last long, and by the end of 1541 Calvin's followers again had the upper hand in Geneva and the reformer was invited back. In that same year he wrote for his new church a kind of constitution or order, called the *Ordonnances Ecclésiastiques*, and in September the municipal council voted to make this document public law of the city of Geneva.

According to Calvin's church order, in addition to ministers who were responsible for presiding at divine worship, for preaching, and for instructing the faithful, there were other church officers, called elders and deacons, whose task it was to keep watch over every detail of the moral life of the citizens, in public and private. As if this were not enough, in that same year the municipal council actually encouraged Calvin to write a new code of civil law. This code provided harsh punishment for what Calvin considered great sins. In addition to heresy and adultery, these also included such delicts as missing divine worship, playing cards, and dancing. Death sentences were handed down for the more serious violations of Calvinist ethics and a number of executions took place. By 1555 Calvin's control over the city was absolute, and in 1559 he founded a theological academy which was very influential in spreading the doctrines of the new reformed church throughout Europe. (In general, in continental Europe, churches of Calvinist origin are called *Reformed* churches.)

Calvin was the most intolerant of the reformers and his hatred of Catholics and their church knew no bounds. Furthermore, he argued that the members of the reformed church had not only the right but also the strict duty to resist Catholic rulers and to do all in their power to replace them with those loyal to the principles of the new faith. Calvin's radical intolerance and his absolute rejection of any distinction between the competences of church and state were responsible for much of the bitterness of the religious wars in France toward the end of the sixteenth century and for many of the horrors of the Thirty Years War in Germany from 1618 to 1648.

On the surface, Calvin's concern for ethics and the "Godly" life looked very much like a revival of the old rigorism of the second and third centuries, but it had deeper roots. Calvin believed that before the beginning of the world God had determined that some human beings would be called or "elected" (chosen) to be given the gift of faith (which he understood as unswerving obedience to the will of God), to accept it, to manifest it in a good Christian life, and then to go to heaven to live with God for eternity. On the other hand, Calvin asserted that before the world began, God had chosen to create other human beings who would *not* be given the gift of faith, and who were therefore rejected by God and would spend eternity in the frightful punishments of hell, giving glory to God by manifesting the justice of his punishments. (One may wonder what the word "justice" might mean in such a context.) This principle of *double predestination*, as it is called, is a distinctive mark of Calvinism, and in this extreme form it was never shared by other Protestants.

This belief in predestination actually seems to have inspired Calvin's followers to behave in such a way that they might persuade others (and most probably themselves) that they belonged to the "elect." Signs of such election were, of course, membership in Calvin's reformed church, and willingness to live the strict, stern, and joyless life of those who did not want to "forget" God.

Calvin died in 1564. The reformed faith which he developed, given a more humane coloring and stripped of his extreme views on predestination, had considerable success in southern Germany, in Alsace, and in France itself, as we will see later. In Scotland, Calvin's version of the Reformation was introduced by John Knox—a man who, in his strict belief in double predestination and in his hatred of joy and spontaneity, was certainly a match for Calvin himself.

7.4 THE ANABAPTISTS

From the very beginning of the Reformation, Luther's *sola scriptura* principle (scripture alone) favored religious individualism. If scripture was the only guide one needed for faith and life, and if vernacular translations were available, then each man and woman was capable of discovering for him/herself the will of God. The kind of piety which grew from these beginnings was intensely personal and strongly associated with a conversion experience, in which one felt the presence and the call of Jesus and came to accept him as Lord. This conversion experience was often marked by a second reception of baptism (as an adult), and it was this which gave the *Anabaptist* movement its name.

The personal religion of the Anabaptists could have no sympathy with empty religious practice, which could easily be used to maintain the status quo, and therefore the movement often manifested radical and even revolutionary tendencies. It did this in Germany when Thomas Münzer tried (successfully for a short time) to establish a kind of primitive Christian society in Münster, in northwest Germany. The nobility of the region realized how dangerous such movements might become, and suppressed the experiment with great brutality.

Münzer was the most radical of these Anabaptist preachers, and he revived a notion which had appeared in the work of Joachim of Fiore in the early thirteenth century (and which had been espoused by other radical preachers since his time): the notion that the "thousand year reign" of Christ is about to begin, and that only those who receive the (adult) baptism of the Spirit will reign with their triumphant Lord. These ideas spread rapidly among the members of the underclass of the day—principally the peasants who had been disillusioned by Luther, and the lowest classes in the German cities.

Münster, in Westphalia (northwest Germany) was destined to be the city in which the thousand year reign of the Anabaptists was to begin. A priest of that city, Bernhard Rothmann, had been won over to the Anabaptist cause, and while Catholics and Lutherans in Münster were battling each other, he was able to preach the Anabaptist gospel almost unnoticed by them, and he won so many converts that he practically had control of the city. Once Rothmann was in control, Anabaptists streamed into the city from all directions, and the rebaptism of adults who flocked to the new faith became something of a fad. In one period in 1534, the number of adult (re)baptisms was running over a thousand a week. The Anabaptist movement became increasingly radical and its leaders took over the city government of Münster, announcing that it was destined to be the new city of God. Under the direction of these leaders, the community began to practice the primitive community of goods which they read about in the *Acts of the Apostles*. Reaching even more adventurously into the Old Testament, they introduced the practice of polygamy.

With the help of some of the civil rulers of the region, the bishop of Münster, who had been driven out, laid siege to the city, and in June 1535 Münster was captured and the Anabaptist leaders were put to death. A general persecution of the sect throughout Germany followed, because the authorities realized that this particular form of "spirit-inspired" Protestantism constituted a great danger to public order.

The Anabaptist movement regrouped after the catastrophe and its members rethought their relation to civil society. The Mennonites, with communities in the eastern and central United States, are their direct descendants. The type of personal faith which this movement cultivated, and which was nourished directly on the word of God, has appeared again and again within Protestantism, sometimes influenced indirectly by the Anabaptists, and sometimes apparently independently of them. Baptists, Methodists, and various evangelical groups are their descendants today.

7.5 THE REFORMATION IN FRANCE

After his sudden conversion to the principles of the Reformation, Calvin had had to leave France. Although the French kings Francis I and his son Henry II were quite willing to play footsie with German Protestants in order to further French political ambitions, they were not prepared to welcome the Reformation in France, and the persecution of Protestants was harsh.

Calvin did all that he could to further the Protestant cause in his native land, and in 1559 French Protestants were able to hold their first national council in Paris. Because the French regarded Protestantism as an import from Switzerland, the land of the "confederates" (in German: *Eidgenossen*), a corruption of this latter word—Huguenots—became the term for these French Protestants of Calvinist persuasion. From the beginning, the movement appealed to the well-educated professional class and to the middle class which was just beginning to appear in the cities. These were the very people who were inclined to despise the superstition of the Catholic peasantry and who were inclined to resent the absolutist pretensions of the Catholic monarchs. As was usual at the time, religious and political questions were inextricably confused.

Shortly after 1560 a number of members of the nobility, including some of the better known political and military leaders of the country went over to Protestantism. The king and the Catholic nobility, knowing Calvin's attitude toward Catholic rulers, felt threatened by this shift in religious allegiance; the result was that from 1562 until 1598 France was torn by religious strife which, during most of that period, broke out into open civil war. The war was fought by both sides with extraordinary brutality, but in 1572 it looked as though some kind of compromise might be reached through a political marriage between the king's sister and Henry of Navarre, the leader of the Protestant party. Catherine de Medici, acting as regent for her son, who was not yet of age, arranged with the leaders of the Catholic forces in the civil war to slaughter those Huguenots who were in Paris for the wedding. The event, known in history as the St. Bartholomew's Eve Massacre, took place during the night of August 23, 1572, and brought death to many members of the nobility in Paris, and to thousands of Huguenots throughout the country. Protestants have never forgiven or forgotten the fact that the newly elected Pope, Gregory XIII, had a *Te Deum*—a solemn hymn of thanksgiving—sung in Rome to mark the occasion (though it is probable that the Pope had merely been informed of a great victory over the Protestants and knew nothing of the slaughter).

Charles IX ruled as king from 1574 to 1589, but he died without leaving any heirs, and royal power passed to a related family, the Bourbons, whose leader was none other than the Protestant lord, Henry of Navarre, who had married the sister of Charles IX. According to French law, Henry could not become king of France unless he converted to Catholicism. This apparently presented no insuperable problems of conscience to the Protestant leader, and his remark on the occasion is classic: asked if he would be willing to convert to Catholicism in order to become king, he answered that "Paris was worth a Mass." France had paid in every way an appalling price in order to remain a Catholic country.

Henry took the name "Henry IV" and ruled from 1589 to 1610. In 1598 the religious wars finally came to an end in France with the issuing of the *Edict of Nantes*. This edict by no means gave the Protestants real equality, but they were granted a limited degree of freedom to practice their religion, and two hundred towns and cities throughout France were given to them as secure places of refuge.

Between 1598 and the reign of Louis XIV, the Huguenots were able to win an increasing number of converts, and for quite different reasons the government and the Catholic hierarchy began to worry. This anti-Huguenot coalition prevailed on Louis to revoke the Edict of Nantes in 1685. Louis complied, and in the act of revocation he demanded that all French Protestants return to the Catholic church. A good index of the strength of the faith of these Huguenots is the fact that over two hundred thousand chose to emigrate rather than to abandon their faith. Many went to Germany and many others went to the British colonies in the new world. Their departure was a serious loss to public life and to the economy of their country.

In later years, with the advent of more tolerant times, some of the emigres returned; together with some who continued the clandestine practice of their faith during the time of persecution, they formed the nucleus of the Reformed Church in France. Never numerically very significant, French Protestantism continues to the present day as a faith which is frequently attractive to members of the professional middle class, and its members are often respected for the seriousness of their religious commitment.

7.6 THE ENGLISH REFORMATION

7.61 From Henry VIII to the Elizabethan Settlement

The Reformation got off to a slow start in England. Henry VIII was as near to an absolute monarch as could be found anywhere in Europe in his day, and he probably sensed the revolutionary potential in the movement of reform (and had ample opportunity to observe its effects in Switzerland and Germany). It was his desire to have his marriage to Catherine of Aragon annulled, and the refusal of the Pope (probably from a mixture of religious and political motives) to accede to his request, which brought about the break with Rome and opened the door (just a crack at the beginning) to the Reformation in England. Henry VIII rejected papal jurisdiction and had himself declared supreme head of the church in England. He was also quite willing to persecute and put to death all those who refused to swear an oath of loyalty to him as supreme head of the church; and those who objected to his confiscation of the lands and wealth of the monasteries in 1535 were treated with a savage cruelty which was unusual even in that brutal age.

Oddly enough, despite all of this, Henry wanted nothing at all to do with Protestantism; as late as 1539 he arranged for the publication of the so-called Six Articles which imposed the death penalty on all those who *denied* transubstantiation, who rejected auricular confession, priestly celibacy, and communion only under the form of bread, and who supported a number of other specifically Protestant demands. It is hard to guess the motives for this spurt of "orthodoxy" on Henry's part. He may have wanted to believe that no matter what other monstrosities he had committed in his lifetime, he had at least remained true to the ancient faith. But it is just as likely that he sensed that in the Protestant principle of the supremacy of personal conscience and in the doctrine of individual interpretation of scripture, there lurked the rejection of the absolutism for which he stood.

A number of the men whom Henry had appointed to high position in the English church were strongly attracted to the very practices which Henry condemned and to the Reformation doctrines of which these practices were an expression. But these men had taken note of Henry's tendency to use direct methods to resolve disputes, and they kept their Protestantism carefully under wraps for as long as Henry lived. When Henry's son, Edward VI, came to the throne in 1547, the country took its first long step in the direction of continental Protestantism, and this move was symbolized in the Book of Common Prayer which was issued in 1549.

When Edward died, he was succeeded by his half-sister, Mary, the daughter of Henry and his first wife, Catherine of Aragon. She ruled from 1553 to 1558 and tried to restore the Catholic faith. But she was not very deft, and she went about it with a brutality which alienated increasing numbers of her subjects. She is known to Catholics as "Mary the Catholic" and to Protestants as "Bloody Mary."

On Mary's death in 1558, she was succeeded by her half-sister, Elizabeth, who was to rule the country for forty-five years. She was the daughter of Henry VIII and Ann Boleyn, the woman because of whom Henry had wanted his marriage to Catherine of Aragon annulled. Elizabeth's own background and the political circumstances of the time led her to persecute Catholics.

7.62 The Elizabethan Settlement

In 1559 the Protestant innovations which had been introduced under Edward VI were restored and the Catholic restoration which had begun under Mary was reversed. In the same year, an oath supporting the monarch as supreme head of the church in England was demanded of all bishops, priests, and public officials in the kingdom. This *Elizabethan Settlement*, as it was called, introduced a kind of moderate Protestantism into England, which was about halfway between the traditional Catholic faith on the one hand and a mixture of elements from Lutheranism and Calvinism on the other. Elizabeth apparently attached considerable importance to *apostolic succession*—the notion that those who are truly bishops must be able to trace their episcopal power back in an unbroken line to the Apostles themselves. If this apostolic succession were to be interrupted, then those who came after would not be true bishops nor would the priests whom they ordained be truly priests and they would lack the power to celebrate a Eucharist in which the Lord was really present.

For these reasons, Elizabeth had her new Archbishop of

Canterbury, Matthew Parker, consecrated by a bishop who had himself been consecrated during the reign of her father, when there was no doubt about the validity of his episcopal consecration. But the validity of Parker's consecration was later to be questioned, on the grounds that at the ceremony a ritual was used which had been written by Cranmer, when he was Archbishop of Canterbury, and which was somewhat Protestant in tone, especially in its view of the nature of holy orders.

This peculiarity of Parker's consecration has led to a number of discussions over the years on the question of the validity of Anglican orders—that is, the question of whether the bishops and priests of the Anglican church, the Church of England, have true episcopal and priestly powers. In the years after the Elizabethan Settlement, when the country drifted more securely into the Protestant fold, many of the priests and ministers of the state church could not have cared less, but in the nineteenth century there was a movement toward Catholicism in the Church of England, and many of the clergy who were affected by this movement began to worry about the validity of their orders. The question was brought to the attention of Pope Leo XIII in 1896, and he appointed a commission to research the question and to report to him. His decision, on the basis of the commission's report, that Anglican orders were not valid was resented by some Anglicans, but was deeply troubling to many others. In the first half of the twentieth century a number of priests and bishops of the Anglican church secretly made the trip to Holland to have themselves reordained by Catholic bishops who belonged to a separatist, schismatic church which had separated from Roman Catholicism at the time of the Jansenist controversy, but about the validity of whose consecration there had never been any doubt.

As a result of this, even if we used the same criteria which Leo and his commission used back in 1896, the actual judgment might be quite different today. However, a theology of holy orders or ministry which has a better New Testament pedigree will certainly provide a more realistic solution to the question of the validity of ministry in the various Anglican and Protestant churches. A marked degree of agreement has been reached in recent years, not only between Catholics and Anglicans (or Episcopalians, as they are called in the United States), but also between Catholics and the more Protestant groups which emerged from the Anglican church in the years after the Elizabethan Settlement.

7.63 The Puritan Movement

For many in England, the Elizabethan Settlement of 1559 had not gone nearly far enough in the direction of Protestantism and they were more than disturbed at the many elements of what they regarded as Catholic superstition which remained in the liturgy and life of the English church. In general, these opponents of the Elizabethan Settlement were iconoclastic in tendency; they wanted to abolish statuary in the churches, the use of vestments for the celebration of the liturgy, most of the ecclesiastical ceremonies, and any kind of invocation of the saints.

As is evident, these *Puritans*, as they were called (because of their demand for a "pure" or untainted church), were more Calvinist in inspiration than Lutheran, and this showed itself particularly in the emphasis they put on having a well-trained clergy: they wanted men who had studied scripture and who could preach the word with power. Another point about these Puritans is that they were not favorably disposed toward the office of bishop. They wanted each parish to be under the control of a group of respected Christians who were called *elders*. This word was a translation of the Greek term *presbyteroi*, which referred to a group that exercised a governing role in some of the churches in New Testament times. This, in turn, led to calling the church order of the Puritans *Presbyterian*, and to a significant degree the Presbyterian churches of the United States have both English and Scottish Calvinist roots.

From the time of the Elizabethan Settlement until after the beginning of the next century, these Puritans tried to persuade Parliament to adopt a new church order based on their religious principles. But since the bishops of the state church sat as *de jure* members of the House of Lords, the Puritans' chances of success were minimal. When King James VI of Scotland became King James I of England in 1603, many Puritans hoped that the new monarch, who had been raised in Presbyterian Scotland, would favor their cause. But James made it clear to them in 1604 that the religious unity of the realm was of prime importance and that for this reason he was not willing to make any fundamental changes in the organization or liturgy of the Church of England.

Puritan ministers were generally well-trained, and the Puritan laity usually led the kind of morally upright life which tends to attract the attention and sympathy of serious people. As a result, Puritanism spread—its spread aided by the fact that Puritans and their ministers did not constitute a dissident religious group outside the Church of England, but, in rather typically English fashion, they were members of the Church of England. Thus many of the ministers of the state church were Puritan in sympathy, and although they could not get rid of their church vestments as quickly as many of them would have liked, they were able to preach their Calvinist version of Protestantism throughout the realm.

Puritans held a strict moral code and were more than suspicious of what they called "worldly pleasures," which might lead to absorption in the world and forgetfulness of God. But unlike Calvin and his more somber continental confreres, many of these English Puritans had a deep love of nature and were able to find God in the beauty of the world. And although their understanding of joy might not strike everyone's fancy today, they did not have quite the same suspicion of joy which characterized the Presbyterian Church of Scotland or the Reformed Church on the continent. All in all, Puritanism represents one of the highest and gentlest forms of moralism that has ever flowered in Christianity. But like all forms of moralism, it was vulnerable to the temptation of self-righteousness and it encouraged a kind of self-salvation by exact observance of religious law.

As the Puritan gospel spread, the Church of England began to divide into two branches—called High Church (with more of the old ceremonies preserved), and Low Church (with a typically Calvinist rejection of ceremony). But there was never a split; rather, in a way only the English seem able to manage, the two movements continued to coexist with a mixture of distaste and grudging tolerance for each other. Things might have continued this way indefinitely, if it had not been for political events which brought the Puritans to power.

In 1641 Parliament decided that the time had come to assert its rights against the king, Charles I. This Parliament had a Puritan majority, and in 1643 its members forced an alliance with Scotland, and in the civil war which followed, the Puritan general, Oliver Cromwell, scored a number of brilliant victories over the royal forces. In 1649, the Parliamentary forces under Cromwell won, and the king was executed. The rest of the story belongs to English secular history, but it was at this time that Puritanism, with all of the iconoclastic tendencies of continental Calvinism, became fully acceptable in the English Church. From that time on, the English church has manifested a broad spectrum of liturgical variety, all the way from the extremely Catholic Anglicans to the various Low Church groups who outdo contemporary European Protestantism in their suspicion of statuary, vestments, and religious ceremonies. The Church of England has always been able to tolerate in its midst theological differences which would destroy other churches more insistent on the conformity of practice with theory.

7.64 The Church in Ireland

Before Patrick's time and for many centuries after, Ireland had been independent of England and it was not until well after the Norman invasion of England (1066) that Anglo-Norman nobles went to Ireland to make their fortunes. In the course of the twelfth and thirteenth centuries, they conquered much of the eastern part of the island and settled there permanently. But the conquerors were outnumbered, and over the years they were assimilated by the native Celtic population and became, if anything, more Irish than the Celts themselves.

When England drifted into Protestantism, as a result of Henry's break with the Pope over the divorce, and as a result of the introduction of Protestant liturgy and theology under Edward VI and Elizabeth, the Irish wanted nothing to do with the reformed faith. Efforts by the crown to bring the English Reformation to Ireland met with opposition, and the Catholic faith of the Celts and Anglo-Normans was on the way to becoming a symbol of dissatisfaction with English rule.

It was not until the reign of James I, which began in 1603, that Protestantism began to spread in Ireland. But this came about not through conversion of the local population, but through a program of colonization in the northern Irish province of Ulster; some of the colonists were English, of both Low Church and High Church, but most were Scotch Presbyterians.

During the war between the Puritan-controlled Parliament and King Charles I, Ireland sided firmly with the royalists, and Cromwell himself crossed over to the island with a large army in order to smash all opposition there. His military campaign was brutal and successful, and it was followed by official persecution of Catholics and their faith by the Calvinist government.

When Cromwell died and Charles II came back from exile in 1660, hopes in Ireland ran high, because the king was Catholic in sympathy (although he would be received into the church only on his deathbed); but the only change in Ireland was that the Presbyterians were forced to give up their authority to the Anglicans. But in 1685 when Charles' Catholic brother became king and ruled as James II, it looked as though Irish hopes would finally be fulfilled. However, James was forced out of England by the "Glorious Revolution" of 1688, which brought William and Mary to the throne. The exiled king tried to use Ireland as a base of operations to regain control in England. But in a series of skirmishes and one great battle in Ireland, his forces were defeated by those of William of Orange (and the North of Ireland Protestants are called "Orangemen" to the present day).

With the victory of the Orangemen came renewed attempts to suppress the Catholic faith. The method used was shrewdly chosen—not very much outright brutality, but the imposition of civil disabilities on Catholics, in order to encourage those with intelligence and promise to convert to Protestantism. Catholics were effectively blocked from political and professional life and were reduced to the status of tenant farmers, heavily taxed to support the state church—an "Irish" clone of the Church of England. The Catholic bishops were driven from the country, and all possible obstacles were placed in the way of the priests who tried to provide religious services for their flocks. But more than ever before the Catholic faith became a symbol of Irish resistance to the hated conquerors, and the overwhelming majority of the Irish have remained fiercely loyal to their church and to the Pope up to the present day.

7.7 THE REFORMATION IN RETROSPECT

By 1570 the Reformation claimed more than two-thirds of the population of Germany and virtually all of England, Scotland, and Scandinavia. It had made strong inroads in the Low Countries, particularly in the northern provinces, in Hungary, and among the nobility in Poland. Although not numerically strong in France (possibly ten percent of the population), the adherents of the new faith were generally well-educated and were, in the main, engaged in business or professional life, so that they exerted an influence out of proportion to their numbers. Wherever it went, the Reformation adapted itself to the character of the people; the form which it took and the way in which it developed reflected the unique religious and political history of each country.

Germany, for example, was not yet a nation, but rather an assortment of tiny to fair-sized states, under the rule of princes who jealously guarded their prerogatives and were usually looking for ways to assert themselves against an Emperor who was much like the chief executive officer of a fairly loose confederation. This situation had two results. First, because the Emperors remained Catholic, the Protestant faith became a way in which the princes could assert their independence; and, second, because of the independence of these princes from one another, the introduction of Protestantism brought into being a large number of territorial churches (Landeskirchen), some more Lutheran and some more Reformed in theology and style, all quite independent of each other, but subject to the local lord both in matters of politics and of religion.

England was already a nation state before the Reformation began. The monarchy was strong, and by the time the Reformation began, the king was ready to assert his absolute power in every domain. As a consequence of this, Henry's dispute with Rome over the divorce was quickly translated into the removal of the entire country from the jurisdiction of the Pope. At least in London and many parts of the south, this move had been prepared for by the preaching of Wyclif and by the Lollard movement of the fifteenth century. In Henry's time the north of the country was more emotionally tied to the old church, but Henry enforced his claim to supremacy over the English church by methods of unparalleled brutality, and he was able to break the opposition quickly. Although Henry's church was not Protestant in the proper sense, the men whom he appointed to high position in the realm had been strongly influenced by the Lutheran Reformation, and by the time of Elizabeth in 1558, the country had moved to a moderate Protestant position.

France was already a nation state by the time that the Reformation began. Unlike the situation in Germany, there was no long-standing general dissatisfaction with Rome and no universal public outcry against the financial exactions of the Roman Curia. For a considerable period in the fourteenth century the papacy had been a French national institution, and the emotional bond between the rulers of France and the papacy, which went back to the time of Pippin and Charlemagne, was probably a strong factor in the loyalty which both peasantry and nobility felt toward Rome. When the Reformation came to France, in the form of Calvinism, it had to germinate on foreign soil—that of Switzerland—and Calvinism always remained slightly foreign to French life and culture.

However, even in France, the Reformation adapted. Although the somber rejection of the world and its allurements is fortunately not one of the facets of the French character, but rather a quite personal trait of John Calvin himself, nevertheless the clarity and logical order with which Calvin summed up the principles and practices of the Reformed faith in his *Institutes* seem quite typically French.

In Scandinavia the old faith had never really had enough time to strike deep roots, and it seems as though the Reformation occurred almost automatically, as a matter of course. The monarchs were won to the Reformation and the new theology and preaching were introduced, while the old liturgy was left largely intact. As a result, without anyone really taking note of it and without serious opposition (although at very different rates in the various countries), Scandinavia found itself Protestant by the end of the sixteenth century.

But although the Reformation took on a unique coloring in every land in which it was successful, and although Luther really had no control over the course of events after 1525, the Reformation remained in the fullest sense of the word Luther's work. The cry for reform of the church in head and members had been rising in northern Europe for centuries, but Luther was the first to give concrete expression to this cry and to translate it into practical proposals for reform. He took an inarticulate longing and gave it an articulate voice; and it was from the absolute seriousness of his search for God and from his consequent discovery of the demanding and liberating word of God in scripture that the Reformation drew its religious substance. There were others who were more gifted organizers, and there were others who excelled, often tragically, in whipping popular enthusiasm to a fever pitch, but it was Luther who discovered the three great "exclusivities" of Reformation theology from which the movement derived its transforming power: *sola scriptura, sola gratia, sola fide*.

Although the Reformation was, in a unique sense, Luther's work, the first tragedy of the movement is that Luther never wanted what the Reformation became in actual fact; he wanted the reform of the one church, but the Reformation resulted in the division of the one church into many opposed and mutually hostile churches.

A second tragedy of the Reformation is that even in Luther's time, the movement which he began from purely religious motives was forced to serve political, social, and economic goals which were alien to its purpose and which often interfered with the religious renewal which he desired. The Reformation touched on every sector of life in its day. It invoked and inspired change in politics, economics and in the structure of society, and each of these areas joined itself to the Reformation in order, consciously or unconsciously, to tap for its own purposes the vitality of the movement. This is why the Reformation often looks, from our standpoint today, like an automatic consequence of those largely secular factors which led to the rise of modern Europe.

The final tragedy of the Reformation is that the Catholic church reacted to it initially with something very much like paralysis; the religious superficiality of the Renaissance papacy was no match for the religious depth of the monk from Wittenberg. By the time the Catholic church began to pull itself together and began to give a genuinely religious and theological response to the questions which Luther raised, the split between Protestants and Catholics was already so wide and so deep that the Council of Trent became, inevitably, an inner-Catholic affair, and an affirmation of the Catholic south of Europe against the Protestant north. This has been tragic for the church and the churches up to the present day. In order to understand why, we will turn in the next chapter to the history of the Council of Trent, of the Catholic reform, and of the Counterreformation.

8

Counterreformation, Reform, and Renewal: The Church from the Reformation to the Eve of the French Revolution

8.1 INTRODUCTION

Historians often argue about whether this period should be called the *Counterreformation* or the *Catholic Reform*. Each of these terms points to something important about the period, and yet each is also incomplete. The word *Counterreformation* often has a pejorative sense and implies that the papacy attempted, with the aid of the absolutist Catholic monarchies of southern Europe and with the help of the Jesuits, to recover the terrain lost to the Reformation and to restore the discredited institutions of the pre-Reformation period. But if the term is stripped of these somewhat naive connotations, it can be a useful description of the period. For it is true that although the Catholic renewal of the sixteenth century had begun very tentatively before 1517, it developed in opposition to the Reformation, and at the Council of Trent the Catholic church defined itself by the emphatic rejection of the major theses of Reformation theology.

Catholic Reform is a useful term, but it seems to imply that the reform of the one church in head and members, which Luther and the other reformers desired but failed to bring about, was achieved within the Catholic church itself in the course of the sixteenth and seventeenth centuries. But what happened during these centuries was not restricted to reform, as that word had been understood about the year 1500; and the church which emerged from the Council of Trent or, more accurately, the church which was a product of the Tridentine reform, was not simply purified of certain abuses. Rather, it was a much more tightly organized, and distinctively Latin church, which defined itself not only against the Reformation, but also against the concerns and the character of northern European Christianity. And yet, particularly during the sixteenth and the early part of the seventeenth century, the church did rid itself of many of the abuses against which the reformers had protested. And when the reform movement reached the papacy shortly before the middle of the sixteenth century, the church was given an entirely new shape and form as a result of the work of these reforming Popes.

Probably the best way to describe what happened to the Catholic church during this period would be to speak of retrenchment and renewal: a defensive step backward to regroup, reorganize, and tighten the chain of command, in order to confront an enemy who had appeared unexpectedly, and in order to win back ground lost in the initial moment of the surprise attack. For initially, the Catholic church reacted to the outbreak of the Reformation with something very much like paralysis: the Popes were indecisive and fearful; the emperor vacillated between, on the one hand, wanting Luther burned at the stake, and, on the other, asking that Rome agree to almost all of the Lutheran demands; religious houses emptied almost overnight; and half of Christendom seceded without any real opposition.

8.2 THE JESUITS

Religious life (in the sense of giving up marriage and the right to dispose of personal property, and doing this "for the sake of the kingdom") has always developed its concrete forms in response to the needs of the church at a particular moment of history, and in response to the signs of the times. And so it was at the time of the Reformation. The papacy was under attack, and Catholics seemed paralyzed by the intellectual and moral vigor of the reformers; but at this very moment a religious order was founded which made absolute obedience to the Pope its distinguishing mark, and which from the beginning exhibited an enormous intellectual energy which catapulted its members into the leadership both of the Counterreformation and of the Catholic Reform. In fact, the success story of the Jesuits during this period is virtually the key to understanding the history of the church from about 1540 to 1700.

8.21 Ignatius Loyola

Ignatius was born in 1491 in a family of the Basque nobility. His early schooling was limited to what would be of use to him in service at the court of the king of Navarre, in northern Spain, and he began his career as an officer in the king's army. But in 1521 he received a severe leg wound during the siege of Pamplona, and he was forced to put his career on hold. During the long recovery in the castle of Loyola he was unable to find the courtly romances which he sought for distraction, and was forced to turn to a translation of a life of Christ, written by a German monk two centuries before his time.

Ignatius was so gripped by the story that he underwent a conversion. To the dismay of his family he gave up his military career, adopted a life of strict asceticism, and went and lived in a cave at Manresa for nine months, where he experienced the ecstasy and the agony of mystical prayer. While there, he prepared the first sketch of a book of instructions on prayer and the life of the spirit, which would later be known as the *Spiritual Exercises.*

Drawn by a desire to visit the sites of Jesus' life and death, Ignatius went to the Holy Land in 1523 and stayed for about a year. The monks who were in charge of the Christian shrines, and who took care of the pilgrims who visited them, did not know what to make of Ignatius, and in the course of the year he began to see that if he was going to accomplish anything in the service of Christ he would need an education.

Returning to Spain, he spent two years in school in Barcelona, learning Latin with boys less than half his age, and continuing to practice his strict, ascetical way of life.

When he had learned enough Latin, he spent two years studying philosophy at the Spanish Universities of Alcala and Salamanca, and while he was there he became something of a wandering street-corner preacher. He came to the attention of the Spanish Inquisition, but escaped with a rebuke and the order not to preach, since he lacked the requisite theological training. To get it, he went to what was still the most prestigious university in Europe—the University of Paris—where he remained from 1528 to 1535.

While studying theology at the University, Ignatius continued to cultivate the life of prayer and asceticism, and he continued to work on his little book of *Spiritual Exercises*. Others began to gather around him and under his direction they made the Spiritual Exercises and dedicated their lives to God—the goal which the Exercises sought. On August 15, 1534, Ignatius and six dedicated followers took private vows of poverty and chastity and joined to these a promise to go to the Holy Land and work there for the conversion of the Moslems. Prudently, Ignatius specified that if the Holy Land venture should prove impossible, the members of his little group would put themselves at the disposition of the Pope and commit themselves to whatever task he gave them.

8.22 The New Religious Order Takes Shape

When one obstacle after another appeared in the way of their journey to the Holy Land, they took this as a sign from God, and in 1539 Ignatius formally requested the Pope, Paul III, to grant his approval for a new religious order. This order would be distinguished by the absence of most of the practices which were part of the life of the older religious orders: common recitation of the Office (the public prayer of the church), living in cloister, distinctive garb, prescribed mortifications, and many others. This new order would be mobile, able to go at a moment's notice to the ends of the earth in the fulfillment of that vow which was its really distinguishing mark—absolute obedience to the Pope in undertaking whatever apostolate he assigned them. In 1539 Paul III approved the new order and in 1540 the official document of approval was issued. The Jesuit order was formally in existence.

8.23 The Constitutions

Ignatius immediately set to work to write the *Constitutions*—the document which is much more than a code of law, and which embodies his basic vision for the Society of Jesus. Foremost, of course, was the fourth vow of obedience to the Pope, which was taken by the inner circle of the order. In addition, all Jesuits were bound by obedience to the superior or General of the order—a position held by Ignatius himself, at the insistence of all of the earliest members. (Because of this title, Jesuits have often been either romanticized or vilified, as though it were the symbol of the military dedication of their order. But the word really has no military connotations at all. It simply refers to the fact that the authority of Ignatius and his successors was not limited to particular areas but that they had *general* responsibility for the affairs of the whole order.)

Many have failed to note that according to Ignatius a principal task of the order was the instruction of children and uneducated people, as well as preaching and the hearing of confessions. Ignatius was shrewd, and he realized that the service of these neglected members of Christian society would be much helped if the Jesuits had the favor of the rich and the powerful. He encouraged his men to win the favor of those who could do either great good or great harm to the cause of the church; but his goal was not power for his order but the service of the Christian people. Occasionally some of his spiritual sons may have forgotten this but the record which Jesuits have made in the service of the poor, the sick, and the neglected from the earliest days of the order is impressive. Peter Claver (1580 to 1654) dedicated his life to caring for the slaves who were arriving by the thousands in the South American port of Nueva Cartagena and who had been subject to inhuman abuse on the journey. John Francis Regis (1597 to 1640) literally wore himself out bringing the good news to the rural poor in the French province of the Auvergne.

The Constitutions breathe the spirit of the *Spiritual Exercises*. Ignatius wanted his men to act always *for the greater glory of God* (the motto of the order) and to be motivated by the knightly desire to serve Christ, their King and Lord, by dedicating their entire selves to him. This dedication was to be deeply felt, and the book of the Exercises suggested ways of strengthening this commitment through appropriate appeals to feeling and emotion; but the service of Christ was to be *intelligent* as well. The Jesuit was to be shrewd, practical, and realistic in making his choices and in developing his talents so that he might be well equipped for whatever task he was assigned by superiors; then, when the decision was made, he was to do all in his power to try to see the decision as an intelligent one and to dedicate himself to implementing it.

8.24 Jesuits and the Counterreformation

Ignatius had not founded his order to combat the Reformation, but the intellectual training of his men and their dedication to the papacy made it inevitable that they would be in the forefront of the Catholic resistance to the Reformation. When the Council of Trent finally did meet, Jesuit theologians played a leading role, and they insisted that no concessions be made to the Protestants, thus giving the Council its distinctive character. At a time when much of Europe was turning from the papacy, the Jesuits bound themselves by a special vow of obedience to the Pope, and they were instrumental in creating the *papal* church of the modern world. In those areas where the Counterreformation was successful, this was achieved to a significant degree through the founding of Jesuit colleges, because these institutions were established, not only in the Catholic heartland, but also in those areas which had been partially lost to the Reformation. The German, Peter Canisius, joined the order in 1543, and successfully led the campaign to keep southern Germany loyal to the Catholic church. He wrote a catechism for Catholics which was in use up to the present century.

Later in the century, Robert Bellarmine, the Italian Jesuit (1542 to 1621), became the first to make the church itself an object of theological study. A skilled controversialist, he undertook to prove that the reformers were wrong in their understanding of the church. In this attempt he strongly emphasized the social and juridical dimension of the church, and defined it in a way which underlined the points which distinguished Catholics from Protestants. In this, Bellarmine was simply continuing a tradition which had been begun by Jesuit theologians at Trent, who urged that the Council make a statement of Catholic doctrine which would be devoid of any spirit of compromise with the teaching of the reformers, and which would define Catholic doctrine in decidedly anti-Protestant terms. As we will see in discussing the Council of Trent, this tendency may have been one of the less happy consequences of Jesuit intellectual dominance in the sixteenth century.

8.25 Other Contributions of the Order

Jesuits first became involved with schools about two decades after the order was founded. The practical needs of the time fostered a growing involvement in this apostolate, and the Jesuit colleges in Germany were a major weapon in winning back territory from the Protestants and in stopping the advance of the Reformation in southern Germany. In 1585 an important document was published, which has guided Jesuit education almost to the present day: the *Ratio Studiorum* or Plan of Studies. It is a clear statement of dedication to the principles of humanistic education, and on the basis of this document the Jesuits became the teachers of the European elite, not only in Catholic countries but in some lands which had gone over to the Reformation and in others which were nominally under the control of the Russian Orthodox Church.

But Jesuits were not simply pragmatic educators; the order fielded a number of creative artists as well. Jesuit architecture and theater were an expression of the Baroque spirit, which is itself a key to understanding the dynamism and appeal of the Catholic reawakening. Finally, as Europe turned its face outward again, to the newly discovered lands of the Far East, it was Jesuit missionaries who scored the greatest successes, and who approached the ancient cultures of that part of the world with an openness and sympathy which might have led to the conversion of entire populations if it had not been for the jealousy of some of the other orders and the tragic stupidity of some of the Popes of the eighteenth century.

8.3 THE BAROQUE

More than in most other periods, the life of the church during this time of reawakening can be described by a word which usually refers to an architectural or musical style. But the Baroque period was more than a time when a certain artistic style was dominant; rather it was a time which brought a new way of looking at the human situation, a new appreciation of the hierarchical order of the world, and a new attempt to unify all creation in such a view. This Baroque world view found expression in almost every area of life. The absolutist, authoritarian monarchies which developed in France and Spain (and in Prussia and Russia which were strongly influenced by French ideas during this period) were the perfect expression of its hierarchical view of the world. Baroque philosophers and theologians were always ready to give a theoretical justification to the "divine right of kings," and the Jesuits were typically Baroque in their emphasis on absolute obedience to the Pope and to the superiors of the order.

In a sense, none of this was really new. The High Middle Ages had certainly had a hierarchical view of the world, and the Popes of the thirteenth century were absolute both in their pretensions to power and in their exercise of it. But for the Baroque period, there was a difference. God and his world of heavenly beings (angels and saints) were no longer on the other side of a great divide. Rather, a *channel* had been opened between heaven and earth and a vision of heaven became possible for human beings below. The light from this vision streamed into the churches of the Baroque era and flooded the devotional life of Catholics of that period. In the Baroque church (in both senses: the building and the institution), the men and women of Catholic Europe left the drabness of the world behind, and they were offered an emotional and even ecstatic encounter with God. The Gesù, the Jesuit mother church in Rome, and all of the other churches which were built in imitation of it, are the artistic expression of this vision.

But when a vision of heaven becomes possible from within this world, there is an element injected into human life which cannot be grasped by merely rational analysis. There is something about the fascinating but awe-inspiring reality of God which must be *felt* and which makes a strong appeal to *emotion*. Ignatius' *Spiritual Exercises* demonstrates this: it was the Jesuit order which brought intellectual vigor to the Counterreformation, but an important part of the meditative prayer of the Jesuit is the "application of the senses" in which the one who prays uses all of the resources of senses and imagination to understand the call of Christ and to motivate himself to respond more whole-heartedly.

Because it was Jesus who opened this channel from heaven to earth, the Baroque showed a new interest in the humanity of Jesus. The Sacred Heart devotion became popular after the visions which were experienced by a French nun, Margaret Mary Alacoque, between 1673 and 1675; this devotion is typically Baroque in its emphasis on the humanity and vulnerability of Jesus and on the strong appeal to the senses which characterizes the art (and pseudo-art) associated with it.

Baroque Christianity was interested in preaching the Gospel to ordinary people, to the very groups which had been neglected in earlier periods. This did not spring from any hidden democratic tendencies of the Baroque world—its vision was far too hierarchical for that—but it did come from the increased attention being given to the humanity of Christ, and it expressed itself in the preaching and charitable work of Vincent de Paul (+ 1660) and in the dedication to educating young men of the poorer classes which found expression in the founding of the Christian Brothers by John Baptist de la Salle, who lived from 1651 to 1719.

During the period of the Baroque, religion became a joyous and even exuberant exercise. There was nothing somber about a Baroque church: beauty was consciously sought, not for its own sake, but because it manifested the glory of God. The practice of religion was made attractive to the senses in every way, and it offered relief from the drabness of life. In the Jesuit colleges great attention was given to drama and Jesuit playwrights produced their own dramas in order to drive home the central points of the theology of the Catholic Reform.

8.4 REFORM BEFORE (OR INDEPENDENT OF) TRENT

There had been talk of reform since before the time of the Avignon papacy, and the first half of the fifteenth century saw the struggle between conciliarists and the papacy over the question of who should initiate and direct such a reform. The Popes who ruled in the two decades after Constance were successful in curbing the conciliar movement and in affirming the principle that ultimate power to reform the church belonged to the papacy. The tragedy was that even though Martin V and Eugene IV were good men, they identified reform of the church with the supremacy of the Pope over the council. As a result it never occurred to them that it was the papacy itself which needed reform, and with the coming of the Renaissance Popes in the years after 1450 this oversight was to have tragic results.

Locally, reform had been carried out in Spain, by Cisneros, as we saw in the last chapter, and this reform extended both to the tightening of discipline in the monasteries and to basic improvements in the training of the secular clergy. It also manifested that savage obsession with the purity of faith which gave Spanish Catholicism its inhuman face for so long a period. Charles V and Philip II both dealt with supposed heretics with a brutality which is difficult for outsiders to comprehend, and the excesses of the Spanish Inquisition can only be explained as the irruption of sadism into the domain of religion.

And yet, around the middle of the sixteenth century, this Spanish church produced two remarkable mystics—Teresa of Avila and John of the Cross, who not only gripped popular imagination in Spain, but who carried through a reform of Carmelite monasticism which spread to other orders and which left its permanent impress on Spanish piety. At about the same time the work of the great painters, Velasquez (1599 to 1660) and Murillo (1617 to 1682), reveal a genuinity of faith and a depth of religious feeling unequaled elsewhere.

In Italy, the capture and pillaging of Rome by the soldiers of the Emperor, Charles V, in 1527 was regarded by many as the judgment of God on the Renaissance papacy, and some stirrings of reform were felt even in the Curia. When Paul III was elected in 1534 it could be argued that reform had finally reached the papacy. Though still in many respects a man of the Renaissance, Paul appointed good cardinals who had the best interests of the church at heart, and it was Paul who finally summoned the Council of Trent to meet in 1545.

In 1540 Paul III had given his approval to the Jesuits, and other orders were founded in the same century. After the Jesuits, it was the Capuchins who had the greatest impact. They spread rapidly, and by about 1650 there were twenty thousand Capuchins living throughout western Europe, from Ireland to Poland, with their greatest strength in the Latin countries, and especially in Italy. They took as their goal the full observance of the Franciscan rule, and they undertook to live in poverty and to bring the Gospel to the people in the cities and villages of Italy. They probably were a major factor in the failure of the Reformation to make much headway there, and they have been popular as confessors and preachers of missions up to the present day.

But except for Spain (where reform was so typically Spanish as to be unexportable), pre-Tridentine reform in the church was always related to the Reformation: it was either an answer to the threat of the Reformation, or a conscious preparation for the Council of Trent, or a development which was to assume its final form only at the Council or the attempt to spread the reform which the Council inaugurated.

8.5 THE COUNCIL OF TRENT

8.51 The Long Delay

One of the tragedies of the Council of Trent is that so many years passed before the bishops were finally summoned to meet. The Council met for the first time twenty-eight years after Luther broke with the church. During this long period of delay, the Reformation spread rapidly, and fronts hardened in a way which might have been avoided if the reformers could have taken part in a council at some time in the 1520's. The Popes of the time were still afraid of the conciliar movement and they saw any council as a threat to their power and position. The fact that Luther had appealed against the Pope to a council in 1518 certainly did nothing to allay their fears. Furthermore, until the time of Paul III, the papacy simply lacked the spiritual depth and drive which would have made it possible to understand the threat posed by the Lutheran Reformation, and to make an appropriate response.

Clement VII was Pope from 1523 to 1534, but he was indecisive, and afraid that a council would give Luther and his followers a public forum from which to attack the papacy. Like so many of the Popes before and after him, Clement gave most of his attention to the defense and extension of the Papal States and seemed to identify the prosperity of the papacy with the health of the church. He was afraid that the Emperor posed a threat to papal lands in Italy and for this reason he entered into an alliance with France against the Empire. In disgust, the Emperor, Charles V, sent his troops against Rome to teach the Pope a lesson. The lesson terminated with the *sacco di Roma*—the plundering and pillaging of the city of Rome by the troops of the Emperor in 1527, which was interpreted by many in that day as the judgment of God against the luxury and corruption of the Curia.

Clement was succeeded in 1534 by Paul III. In disposition still very much a man of the Renaissance, Paul can be called the first of the reforming Popes for two reasons: first, he appointed a number of brilliant and dedicated churchmen to the college of cardinals, and, second, he summoned what would eventually be known as the Council of Trent. Among his appointments to the cardinalate, especially worthy of note are Contarini, a moderating voice at the Council, Caraffa, who would succeed him, and the two Englishmen, Pole and Fisher. Paul had originally summoned the Council to meet at Mantua in 1537, but Francis I of France did all that he could to block the meeting of the bishops, fearing that the Council would strengthen the unity of the Empire. Finally the Council met in Trent in December 1545.

8.52 The Task of the Council

The bishops who assembled in Trent were not entirely in agreement about the purpose of the Council. There were still a few hard-line conciliarists who wanted the Council to undertake the work of reform on its own responsibility, but the great majority recognized the Pope as the highest authority and agreed that the task of reform belonged to him. There were more serious differences about the proper task of the Council. For the Emperor, the principal task was to effect moral reform in the church (especially the Curia) and to bring about reunion with the Protestants in Germany. For the Pope, the pressing need was to clarify questions of doctrine and to determine exactly the traditional teaching of the church on the points which were being disputed by the Reformers. (The Pope was quite correct on this point, because Luther had split with the church primarily over the dogmatic questions of the nature of faith and grace, of the efficacy of the sacraments and of the nature of the church.) On the procedural question, a compromise was reached, and it was decided that questions of dogma and questions of reform would be discussed simultaneously.

At the first session of the Council there were no bishops from Germany and the overwhelming majority were from Latin Europe; and although some bishops from northern Europe were present at the later sessions, up to the final meeting in 1564 the Italians constituted an absolute majority. It is often asserted that the Council was a purely Catholic affair, which saw its task as that of stating Catholic doctrine accurately and clearly, so that it could be sharply distinguished from the teaching of the Reformers; but such a statement is anachronistic. It assumes that the Council was from the very start faced with the fact of a Christianity which was divided into mutually exclusive and opposing churches. This was, to be sure, *coming* to be the case in 1545, but the final split between the churches (at least as far as Catholics and Lutherans are concerned) was to some extent the *result* of Trent. The problem of Trent was (and *is*) that the Pope and the bishops from the Latin countries identified Latin Catholicism, and its customs, its devotions, its whole religious ethos, with Christianity pure and simple. They had been doing this for centuries with the Orthodox churches of the East, and it was a hard habit to break. The bishops of the southern lands were horrified when German Catholics, as well as Protestants, had asked for a married clergy and for the granting of the chalice to the laity. But if Latin Catholicism had been willing to yield on these two points (which touch only *discipline* and not faith) in 1525 or 1530, it is possible that genuine reform could have been achieved in the *one* church.

8.53 The First Period

Although the sessions of the Council were spread out over almost twenty years, little more than two years were spent in actual meetings. The first period began in 1545 and ended in 1548, and it quickly became clear that doctrine was going to be defined *against* the position of the reformers, although none of them would ever be mentioned by name. Against Luther's *sola scriptura* principle, it was asserted that the faith of the Christian and the practice of the church were based on scripture *and* tradition—the latter word seemed to mean "teachings and practices which had been current in the church from the beginning and which had been handed down to the present day." Oddly enough, the Council took no position on the question of whether these were really *distinct* sources, in the sense that tradition contained some material which was totally absent from scripture, or whether they were *complementary*, in the sense that authentic tradition was simply the correct interpretation of scripture down through the years.

When the Council turned to the question of *justification*—that is, the question of what one must do in order to have the right relationship with God—there were a number of cardinals who saw the strength of Luther's position, and who were willing to go much farther in accepting his views than the Council finally did. Cardinal Caraffa and the Jesuit theologians prevailed, however, and the Council asserted that, although justification is the pure gift of God, which human beings cannot merit by their own works, nevertheless, when we are so "justified," we receive the gift of sanctifying grace, which produces an interior change in the soul. In virtue of this it is possible to perform good and meritorious works which, *together with faith*, bring about our salvation. In this, the Council thought that it was rejecting Luther, but it was addressing a somewhat different problem, in language which was inevitably going to be misunderstood by Lutherans.

At this same session the Council took up the question of the sacraments and affirmed that the sacraments work, not because of the faith of the recipient but because of the inner power of the sacramental rite itself ("ex opere operato" = "from the performance of the sacramental action"). In one sense this was a reaffirmation of teaching which had been generally accepted in the church from the time of Augustine's victory over the Donatists. But it was also a position which could easily be misunderstood, and which had led, in the centuries before Trent, toward a popular perception of the sacraments as magical acts which could work independently of faith. (It is possible that the failure of churchmen to dedicate themselves wholeheartedly to instructing the descendants of those who accepted the faith at the time of the mass conversions was due in part to such a magical view of the efficacy of baptism and annual communion.)

In March 1547, the Pope transferred the Council from

Trent to the north Italian city of Bologna. The pretext was that a plague had broken out in Trent and that Protestant armies in the vicinity threatened the security of the bishops; the actual reason probably was that the Pope wanted the Council removed from territory which was under the Emperor's jurisdiction and to a place where he, the Pope, would be in more complete control. The Emperor was furious, beause he had finally gotten control of the rebellious German princes and was convinced that he would be able to get the Protestants to take part in the Council. However he knew that they would never agree to go to Italy. At this very moment, when it was vital that the Pope and Emperor work together to heal the wounds of Christendom, the Pope began to plot with Henry II of France, against the Emperor, for the incredibly short-sighted purpose of protecting the integrity of the Papal States in central Italy. Finally, on September 14, 1549, the Pope suspended the meetings of the Council (which had actually come to an end a year before). Another *sacco di Roma* was probably prevented by the timely death of Paul III.

8.54 The Second Period

The new Pope, Julius III, was not particularly interested in reform, and he represented a partial return to the Renaissance papacy. But at least he and the Emperor were not prepared to make war on each other, and it was at his command that the Council met, again in Trent, from 1551 to 1552. At this session for the first time there were a few German bishops present. The Council turned first to the sacrament of the Eucharist and decreed, principally against the Calvinists, that the Lord was really and truly present when the Eucharist is celebrated, and that what happens at the Mass is properly called *transubstantiation*—that is, that the underlying reality of the bread and wine is changed into the underlying reality of Jesus Christ, but that the appearances of the bread and the wine remain. Unfortunately the Council made no attempt to distinguish the New Testament teaching on the real presence (with which the Lutherans agreed) from ways of interpreting and explaining that presence which were conditioned by early medieval philosophy and by a preoccupation with the elements of bread and wine which really did not have a good basis in the New Testament. At the same session, the Council defined penance and extreme unction (the anointing of the sick) as two of the seven sacraments, asserting that they had been instituted by Christ and that they could be administered only by a priest.

In January 1552, as a result of some arm-twisting by the Emperor, a number of Protestant delegates arrived at the Council, and Charles V probably felt that now the Council could get to work on its main task, which was that of reform and reunion. But by now the *kairos* of history, the right time to act, was long past. The Council had already committed itself to a number of positions which the Protestants could not possibly accept (and which represented a distinct narrowing of what had been commonly accepted in the church up to the beginning of the sixteenth century). As a condition of their participation, the Protestant delegates demanded that debate on all the earlier decisions of the Council be reopened, and that the questions be decided on the basis of scripture alone. They further demanded that the Council conduct its meetings independently of the Pope. The Pope and the bishops of Latin Europe were not about to accept these conditions (and the Protestants probably did not expect that they would). In April 1552, there was yet another uprising of Protestant princes against the Emperor, and the resulting turmoil brought this session to an end.

8.55 The Third Period

The Council of Trent did not meet again for nine years, and when the bishops came together in Trent in 1563, again there were no Germans present. At this meeting the sacrificial character of the Mass was affirmed, and the bishops asserted that the Mass itself had infinite satisfactory value—that is, that the offering of Christ as victim to the Father has the power to take away, in whole or in part, the punishment which we would otherwise have to make good in purgatory. Purgatory itself was defined as a real state of suffering in which those destined for heaven paid the penalty of suffering which was due, even after their sins were forgiven. The Council affirmed that ordination to the priesthood and marriage were also sacraments, instituted by Christ and endowed with the power to give grace. Finally, indulgences were explained and justified, and the cult of saints and the veneration of relics was defended. At this third session, the anti-Protestant feelings of the majority of the bishops were evident, and of all of the sessions, it was the one whose decisions had the weakest New Testament roots. Unfortunately it was also the session which provided most of the issues and terms in which Catholics have understood their church in the centuries since Trent. On January 21, 1564, Pope Pius IV approved all of the decrees of all of the sessions of the Council, and the Council of Trent formally came to an end.

8.56 The Significance of the Council of Trent

On the positive side, the Council of Trent put an end to some of the worst abuses of the late medieval and Renaissance church. The selling of indulgences was stopped and the Council made some clear statements about the veneration of saints and their relics which, in principle at least, struck at superstitious elements of popular devotion. In its decree on justification, the Council strongly underlined the absolute gratuity of God's gift of grace; it was this which led Harnack to affirm that if Trent's decree on justification had been available in 1517, the Reformation would never have happened.

Still on the positive side, there was a calmness and civility about the Tridentine decrees which contrast favorably with the harsh intolerance which appears, at least at times, in the writings of the reformers, and ranges from Luther's vulgarity to Calvin's chilling intransigence. Furthermore, although all scriptural exegesis in those days was, as we would say today, strongly *fundamentalistic*, Trent's rejection of the *sola scriptura* principle, whether for the right or the wrong reasons, made its decrees less vulnerable to this criticism.

On the negative side, Trent obviously set out to define

the Catholic faith *against* the position of the reformers, and it failed to take note of two facts. First, the church against which Luther rebelled from 1517 on was, in some respects, no longer fully *Catholic*, and in criticizing it Luther took his stand on the basis of some ancient and genuinely Catholic teaching which had been neglected or even forgotten during the late medieval period. Second, Luther and some of the other Reformers were speaking for the non-Latin Catholicism of northern Europe, and Trent had no understanding of the ethnic and temperamental differences which separated the north from the south. To the end, Trent confused the religious "style" of the south in dogma, discipline, and devotion with the Catholic faith itself.

Trent was intent on labeling the teaching of the reformers as heretical, and with few exceptions the bishops who voted for its decrees showed no understanding of the genuinely religious substance and theological depth of Luther's rediscovery of Paul's teaching on justification. Neither did they seem to see how easily the traditional teaching on the efficacy of the sacraments ("ex opere operato") could be misunderstood and could lead to superstition in the reception of the sacraments. Especially during the third period, the bishops came close to defining the religious life of the Catholic in terms of devotions and practices which had almost no New Testament pedigree (devotion to the saints, veneration of relics, the gaining of indulgences). The result was that, almost up to the present generation, the convert instruction manuals used by Catholics emphasized precisely such things, and inevitably suggested that they were at the center of Catholic faith.

On more serious questions of doctrine, Trent's emphasis on the Mass as a satisfactory sacrifice and on the propriety of private Masses often led to the view that Mass was a ritual act to be *observed*, and this led to the neglect of the Mass as a communal meal of the people of God, at which they celebrated the presence of their Lord. Trent's eagerness to condemn Luther's definition of faith, which was not in accord with that of the great scholastic theologians of the medieval period, blinded the bishops to the fact that Luther's doctrine was genuinely Pauline. Finally, Trent's assertion of the doctrine of merit and of the necessity of both faith and good works for salvation (as though they were two quite distinct contributing factors) led to something very much like Pelagianism both in popular piety and in the quest for moral perfection in some of the religious orders.

In summary, largely because of the efforts of the Jesuits, the Council of Trent became a clear statement of Catholic doctrine in a form which maximized its distinction from Protestant teaching. Furthermore, the Council marked the definitive triumph of the papacy over the conciliar movement, because it put the execution of its reform decrees firmly in the hands of the Pope. The result was that the Council of Trent was a Latin affair—the affirmation of the traditional concerns and even the traditional ethos (here: religious value system) of southern, Latin Europe against the concerns, customs, and culture of the north.

Ecumenical theology today cannot start with the more polemic statements of the reformers, any more than it can start with the more negative statements of the Council of Trent. The contemporary quest for Christian reunion can only succeed by "redoing" the Reformation, and by recognizing the exaggerations and one-sidedness of both Catholics and Protestants during the sixteenth century. The reformers took with them, when they left the Catholic church, many teachings and practices which were genuinely Christian and Catholic, but which have become suspect in post-Tridentine Catholicism *precisely because the reformers emphasized them.* During the same period, the Catholic church kept a number of teachings and practices which had come down to it from Christian antiquity, but which have become suspect in post-Reformation Protestantism *precisely because Catholics emphasized them.* Today, to the extent that both groups can affirm their common patrimony, they will find that whatever one may say of the differences which may divide them, they are probably not great enough to justify the existence of separate and mutually exclusive churches.

8.6 REFORM AND RENEWAL AFTER TRENT

8.61 The Counterreformation

The period from the close of the Council of Trent to the end of the century can properly be called the *counterreformation*, although the *political* consequences of this latter movement were not made final until the Peace of Westphalia in 1648. By 1550 the reformers and the Council of Trent had talked themselves into accepting the existence of distinct and hostile churches, each of which claimed to embody the fullness of Christian truth. At the same time, the Jesuits were fighting the good fight in their own way; Jesuit colleges were founded in France and in Germany (the Empire); and in central and southern Germany, as well as in Austria, they were instrumental in winning back many territories which had partly gone over to the Reformation. Jesuit colleges throughout Europe were attended by the sons of princes and by others of the elite, and they turned out a number of graduates who were able promoters of the Latin Catholicism of Trent. The Jesuits, with their strong practical instinct, pressed the papacy to provide political and (indirectly) military support for Catholic princes in Germany and Austria who, for whatever reasons, were committed to stopping the advance of the Reformation.

The Italian Jesuit, Robert Bellarmine, was one of the most famous controversialists of his day, and developed an understanding of the church which made it easy to distinguish Catholics from Protestants. In accordance with the decrees of Trent, seminaries for the training of priests were established throughout western Europe. In France (after 1600, because of the delay which resulted from the religious wars) new religious orders were founded, and a concerted attempt was made to bring the Gospel to the masses. Jesuits were active in all of this, and toward the end of the seventeenth century, a doctrine or teaching called Jansenism appeared, which had a pronounced anti-Jesuit bias. The Jansenist movement had many roots, but it was to some extent a reaction to the Jesuits and a rejection of the Baroque spirit which their order embodied.

The Inquisition had been established in Rome in 1542, and after the Council of Trent was over, the officials of the Roman Inquisition began to oversee the work of Catholic theologians and to control Catholic intellectual life in a way which has frequently been a scandal up to the present day. At the time, of course, neither liberty of conscience nor academic freedom was recognized as a value, and church authorities acted as they did because they felt they were involved in a life and death struggle for the purity of the faith.

8.62 Popes of the Counterreformation

Pius V was elected two years after the end of the Council, and he reigned for six years, until 1572. He continued the reform of the college of cardinals, not simply by making new and very strong appointments, but by involving the college itself in the work of reform. He set up a number of *congregations*—practically speaking they were standing committees, staffed by cardinals—to direct the work of the foreign missions, to oversee the performance of the bishops in their dioceses, to insure the maintenance of discipline in the religious orders, and to arrange for the establishment of *seminaries*, the schools in which the candidates for the priesthood were to be trained. It was during the pontificate of Pius V that a new Missal was issued, which contained the revised text of the Mass, together with exact instructions for its celebration, as well as a new Breviary—the book of the official prayer of the church which was an important part of the daily prayer of the priest.

In the political realm, Pius V was not as fortunate. In 1570 he excommunicated Queen Elizabeth of England and freed her subjects from their oath of allegiance to her. By this time, such an act was without meaning, and the only effect it had was to make the already difficult position of English Catholics almost impossible. On the other hand, in 1571 the forces of Christian Europe, under the leadership of an Austrian prince, won a great victory at Lepanto over the Ottoman

Turks, finally putting a stop to the Moslem advance in Europe—something which had been a goal of papal policy since the middle of the fifteenth century. Pius' policies were continued during the long pontificate of Gregory XIII (1572 to 1585), who was a strong supporter of the Jesuits, as well as during the reign of Sixtus V who was Pope from 1585 to 1590.

8.63 New Forms of Catholic Life in the Spirit of Trent

One of the first positive effects of the Council of Trent was the new spirit of dedication and responsibility which many bishops began to manifest in the management of their dioceses. Charles Borromeo, who was bishop of Milan from 1560 to 1584, is typical of many. He visited the parishes of his diocese regularly and issued a constant stream of instruction and exhortation to his priests concerning the dignified celebration of Mass and the proper administration of the sacraments.

As we have often noted, the establishment of new Jesuit colleges in Germany resulted in winning back territory which had gone over to the Reformation in Bavaria, and farther to the north, in Mainz, Trier, Würzburg, and Fulda. The Jesuits were very active in Poland, founding their first college there in 1565, and it was above all due to their influence that the upper classes in Poland remained Catholic.

In France, the Catholic-Huguenot religious wars delayed the Catholic Reform, but even there the Jesuits had established their College of Clermont in Paris in 1550. From the beginning this was resented by the theologians at the Sorbonne (University of Paris). The latter group continued the conciliarist and somewhat anti-papal traditions of the University and they felt that the Parisian Jesuits constituted a bridgehead of papal power in the very heart of France. This unfortunate opposition continued for many years, and the University collaborated in the suppression of the Jesuits at the end of the eighteenth century. Late in the sixteenth century several Jesuit colleges were established in other parts of France, and by 1640 there were over fifty Jesuit colleges in the country. By 1603 the King, Henry IV (of "Paris is worth a Mass" fame), had a Jesuit confessor—a development which probably made the order suspect in some quarters.

In the early seventeenth century in France, both the Benedictines and the Cistercians underwent periods of spiritual renewal and rededication to the monastic ideal. Another influential figure was Francis de Sales (1567–1622), who was bishop of Geneva from 1602 until his death. Unable to live in the city because it had become a Calvinist bastion, he set up headquarters in Annecy, a French city not too far away, and became famous as a spiritual writer and director. His *Introduction to the Devout Life* was very influential on the spirituality of the religious orders at least up to the time of the Second Vatican Council.

At about the same period, another French priest, de Berulle (1575 to 1629), founded a new school of piety which had strong Augustinian roots, emphasizing the transcendent holiness of God, the total unworthiness of man, and the unbelievably amazing character of the incarnation which was consequent on this. De Berulle's piety was typically Baroque in its emphasis on the humanity of Jesus, and he developed a kind of Catholic version of the theology of the cross, in which one's sharing of the life and death of Jesus led to the conquest of self and even to a kind of self- annihilation. This spirituality spread in France through a school which de Berulle had founded in 1611 for the training of priests. A slightly later contemporary, Olier (1608 to 1657), had an even greater impact on the church in France and in the United States through his founding of the Society of St. Sulpice—a congregation of priests who were dedicated to providing trained professors for the seminaries which were appearing everywhere, as directed by the decrees of Trent.

One of the finest examples of the spirituality of the Baroque was Vincent de Paul (1578 to 1660). He devoted himself to preaching, instructing the laity, and giving retreats to the rural population of France, which had been neglected over the years. He was a man of enormous energy. In 1625 he founded the Congregation of the Priests of the Mission to continue his work of evangelizing the poor and his men also dedicated themselves to the education of future priests. At the time of the French Revolution over a third of the seminaries in the country were being run by these *Vincentians*, as they were called. In 1633 he founded the Sisters of Charity, who continued his work with the destitute in the cities.

About the year 1650, a number of priests began to realize that preaching the Christian message to the lower classes in the cities could be effective only if the people of these classes had received basic training in reading and writing. Some of these priests may also have been dimly aware that these same people could be rescued from that grinding poverty to which their class was condemned only if they acquired some learning. The school had always been a democratizing influence, and it was about to become one again.

There were, of course, some grammar schools in the larger cities, but methods were antiquated and there was a constant shortage of teachers. A priest, Nicholas Roland, tried to establish a network of schools for the poor in various cities of northern France, and, after his death, followers continued his work, but without much success. One of them, Adrian Nyel, arrived in Rheims in 1681, to see if it would be possible to establish a school there, and both the place and the time were providential. He met a wealthy priest attached to the cathedral staff, John Baptist de la Salle, who not only offered Nyel a place to stay, but who became interested in his work and helped him open a free school for boys in Rheims. De la Salle not only financed the venture, but he became more and more committed to the work of the teachers, living with them and teaching in their school. (This caused a break with his own family: they were from the high nobility and regarded this association with those of the lower classes as unworthy of a member of their family.)

In 1684 de la Salle gave up his inheritance and put the money at the disposal of the famine-striken people of the region. In the same year, with twelve of his teachers, he took vows to commit himself for life to the teaching of the poor. Later in the same year he opened what was to be the first teacher-training institute in history.

In Paris, in 1688, de la Salle began to employ a revolutionary new teaching method. Instead of forcing them to learn Latin, he trained boys in French; instead of the wasteful practice of having a teacher move from one individual to the next, he developed a system of classroom instruction; and for the first time textbooks were provided. By 1691 there were over 1,000 students in his school in Paris, and he was beginning to put in special courses for older adolescents who were already working, and for adults. In that same year he wrote his famous *Conduite des Ecoles* (The Running of Schools) which was based on his rich experience and most successful educational innovation. Because opposition in Paris threatened the peaceful development of his schools, he transferred headquarters to Rouen. It was not until 1724 that his followers, who were now practically a new religious order, received permission to incorporate under French law, and in the following year their order was approved by Pope Benedict XIII.

8.64 Jansenism

Jansenism was an unhealthy manifestation of counter-reformation piety which in many ways harked back to the rigorism of the church of the second and third centuries and which was an expression of that concentration on ethics and the moral life which characterized Latin Christianity almost from the beginning.

Cornelius Jansenius (1585 to 1638) had studied at the University of Louvain, in Belgium, at a time when the Jesuits there were embroiled in a great deal of controversy, and he had imbibed from his teachers a lasting hatred of the order, whose theology was at opposite poles from his own. He was ordained and became bishop of Ypres, in Belgium, in 1636, the same year in which he wrote his major theological work, the *Augustinus*.

At another time, and with a personality conditioned by other experiences, Jansenius could easily have become a second John Calvin. He taught a kind of exaggerated version of Augustine's theology, concentrating on the very themes of the later Augustine which had never become the common property of Christian theology: the total depravity of man, consequent on original sin, and the arbitrary act of divine pre-destination, which awarded grace to some and kept it from others. Jansenius was horrified at the practice of frequent communion (which the Jesuits advocated), because he was convinced that the sacrament was being profaned by those who had not made the exacting preparation which so exalted an act demanded.

This kind of elitist rigorism proved attractive to many who were seeking perfection in religious life, and it became virtually the official theology of a convent of Cistercian nuns at Port Royal, who became the center of a movement of pious rigorism which was to have destructive effects into the twentieth century. The brilliant philosopher Blaise Pascal (1623 to 1662) was a member of the circle of admirers who gathered at Port Royal for discussion and mutual encouragement. It was Pascal who identified the Jesuits as the most dangerous opponents of Port Royal and of the Jansenist movement, and who wrote his *Provincial Letters* in order to try to discredit the order in the eyes of his countrymen.

Largely at Jesuit urging, the Pope condemned a number of statements from Jansenius' *Augustinus* in 1653, and in 1661 all of the French clergy were required to sign an anti-Jansenist formula. There were debates for years on whether the Jansenist doctrines were condemned in the sense in which Rome understood them or in the (assertedly different) sense in which Jansenius had meant them, and in 1713 the Pope condemned them in every sense. Formally and officially this put an end to the discussion, but the opposition of Jansenists to Rome made them allies of all in France who wanted to trim papal power, and many of the bishops of the country were quite sympathetic to Jansenism for a variety of reasons. From the late seventeenth century on, although the doctrines of Jansenius were no longer being openly taught, there was a climate of Jansenism which was widespread among those of the upper classes who took their religion seriously, and this climate penetrated the seminaries and spread widely from there.

Around this time a number of Irish students who had no opportunity to study for the priesthood in their own country went to France for their seminary training, and they brought back to their own country a kind of rigorism to which the Celtic spirit is often prone. From there, this kind of hidden Jansenism spread to the church in the United States, which was, in the later nineteenth and early twentieth centuries, staffed to a great extent by Irish priests.

After the condemnation of Jansenius in the early eighteenth century, a number of priests and bishops who were unable to accept Rome's decision set up their own schismatic church in Utrecht in Holland, where they exist to the present day as the church of the Communion of Utrecht. Their ordinations and consecrations have always been regarded as valid by Roman Catholic authorities, and over the years they have been joined by other dissident groups, including those who were unable to accept the decision on papal infallibility of Vatican I. It is to the bishops of this church that a number of Anglican clergymen have gone in this century for secret reordination, when they began to doubt that apostolic succession had been maintained at the time of Parker's consecration during the reign of Elizabeth I.

8.7 THE MISSIONS FROM 1500 TO 1750

The church is *essentially* a missionary organization. Jesus knew that he himself had been *sent* (Latin *missio* = "sending") to proclaim the good news, and the earliest communities turned to their Jewish brethren and then to the gentiles in order to fulfill a task which they knew was inherent in their faith. For their faith could not be the private property of religious or ethnic elites. Christianity was for rich and poor, slave and free, for the masses and for the cultured elite. There is something in Christianity (and very near its center) which cuts across all of these barriers, relativizing them without eliminating them. For this reason, Christianity does pose a threat to other faiths, as they are commonly understood by their devotees, just as it is a threat to all political systems and cultural traditions which make any of these barriers absolute.

The problem of adapting the Christian message to new

and different cultural traditions is as old as the faith itself. The first great doctrinal dispute in the nascent church arose over the question of whether the religious and cultural traditions of the Jewish Law were to be imposed on gentile converts as a condition of their becoming Christian. And the solution which eventually prevailed represented a radical break with the understanding of itself and its mission which had characterized the very earliest church.

But no sooner was the question of the relation of the gentile converts to the Law settled than other, more subtle problems of terminology surfaced. The earliest community had expressed its understanding of the mystery of Jesus by calling him *Messiah*. In the literal sense, this title could be translated into Greek as *Christos*, but in this new cultural context it no longer said anything important about Jesus and rapidly became his second name. As a result, other terms from the Hellenistic-Jewish milieu, such as *Kyrios*, Lord, or from the Greek world, such as *Soter*, savior, had to be used, if the *content* of the new faith was to be maintained in the new context.

The earliest church was still very flexible, and the transformation which the church underwent in its first thirty years was total. But by the time of the mass conversions of the Germanic invaders, starting with that of Chlodwech and his army in 499, and then proceeding through the forced imposition of Christianity on conquered populations by Chlodwech in Burgundy and in the south of France, to those of Charlemagne in Saxony and the eastern marches, no significant adaptation of the Christian message to the language and culture of the subjugated people was made. Latin was the language of culture and of faith, and it was assumed that those who had become Christian at the time of the mass conversions would sooner or later learn it, and thus come into a Christian inheritance which had never had to change its garb in the attempt to adapt to them. It is arguable that it was precisely this failure of Latin Christianity to adapt its message to the Germanic converts which allowed the more dangerous elements of pagan polytheism to live on under a thin Christian veneer.

Events in the Middle Ages, particularly the excommunication of Michael Cerularius in 1054 and the sack of Constantinople in 1204, led to the permanent estrangement of eastern and western Christendom, and made of the Catholic church a purely west European phenomenon. After the Reformation and Trent's response to it, the Catholic church of the West became an almost entirely Latin organization, and from the sixteenth century on the Catholic church has often had a rather foreign appearance in the Germanic lands of northern Europe. This was a problem which reached its peak in the nineteenth century under Pius IX, when "Romanità"—Romanness—became virtually the fifth mark of the church (and one which weighed more heavily than the other four!).

At the time of the great discoveries, principally the work of Portuguese, Spanish, and Italian navigators between the years 1486 and 1567, religious motives for opening the new frontier often seemed important, but what passed for religion was simply a part of the Latin culture of each of the colonizing powers. And no one seemed capable of distinguishing Christian faith from the concrete form which it had taken in the late medieval period in these three countries.

There was a close link between the missionaries and the armies of the conquistadores, and most missionaries obviously felt that the destruction of the native culture was a condition for the natives' acceptance of the Good News. Not many attempts were made to integrate Christianity into the native culture, because very few seem to have felt that it was worth the effort, if they thought about it at all. When Christianity met either primitive cultures, or relatively advanced cultures without a real literary tradition—as was the case in Mexico, Central and South America—the result was a Christian facade, behind which the old paganism was able to exist in many areas up to the present day. But when Christianity encountered the high and ancient civilizations of India and China, the usual result was that the new faith appeared as part of an alien culture, which might be embraced by some out of opportunistic motives, but which was despised as a foreign body by upper and lower classes alike. Particularly in the Americas, the members of the older orders as well as the Jesuits often showed real concern for the native populations and tried to protect them from oppression and exploitation by the representatives of the colonizing powers, but for all of their good intentions and personal kindness, the missionaries usually were intent on exporting Portugese or Spanish Catholicism to a new setting.

8.71 The Jesuit Missions in China and India

There were two great missionary endeavors which were an exception to this sad pattern. The first was the work of the Italian Jesuit, Matteo Ricci (1552 to 1610). Ricci arrived in China before 1600, and quickly came to the conclusion that if Christianity was to make any progress in this land of ancient culture, he would have to show that Christian faith was worthy of the attention and the loyalty of educated and cultivated men. To this end, Ricci immersed himself completely in the Chinese cultural world, learning the language, and adopting the garb of a Chinese scholar. Not content with externals, Ricci went on to become a recognized Chinese scholar and to win the respect of the Mandarin class in Beijing. By 1600 he had set up a quite modern astronomical observatory in that city, and he had become a friend and confidant of the Emperor. In 1610 there were two thousand Chinese Christians in and around the capital.

After Ricci's death, his work was continued by a German Jesuit, Adam Schall (1592 to 1666). Schall became a respected Mandarin, and in 1645 he was appointed imperial astronomer. With the permission of the Emperor he built a church in Beijing in 1650, and by his death in 1666 there were over a quarter of a million Christians in China.

But trouble was brewing. Ricci and Schall had not only adopted Chinese customs themselves, but they had allowed the Chinese converts to continue practices which might look religious to the outside observer, but which seemed to them to be integral parts of Chinese culture—such as the respect shown to the philosopher Kung Fu Ce (Confucius) and the reverence shown to the traditions and persons of one's ncestors.

However, the Jesuits were not the only missionaries in

China; and Franciscan and Dominican missionaries there complained to their superiors and to the papacy about these practices. Their motives were probably mixed, and jealousy undoubtedly played a role. But more important was a kind of cultural bias which prevented them from seeing cultural adaptation as anything less than treason to the faith. In 1645 Pope Innocent X forbade the whole Jesuit policy of accommodation (adaptation of the Christian message to foreign cultures). Although Jesuit authorities succeeded in having this rejection mitigated, in 1693 it was issued in a new and more absolute form, and finally, in 1742, Pope Benedict XIV issued a final prohibition which ended any further attempts at accommodation.

Unfortunately, this tragic near-sightedness in high places also meant the effective end of the China mission. The Chinese Emperor himself was mystified at the stupidity of the highest authorities in the Catholic church, and he wondered aloud how the cultivated and respected Jesuit scholars whom he knew could possibly find a home in so narrow and constricting an organization as the church. The Jesuits of the China mission must have had similar thoughts, but they obeyed the Pope's order.

Shortly after Ricci began his experiment in China, another Italian Jesuit, Robert De Nobili (1577 to 1656) arrived in South India and made some observations which were quite similar to those which had set Ricci on his path of accommodation. By 1605 De Nobili was living as a Brahman, having adopted the garb and the style of life of a Hindu holy man. He realized that if Christianity were presented simply as a European faith, it would have no chance in India. He lived apart from other Europeans (and even from his fellow Jesuits), and he began to develop a theological terminology and liturgy for Christianity which would adapt it to the ancient religious culture of India. He learned Sanskrit, the sacred language of Hinduism, and he tried to present Christianity as the perfection of everything which was good and true in Hindu thought. By 1650 there were four thousand Christians in Madura, but by the end of the century the India mission was in ruins, the victim of the same outbreak of jealousy and stupidity on the part of the other orders, and of the papacy, as the China mission at the same time. In 1742, Benedict XIV condemned the Malabar rites of India at the same time as the Chinese rites. Christianity has remained an essentially foreign faith in India up to the present day.

The flexibility which Christian faith had shown in its earliest days, in courageously emerging from its Jewish cocoon and going out to face the incredible task of converting the entire Empire, had been lost. It was not until the present century that the theory and practice of foreign missionary activity were to begin to catch up with the brilliant innovations of Ricci, De Nobili, and Schall.

8.8 REACTIONS TO THE CATHOLIC REVIVAL

8.81 Introduction

The Council of Trent had made the Catholic church into the *papal* church. The Council had put the task of reform firmly in the hands of the Popes, and the Popes had accepted the mandate and acted on it. As a result, by the end of the sixteenth century, the Popes were exerting a spiritual power greater than any which they had had since the High Middle Ages. But there was a negative side to this as well. The Catholic church was becoming a very centralized institution. Papal jurisdiction was being extended in all Catholic countries, not only at the expense of civil authority, but at the expense of the local episcopacy as well. The members of the Curia, the church's central administration, often dealt in a high-handed manner with local bishops, and the papacy pushed for the establishment of what are called *Nunciatures* or papal embassies in the capitals and some major cities of Catholic countries. These Nunciatures were staffed by papal officials whose task was to report to Rome on local conditions, and who were committed to the extension of papal power throughout all of western Europe.

8.82 Trouble in France

It was in the France of Louis XIV, who reigned as a minor from 1643, and then in his own right from 1661 to 1715, that strong opposition arose to what was regarded as papal pretension and curial meddling. In 1638 a book with the title *The Liberties of the Gallican Church* was published. The author affirmed that it was the French king and he alone who had the power to summon a council of the French church (the only one which mattered in its view!) and went on to affirm that it was legitimate for a Catholic to appeal to a council against the Pope, and that the enforcement of any papal laws in France depended on the permission and approval of the king. The two brilliant and powerful cardinals, Richelieu, who served from 1624 to 1642, and Mazarin, who served from 1643 to 1661, agreed with these policies, and their position as Secretary of State gave their opinions much weight as they did all in their power to loosen the bonds which linked the French church to Rome.

The movement continued in France, and in 1682 the so-called *Four Gallican Articles* were proclaimed in the name of the clergy of France. Two of these asserted the old doctrine of conciliarism—the teaching that the council is above the Pope and possesses highest legislative authority in the church; and two were a rejection of the claim of infallibility which Popes had been making on and off since the time of Gregory VII and his *Dictatus Papae* of 1073.

8.83 Trouble in Germany

In this period, German culture and intellectual life were strongly influenced by that of France, and a number of German bishops in the seventeenth century were annoyed by what they regarded as curial meddling. They felt that bishops should not be treated simply as proconsuls who were appointed to carry out the policies of the Curia, but that they were independent successors of the Apostles, with full power in their own dioceses.

In 1763 an auxiliary bishop of Trier, named von Hontheim, wrote a book with the title *On the State of the Church and on the Legitimate Power of the Roman Pontiff*, under the pen-name or pseudonym of "Febronius." He argued that papal authority was far more limited than the Popes of the time were willing to admit, and he urged the establishment of quite independent national churches which would express their universality, not by loyal adherence to the Pope, but by the fact that bishops from these national churches would meet periodically in general councils, which possessed ultimate authority in the church.

In 1786, when the Pope established a Nunciature in Munich, the archbishops of the major imperial cities of Cologne, Mainz, Trier, and Salzburg objected strongly to the move, fearing that the papacy was attempting to limit their authority and to take control of the internal affairs of the German church. In Austria at the same time, Joseph II, who ruled from 1780 to 1790, wanted absolute authority over the Austrian church. He suppressed a number of monasteries, and did everything in his power to break the tie which bound the church in his country to Rome. He played very much the role of the enlightened anti-clerical and did great harm to the Austrian church.

This was the period of the Enlightenment, and unfortunately churchmen had no idea of how to cope with its challenges, and often dealt with them in an inept and counterproductive way. The new ideas had come principally from England to the continent, and were mediated to Germany from France. In Germany, the leading philosophers were Leibniz (1646 to 1716) and Wolff (1679 to 1754). In the name of reason, philosophers of the Enlightenment opposed traditional authority, and often called into question the possibility and the necessity of divine revelation. They were not necessarily anti-Christian, but they usually felt that a kind of moralizing version of the faith, without dogma (binding doctrines), would be an ideal. There is much in the Enlightenment's esteem of reason which seems today to be almost touchingly naive, but it did offer a healthy critique of superstition, of the fascination with miracles, and of the exaggerated veneration of the saints. The Enlightenment showed how much medieval baggage was still being carried by the post-Tridentine church, and at the same time it offered a valuable criticism of the hierarchical world view of the Baroque period.

8.84 The Suppression of the Jesuits

As the Catholic monarchies of southern and western Europe began to turn against the papacy and to try to curb the exercise of papal jurisdiction within their territories, it was inevitable that they would turn against that order which was distinguished by a special vow of obedience to the Pope—namely the Jesuits. By 1750 there were 22,000 members of the Jesuit order worldwide. Jesuits were often in positions of influence and power, and the success of the order had given its members an esprit de corps which often looked to outsiders very much like arrogance.

But the order's position was not as strong as it seemed. Jesuit missionaries in South America had protested against the exploitation of the Indians, and in order to prevent it, they had begun another innovative experiment in Paraguay—the so-called *Reductions*. These were model villages where the Indian converts could live in peace and relative prosperity without being exploited by the European colonizers and without having to confront the challenge of European civilization for which they were not prepared. The Jesuits even developed an alphabet for writing the native language of the Indians and translated the scriptures into the native tongue, using much care to find proper words to express the biblical thought and adapting the scriptural message to the whole world view of the Indians. However, there were many in the new world who had come precisely to exploit the Indians and they resented Jesuit policy in regard to them. They spread the rumor that the order was setting up a state within a state and training vast armies of Indians who would provide a secure power base for the Jesuits, and perhaps even rise up in revolt against the colonizing powers. The accusations were absurd, but they were used as a pretext by the Portuguese Secretary of State, the Marquis de Pombal, to suppress the Jesuit order in the overseas dominions and in Portugal itself with great cruelty and brutality in 1757.

In France, the situation came to a head as a result of some unfortunate financial dealings of one of the Jesuit provincial superiors who had dabbled in West Indian trade. The affair made headlines at the time, and anti-Jesuit sentiment which had been latent since the time of the Jansenist conflict in the preceding century found a welcome outlet in this new *cause celebre*. As a result, the order was suppressed in France in 1764. During the next nine years, Portugal, France, Spain, and the Kingdom of Naples-Sicily talked darkly of schism and even threatened to attack the papal states if the Jesuits were not suppressed worldwide. On July 21, 1773, Clement signed the papal document which resulted in the suppression and, as many thought, the end of the Jesuit order.

Oddly enough, the parts of Europe where the order was never really suppressed were Protestant Prussia and Ortho-dox Russia; the absolutist monarchs reigning there had too high an esteem of the Jesuit schools within their domains to allow the promulgation of the papal document of suppression. Early in the next century the order rose from the ashes and reappeared in most of the countries of Catholic Europe, much chastened by the experience, and in many ways a very different organization from what the old Society had been.

8.9 LOOKING BACK OVER THE PERIOD

After Trent, the Catholic church in western Europe manifested great vitality for a rather brief period. Even in France, where the religious wars had delayed it, the Catholic renewal was losing momentum by the middle of the seventeenth century, and opposition to the decidedly papal character of the post-Tridentine church was growing. It is not easy to explain why the Catholic revival after Trent was of relatively short duration, but was a powerful influence for only about a century and had spent its force in less than a hundred and fifty years.

Unlike their medieval predecessors, the Popes of this pe-

riod did not crave civil or temporal power outside of the Papal
States. Consciously or not, they realized that the day for such
policy was past, and these post-Tridentine Popes were not
sacrificing their mission of spiritual leadership because they
were lured by money or power. It is true that although the
power they sought was spiritual, these Popes mimicked the
methods employed by secular powers of the time, and they
tried to centralize the administration of the church in Rome
and in the papacy. This not only caused much resentment at
the time, both in the absolutist states and in the church, but it
had harmful after-effects which have lasted almost to the
present day. But despite this fact, it is probably better to look
for an explanation of the loss of momentum in Catholic renewal after Trent more on the level of theology and religious
practice than on the level of papal policy.

Trent had never been willing or able to recognize, or to
sympathize with, the deep religious concerns of the Reformation. The Catholic response to Luther at Trent and after
was generally in the hands of skilled controversialists who re-
lied too strongly on *tradition* (understood as the customary
teaching and devotional life of the late medieval church) and
not enough on the prime source of Christian life, scripture itself. Luther was undoubtedly one-sided, but there was a profound truth in the three great exclusivities of the Lutheran
Reformation—*sola scriptura, sola gratia, sola fide*. In the attempt to combat the Reformation, the bishops at Trent and
the theologians of the post-Tridentine period developed a
Catholic religious culture in which too many of the old medieval abuses in matters such as a superstitious approach to
relics, an unhealthy fascination with the "miraculous," and
overemphasis on the cult of the saints and on private devotions could continue unabated. Furthermore, the Popes of
the seventeenth century still thought of themselves as Renaissance princes. While none of them practiced the gross im-
moralities of an Alexander VI, in their dedication to
nepotism they were his equals. They felt they could best defend the Catholic faith by making Rome the artistic and architectural capital of the world, thus transferring the
mystique of imperial Rome to the visible head of the Catholic

church. The sculpture and buildings produced by Bernini (1598 to 1680) are magnificent, but they manifest the wealth and the somewhat antiquated splendor of a papacy which had forgotten its spiritual mission. The church was not well served by these Popes whose vision was directed to the imaginary glories of the past, and it is not at all surprising that Innocent X, in 1654, showed no understanding for the achievements of Jesuit missionaries on the frontiers of Christianity in the Far East.

In general, the brevity of the Catholic revival after Trent sprang from the failure of churchmen and theologians to anchor that revival on the genuine Catholic substance of the ancient church and from their failure to see that the church against which Luther rebelled was no longer integrally Catholic. In the wake of Trent, the Catholic church showed a tendency to define itself in purely anti-Protestant terms, without realizing that this often meant a loss of genuine Catholic substance. As a result of these negative and defensive stances, the official church was still fighting the counterreformation well into the twentieth century, and in many ways this quite anachronistic struggle came to an end only at the time of the Second Vatican Council. As the eighteenth century came to an end, the church was heading for crises, external and internal, which would tax its capacities to the limit and beyond, and which would inflict upon it losses even greater than those of the Reformation era.

9

From the French Revolution
to Vatican II

The Council of Trent had entrusted the Popes with the task of carrying out its reforms, and until the end of the sixteenth century these reforming Popes did their work well. But once that century ended, the papacy reverted to its old ways, in the apparent belief that the luxury and elegance of the papal court would be a sign to the world that the Popes were truly the vicars of Christ and that the defense of the territorial integrity of the Papal States was the highest duty of the Bishop of Rome.

9.1 INTRODUCTION

Through the seventeenth and most of the eighteenth centuries, the Popes tried to reassert their control over the church in those countries (or parts of countries) which had remained Catholic. As we saw in the last chapter, their efforts did not meet with much success. During both of these centuries the papacy looked wistfully to the past and nourished the unrealistic dream of restoring the papal power and prestige of an earlier day, when all Europe was united in allegiance to the Pope. This nostalgia for the days of old blinded these Popes to the crisis that was brewing throughout Western Europe.

9.2 THE FRENCH REVOLUTION

The French Revolution was the most important event in church history since the Reformation, and it presented churchmen with problems which they were unable to master throughout the nineteenth century and well into the twentieth. For this reason it merits detailed treatment.

9.21 The Background

The church of the eighteenth century seemed to have recovered rather well from the Reformation, but its strength was illusory. Trent itself had defined Catholic Christianity in too exclusively anti-Protestant terms, and there was far too much concentration on superficial manifestations of typically Latin piety. Life in Western Europe was changing rapidly in every area of life. The middle class was growing and was becoming better educated, and this meant that the days of the absolutist monarchies were numbered. Some of the theorizing of the Enlightenment on human rights was beginning to trickle down to the lower classes, and, particularly in France, they were becoming restless under a social and economic order which kept them permanently on the lowest rung of the ladder.

Europe was on the brink of profound change, but those in control of the Catholic church were incapable of a creative response. They spent much of their time looking backward, to a golden age which they often identified with the thirteenth century, but which had never really existed. The Papal States had become an obstacle to the independence and universality of the papacy, but the Popes of the time were utterly unaware of this. They thought of their territories in central Italy as being an indispensable base for independent papal power in the spiritual sphere; but, in fact, these States involved them incessantly in internal Italian political squabbles and forced them to define their relation to the great Catholic powers in purely political terms.

Jansenism, which had been rejected on the level of theology and doctrine, was still strong among the self-styled spiritual elite in France and Italy, and was nourished by dissatisfaction with the mediocrity of much Christian life in the period. In the Latin countries and in Germany, high church offices were exclusively in the hands of the upper classes, and these offices were regarded as appropriate sinecures for the younger sons of the nobility, who often had no conception of what a good bishop should do or be. Life in the religious orders is usually a good index of the religious health of an age, and in the eighteenth century the monasteries often offered nothing more than secure mediocrity. The monks were commonly regarded as a drain on the economy, socially unproductive, and many committed Catholics felt that these monks were not of much value to the church either.

The church was torn by the question of what to do about the Jesuits. Suppressed by Clement XIV in 1763, they were carrying on a half-clandestine existence in the Russian Empire, where Catherine the Great had not allowed the promulgation of the Bull of Suppression. There were many in the church who wanted the suppression to be made permanent, but there were others who felt that the initiative and commitment which the Jesuits had shown in the late sixteenth and throughout the seventeenth centuries were precisely what the period needed. Unfortunately, when the order was reinstated, it showed little resemblance to the Society of pre-suppression days, and its most passionate opponents had little to fear. In 1775, Clement XIV died, and the new Pope, who took the name Pius VI, had no grasp whatsoever of what the times called for. Unfortunately, this was to be true, in varying degrees, of all the Popes who reigned during the next century, up to the time of Leo XIII in 1878, although his successor, Pius VII, was in some ways a rather able man.

9.22 France on the Eve of the Revolution

The French church of the mid-eighteenth century was not healthy. Churchmen felt secure in a close union of church and state, which they used to bolster their dreams of independence from Rome. The church owned about ten percent of the land in France, and this gave it enormous wealth, and, as long as the old semi-feudal order lasted, equally great power. And although loyalty to the church was still strong in most of the rural areas of the country, many members of the intellectual elite and the growing middle class despised the church. Those virtues which were highly prized by the Enlightenment, such as respect for freedom of conscience and for the rights of man, were notably absent from church life. Furthermore, the clergy were divided among themselves. The higher clergy (the bishops and abbots) were named by the king, and came exclusively from the nobility. The parish priests came mainly from the lower echelons of the middle class, and they were ready for reform in the command structures of the church.

9.23 The Initial Phase

In the summer of 1789, the Estates General, a consultative body with a majority of higher clergy and members of the nobility, met to try to cope with growing unrest in the country. Initially, the members of the nobility seemed to feel that they could use popular unrest and the financial embarrassment of the regime to secure some power for themselves but they misjudged the situation and did not realize that control of the revolt was soon to pass from their hands to those of the middle and lower classes. Taxes on these latter groups had become more oppressive than ever, and they were being used to support the upper classes in luxury. This, of course, had been true for a long time, but by the year 1789 the Enlightenment's ideals of freedom and equality had become more generally known and were gripping the imagination of even the poor. The situation in France was so unstable that even the nobility realized that their own privileges would be threatened if they did nothing, and they acquiesced in the decision of the delegates of the middle classes to turn the Estates General into a Constitutive Assembly which would have the task of proposing and legislating fundamental reforms in government and in the economic life of the country.

Since the French church owned about ten percent of the land in the country, it could not long avoid the attention of the Constitutive Assembly. The members of the middle class, who were in control of the latter body at this point, were by no means anti-Christian, but they felt that the church was in need of reform, and they were convinced that many of the institutions of the French church were not in tune with the spirit of the times. In this they were correct. However, it was the pressing need of money which led the Constitutive Assembly to seize the property of the church late in 1789 and to decree in the following year the suppression of all religious orders which were not engaged in teaching or in hospital work.

Gallicanism, that centuries-old tendency to think of the French church as a national institution with only the most tenuous links with Rome, had led most Catholics in France to accept governmental control of the church as a matter of course. And, therefore, it seemed natural enough when the Assembly, on July 12, 1790, passed a law called the *Civil Constitution of the Clergy*. This law specified that the government was to pay the salaries of the priests (on condition that the latter made no charge for the administration of the sacraments). It further provided that pastors should be chosen by the members of the parish and that bishops should be chosen by electors who were themselves chosen by the populace at large. It was further specified that no papal approval would be needed for the newly elected bishops to exercise their powers. It is interesting to note that the Constitution was called *Civil*, because those who proposed it felt that it did not touch religious or spiritual matters directly, but was concerned only with the relations of the church and churchmen to civil society.

On December 26, 1790 a new law was passed which demanded that all members of the clergy take an oath to support the king and the Civil Constitution of the Clergy; if they refused, they were to be deprived of their offices. To the surprise of almost everyone, about half of the parish priests and almost all of the bishops refused to take the oath. From this moment on, for almost ten years, the clergy in France was to be divided into two, often mutually hostile, competing groups: those who had taken the oath and were called the *con-*

stitutional clergy and those who refused the oath and were called the *réfractaires*.

Pius VI had been very unhappy with the Civil Constitution of the Clergy, but he had kept his feelings to himself in order not to make things more difficult for the king. But in the face of incipient schism in the French church, in May 1791 he condemned the Civil Constitution, and, most unfortunately, he condemned at the same time another document which had been issued by the Constitutive Assembly—the *Declaration of the Rights of Man*. This confusion of the proper independence of the church in its own sphere with the suppression of enlightened ideas about freedom of conscience was to do enormous harm to the French church and to the Catholic cause throughout Europe during much of the nineteenth century, because it confused loyalty to the Catholic church with loyalty to the *ancien régime*.

9.24 The Revolution and the Reign of Terror

From about October 1791 control of the Assembly passed into more radical hands, and real persecution of the *réfractaires* began. Then, on August 10, 1792, the mob took control, in what can really be called a second revolution. At this point it became clear how alienated the church had become from the poorer classes in the cities, and how great a capital of hatred had been accumulating against the church for centuries. Before the end of the year all of the religious orders were suppressed and thirty thousand of the clergy who had refused to take the oath of loyalty to the Civil Constitution were deported. But even the so-called "constitutional clergy" (those who had taken the oath) were not spared, and their churches were closed in the wave of de-Christianization which swept the country during the next two years. At the very time that the churches were closed to Catholics, in a kind of tragi-comic parody of man's insatiable need for religious absolutes, the "Goddess Reason" was worshiped in some church buildings when the altars had been removed.

By 1795 the Revolution itself had devoured some of its

more radical elements and the pretentious silliness of the religion of reason was, if not abandoned, at least less evident in public life. Freedom of worship was allowed, but the French church was in a state of utter confusion. Most of the clergy who remained were "constitutional," but they were not generally respected or accepted by Catholics. Many of the réfractaires had been deported, but those who remained would have nothing to do with their brethren who had taken the oath to support the Civil Constitution. Furthermore, Catholics were, in general, suspected of opposing the Revolution, and because the country had been busy for several years both in exporting the Revolution and in defending it against foreign assault, opposition was equated with treason. In 1797 the government demanded that all civil officials as well as the clergy take an oath of hatred against the king. The majority of the clergy refused, on the grounds that it was blasphemy to call upon God to witness such an act. Relations between the church and the government remained poor, and many priests were imprisoned or deported, but there was no renewal of the worst excesses of the reign of terror. From about 1797 on, the French church began to recover very slowly from the shock. The shortage of respected priests had led some of the laity to take responsibility for their own faith and that of others, and some of them began to band together in groups which would become new religious orders when the times allowed it.

9.25 Exporting the Revolution

The French Revolution was never a purely French phenomenon which was then imposed on France's unwilling neighbors by force of arms. It was an inevitable consequence of factors in European history which had been fermenting for centuries. When it broke out in France, there were groups in the neighboring lands who were prepared to welcome it, particularly in Switzerland, Holland, and north Italy. (Holland's situation was unique, because here it was precisely the Catholics who welcomed the Revolution: to them it meant relief from the oppression of the Protestant ruling class and the freedom to practice their faith in peace.)

Of course, the welcome accorded the Revolution varied from country to country. In Italy there were many progressive Catholics who welcomed it, because, among other reasons, they thought it would put an end to the hopelessly backward economic and political system in vigor in the Papal States, which they felt to be a scandal. These progressive Catholics were annoyed at the arch-conservatism of the Popes and at their alliance with the most reactionary forces of the time. However, when the Revolution in France turned against the church, as it did in 1793–1794 and again, though not as brutally, in 1797, this tended to undermine the position of these Italian progressives. As we will see, the young general, Napoleon, who was leading the French revolutionary armies in north Italy at the time, saw this, and it may have been the occasion of an important insight on his part.

9.26 The Papacy

Pius VI was unfortunately unable to distinguish the anti-clerical and anti-Christian excesses of the more radical Jacobins from the Enlightenment's esteem for freedom and human rights, and he roundly condemned both. There was much sympathy for the Revolution in the Papal States, and when the young general, Napoleon Bonaparte, appeared there at the head of a French revolutionary army in 1796 he was greeted by many as a liberator. The French army occupied part of the Papal States, and the Treaty of Tolentino in 1797 gave the best part of the papal territories to France. But to many Italians, the French were nothing more than a foreign army of occupation, and in 1797 revolt flared against the French in some parts of the Papal States. Urged on by anti-clerical sympathizers in Rome, the French occupied the rest of the Papal States and declared a "Roman Republic." In 1798 Pius VI asked the crowned heads of Europe for help and Napoleon reacted by having the Pope deported to France in 1799, where he died later that same year.

The conclave to elect a new Pope was held in Venice in 1799, because that part of Italy was under Austrian control and freedom from interference by revolutionary forces could be guaranteed. The new Pope took the name Pius VII, and turned out to be one of the more capable Popes of the period. He was a forceful personality—in some ways even forward-looking—and he was able to return to Rome and take up residence there in August of 1800.

As the revolution ran its course, alternating between mindless violence and sporadic returns to relative sanity, the higher clergy longed for the return of the old regime and the reassertion of strong central authority. What they got was not a king but a military dictatorship under Napoleon, who was quite willing to make deals with churchmen if they could help him use the institutional church as a tool of imperial policy, and who was more than willing to humiliate the Pope in the process.

9.27 The Concordat with Napoleon

Since November 1799 Napoleon had been effectively dictator in France and it was clear that he wanted to resolve the problem of the relationship of the church and state there. His motives were clear: he was enough of a realist to see that Christianity could not be destroyed in France (at least at that moment in history), and he felt that peace with the church would further his European ambitions. Of course the problems which had to be solved were enormous. The clergy were still divided into two groups which wanted nothing to do with each other. The majority of the non-constitutional bishops were living in exile, and the constitutional bishops and their priests were, by and large, not accepted by the Catholic populace.

In 1800 Napoleon's representatives and those of the Pope negotiated a *Concordat*—that is, a treaty between France and the papacy which regulated the position of the church in France and specified the rights and duties of the Pope in regard to the French clergy. The Concordat was an interesting compromise: it affirmed that Catholicism was the religion of the majority of Frenchmen; it noted the agreement of both signatories that the bishops who had held power during the ancien régime would all hand in their resignations; and, finally, it specified the method of choosing the bishops and of investing them with authority.

The Concordat was a brilliant stroke on Napoleon's part, but he realized that it would not make him popular with the more radically anti-clerical groups. Largely as a sop to the latter, he added, on his own authority and without papal consent, seventy-seven "Organic Articles" to the Concordat, which placed the French church more securely under the thumb of the government. The bishops were to be controlled by a new "ministry of cult," and their communication with each other and with Rome was severely circumscribed. However, they were given total authority over their priests. The Pope protested in vain against what he regarded as a one-sided alteration of the Concordat.

The Concordat regularized the position of the church in France but it left churchmen faced with a monumental task of reconstruction. There was a great shortage of priests, and although the government undertook to pay their salaries, the seminaries and monasteries had all been suppressed and there were no funds available to finance institutions for the training of the clergy. Nevertheless revival began slowly. Although in 1804 the government suppressed those religious orders which it felt made no contribution to public welfare, in general, government officials were much less hostile than they had been immediately after the Revolution, and they actually encouraged the foundation of some new orders of women who were engaged in teaching or nursing. Little by little a religious revival took shape. New catechetical methods were developed to train young people, and parish missions were held to make up for the years when people had been without religious instruction and services and when de-christianization had gone very far. The revival had some success with the intellectuals, and Chateaubriand's remarkable work *The Genius of Christianity* was symbolic of this success (and of its limitations).

9.28 The Secularization in Germany

The great *secularization* of 1803 was one of the most important events in the history of the Catholic church in Germany, but it is appropriate to handle it here because it was an immediate consequence of the French Revolution. Napoleon's victory over the forces of the moribund Holy Roman Empire was sealed in the Treaty of Lunéville in 1803. This treaty gave all of Germany west of the Rhine to France, and resulted in the immediate secularization of all properties of the church in that region. In addition, the treaty specified that those German princes who had lost territories in that area would be compensated by receiving lands from other parts of the Empire. It was obvious to everyone that these lands would be taken from those owned by the church and by the religious orders.

In general it is probably fair to say that this section of the Treaty of Lunéville was not motivated by hatred of Christianity or of the church. There was a general feeling on the part of many serious Catholics that the church had grown too wealthy and that the wealth in its hands was unproductive and sometimes a scandal. Many felt that it would be good for the church to be divested of its wealth and property, so that it might come to resemble more closely the Lord to whom it was paying lip service. However, it was without doubt the need to secure the adherence to the Treaty of those princes who had lost their territories west of the Rhine which really motivated the great secularization.

The imperial electors appointed a commission (the Reichsdeputation) which was given the task of working out the details of compensatory land grants. The agreement which they reached (the Reichsdeputationshauptschluss—for obvious reasons we will refer to it as the *Decree of the Imperial Electors*) went far beyond what many had envisioned at the time of the Treaty of Lunéville. It provided for the seizure of virtually all of the property of the prince bishops, all monasteries, and all church buildings and institutions which derived their income from foundations—that is, land and property set aside for their support.

The Decree of the Imperial Electors brought the immediate closing of eighteen Catholic universities and this struck a blow at Catholic culture and intellectual life from which the church in Germany recovered only after many years. In all areas, church life was almost paralyzed by this removal, at one stroke, of all means of support. However, as we will see in the next section, the church did recover, and in the long run the end of the old and comfortably secured existence worked to the benefit of church life in Germany by making room for the creative involvement of the laity. One of the conditions of the agreement was that in return for the church's acceptance of the secularization of its lands (church authorities really had no choice, and no one asked them!) the Empire (that is, the Holy Roman Empire which itself had only three years left) would undertake to pay the salaries of the priests. In one form or another this has continued to be the case. Through the entire period of Hitler's rule and up to the present day, Catholic priests in Germany have been paid through an indirect subsidy which is granted to the church by the government and which is collected in the form of a surcharge on the income tax.

9.3 FROM THE CONGRESS OF VIENNA TO THE EVE OF VATICAN I

When the crowned heads of Europe met in Vienna in 1815, after the Napoleonic wars, their one purpose was to restore the old order and to banish the specter of revolution. Metternich, the Austrian foreign minister, had worked out a plan of restoration which seemed promising, but which was destined to last for little more than thirty years. The period from 1815 to 1830 (and sometimes even up to 1848) is often referred to as the *Restoration*—a term which applies quite well to the situation in France and in the Papal States, but which is of little use elsewhere; particularly for the church, the point of departure in 1815 was quite different in each country.

In France and in Italy, the authorities cultivated the illusion that they could restore the old order unchanged. They thought of the French Revolution as an isolated outbreak of a disease which could be cured by proper (if painful) treatment, and they failed to see that the Revolution was a symptom of a changed condition of the body, which could in no real sense of the word be "treated," but was rather a new situation to which they would have to adapt. They did not understand that the Revolution was the inevitable consequence of Europe's coming-of-age, and that the philosophy and political theory of the Enlightenment necessarily led to the events of 1789.

9.31 Restoration in France

It was obvious, in 1815, that French Catholics wanted nothing to do with the Revolution and its ideals and values. They had suffered too much under the Reign of Terror, and they were disillusioned by Napoleon's attempt to use the church for purely political purposes. As a result, they suspected even those who paid only lip-service to the ideals of the Revolution. They were ready for the restoration of the old order, and, to some extent, that is what they got. Under the restored Bourbon monarchy, Catholicism became the state religion again, and freedom of religion was curtailed. The union of throne and altar was restored, but there were two significant differences. First, many of the intellectuals, the middle class, and most of the urban lower classes had been won to the ideals of the Revolution, and they were totally out of sympathy with the monarchy and the church. Second, and of greater importance for the church at large, it became evident that Gallicanism had been a casualty of the Revolution— at least seriously wounded, if by no means dead. Events since 1789 had taught the French bishops that they could never again rely on a French government for support in their quest for independence from Rome. In fact, many of them were beginning to see that it was only a strong link with Rome that could give them support against the unpredictable incursions of the governmental bureaucracy into church life.

The first expression of this new feeling toward Rome can be found in the work of the layman, Joseph de Maistre, whose essay *On the Pope* was the opening salvo in the campaign of French ultramontanism (for the moment, think of this word as meaning "the position of those who support a strong papacy"). De Maistre was a passionate supporter of the monarchy, and argued that it was the form of government intended by God for both church and state. Furthermore, the Pope was destined by God to be the sovereign lord of all earthly monarchs, and his authority was guaranteed by the divine gift of infallibility—protection from error in all of his utterances. (As we will see, the prudent limitations of papal infallibility which were decreed by the First Vatican Council dealt a severe blow to the hopes of the exaggerated ultramontanes who were the intellectual heirs of de Maistre.)

When Charles X became king in 1824, the union of throne and altar became stifling, and it should have been obvious to one and all that this anachronistic rejection of the positive values of the Revolution could not continue. In 1830 the *July Revolution* put an end to Charles' reign, and replaced him with a king more open to the modern world. At the same time, it became clear that the very group which would be most influential in society—the middle class—had been disgusted with the attempts of the king and his Catholic supporters to restore the *ancien régime*, and were, in fact, quite estranged from the church.

At this juncture, a remarkable man appeared—the priest, Robert de Lamennais—and he offered French Catholics a radically new interpretation of the problems and possibilities of their church. Lamennais urged Catholics to accept the positive ideals of the Revolution, including freedom of conscience and the separation of church and state, and he argued that it was precisely in a society based on such ideals that the church had the best chance to preach its message in a manner which the modern world could appreciate and accept. But at the same time, he argued that it was only when the local church was firmly linked to the papacy and drew from it inspiration and life that the church could be truly independent and could fulfill its role in society.

Lamennais was frankly ultramontane, but in a way very different from de Maistre. For the latter, it was the monarchical principle which justified both the divine right of kings and the infallibility of the Pope. Lamennais, on the other hand, envisaged the alliance of the Pope with a free people who accepted the Revolution's Declaration of the Rights of Man. In 1830, he and a number of liberal Catholic friends began the publication of a journal called *L'Avenir* (The Future), in which these ideas were defended forcefully and eloquently.

But Lamennais and his friends were too forward-looking for the arch-conservatives who formed the overwhelming majority of the French episcopacy. These bishops forbade Catholics to read the journal and prohibited its publication. Lamennais and his friends appealed to the Pope, but they should have known that their cause was hopeless. Gregory XVI was so reactionary that, in comparison, the French bishops looked rather liberal, and in 1832 he issued the encyclical *Mirari Vos* which condemned *L'Avenir* and the whole liberal Catholic movement. Lamennais was almost a century ahead of his time, and, after him, "official" Catholicism in France retreated into a royalist, anti-republican, pietistic ghetto, which led to the defection from the church of almost two-thirds of the population by the time of the Second World War.

With the suppression of liberal Catholicism, the energies of the Catholic elite turned inward, but in a quite productive way. In 1833, some of those who had been associated with *L'Avenir* joined with others and began to live according to the Benedictine rule at the abbey of Solesmes, which had been deserted since the time of the Revolution. The abbey quickly became the center of a new liturgical movement which emphasized the mystical union of Christians with the church—a union which was nourished by living the mysteries of the life, death, and resurrection of Christ in the liturgical ceremonies of the year. The abbey of Solesmes became a center of research into the sources of the ancient *Gregorian Chant*, and the careful and critical work of the monks led to a restoration of these stately cadences in the churches of France, and, as the movement spread, in other parts of Europe.

9.32 Restoration in Italy

In Italy, the three Popes of the restoration period were good men, but in varying degrees they were out of contact with the world of their own day, and their utterances betray a kind of petulant and ill-tempered rejection of the modern world which, with few exceptions, would plague the papacy until recent times.

However, although Pius VII was very conservative, he was intelligent, and quite aware of the events of the day. He reigned until 1823, and he pursued a deliberate policy of strengthening the ties which bound the local churches to Rome, and thereby increasing the authority of the Pope and the Curia. The new climate of opinion in Europe after 1815 helped him in his efforts. Even those circles which had no use for the Restoration had felt a great deal of sympathy for Pius VI, who had been dragged off to France as an old man and had died there, and the years of confusion after the Revolution had left most Europeans with a new esteem for law and order.

When Pius VII died in 1823 he was succeeded by Leo XII—a good man with genuinely religious concerns, but hopelessly out of touch with the political realities of his day, and totally committed to the union of throne and altar as the final solution of all problems of church and state. His reign was brief, as was that of his successor, Pius VIII.

The situation of the church in Italy throughout the nineteenth century (and well into the twentieth) was complicated by the fact that Italy had never become a nation-state. Soon after the Congress of Vienna it became clear that sentiment was growing in favor of national union, and this immediately raised the question of what to do about the Papal States, which occupied the central third of the peninsula. The situation was further complicated (or rather exacerbated) by the fact that the papal regime was not only undemocratic, but backward in the extreme. (Gregory XVI would not allow the introduction either of gas lighting or of the railroad lines into the Papal States!)

In 1831 Italian nationalists rose in revolt in Bologna (part of the Papal States). Even though the revolt failed because of a lack of popular support, it did draw the attention of all of Europe to the backwardness of the administration and to the police-state tactics of the papal commissars. Metternich himself (the Austrian foreign minister, and an intelligent conservative) urged the Pope to modernize the administration and to allow the inhabitants some control over their lives. Apart from a few ineffectual gestures, Gregory XVI did nothing, and when revolt flared in 1832, it was put down with a great show of force. After 1843 the revolts were constant, and they were just as constantly suppressed, often with the support of Austrian troops, and with a brutality which embarrassed Catholics throughout Europe.

With this as a background, it is easy to see why the leadership of the Italian national revival, the *Risorgimento*, was firmly in the hands of anti-clericals well into the 1840's. What is surprising is that even before the death of Gregory XVI, some Italians were beginning to think of Catholicism and of the papacy as Italian national treasures, and that they were beginning to wonder if it might not be possible to build a new Italy, united in loyalty to the church and to the Pope. The election of Pius IX in 1846 and his apparent initial sympathy for these ideas led some to propose a confederation of Italian states under the presidency of the Pope. They were rudely disillusioned in 1848, and the virulent anti-clericalism which has never quite disappeared from Italian public life has been the enduring legacy of their disillusionment.

9.33 Reconstruction in Germany

In Germany the church had been stripped of virtually all of its lands and universities at the time of the *Secularization*— that is, the confiscation of ecclesiastical property which followed on Napoleon's victories and which was itself followed, three years later, by the demise of the Holy Roman Empire. Divested of its lands and property, the church initially seemed crippled, but as the years passed, reconstruction began and the German church found that it had an unsuspected vitality.

Some more perceptive minds began to realize that the secularization had been a blessing in disguise.

After the Congress of Vienna, Germany was still not a nation-state, but rather a loose confederation of relatively independent principalities and free cities, known as the *German League*. Several factors worked together to strengthen the hold of the papacy on the church in this German League. First, the kings and chancellors of the various states preferred to deal with the Pope, who lived some distance away and who had little or no power to interfere in what they regarded as their internal affairs. And, second, the papacy itself had had enough of the independence of German churchmen and theologians ever since the Reformation. As far as the Pope was concerned, the division of the church into small local units which had little contact with each other was desirable. Therefore, the Curia entered into concordats (contractual arrangements) with the various German states, which regulated the position of the church within each and which recognized the rights of Pope and Curia to exercise a certain control over church affairs there.

In Germany, the style of the nineteenth century was *Romanticism*—in music, in literature, and in church life. The excesses of the French Revolution had led many to think of rationalism as intellectually and morally bankrupt. For the Romantic movement, reason was a bit suspect, and mystery had been rehabilitated. Whatever the Enlightenment despised, Romanticism admired, and this led to a new esteem for the medieval period, and to a wistful longing for that time when European Christendom professed the same faith. In many respects, the Romantic period showed important "Catholicizing" tendencies. Not only Catholics, but Protestants as well, moved away from the individualism of the Enlightenment (and the Reformation), and rediscovered the role of the church as community, and of tradition as this community's living link with the past.

The Romantic revival in the Catholic church in Germany received powerful impulses from the so-called *Circles*—groups of committed Catholics who met regularly for discussion and mutual encouragement, and who understood that

Christian existence was more than obedience to a moral code, or acceptance of an abstract dogmatic system. They understood Christian existence as a new kind of *life*, and they wanted to become more aware of this life, and to savor the mystery of its growth and development. The movement had begun just after 1780, but it peaked in the Circle around Hofbauer, after 1810, and around Sailer in the same period. These Circles (with the exception of Hofbauer's) were ecumenical; Protestants were drawn into Romanticism's admiration of the medieval period, and many well-known Protestants converted to Catholicism at the time.

Romanticism's esteem for the "organic," for the vital principle in things, for life, together with a certain latent anti-intellectualism, sometimes led to a vague and gushy piety, and Romanticism itself was based on a picture of the medieval world which was highly idealized. But in many ways, the Romantic movement prepared the way for a new understanding of *church* later in the nineteenth century, and for the liturgical movement in the twentieth century.

At this same time, the Catholic faculties in the German universities set a new course in theology. They felt that the time had come to break with the sterile scholasticism which had been in vogue since Trent. Men like Hermes and Günther felt that the scholastic (and originally Greek) notion of immutable truth, which inhabits its own domain above the world and is immune to the changes of time and history, was unreal. They were impressed by the philosophy of Kant and by the earliest stirrings of German Idealism (which would issue in the work of Fichte, Schelling, and Hegel); and they decided to reopen the question of the relation of reason to the mysteries of the faith on this new basis.

The Catholic theologians at Tübingen gave scholarly and systematic expression to Romanticism's love of the past and their interest in history led them to interpret the church of their day as the product of organic development. They turned away from the juridical categories which had been used to understand the meaning of the church from the time of Bellarmine, and they rediscovered Paul's image of church as the body of Christ and as an organism in and through which the living Christ is present throughout time. This led to a strong emphasis on ecclesiology (the theology of the *church*)—a theme already evident in the work of Sailer (1751–1832), but one which reached full development in the work of Möhler at Tübingen around the middle of the nineteenth century.

Developments in the church in Germany were decisively affected by a dispute which broke out in Cologne, between the Prussian government and the bishop, Droste-Vischering. The dispute was kindled by Protestant resentment at the church's way of dealing with mixed marriages (between Protestant and Catholic), and particularly with the church's demand that the Protestant party promise to have all children brought up as Catholics. In the early 1830's it seemed as though a solution might be negotiated. But then the government stiffened its position and demanded that the bishops send all of their correspondence with Rome through the Prussian censor in Berlin. The bishop of Cologne refused, and was put under house arrest in 1837. The dispute was not resolved until 1841, with the accession of a new Kaiser, Friedrich Wilhelm IV, whose affinities with the Romantic movement made him much more sympathetic to the Catholic cause. The Cologne Dispute is important, because it did more than anything else to make ultramontanism respectable in Germany. Many German bishops began to see that the link with Rome was the only way of insuring that church questions would not be decided by the Prussian bureaucracy.

9.34 England

At the time of the French Revolution and the Reign of Terror, almost five thousand French priests sought and found refuge in England (and actually received regular financial support from the English government!). The presence of these priests did much to rehabilitate Catholicism in the eyes of many Englishmen, and in the early nineteenth century a number of the English Catholic institutions which had moved to France at the time of the brutal persecutions during the English Reformation were able to return quietly to the mother country.

England prided itself in this period on being a modern, liberal state—a constitutional monarchy—and the anti-Catholic legislation which had been on the books since the Elizabethan Settlement was something of an embarrassment. Serious attempts to bring about Catholic emancipation (that is, the removal of all laws which prevented Catholics from voting or from being elected to public office) had been made by an English Prime Minister as early as 1800, but it was actually Daniel O'Connell's *Catholic Association* in Ireland which finally tipped the scales by forcing the English government to recognize him as an elected member of Parliament. In 1829, Catholics were granted emancipation throughout the British Isles.

In the 1830's a movement began in England which was to have important effects, not only on the Catholic church in England, but on the ultramontane movement, and on the triumph of ultramontanism in 1870. Some priests and bishops of the Church of England (they belonged to the so-called *High Church*) began to call for a church which was more Catholic and less Reformed. A number of these priests were associated with the University of Oxford, and the movement came to be called *The Oxford Movement*. The Anglican priest, John Henry Newman, was the most eloquent of their number, and during the 1830's he wrote a number of essays ("Tracts") defending his point of view. The bishops of the Church of England (the state church since the time of the Elizabethan Settlement) were worried by this trend and tried to curb the activity of these "Tractarians."

Newman was very disappointed at the cautious and rather negative attitude of the Anglican bishops, and then two things happened which led him to break with his own church. First, his historical studies of the christological heresies of the early church forced him to raise the question of what heresy really was and what the remedies against it might be. The attempt to answer these questions led him to affirm the teaching authority of the church, divinely protected from error, and centered in the Bishop of Rome. The second thing that led Newman to break with his church was the fact that in 1841 the Anglican church had joined the Prussian Lutherans in co-founding the Diocese of Jerusalem; and by this time Newman had lost all confidence in a church that could make common cause with the Lutheran Reformation.

In 1845 Newman was converted to Roman Catholicism, and in 1850 and 1851 there was a wave of conversions of leading figures of the Church of England. Most notable among them was Manning. He quickly took a leading position in the Catholic hierarchy (which had been restored only in 1850) and his strong ultramontane sympathies passed into the tradition of English Catholicism. Pius IX made him Archbishop of Westminster in 1860, simply imposing him on the English hierarchy, without giving them any say in the matter. Manning was able to provide invaluable support for the ultramontane cause by furthering the careers of those who were supporters of the movement.

9.35 The Church in the United States

At the time of the American Revolution, Catholics made up a tiny minority of the population: about twenty-five thousand out of approximately four million. But they did have one advantage which was enjoyed by almost no other Catholics in the world: they had freedom to practice their religion, not only in the sense that there was no anti-Catholic legislation to cope with, but in the more important sense that the American principle of the separation of church and state spared them the stifling embrace of a "Catholic" monarch and his meddling bureaucracy—still very much a reality in Spain, Austria, and to some degree in France.

At the time of the Revolution, the affairs of the church in the former British colonies were being administered by a papal representative in England. Since the newly independent colonies were not likely to accept such an arrangement, Rome appointed the former Jesuit, John Carroll (1735–1815), as Apostolic Administrator, and put him in charge of the American mission. Carroll persuaded the Curia that he would have the authority needed to cope with conditions in the new country only if he were consecrated bishop; Rome agreed, and he was consecrated in 1789.

Despite a drastic shortage of priests, the church prospered, and by 1815 there were more than a hundred and fifty thousand Catholics. There were problems, of course, and one of them was connected with that very separation of church and state which was otherwise so helpful. In the eyes of the law, religion in the United States was a private affair, and the law did not provide for church ownership of property as such. This led to the practice of constituting the laymen of the parish as a corporation, in which the ownership of church buildings and land were vested. From about 1780 to 1830 this led to a number of disputes, as the lay trustees of individual parishes claimed the right to choose their priests and to mediate disputes between the bishop and various dissident pastors—a kind of laicized version, in miniature, of Gallicanism and Josephinism. One of the principal reasons for which Carroll had sought consecration as bishop in 1789 was to be able to cope with this *lay trusteeism*. It was finally laid to rest about 1830, when laws were passed in a number of states which enabled the bishop of each diocese to be the legal owner of all of the property of the diocese.

America remained mission territory during much of the nineteenth century, and in the early years French priests and bishops (some of whom had left France at the time of the Revolution, and others of whom had been working in the French colony of Louisiana, which became part of the United States in 1803) were the mainstay of the American clergy. They were dedicated men, but sometimes their lack of a firm hold on the language gave the church a foreign, un-American look, which made some Protestants suspicious. The Irish potato famine of the 1840's brought many Irish immigrants to America, and from that time on, Irish priests assumed a more and more important role in the American church. They brought with them an excellent command of the English language (considerably better than that of most of the English-speaking population of the United States!), as well as boundless energy. They soon were providing the majority of American bishops, and in many dioceses of the western United

States the link with Ireland is indispensable even today. In the 1830's and 1840's, Protestant bigotry became a threat to life and limb for Catholics in some areas and there were serious outbreaks of anti-Catholic violence. (To some degree these had economic, rather than religious grounds—the Protestant working class in many of the cities felt threatened by the arrival of poor Catholic immigrants who would work for less.) In this somewhat hostile environment, Catholics found in their faith the factor which preserved their identity and served as a link between the old country and the new.

Because the public schools in the United States were largely under Protestant control, the Catholic bishops decided to build their own school system, and these parochial (parish) schools proved to be an indispensable help in providing basic instruction and in preserving the faith of the Catholic masses. However, the concentration on basics in education left little energy for the development of real scholarship and for the emergence of an intellectual elite—problems which remain to the present day. Furthermore, the bigotry which the immigrants met in many areas led many Catholics to retreat into something of a cultural ghetto, in which they remained until after the Second World War. However, the overall record of the church in America has been remarkable and no group of Catholics in the world has shown greater loyalty to the church or greater willingness to make enormous sacrifices to foster and preserve the faith than have the Catholics of the United States. In doing so, they have shown how beneficial to Catholic life the principle of the separation of church and state can be.

9.36 The Reign of Pius IX up to the Revolution of 1848

In Europe, change was in the air. In 1848 Metternich's grand plan for the restoration of the old order in Europe collapsed, and revolution broke out in a number of places on the continent. In France, which had already had its revolution in the years after 1789, and which had then replaced one king with another in the so-called July Revolution of 1830, the revolution of 1848 flared up briefly, but after three years of revolutionary rhetoric the restoration of the monarchy (under an emperor) in 1851 brought back the privileges, if not the power of the church. On the surface, at least, restoration continued and this "Second Empire" did nothing to disturb the class system and the gross inequities in the distribution of wealth which lived on behind the facade of "liberty, equality, and fraternity."

In Italy, on the other hand, the revolution of 1848 was far more important, because it linked the demand for economic and social reform with the growing desire of Italians to form their own national state. In the beginning of the movement it looked for a time as though all Italy might unite under the Pope as both spiritual and political leader, to throw off the yoke of Austrian domination in the northern part of the country. As long as the *Risorgimento*, the revival of Italian national consciousness, could be thought of in medieval terms as the assertion of papal power against the Empire (and Austria was all that was left of the medieval Holy Roman Empire!) Pope Pius IX played footsie with the movement and was, for a brief moment, the darling of Italian patriots. But as soon as these same patriots showed that they had learned the lessons of the French Revolution and demanded both respect for civil rights and a republican constitution even in the Papal States, the Pope, as we have seen, turned against them. For three critical decades of the nineteenth century, the Catholic church was to be ruled by a man of undoubted piety who was totally incapable of understanding the great issues of the day and whose only policy was to retreat to the citadel and brood on the evils of democracy and modernity.

Pius IX was less obviously but no less deeply estranged from the modern world than his predecessor, Gregory XVI. And yet, the image which the Catholic church has had of itself, as well as the picture which it has projected to the non-Catholic world from the mid-nineteenth century to the present, has been largely determined by developments in the church of his time—developments which he sometimes initiated and at other times adroitly managed. At the very moment at which democratic movements were far advanced in some European countries and were beginning to stir in all of the others, the Catholic church turned against the tide, and created a kind of papal absolutism which, paradoxically, rested on a broad consensus of the worldwide church.

This seeming paradox is easily explained if we see it as a late and continuing reaction to the French Revolution. This also explains why the trend toward papal absolutism was so much stronger in France than in Germany. In France and in those lands to which the Revolution was even temporarily exported, churchmen quickly learned how vulnerable they were to the new popular regimes which rapidly became both anti-clerical and anti-Christian. They realized that their only support was a strong papacy, to which all Catholics gave their unquestioning loyalty, and which enjoyed a prestige that was not without effect, even on the non-Catholic states of Europe and the Americas. Their thinking was a mixture of common sense and old-fashioned triumphalism.

We have already seen that the autocratic administration of the Papal States had led to repeated uprisings between 1831 and 1846, which were brutally suppressed, usually with the help of Austrian troops. More than anything else, this made most of the leaders of the Risorgimento into enemies of the church. However, even in the reign of Gregory XVI, there were a few literary men and philosophers who thought of Italian national unity in terms of a confederation over which the Pope would preside.

When Pius IX was elected, one of his first acts was to free the political prisoners who had been jailed during the various revolts of the preceding decade. Italian patriots interpreted this as a sign that the Pope would give his blessing to a war of liberation against the Austrians who controlled much of the north (apart from Piedmont) and against the Bourbon monarchy in Sicily. In the Papal States themselves, the situation was very unstable, because the liberals there were afraid of an Austrian takeover of the papal territories, which would effectively divide Italian freedom fighters in the north from those in the south. At this juncture, Pius IX gave a speech in Rome in which he lamented the outbreak of hostilities. Italians did not seem to note the substance of the address, but heard only his final words: "Almighty God, bless Italy, and preserve its most precious gift, the faith," and from this they concluded, somewhat irrationally, that the Pope was ready to lead them in a holy war against Austria.

Of course the Pope was ready to do nothing of the kind, and should have chosen his words with greater care. Austria was about ninety-five percent Catholic, and Austrian troops had been protecting what Pius' predecessor regarded as papal interests since the 1830's. Furthermore, the Pope was aware that his office was supranational, and that the loss in prestige would be incalculable if he were to support the national interests of Italy against those of another country. Unfortunately, he did not draw the obvious conclusions in regard to his sovereignty over the Papal States. But some of the Italian patriots did, and they began to suggest that if the Pope wanted to be international rather than Italian, then he should have the decency to let the Papal States take their place in a united Italy.

9.37 The Revolution of 1848

In any case, the liberals and patriots were disillusioned by Pius IX. Unfortunately, one of their more radical members chose to express his disillusionment by murdering the Prime Minister of the Papal States on November 15, 1848. The Pope thought that revolution was around the corner, and fled to Gaeta, near Naples, while the cardinal whom he had appointed as his Secretary of State put down the rebellion in the Papal States with the help of Austrian troops. Pius finally returned to Rome in 1850, an implacable foe of the revolution and Risorgimento, and hated and despised by most Italian patriots, who regarded him as no better than a traitor to the cause of a united Italy. For the rest of his reign, Pius had to bear the brunt of their hatred, and by the end of 1870 the Papal States were taken from him—a loss which was finally accepted by another Pope some fifty-nine years later.

The Italian kingdom of Piedmont, in the north, was a progressive state, a constitutional monarchy since 1848, and had the political power which most Italians saw as the key to their liberation from Austria in the north and from the Bourbons in Sicily. Aided and abetted by Pius IX's reactionary policies in the Papal States, anti-clericalism grew in Piedmont, and in 1855 all monasteries were suppressed and all religious houses, whose members were not immediately involved in hospital work or in teaching, were closed. The Pope, of course, excommunicated everyone connected with the take-over, but these "spiritual" weapons had lost their effectiveness; those who were excommunicated despised the papacy and no longer placed any value on being in communion with the Pope and his church.

Cavour, the Prime Minister of Piedmont, was not really pleased with these developments, but the situation was soon taken out of his hands. In 1858 the French Emperor, Louis Napoleon, offered his help to Cavour if Piedmont wanted to drive the Austrians from north Italy. The war broke out in 1859, and the combined French and Piedmontese forces succeeded in driving the Austrians from most of north Italy, with the exception of south Tyrol. This victory was the signal for revolt throughout Italy, above all in the Papal States, and from 1860 to 1870 revolutionaries there, supported by Piedmont, succeeded in taking about two-thirds of the territory and incorporating it into the new Kingdom of Italy. What was left of the Papal States was kept in existence only by the presence of French troops in Rome. With the outbreak of the Franco-Prussian War in 1870, the French troops left for home and the Piedmontese forces entered the city. Pius IX became a voluntary "prisoner of the Vatican" and stubbornly refused all reconciliation with the new Italian government. The so-called "Roman Question" had reached its most critical form, and was to be an unfortunate burden for both the papacy and the church for fifty-nine years.

In France, the Revolution of 1848, which brought the Second Republic, had Catholics worried for a time, but there was no repetition of the Reign of Terror. The new government was quite well disposed to the church, and moderate republicans were able to keep the radicals tethered in the backyard, where they could practice their revolutionary rhetoric, but were not an embarrassment to the regime, which needed Catholic support if it was to survive.

The Second Republic failed, not because it was anticler-

ical, but because it adopted just enough of the socialist program to unsettle both the upper classes and the peasantry,
both of whom regarded any threat to private property as an
assault on the holy of holies. These two groups set the tone in
the church at the time, and when the elected President, Louis
Napoleon, proposed a referendum in 1851, on the question
of whether he should become an hereditary monarch, he received the enthusiastic support of Catholics and their church.

The situation in Germany was very different. There, too,
the revolution of 1848, although it did not bring the national
unity which many German patriots desired, did bring more
liberal constitutions to most of the kingdoms and principalities which made up the German League. Most important
were freedom of association and a limited freedom of the
press, and German Catholics made good use of both. It was
around this time that Catholic political parties began to appear in the newly powerful parliaments of the European
states, although it was in Germany that these parties were
most effective in securing freedom for the church and creating a favorable climate for Catholic life.

However, in Germany, too, there were problems with the
relations of church and state. The growing Prussian state, in
which the Lutheran faith was not only the official religion but
also an important prop and support of the authoritarian regime, acquired a number of Catholic subjects by conquest or
treaty in the first half of the nineteenth century. Initially,
Prussia negotiated a concordat with the papacy which recognized and regulated the Catholic church within its domains.
However, the loyalty of German Catholics to Rome and their
tendency to look to the Pope for support when they felt they
were being discriminated against by the Prussian state irritated the absolutist rulers of Prussia. In time, they and their
Chancellors came to regard Catholicism as a kind of fifth column, and an obstacle in the way of developing a truly German
national consciousness. After the publication of the Syllabus
of Errors, Bismarck, the Chancellor, decided to "Germanize"
the Catholic church in Germany, by separating it from Rome.
The resulting *Kulturkampf* had the opposite effect: it drove
the Catholic hierarchy of the Prussian-ruled parts of Ger-

many into the arms of the Pope, and later in the century Bismarck himself was to see that his plan had no hope of success.

9.38 Pius IX and the Ultramontane Movement

Pius' own naiveté in the face of the revolution of 1848 in Italy made him an opponent of liberalism in all of its forms, and his pontificate, which had begun with such promise, became in many respects a repetition of that of Gregory XVI. The Pope began to think of the papacy and the church (which he did not always distinguish clearly) as the last bulwark against the collapse of the western world under the blows of revolution, liberalism, and democracy, and he sought allies for the cause among Catholics throughout Europe. He found them in France, England, and Germany for quite different reasons, and those who shared this "bulwark mentality" joined in the final stage of the ultramontane movement which triumphed at the First Vatican Council in 1870—precisely at the moment when the temporal power of the papacy was lost forever. It is now time to look at the antecedents of the ultramontane movement.

The movement known as *ultramontanism* had complicated roots. Napoleon played a role by calling on Pius VI to secure the resignation of the pre-revolutionary bishops of France. De Maistre derived his version from his own extreme monarchist philosophy. Lamennais' ultramontanism had two roots. The first was his vision of the alliance of the Pope with the people against the reactionary thinking of the French Restoration; the second was the fact that he and his followers saw that a strong link with the papacy would mean the end of Gallicanism, to which they traced all of the problems of the French church. Gregory XVI made it quite clear that it was Lamennais' liberalism which was condemned in the letter *Mirari Vos*, and not his ultramontanism (although this word obviously meant something quite different to each of them).

In Germany, ultramontanism was fostered by the Romantic movement, with its idealized view of a medieval Europe united in religious loyalty to the papacy. But the most decisive influence came from the interference of Prussia in

Cologne in 1835 and 1837—events which we have noted above. In England, the men of the Oxford Movement were drawn to Roman Catholicism precisely because they felt the need of a strong authority principle in the church, which would put an end to the doctrinal fuzziness which so pained them in the Church of England. They and many other English Catholics also thought that the time had come to restore the hierarchy, and they knew that only a strong Pope would be in a position to make such a move. Finally, Pius IX himself apparently felt that if papal infallibility became the *official* doctrine of the church (it was by no means *new*, but was already old when Gregory VII had stated it in his *Dictatus Papae* in 1073), then he would be in a much stronger position to battle those forces which he saw as undermining the position of the church and as destroying civilization. And obviously the best way to secure the approval of a council for such a doctrine would be to promote the ultramontane movement and then to make sure that it was overwhelmingly represented at the eventual council. We will see how this policy worked in various countries.

It was in France that ultramontanism was strongest, and it was zealously propagated by the followers of Lamennais, who shared his detestation of Gallicanism (although they by no means accepted his somewhat romantic notion of the alliance of the papacy with the people). In the 1840's the first French bishops were won for the new cause, and they quite demonstratively turned to Rome and to the Curia with questions on liturgy and discipline. It was at about this time that the moral theology taught in Rome (either that of the tradition of Alphonsus Liguori, or the even more liberal Jesuit version) began to replace the rather Jansenistic moral teaching which had been in vogue in French seminaries since the seventeenth century. One of Rome's shrewdest moves at the time was to support the rights of the parish priests of France against the arbitrary exercise of power on the part of the bishops (particularly if the bishops were of Gallican sympathies). These bishops were by no means as independent as their predecessors of a century before, but they were still Gallican enough to cherish the absolute control over the parish priests which the concordat gave them. Rome's policy in this matter secured important allies for the future.

The papal Nuntius in Paris from 1843 to 1850, Fornari, was dedicated to the cause of ultramontanism. He got along well with the government official in charge of church affairs, and he was able to urge the advancement of priests with known ultramontane sympathies into the French episcopate. He gave his support to those priests who had complaints against Gallican-minded bishops, and he arranged to have theological works which supported the Gallican cause put on the Index of Forbidden Books.

When a number of French bishops reacted strongly against this campaign, the Pope (by this time Pius IX) took firm control of the movement, not only in France, but throughout the Catholic world. Fornari's success in France encouraged Pius IX to simply appoint bishops, without paying much attention to the wishes of the clergy or the hierarchy in the various countries; and where concordats limited his power of direct appointment, he did not hesitate to veto those who lacked appropriate ultramontane credentials. The very fact that he had already been Pope for twenty-four years when the Vatican Council met meant that he was the one who determined the character of the worldwide episcopacy. In 1869 there were seven hundred and thirty-nine Catholic bishops in the world, and only eighty-one of them came from the time of his predecessor, Gregory XVI.

The ultramontane campaign advanced simultaneously on many fronts. Early in the nineteenth century, there had been something of a revival of Thomistic theology in the theological seminaries in Rome, and from the 1830's on, it was zealously promoted by the Jesuits there. From Rome it came to Germany by two routes: it was brought back by the Jesuits and those whom they had trained at the Gregorian University; and it was favored by the authorities of the Diocese of Mainz, who had a seminary for the training of their priests and did not send them to the university, as was the usual practice in Germany. These ultramontane forces in Germany were suspicious of the atmosphere of open discussion and free research which distinguished even the Catholic faculties of theology at the German universities, and they engaged in the contemptible practice of denouncing anonymously those whom they suspected of anything less than total commitment to their brand of ultramontane orthodoxy.

Ignaz von Döllinger, a Catholic priest who was teaching at the University of Munich, opposed these German ultramontanes, and in 1863 he gave a series of lectures in Munich in which he criticized the papacy for preserving the outmoded institution of the Papal States. This touched a sensitive nerve and made a permanent enemy of the Papal Nuntius in Munich, who began to send reports to Rome, accusing Döllinger of wanting to replace the teaching authority of the Pope with that of the German university professors.

There is no doubt that much of the neo-scholasticism which Rome was propagating at the time was little more than the sterile repetition, not of the theology of Thomas Aquinas, but of the work of inferior minds who had watered down and systematized what they thought Thomas had said, and then packaged it in a series of dogmatic theology manuals. And there is no doubt that Rome was propagating neo-scholasticism, not because of its theological depth or systematic brilliance, but because it offered a common denominator, on the basis of which seminary instruction could be standardized and unified throughout the Catholic world. However, neither is there any doubt that in the hands of its most gifted practitioners, neo-scholasticism offered one fascinating solution to the problem of the relationship of faith and reason. And there is no doubt that, as scholasticism turned for nourishment directly to the writings of Thomas Aquinas, it gained enormously in depth and brilliance.

The ultramontane movement prized uniformity in all areas of Catholic life, and its partisans usually confused this uniformity with the universality of the church. This is quite clear from what might be called the "Latinizing" of Catholic piety in the nineteenth century, and it showed itself in two ways. The first was the great development of Marian piety, culminating in the dogmatic definition of the Immaculate Conception in 1854; and the second was an emphasis on what might be called a piety of religious *practices* or a piety of religious "busy-ness."

Marian piety developed in response to a series of reported appearances of the Blessed Virgin in France, from about 1830 on. The most famous was the appearance to Catherine Labouré in Paris, in 1830, which marked the beginning of the wearing of the "Miraculous Medal" by generations of Catholics, and which led to repeated requests on the part of the French bishops for a papal definition of the Immaculate Conception of Mary. On December 8, 1854 Pius IX read the formal declaration that belief in the Immaculate Conception of Mary was henceforth an essential part of Catholic faith, and that denial of this teaching made one a heretic. It was a decision which has had negative effects on the ecumenical movement up to the present day.

The appearance of the Blessed Virgin to Bernadette Soubirous at Lourdes, on February 11, 1858, looked to the Pope, to the bishops of France, and to most of the ordinary faithful like the confirmation from on high of the papal definition of 1854. Mary identified herself to Bernadette as the Immaculate Conception, and within a few years a number of remarkable cures at the grotto of Lourdes confirmed the infallibility of the Pope in the eyes of many of the Catholic faithful throughout the world.

Apart from the Marian apparitions, the ultramontane movement resulted in the spread of many practices of piety throughout the church. Two are particularly worthy of note: the perpetual adoration of the sacrament of the Eucharist (which was taken out of the tabernacle and exposed to the view of all), and the devotion to the Sacred Heart of Jesus. This latter devotion has a very solid core—a strong emphasis on the humanity of the Lord, as Karl Rahner has shown. However it quickly became associated with the "promises" made to a French nun, Margaret Mary Alacoque, and to practices such as the "nine first Fridays" (to guarantee final penitence), which could easily degenerate into superstition.

There were a number of psychological factors which favored the ultramontane movement in the years after 1850.

Pius IX was treated with contempt by Italian liberals and anti-
clericals, and this won him a great deal of sympathy outside
Italy. Rome had become a center of Catholic pilgrimage during the nineteenth century, and Pius knew how to meet people and to win them to personal loyalty to him. He had an
attractive personality, and he was more popular than any
Pope in history before him. Furthermore, there was a general
feeling among Catholics in most parts of Europe and North
America that a strong papacy was the best guarantee for the
independence of the church in all of the countries of the
world.

9.39 The Syllabus of Errors

At this precise point, Pius IX took a step which was perfectly consistent with his own views, but which seemed likely,
at least to many observers, to jeopardize the future of the ultramontane movement. As we have seen, the Pope turned definitively against political liberalism (and against almost all
currents of modern thought) in 1848. He was convinced that
this liberalism had sprung from the *rationalism* of the Enlightenment, and that this, in turn, had been a consequence of the
individualism which Europe had learned at the time of the
Protestant Reformation. Pius IX held tenaciously to this
somewhat simplified view of the history of ideas, and when
the Jesuit journal, *Civiltà Cattolica*, began, in the 1850's and
1860's, to push for a formal papal definition rejecting all of
the errors consequent on rationalism, Pius was quickly won to
the cause. He appointed a number of commissions to study
the question, and there was much debate over the scope of the
proposed declaration. There was also a good deal of opposition from bishops in countries with large Protestant populations, because the bishops feared that a global condemnation
of liberalism and freedom would make the position of the
church in their countries difficult.

Pius IX might have been willing to shelve the plan, in
view of these objections, had it not been for two addresses
which were given in the year 1863. The first was a speech by
Montalembert in Belgium, in which he gave a stirring defense

of the liberal Catholicism of Lamennais, under the title of "The Free Church in the Free State." The second was a talk by Ignaz von Döllinger, in Munich, in which he demanded that Rome respect the right of the Catholic theological faculties in the German universities to free research and discussion. This was too much for Pius IX, and in 1864 he issued the encyclical *Quanta Cura*, listing eighty of the most serious and prevalent errors of the day (the *Syllabus of Errors*). The list ended with the condemnation of those who supported absolute freedom of religion and freedom of the press, and of those who defended the proposition that the Pope must adapt himself to the conditions of modern life.

The reaction of Protestant Europe was swift and very negative. Non-Catholics in England regarded the whole incident as laughable (perhaps the most appropriate reaction). But it was in France that the encyclical received the most interesting response. Bishop Dupanloup of Orleans, who had opposed the publication of the *Syllabus*, now wrote an "interpretation" of the document, which watered down its most exaggerated assertions, and gave a benign "explanation" of its most sweeping condemnations. Dupanloup was politically shrewd, and he wrote his interpretation in such a way that it won the cautious approval of the Pope himself. In the face of Dupanloup's "interpretation," Catholic opposition to the *Syllabus* (at least outside Germany) faded very quickly. The road was now clear for the triumph of ultramontanism.

9.4 FROM THE FIRST VATICAN COUNCIL TO WORLD WAR I

After the Congress of Vienna, the ultramontane movement gained strength in the various European countries for quite different reasons. As it did, many French Catholics began to argue that the time had come to make the old teaching on papal infallibility into a matter of formally defined Catholic faith. These suggestions were not at all unwelcome to Pius IX, who was quite convinced of his infallibility (and not only in matters of faith!). In 1854 he had, on his own authority, defined the Immaculate Conception as a doctrine to be held by all Catholics, and when, in 1867, he announced that he was summoning a council to meet in 1869, it seemed certain that the question of papal infallibility would be on the agenda.

The First Vatican Council is one of those great paradoxes of church history. In 1820, fifty years before it occurred, no one would have dared to predict that in that same century an overwhelming majority of the bishops of the world would solemnly declare that the Pope was, at least under certain conditions, infallible. But in another sense, Vatican I was the natural, even inevitable result of the ultramontane movement. And yet, when the Council met and made its decision, the decree *limited* papal infallibility far more than most of the ultramontanes wanted, and the Pope himself was probably quite disappointed.

The definition of infallibility at Vatican I has become a serious *ecumenical* problem, and both Catholics and Protestants have felt that it is the single most serious obstacle in the way of Christian unity. It was for this reason that Hans Küng's book, *Infallible? An Inquiry*, which was published in 1970, and which questioned the doctrine, created such a stir at the time, and it is for this reason that Rome has tried to discipline Küng in the intervening years.

9.41 Preparing for Infallibility

The progress of the ultramontane movement from the 1830's on led inexorably toward a pronouncement on papal infallibility. Even in Germany there were some developments which favored such a course. The bishops there had already learned how useful it was to be able to rely on Rome when the Prussian government tried to meddle in church affairs. Furthermore, during the course of the nineteenth century, German Jesuits and their former students at the Gregorian University in Rome did everything to impress their particular view of papal primacy on the laity in Germany. The parish missions conducted by these priests emphasized a counterreformation and even anti-Protestant piety, and instilled a sense of personal loyalty to the Pope in all of the faithful.

In France, Louis Veuillot, one of the most radical ultra-montanes, used his newspaper, *L'Univers*, as a pulpit from which to preach a type of papolatry which is almost sickening today. In Italy, the Jesuit journal, *Civiltà Cattolica*, followed the same course. And in all countries, the supporters of the ultramontane cause did not hesitate to employ the practice of secret denunciation in order to discredit their opponents and block their advancement in the church.

The dogmatic decision on the Immaculate Conception which Pius IX issued in 1854 should also be seen as part of the preparation for infallibility. It is true that the Pope had asked the bishops of the world for their views on the matter in the years before his decree, but when the decision was made, no allusion was made to his acting in concert with the bishops or as head of the episcopal college. *The Pope* made the decision and then communicated it to the bishops and the Catholic world.

In 1864, Pius IX asked the cardinals what they thought of the idea of calling a council, and, perhaps surprisingly, he did not mention the possibility of including papal infallibility on the agenda. Rather, the council was to be the crowning triumph of the church over liberalism in all of its forms. However, many members of the Curia were quite worried about the coming council. They feared the French bishops, who were no longer openly Gallican, but whom curial officials suspected of lingering anti-Roman sentiments; and even more they feared the German theologians, whose historical studies could easily undermine the ultramontane structure so laboriously assembled during the preceding decades. The Curia did what it could to avert both "dangers," and the Pope cooperated by appointing almost exclusively supporters of the ultramontane cause to the preparatory commissions.

Although many of the laity throughout Europe had been won by the ultramontanes, there were still serious divisions among the bishops and theologians, as well as among the well-educated laity. However, the ultramontane party was convinced that the time had come to settle all problems for the church then and in the future by pronouncing the Pope infallible. The Jesuit periodical *Civiltà Cattolica*, alluding to the situation in France, suggested that what all *real* Catholics wanted was a short council which would affirm the truth of the *Syllabus of Errors* and would then proclaim papal infallibility *by acclamation*(!). Such excesses enraged a number of French and German bishops, as well as almost all of the Catholic theological faculties of the German universities. These men had serious reservations about the doctrine on what they considered to be solid grounds, and they had nothing but contempt for the simplistic adoration of the papacy which they found on the pages of *L'Univers* and of *Civiltà Cattolica*.

The position of these opponents of infallibility was moderate, and really had nothing to do with Gallicanism, Febronianism, or Josephinism. Rather, they felt that the trend toward centralization of all power in Rome was not healthy for the church. In their eyes, the episcopal office was a matter of divine foundation and divine law, and they felt that any move which lessened the power of the bishop to act as a successor of the Apostles in his own diocese was an attack on the essential structure of the church. Furthermore, particularly in Germany, they did not like the attempt of Rome to make Catholic piety uniform on the Latin or Italian model. They felt that this model overemphasized external pious practices, "devotions" and the like, at the expense of genuine faith and inner religious depth. Many of these opponents of infallibility (and, again, this was true particularly in Germany) also felt that freedom of theological research would benefit the church and they were convinced that Rome was intent on curbing this freedom. They were afraid that an "infallible" Pope would repeat the *Syllabus* and thus demand rejection of the whole modern world as a condition of remaining Catholic. Finally, the historical studies of the university professors had convinced them that there was overwhelming historical evidence against papal infallibility.

Four months before the council was due to meet, Ignaz von Döllinger, a priest at the University of Munich, began a series of articles in an Augsburg newspaper, in which he accused the Pope and the Jesuits of trying to force both infallibility and the jurisdictional primacy of the papacy on an unwilling church. Döllinger had been driven to distraction by the papolatry of the ultra-ultramontanes, and he used strong language, referring to the attempts of Popes to exercise supreme power in the church as "usurpations . . . (and) . . . an ulcer which distorts and chokes the church." Needless to say, his words polarized opinion within Germany almost immediately.

In France during the Second Empire (under Louis Napoleon, from 1851 on), the opponents of ultramontanism had been able to undo some of the work of the Nuntius, Fornari. Maret, the rector of the Sorbonne, was on good terms with the Emperor, and he was able to influence the nomination of bishops. By the time of the Council, eighteen of the bishops of France had been chosen this way, and they were almost all opponents of the ultramontane cause. On the very eve of the Council, Maret's book, *On the General Council and on Religious Peace*, was published. In it he affirmed that the Pope, as an individual, isolated person, was not infallible, and that there was no place for despotism in the church. At the same time, Bishop Dupanloup, the respected head of the diocese of Orléans, let it be known that he regarded it as "inopportune" to define papal infallibility at the time.

9.42 The First Vatican Council Begins Its Deliberations

Seven hundred bishops assembled on December 8, and many of them came from parts of the world which had never been represented at such a gathering before. However, more than a third were Italians, and, taken together with the French, they constituted an absolute majority. It became clear that there would be two strongly opposed parties represented at the Council.

The ultramontanes were led by the English cardinal, Manning, and by the Superior General of the Jesuits, Beckx. They were firmly convinced that a decree on infallibility would not add anything new to Catholic faith, as it had been traditionally understood. Rather, such a decree would simply take note, at a most appropriate historical moment, of something which had been part of Catholic faith from the beginning and which, in addition, was firmly anchored in scripture.

The leaders of the ultramontane faction never tired of pointing out that the scholastic theologians of the Middle Ages had, almost without exception, accepted the doctrine of papal infallibility and regarded it as part of the faith. However, what seems clear is that the ultramontanes confused the *scholastic tradition*, and, later, the *canon law tradition* from the time of Aegidius Romanus (Boniface VIII's canonist), with the tradition of the church as such. The ultramontane party was notoriously weak in scholars who were acquainted with the situation of the church and the papacy in the earliest times, and many of them seemed to think that the history of the church had begun with the pontificate of Gregory VII.

The party which opposed the definition of infallibility was smaller, although not numerically insignificant. It included the more liberal members of the French episcopacy, as well as those who, though by no means Gallican, thought that there should be some limit on papal power. This included Dupanloup and those who respected and followed him. There were many German bishops in this opposition party. Some of them had taught in the universities before their consecration, and most of them kept close ties to university theology and were influenced by it. Most of the *uniate* bishops of the East (that is, those bishops of the eastern rite churches which recognized the primacy of the Pope in the sense in which one could speak of such primacy prior to 1870) belonged to the opposition party; they were afraid that any further concentration of power in the hands of the Pope would result in increased attempts to Latinize the eastern churches, by imposing changes in ritual, and by inflicting on them a code of canon law which was utterly alien to their customs and traditions.

The members of the opposing party did not really question the doctrine of the *primacy* of the Pope as head bishop of the church, but they were convinced that the Pope could only make binding decisions when he acted in concert with his fellow bishops. The real leader of this group turned out to be an English layman, Lord Acton. Acton, of course, could not even be present as an observer at the deliberations of the Council, but he was active in putting the opponents of the definition in contact with each other and in devising effective policy, so that his group, despite its numerical inferiority, might be able to affect the outcome. Acton saw that if the opponents of the definition could win the French Emperor, Napoleon III, to their side, they would have a very strong card to play: everyone, including Pius IX, realized that it was only the presence of French troops in Rome which guaranteed papal sovereignty over what was left of the Papal State (that is, those parts which had not yet been annexed by Piedmont and made part of the new Italian nation).

When the bishops began their deliberations, although the infallibility question was uppermost in everyone's mind, it was not actually on the agenda of the Council. Pius apparently felt that it would be bad form if he forced the question of his own infallibility on the Council fathers. But there is no doubt that he gave his full support to those ultramontanes who circulated a petition at the end of December, requesting that the question of infallibility be put on the agenda. By the end of January, there were already four hundred and fifty signatures on that petition—almost two-thirds of those entitled to vote. It is safe to say that practically every one of those signatures represented a vote in favor of the definition of infallibility.

Beginning on December 17, 1869, a series of articles by Döllinger, entitled "Roman Letters," began to appear in some of the German newspapers. Although Pius IX had imposed secrecy on the bishops, it was clear that Döllinger was very well informed about the deliberations at the Council, and his articles were eagerly read, because they contained the only available information about what was happening there. Lord Acton, of course, was at work here. He got his information from bishops who were friends of his and who did not accept the Pope's right to bind them to secrecy, and then he passed the information on to Döllinger.

The Council did not begin with the question of infallibility, but with a proposal which condemned the errors of rationalism. As the meetings dragged on and the speeches became interminable, the ultramontanes began to fear that the Council would never get to the question of infallibility, and in March some of them began to circulate a petition which asked that the question be moved forward on the agenda so that it might be treated without further delay. And so it was that on May 13, 1870, discussion opened on the proposed definition of papal infallibility (part of a larger proposal which dealt with the teaching authority of the Pope and with his jurisdictional primacy).

Events at the Council had already convinced opponents of the definition that the ultramontanes had more than enough support to win, with more than a two-thirds majority, *on the question of infallibility itself.* They saw that their only effective argument was to point out that this was an inopportune time to issue such a decree because of the harm it would do to the church in the non-Catholic world. Undoubtedly they hoped that if the question could be shelved, the ultramontane movement would lose momentum, and that if the issue ever came up again, it would be settled in a way more to their liking.

Throughout the rest of May, through June and the early days of July, discussion continued and the debate was thorough. Although the opposing party had been excluded from the work of practically all of the preparatory commissions, at the Council they were given the full opportunity to present their case—something that was done in a particularly cogent and effective way by Hefele, bishop of Rottenburg, in southwest Germany, and himself an accomplished church historian.

It seems clear that in the course of these discussions, all but the most extreme members of the ultramontane party came to see that their own position needed some clarification. They saw that some limitations had to be imposed on papal infallibility and that some way had to be found of insuring that infallibility would not be claimed for every statement of every Pope on every topic. On the other hand, the opponents of the definition came to see that the principle of divine guidance for papal teaching, in at least some circumstances, was not simply an invention of the Jesuits, but was a widely accepted part of church tradition. They came to understand that the point which they really wanted to make was that, regardless of the role which the Pope should play, he is not to be *identified* with the church.

Still, no resolution of the disagreements was in sight. The opponents of the definition had, despite their numerical inferiority, made a number of good points, and on June 18, Guidi, the Superior General of the Dominicans, proposed a compromise formula. He suggested that what should be debated was not the infallibility of the *Pope*, but rather the infallibility of his *doctrinal decisions*. In Guidi's view, these decisions were infallibile, precisely because they were made by the Pope, *acting in concert with the other bishops* and not independently of them; the Pope could only teach infallibly when he acted in union with his fellow bishops and when he respected the tradition of the church. Pius IX reacted angrily to Guidi's intervention, and reminded him, in a personal confrontation, that "La tradizione son' io!—I am the tradition!" But it was actually Guidi's suggestion which appeared in the title of the fourth chapter of this new constitution, which was *not called* "On the Infallibility of the Roman Pontiff" *but rather* "On the Infallible Teaching Authority of the Roman Pontiff"—an apparently small but actually very significant difference. It was the Irish bishop, Cullen, a strong supporter of the definition, who then proposed that infallibility be limited to the *doctrinal* decisions of the Pope. This was the intervention which broke the logjam.

Although the interventions of Guidi and Cullen had imposed limits on infallibility which were very unpalatable to extreme ultramontanes and to Pius IX himself, it was evident that the Council was moving quickly in the direction which these interventions suggested, and the members of the opposing party saw this clearly. As the time for a vote approached, fifty-five of the bishops who opposed the definition left the Council and returned to their homes, in order to avoid angering the Pope even more by voting against the decree. On July 18, the Constitution on the Infallible Teaching Authority of the Roman Pontiff (it bore the Latin title *Pastor Aeternus*) was formally read and approved by an overwhelming majority of the assembled bishops. The key statement in this document is that the Pope teaches infallibly

when he speaks *ex cathedra* (literally "from the papal throne")
in a matter of faith or morals. The bishops at the Council
seem to have understood the phrase *ex cathedra* as describing
the Pope's words when he speaks precisely as supreme pastor
and teacher, with the professed purpose of affirming a doctrine that is a matter of Catholic faith, which is binding on all
who wish to profess that faith.

In August, the Council recessed, in order to give everyone a chance to recover from the heat. Before the Council
could reassemble, the Franco-Prussian War had begun, and
the bishops of France and Germany had to return to their
own countries. The German bishops took the opportunity to
meet in Fulda. Many of them had opposed the definition, ar-
guing that it was at least inopportune, but now they realized
that the decision was one which they could live with, and they
recommended it to their people. With the outbreak of the
war, the French contingent which was protecting the city of
Rome and its suburbs returned to the homeland, and the
Piedmontese forces marched on Rome and took the city on
September 20. One month later, the Council was adjourned
indefinitely by the Pope. It was never reconvened, although
Vatican II might be thought of as its continuation, in a totally
different situation and in a wholly new world. Vatican II did
take up questions which were scheduled for discussion at the
First Vatican Council, and there is no doubt that in its own
way, Vatican II tried to redress the balance of power, which
had shifted dangerously in the direction of papal absolutism.

9.43 After the Council

In France, attention centered on the war with Prussia,
and this hastened the acceptance of the definition of papal infallibility. Furthermore, those who had originally opposed
the definition realized that Veuillot and his party had not gotten what they wanted, and the opponents of the definition
were pleasantly surprised by this. They began to see how strict
the limits were which had been imposed on papal infallibility
by the Council, and they felt, not incorrectly, that they had
gotten away relatively unscathed.

In Germany, on the other hand, there were serious difficulties. The bishop of Rottenburg (near Tübingen), the respected church historian mentioned above, not only felt that the decision was inopportune; even more, he was convinced that there were serious theological and historical arguments against it. After a lengthy struggle with his conscience, he finally promulgated the decree in his diocese in April 1871. The opposition in the Universities was more serious. The Catholic professors who opposed the definition held meetings throughout the spring and summer of 1871 to stir up opposition and to try to win the German bishops to their cause. Rome promptly excommunicated the leaders of the movement, but this simply drove them into schism. At a congress in Munich in September 1871, some of the dissident professors and their followers proclaimed the existence of an "Old Catholic Church"—that is, a church which would be true to the traditional teaching on the relationship of Pope and Council, and would reject what they regarded as the innovations of the Vatican Council which had just ended.

By 1873 the Old Catholics had their own bishop (consecrated by the Jansenist bishop of Utrecht, in order to secure a valid claim to apostolic succession) and from then on, the church has gone its own way. It was used by Bismarck during the Kulturkampf, in order to divide Catholics and in order to further the Chancellor's dream of a German national church, independent of Rome (and which could probably be coaxed into some kind of ecumenical union with the Lutheran Church of Prussia). The Old Catholics were often criticized for some of the reforms which they adopted during the 1870's, such as the abrogation of the laws of fasting and abstinence and the simplification of the liturgical calendar. Oddly enough, some of these same reforms were undertaken by the Second Vatican Council, and other reforms of the Old Catholics have remained on the agenda after Vatican II, and are still debated in the Catholic church today. (Vatican II also dealt with the relation of the Pope to the bishops in a way which considerably mitigated the one-sided papalism of the Council of 1869–1870. It is not too unlikely that many of those who were upset by the decree on infallibility would be able to find a quite comfortable home in the Post-Vatican II church of today.)

Vatican I created some major problems for ecumenical theology, and the infallibility decree of Vatican I is the neuralgic point in the search for Christian unity today. It is certain that if we contrast the way in which Catholics affirmed infallibility and jurisdictional primacy from 1870 until the late 1950's, with the way Protestants rejected it during the same period, the doctrine would present an insurmountable obstacle to Christian unity. However, there is an understanding of papal primacy which has been spreading in Catholic theology since even before Vatican II (and which to some degree was part of the hidden agenda of a number of bishops at that Council). Those who hold this view feel that the *term* "infallibility" and the whole conceptual apparatus used to promote and defend it have been unfortunate developments, not only from the standpoint of Christian unity, but in terms of the Catholic faith itself. Both the *term* infallibility and the apparatus used to defend it reflect a proposition-centered view of faith which is alien to the New Testament, but which was the perfect expression of the papal church of the nineteenth century, particularly at the time of Pius IX. However, once this is admitted, there is another question which has to be raised: if the church has the task of speaking the message of its Lord into the ever-changing present situation, how is this message to be preserved from distortion and dilution? Christian tradition has insisted from very early times that the Bishop of Rome plays an important role in discharging precisely this task. It has affirmed that it is he who is called to do for the whole church what each bishop is called to do in his own diocese—namely, to preserve the ancient teaching intact and to pass it on to his successors, who will continue to fulfill this task as long as the church endures.

In the course of history, the Bishop of Rome has fulfilled this task in union with the other bishops, and he often did it precisely because other bishops asked him to formulate this traditional teaching. If the phrase *ex cathedra* of the Vatican I decree on infallibility is interpreted as involving just this kind of cooperation, then papal teaching would be infallible precisely when the Pope speaks as head of, and in concert with, the college of bishops—that body which has the responsibility of preserving and articulating the original message. Such an interpretation has a very good New Testament pedigree, and it would put an end to the one-sided papalism which peaked, at least in recent times, during the reign of Pius XII.

9.44 The Closing Years of the Reign of Pius IX

The opposition to the First Vatican Council's decree on infallibility came almost exclusively from university circles and from a very small sector of the educated laity in Germany. The last of the bishops to hold out finally accepted the decree in December 1872. Strangely enough, at the very moment when the temporal power of the papacy had reached the vanishing point, Pius IX was able to exert more power *within the church* than had any Pope since the High Middle Ages.

Even before the Piedmontese army had taken the city of Rome, the King of Italy had offered the Pope a small piece of territory within the city of Rome which would be completely under papal sovereignty, and which would therefore be a guarantee of papal independence. (What he offered was something very much like what Vatican City became after the Lateran Treaties of 1929.) But Pius IX refused, and in November of that same year he excommunicated everyone who was involved in the Piedmontese takeover. This accomplished nothing other than the strengthening of those anti-clerical tendencies which were already quite evident in Italian public life. It was not until 1929 that this so-called *Roman Question* was settled to the satisfaction both of the papacy and of the kingdom of Italy.

At the same time, trouble was brewing for the church in Germany. Bismarck had been irritated by the Syllabus of Errors as well as by the infallibility decree of Vatican I, and he began to look on the delegates of the Center Party (the Catholic political group in the Prussian parliament) as a kind of papal fifth column, inimical to the best interests of Germany. Beginning in 1873, a number of laws hostile to the Catholic church were enacted. The first, in 1873, interfered with the bishops' exercise of jurisdiction in their dioceses. In 1874 some bishops who strongly resisted Bismarck's policy were arrested. In 1875 obligatory civil marriage was introduced, and in that same year all payments to the Catholic clergy on the part of the Prussian state were suspended. Bismarck's policy was intended to Germanize the Catholic church in Prussia, and to pry it away from union with Rome; he thought of it as the struggle of German culture against Mediterranean or Latin culture, and hence the name *Kulturkampf*. Bismarck's policy was misguided, and it was based on a thorough misunderstanding of the import both of the Syllabus and of Vatican I. But Pius IX's reaction was equally imprudent. In 1873 in a letter to Kaiser Wilhelm I, he asserted his pastoral supremacy and jurisdiction not only over Catholics, but over all of the baptized (including, of course, Bismarck and the Kaiser himself!). Although quite in accord with the teaching of canon law, this approach was not calculated to calm the rising storm. Furthermore, in 1875, Pius IX declared that all of the legislation of the Kulturkampf was null and void, thereby making it practically impossible for Bismarck to back away from his program without losing face.

9.45 Leo XIII (1878 to 1903)

Rarely has a new Pope been faced with problems as complex and as apparently insoluble as those which confronted Leo XIII on his election in 1878. Pius IX had painted himself into a corner with his hard line on the Roman Question, and his imprudent handling of the Kulturkampf had virtually ruled out the possibility of a face-saving compromise. European liberals were still irritated by the Syllabus, and in France the Third Republic was about to banish all vestiges of France's Catholic past from the public life of the country. Republican forces had come to power in 1879, and over the next twenty-five years a good deal of anti-Catholic legislation was passed. The new laws aimed at excluding the church from education and expelling the religious orders from French soil, and, finally, at the elimination of the church as a factor in the public life of the country. Ever since this time, the phrase "separation of church and state" has had extremely negative connotations for French Catholics. Leo XIII urged French Catholics to make their peace with the Revolution, but they had not been able to do it, and the hostility of the Third Republic was to some degree the result of this boycotting of the republican cause by Catholics.

Leo was a forceful personality and a realist. He did not want to condemn the modern world; he wanted to reach an understanding with it, and one of the first signals of this new openness on the part of the papacy was Leo's appointment of Newman to the College of Cardinals in 1879. Leo was the first Pope to concern himself with the social problems which had resulted from the rapid industrialization of Europe in the nineteenth century, and in this respect as in all others, he broke with the reactionary policies of his predecessor. He was also a very successful diplomat and his intelligence and tact led to the termination of the Kulturkampf in Germany. In the years that followed it was obvious that he had won the respect of both Bismarck and the Kaiser. In 1888 Kaiser Wilhelm II visited the Pope in Rome, and in 1902 the Prussian regime gave its approval to the founding of a faculty of Catholic theology at the University of Strasbourg.

Leo never made use of the infallibility which had been defined at the Vatican Council—a very wise move which contributed to the prestige of the papacy. He was the first "encyclical Pope" and he issued a number of these general letters to the whole church. They dealt with the pressing problems of the day, and in most of them both his concern for the church and his realism were evident. Unfortunately, however, one of these letters led to the isolation of Catholic theology from modern thought for almost seventy years. In 1879 he strongly reaffirmed the support of the church for the theology of Thomas Aquinas and made him something like the official theologian of the church. This led quickly to a revival of the scholasticism of the thirteenth century in Catholic centers outside Germany—most notably in France, Canada, and the United States. This *Neo-Thomism*, as it was usually called, was by no means an intellectually sterile exercise in nostalgia; it rather attempted to use the method and the fundamental

insights of Thomas Aquinas to deal with philosophical, theological, social, and political problems of the day. At its best it
demonstrated a kind of intellectual discipline and care for the
definition of terms which are a permanent necessity for all
who try to think seriously. But like all styles which incorporate
the word "neo-" in their names (Neo-Gothic, Neo-Roman-
esque, etc.), its achievements remained magnificent *tours de
force* and did not offer creative solutions to the problems of
the day. The subjection of man to history is the insight which,
more than any other, characterizes the modern age, but neo-
scholasticism, with its concept of static truth, had no sympathy
with or understanding of the category of history. It was because of this weakness that neo-scholasticism had such destructive repercussions on biblical scholarship in the Catholic
church.

There is no doubt that Leo's own strong personality and
the requests for his intervention in national church affairs
throughout Europe brought about an ever-greater centralization of power in the church. Under later pontificates, particularly that of Pius XII, this led to the practical supremacy
of the Curia over the world-wide episcopate—an unfortunate
development which would not be corrected until the time of
John XXIII and the Second Vatican Council.

Leo XIII is sometimes faulted for his founding of the
Pontifical Biblical Commission in 1903. It is true that the
Commission itself (discussed below under another heading)
was a serious mistake which delayed the acceptance of modern biblical science in the Catholic church by about forty years
and made those Catholic exegetes who accepted its decrees
the laughingstock of their Protestant confreres. However,
Leo was ninety-three years old at the time and the Biblical
Commission and its outdated decrees should really be blamed
on archconservative officials of the Curia who were eager to
bring back the reactionary intransigence of Pius IX.

The same Curial conservatives were responsible for the
condemnation of the movement in Germany, known as *Reform Catholicism*. The major work of the movement was a book
by Herman Schell, of the Catholic faculty in Würzburg, published in 1897 with the title *Catholicism as the Principle of Prog-*

ress. In it, Schell broke no new dogmatic ground, but he did urge that political and cultural "Romanism" not be confused with either Christianity or Catholicism, and he pleaded for a broader view of the meaning of the word "Catholic," pointing out that its proper meaning was not "uniform" but "universal." Reform Catholicism was a healthy reaction to the centralizing and uniformitizing tendencies that were dominant in the church at the time, but no bishops were won for the cause, and it remained a phenomenon of "university theology." Schell's works were put on the Index of Forbidden Books in 1899.

9.46 Americanism

An event which took place in the same year—Leo XIII's condemnation of "Americanism"—makes this an appropriate place to review the history of the church in the United States during the latter half of the nineteenth century. The church had grown enormously, particularly since the late 1840's, with the influx of Catholic immigrants from Ireland and from Catholic countries of southern and eastern Europe, even though by 1880 Catholics formed only about ten percent of the population. The development of a Catholic grammar school system, supported by the donations of the laity and staffed, in the main, by sisters, had done more than anything (except, perhaps, the hostility of the overwhelmingly Protestant environment) to preserve the faith of the Catholic immigrants. As the years passed, the Irish element in the American church became ever more dominant, and it was partially because of this that there was never any serious opposition of the working classes to the church. Most of the bishops had themselves come from working class families, and the parish priests were wholly involved in the lives of their flocks. Toward the end of the century, the Knights of Labor, a society founded by an Irish Catholic and supported by Catholic workingmen, attracted Rome's unfavorable attention, and it was finally placed on the list of forbidden societies, despite the attempt of Cardinal Gibbons and others to prevent this unnecessary irritation. But the harm done was minimal. Although the need clearly existed, the union movement's time had not yet come, and the papal condemnation did little to disturb the loyalty of Catholic workingmen to their church.

There were, of course, problems for the church in the late nineteenth century—some of them caused by the ethnic mixture in American Catholicism, and others caused by the strong and at times abrasive characters of the leading American bishops of the period. Unsettled conditions in Europe had brought millions of immigrants, many of them Catholic, to the United States throughout the nineteenth century. From the 1840's to the 1870's the Irish were the largest group; in the 1870's the Germans passed the Irish in the number of annual immigrants; and from the 1890's on, the overwhelming number of new arrivals were Italian.

The city parishes were largely in the hands of priests of Irish origin (frequently Irish born), and they had no way of offering the German and Italian immigrants either pastoral care in their own language or the style of church life to which they had been accustomed in the old country. Furthermore, when the immigrants (especially the Germans) did not remain in the cities but settled in rural areas, there were few parishes and little opportunity to practice the faith. Inevitably, a number drifted away and were lost to the church.

In 1874 a wealthy Catholic member of the German parliament, Peter Paul Cahensly, made a trip to the United States and became alarmed at the widespread loss of faith among his countrymen. Back in Germany, he founded a society which was dedicated to promoting the spiritual welfare of German immigrants by sending them priests who spoke their language. At one of the meetings of this society in Lucerne in 1890, Cahensly made the quite unrealistic assertion that over ten million Catholics had already been lost to the church in the United States because of the inadequacy of the pastoral care available to them. He later upped the figure to sixteen million, and suggested that the only way of coping with this problem was to put those areas of the United States which were populated by European Catholics (he meant "non-Irish" Catholics) under the direct jurisdiction of bishops of those countries from which they came. The American bishops (by this time the overwhelming majority were first or second generation Irish) resented deeply this assault on their jurisdiction in their own country, and Leo XIII prudently rejected the proposal, although he urged that, where they were needed, national parishes which catered to the religious needs of the ethnic minorities should be established or continued. Some of these national parishes have continued to the present day, although as the children of the immigrants learned English, they were often, at least by the third generation, more comfortable in the English-speaking churches, particularly if the latter were not too aggressively Irish in custom and style.

The Irish-American bishops were pursuing a "melting-pot" policy from the 1860's on. They themselves, as well as their flocks, had arrived in the new world already speaking English, and their sound instincts told them that unless the Catholic church here looked and sounded like an American institution, there would be no hope, either of breaking down the anti-Catholic prejudice which was a fact of American life well into the twentieth century, or of winning any significant number of converts.

The principal architect of this policy was the future cardinal—James Gibbons (1834–1921), who was already a bishop in 1868 (and in the following year was the youngest bishop at the First Vatican Council). Without being offensively political, he was thoroughly American, and he won a great deal of respect for the Catholic church among non-Catholics. Some of his statements sound quite chauvinistic to us today, but in the framework of the world in which he lived, they made good sense. Gibbons was respected in Rome, and although the Pope and the Curia did not always follow his sound advice, he was able to ward off some of Rome's more imprudent initiatives. Even the one area in which he failed (Rome's condemnation of "Americanism"—see the section below) was a sudden (if very unfortunate) storm which did a limited amount of damage.

John Ireland (1838–1918) was a man of quite different temperament, although he and Gibbons agreed on most of the issues which were important for the church in the United States. Ireland had received his seminary training in France, and this contact with the church in Europe, together with his native shrewdness, made him a much more clever tactician in dealing with the Curia. He was a bit of a super-patriot and his commitment to the American principles of freedom of religion and the separation of church and state proved irritating in the extreme to conservative French Catholics who were shivering in the chill winds which blew in the Third Republic in the 1890's.

But even the Irish majority among the American bishops were not united. Gibbons and Ireland formed a liberal, americanizing wing, but John Corrigan (1839–1902) and James McQuaid were the leaders of a more conservative group. Corrigan was archbishop of New York from 1885, and he had little sympathy for Gibbons and for the latter's enthusiastic support of the American way of life. Of course even a Pope who was as much of a realist as Leo XIII found it difficult to share the enthusiasm of Gibbons and Ireland for freedom of conscience and for the separation of church and state, and in a generally laudatory letter which he wrote to the American hierarchy in 1895, Leo intimated that a situation in which the government positively favored the church was really the best solution of all. Things probably would have not gone beyond this mild disapproval, had it not been for the publication of a biography of Isaac Hecker (in 1891 in the United States and 1897 in France).

Hecker was a convert who entered the Redemptorist order and was ordained to the priesthood. After a while, he found that he was unable to pursue the apostolate to which he felt he had been called, and he obtained papal permission to found a new order, the Paulists. Hecker and his order distinguished themselves in the development of new forms of apostolic activity which were geared to American conditions and which respected the American character. However, despite this fact, the appearance of the biography of Hecker in 1891 was not really a major event in the American church.

Unfortunately, the French translation of 1897 *was* a major event—for the American church. A priest named Klein, who was teaching at the Institut Catholique in Paris, translated and edited the biography, and was imprudent enough to present Hecker as a model to French Catholics. Klein also suggested that the American approach to democracy and toleration should be accepted by French Catholics. This infuriated the ultra-conservatives there, and one of them wrote a book which questioned the orthodoxy of the American approach. The dispute was soon reported to Rome, and Leo XIII appointed a commission to investigate the problem. Significantly (and typically) no American bishops were invited to Rome to give their views. The papal letter which dealt with the problem was written, in the main, by an Italian Jesuit, Mazzella, whose knowledge of the American scene was limited to what he had gathered while teaching at Woodstock—a Jesuit seminary near Baltimore, which was hermetically sealed off from the realities of American life.

Leo's letter condemned, as he said, "what some have called 'Americanism,'" but, as is evident from the content of the letter, this "Americanism" was of French provenance, and was an invention of ultra-conservative Catholics who despised democracy with all its works and pomps. The Pope condemned all those who asserted that those dogmas which are not readily intelligible should be downplayed in preaching, and that it would be better if church authorities refrained from making authoritative statements in matters of faith and morals. Also condemned were those who emphasized the natural virtues (of value for practical life) at the expense of the supernatural virtues of faith, hope, and charity, as well as those who questioned the appropriateness of perpetual vows for members of religious orders, or who doubted the value of religious vocations to the contemplative life.

Gibbons, Ireland, and their supporters had gotten wind of the letter too late to do anything to stop its publication, and they were shocked by it. Both of them were convinced that there were no bishops or priests, no theologians or laymen in the United States who held any of these positions. Ireland was shrewd enough to thank the Pope for the letter and for the clarity which it brought, pointing out that it distinguished between a false Americanism and the genuine Americanism (which he and Gibbons embraced). Corrigan (the archbishop of New York) and McQuaid (bishop of Rochester) were pleased by the letter, and regarded it as the confirmation of their own position.

Largely because of Ireland's clever response and because of Gibbons' prestige, both in the United States and in Rome, the storm blew over rather quickly. But there were some lasting bad effects, and one of them was a kind of nervous conservatism in dealing with the Curia which characterized the American hierarchy for many years. In addition, Jesuit participation in framing the letter, and widespread Jesuit support of Bishops Corrigan and McQuaid, also led to troubled relations between the diocesan clergy and the Jesuits in the United States through the early decades of the twentieth century. (Symptomatic of this was Jesuit opposition to Catholic University, from before its opening in 1889 until almost the time of the Second World War.) This imposed a degree of isolation on the American Jesuits which was unfortunate, precisely because of the contribution the order could have made to the intellectual life of the American Catholic church.

9.47 Pius X (1903–1914) and Religious Reform

During his long reign, Leo had increased the prestige of both the church and the papacy. He was a skillful diplomat, and he used his sound political judgment to solve most of the problems he had inherited from Pius IX. When Leo died in 1903, his Cardinal Secretary of State, Rampolla, was regarded by many as a leading candidate, although there were many who felt that what the church needed was a Pope who would be more concerned with inner church life and less with the political impact of the papacy. However, at the conclave, these disagreements became quite irrelevant. When it appeared that Rampolla might be elected, the archbishop of Krakow rose, and, in an echo from the imperial past, announced that the Austro-Hungarian Empire would veto the election of Rampolla. The cardinals then quickly agreed on Giuseppe Sarto, the Patriarch of Venice, who took the name Pius X and reigned as Pope from 1903 to 1914. It is possible that the desire of many of the cardinals for a less political and more "religious" Pope was even more effective in denying Rampolla the papacy than the archbishop's veto had been.

Pius X was, in this sense of the word, a religious Pope, and at least at the beginning of his reign, he did not disappoint the hopes of those who voted for him. In a series of decrees which revealed the hand of the skilled administrator, he initiated reforms in seminary training and in priestly life in Italy, and he reorganized the curial bureaucracy in a way which made it a much more effective tool of papal policy. He then set up a commission to revise canon law, and even though the new Code of Canon Law which was the result of this commission's work was to take effect only in 1918, it remained Pius' achievement and was in the hands of his appointee, Cardinal Gasparri, up to the time of the publication of the new Code.

But it was in the area of liturgy and sacramental life that Pius' reforms touched the lives of most people in the church. He was intrigued by the work on liturgy and Gregorian Chant which had been done by the monks at Solesmes, and from the year of his election he issued a series of decrees on church music which were designed to made the Mass more of a liturgical act and less of an operatic spectacle. Later decrees simplified the liturgical calendar, lessening the role of the saints, and making the celebration of the mysteries of Christ's life, death, and resurrection much more prominent and central to Catholic worship.

Most important were Pius' decrees on frequent communion and early communion for children. In his day there were still serious disagreements on the role of the Eucharist in Catholic life. Many saw it as a reward for those who had achieved a relatively high degree of sanctity, and they demanded a level of theological awareness and moral purity from those who approached the altar, which kept down the number of communicants and made daily communion extremely rare. Pius X belonged to another school, which saw the Eucharist not as a reward for the saintly, but as nourishment for those who were struggling to lead a Christian life. Between 1905 and 1910 he issued decrees which urged frequent communion, and established the principle that the basic requirement was freedom from mortal sin and the desire to receive the grace of the sacrament in order to live a full Christian life. These decrees further urged the lowering of the age at which children began to receive the Eucharist, and asserted that as long as they knew the difference between the eucharistic bread and ordinary bread, and desired to receive the former, they should be admitted to the sacrament. The Jesuits put themselves at the forefront of the new movement and campaigned for frequent and even daily communion in a way which was perfectly in accord with the wishes of Ignatius Loyola himself.

9.48 The Church in France

Pius X inherited a bad situation in France, but he did not handle it adroitly. The position of the church in France at the end of the nineteenth century was largely a result of the passionate hostility of the majority of French Catholics to the ideals of the French Revolution. Since before the time of Lamennais, Catholics had been split into two very unequal groups—a small group of liberal intellectuals, almost without influence in the official church, and a far larger group of arch-conservatives, who looked with horror on the Revolution and on the notions of toleration and freedom of conscience which it represented.

Since before the Revolution, many in the middle class and most of the intelligentsia had been estranged from the church, which they regarded as a relic of the unenlightened medieval past. Both the Bourbon monarchy of the Restoration (1815 to 1830) and the monarchy of the "July Revolution" (1830 to 1848) had restored the French church to its position of privilege, if not of power, and this policy continued with the creation of the Second Empire in 1851. In most parts of the country, the peasantry remained loyal to the church, and the nobility, consciously or unconsciously, made use of the church, because it was one of the most reliable props of the old social order. But the urban proletariat had been won to the slogans, if not the ideals, of the Revolution, and the upper middle classes, especially those in the professions, the government bureaucracy, and the arts, were increasingly alienated from the church, from Christianity (which they unfortunately identified with the church as they saw it), and from the "God" for whom conservative church-men claimed to speak.

The defeat of France in the Franco-Prussian War brought the Second Empire to an end, and the Third Repub-lic was born on a wave of revulsion against the shallowness, the injustice, and the clericalism of a social order with which the church seemed to be inextricably involved. From 1876 on, the leaders of the Third Republic were, in the main, hostile to the church, and they were bent on eradicating its influence from, and even its presence in, the public life of the country. In 1886 the teaching of religion in the schools was banned, and from that moment on, Catholics turned even more res-olutely against the Republic. Finally, in 1905 and 1906, leg-islation was passed which separated church and state. This brought to an end the public celebration of church holidays and suspended all government support of the church. It now became clear that churchmen had been living in a dream world through much of the nineteenth century and had felt that that century's slightly modernized version of the *ancien régime* would last forever. Pius X reacted with futile protests and with condemnations of the separation of church and state and of all of those responsible for it. To underline his dissat-isfaction with affairs in France, he went on to condemn, in 1910, a Christian youth movement, known as "le Sillon," which he suspected of being too sympathetic to the ideals of the Revolution. As in other questions touching the French church, he was woefully misinformed in this matter. In the face of this type of papal policy, it is not surprising that rela-tions between church and state in France remained thor-oughly unpleasant until the time of the First World War.

It would be impossible to turn from France at this mo-ment in its history without mentioning one of the most re-markable figures which the piety of that country has produced—Theresa of Lisieux (also known as Theresa of the Child Jesus). Very few seem to realize, even now, that Ther-esa's approach to spirituality represented a sharp break with the devotional tradition of the Catholic church in the Latin countries. In the century in which Marian devotion was on the rise, and in the very country in which Marian apparitions multiplied throughout the nineteenth century, Theresa's piety was centered on Jesus and on him alone. Departing from the post-Tridentine emphasis on devotion to the saints, Theresa turned directly to God, precisely as he was present in the weakness and powerlessness of his Son. And in a period in which Catholic piety was always in danger of finding, in external religious practice, a way of self-salvation, Theresa emphasized the absolute impossibility of saving oneself and the absolute necessity of throwing oneself on the mercy of God, and she did this in a language which was, at times, almost reminiscent of Luther.

9.49 The Modernist Crisis

Pius X's efforts to renew the interior life of the church were quite successful, but his defense of what he regarded as theological orthodoxy was nothing less than a scandal, and it delayed for more than fifty years the rapprochement of Catholic thought with that of the modern world. The "Modernist" crisis was the result of Pius' meddling in areas in which he was totally incompetent.

In the course of the nineteenth century, historical studies, both of scripture and of the development of doctrine, had made great progress in the German universities. Much of the work had been done in the Protestant faculties, but in Tübingen, exceptionally good work had been done by Catholic theologians as well. These studies made it clear that there was much in the doctrine and dogma of the Christian churches which had not existed unchanged from the beginning, but which had assumed its present form as a result of slow evolution over the years. These studies also made it clear that scripture was totally misunderstood if it was read as a naively literal account of events which were historical in the modern sense of the word. This new appreciation of the role of history began to win adherents among Catholics even outside Germany at the very end of the nineteenth century, and a collision with those elements which were committed to the scholastic concept of supra-historical and unchanging truth was inevitable.

In France, the priest and scholar, Alfred Loisy (1857–1940) used this new approach to help in the understanding of both scripture and church. He found no sympathy in Rome, either for his radical biblical criticism, or for his assertion that the church had not been immediately founded by Jesus, but was rather the result (and the quite *appropriate* result) of what Jesus had said and done. Loisy's books were placed on the Index of Forbidden Books in 1903. At about the same time, the English convert and later Jesuit, George Tyrrell (1861–1909), developed a notion of church which distinguished it from both papacy and hierarchy, and understood it as the community of those who hearkened to the presence of God, and who, in this process, achieved a deeper understanding of themselves and their task. To the Pope and to the curial officials who had been trained in textbook neo-scholasticism, such ideas were not only incomprehensible but extremely dangerous as well. (Strangely enough, no one seemed to notice at the time that the works of these so-called "Modernists" had been written, not with the purpose of changing Catholic dogma, but rather with the intention of refuting many of the positions of late nineteenth century liberal Protestantism.)

In 1907, Pius X published what might be called a new "Syllabus of Errors"—sixty-five theses which rejected the positions of Loisy, Tyrrell, and a number of Italian theologians concerning the role played by history in the writing of the bible, in the development of dogma, and in the life of the church. Later that same year, in the encyclical letter *Pascendi Dominici Gregis*, the Pope condemned what he called "Modernism." According to Pius, Modernists questioned the possibility of rational proofs for the existence of God, and argued that religious truth was nothing more than a response to human psychological needs. He claimed that the Modernists found in the dogmas of the church nothing more than the result of viewing changing human experience in the light of faith, and that they traced the origin of the sacraments to the human need for a concrete embodiment of faith.

From reading the letter, one could conclude that the

"Modernist" theologians had a clearly defined theological program, and that they had devised a diabolically clever plan to foist this program on the church by writing works which destroyed the foundations of the faith, and by insinuating themselves into key positions in the seminaries and the Catholic universities. Over the years it has become evident that "Modernism," in this sense, never existed outside of the minds of Pius X and his curial advisors. Modernism, as a theological program, was the invention of the Holy Office (successor to the Roman Inquisition).

But if Modernism was a figment of the conservative imagination, the reaction of Pius X was not. In addition to Loisy and Tyrrell, a number of other theologians were excommunicated, and an inquisitorial reign of terror began. A rigid censorship of theological writings was introduced, and spies were everywhere, nostrils aquiver for the slightest scent of the "modernist heresy." Competent theologians were slandered, and the reputations of men who were deeply loyal to the church were ruined. The Pontifical Biblical Commission had been founded under Leo XIII, in 1902, but from 1906 on, it handed down a number of decisions which dealt mainly with the Old Testament. These decisions were an embarrassment to Catholic scholars like the brilliant Dominican, Lagrange, who had been writing scholarly commentaries on the New Testament since 1890—commentaries which have not lost their value even after almost a century. In 1910 Pius X imposed an "Anti-Modernist Oath" on all seminary teachers and professors of Catholic theology (the oath was to be renewed annually!), on all priests, and on all candidates for the priesthood before their ordination. Although the worst excesses of this witch hunt lasted only until the death of Pius X, it had an unsettling influence on Catholic theology, especially in the twenties and thirties, and it was finally laid to rest only at the Second Vatican Council. (And, even today, the Curia tends to deal with theologians in a way which is a mockery of the judicial procedures that are accepted in all of the western democracies as essential for the protection of human rights.) As if this were not enough, Pius X then closed out the year 1910 with an encyclical letter in honor of Charles Borromeo, an

Italian bishop of counterreformation times, which was so na-ively and offensively anti-Protestant that it caused widespread protest among both Catholics and Protestants in Germany and was not promulgated in the Catholic churches there. The comment of the Jesuit superior general about Pius X was very near the mark: if there was one virtue which he lacked in an heroic degree, it was prudence.

9.5 FROM WORLD WAR I TO THE EVE OF WORLD WAR II

9.51 Benedict XV (1914–1922)

The next Pope was a man of intelligence and breadth of view, whose energies were absorbed in trying to prevent the First World War, and then in trying to mitigate the suffering of the innocent, once it had started. From the first year of his pontificate, he did all that he could to put an end to the anti-modernist witch hunt, although here the limits which even a Pope faced when confronted with the intransigence of his Curia became evident. In another area, although the unset-tled conditions of war made a solution of the Roman Question impossible for the moment, he practically terminated the pol-icy which ordered Italians to boycott the public life of their country, and he let it be known that he was not opposed in principle to a "Vatican City-style" solution of the Roman Question (that is, acceptance by the Pope of a small plot of land in Rome which would belong to him and would guar-antee his independence as well as the supra-national charac-ter of his office).

France and Italy had opposed Benedict's peace-making efforts just as effectively as had the powerful militarist clique in Germany, but then, when he insisted on remaining neutral during the war, the Pope was roundly criticized in both France and Italy for what the local chauvinists saw as his pro-German stance. His efforts on behalf of civilians and pris-oners of war were quietly effective, and without intending it, he won much prestige for the papacy. After the war, the climate in France improved considerably. Catholics had given their total support to the war, and had even interpreted it as a crusade against Protestant Germany, and the canonization, in 1920, of Joan of Arc, France's national heroine, pleased Frenchmen of all religious persuasions and none.

Benedict was one of the first to discern the importance of stripping the church in Asia and Africa of its colonialist image, and he fostered the development of a native clergy in the mission countries. He was in every respect a man of fine character and breadth of vision, and far ahead of his time. It is unfortunate that his pontificate lasted for only eight years and that so many of his initiatives were frustrated by the confusion of war.

9.52 Pius XI (1922 to 1939) and the Liturgical Movement

Pius XI was elected in 1922 and he became Pope in a world very different from that which had existed up until 1914. The experiences of the war and of the breakdown of the old European social and political order led many Catholics to see how damaging the papacy's rejection of the modern world during the nineteenth century had been. It also led them to see that it was the alliance of churchmen with political and social conservatism which had brought about the almost total alienation of the urban working classes from the church.

The new Pope was a man of contrasts. A noted mountain climber, he was also a patron of the arts and of ecclesiastical learning. On the one hand, he continued the uniformitizing tendencies of his pre-World War I predecessors (his letter *Deus Scientiarum Dominus* of 1931 is a good example—it aimed at securing the uniformity of seminary training throughout the world); but on the other hand, he recognized that there were currents moving in the church which had to be acknowledged, and which it might be possible to domesticate. He had taken note of the prominence of laymen in the Catholic associations of Germany, and he was well aware of the call of "Reform Catholicism" there about 1900 for the recognition of the maturity of the laity and of their need to be liberated from clerical tutelage. His approval, in 1925, of the movement known as *Catholic Action* is an interesting case in point. The definition ("the cooperation of the laity in the work of the hierarchy") was still thoroughly clerical, and yet he did recognize that the laity were claiming an active role in the church, and he decided that, within strict limits, this should be granted to them. His attitude toward the growing liturgical movement was similar—a kind of cautious approval. This movement was so important, and it has led to such sweeping changes in recent times, that it is worth taking a brief look at its history and the way the Popes dealt with the movement.

From the time of the Reformation on, calls for liturgy in the vernacular had never really been stilled in Germany. They were renewed by Wessenberg in the eighteenth century, and by the Tübingen theologian, Möhler, in the nineteenth century. These proponents of the vernacular saw in it the key to real *participation* by the laity in liturgy. For a long time, this tendency was checked by that drive for uniformity which was a hallmark of the ultramontane movement and which saw in the Latin language the divinely ordained guarantee of loyalty to Rome and to the Pope. It was also checked by the revival of Gregorian Chant at Solesmes, which, under the cover of liturgical renewal, had not really encouraged lay participation in the liturgy, but rather had made of liturgy a kind of sacred spectacle which worked "ex opere operato" for the good of the church, with or without a lay audience of passive spectators.

The modern liturgical movement really began with the reading of an important paper by a Benedictine, Dom Lambert, at a congress at Mechelen, Belgium, in 1909. The paper pointed out that the Mass should be (and had been, in the early church) the act of the whole Christian people, and that the participation of the laity was vitally important for them and for the whole church. "Romanità" was still too firmly in the saddle for the vernacular movement to enjoy quick success, but the new approach led to the introduction of the "dialogue Mass" on some occasions after 1920. (In the dialogue Mass the whole congregation joined in reciting the responses which had previously been muttered almost inaudibly by the altar boy, or even by the priest himself.) Sporadic use of the dialogue Mass led slowly to a new understanding, at least on the part of various "lay elites," of what liturgy was really about; but through the twenties, the movement was largely confined to academic and somewhat esoteric circles. As we will see, it was not until the historical and theological work of scholars like Jungmann, before and after the Second World War, that the liturgical movement achieved a clear understanding of its purpose and possibilities.

9.53 Problems in France Again

After the First World War, anti-clericalism lessened in France, partly because even the most convinced partisans of the republic could not deny the patriotism of the clergy during the war. A number of Catholic schools were opened and some excellent work was done in speculative theology and biblical studies. Unfortunately, the continued campaign of integralists (arch-conservatives) in the Biblical Commission and the Holy Office (successor to the Roman Inquisition) against a constructive engagement of Catholic thought with the modern world cast a pall over these efforts almost up to the time of the Second Vatican Council.

However, Pius XI had problems of another kind with the French church. He had a good sense of the universality of the church, and he did not hesitate to act when he saw tendencies which threatened that universality. A good example is his condemnation, in 1925, of the French Catholic movement known as *Action Française*. The position of the church in France was much changed by 1920, and, as we have seen, the enthusiastic patriotism of French Catholics during the First World War had won much respect for the church and the clergy. However, this patriotism itself was a symptom of the chauvinistic tendencies which were characteristic of French Catholicism; and particularly those with conservative or royalist leanings were given to identifying the French church with the universal church. All of these tendencies were concretized in a movement known as *Action Française*, which dated back to 1899, but which gained great influence on the resurgent tide of patriotism which followed on France's victory in the First World War. Pius XI's condemnation of the movement caused a crisis in France and made him very unpopular with the conservative wing of the French church, but he saw that the movement was using the faith as a prop for an outdated view of the political and social order, and that such a view would do immense harm to the church in France unless he took a strong position. The trouble which the church in France had during and after the Second World War, as a consequence of the support of the Vichy regime by a number of French bishops, showed that Pius' judgment was correct. French Catholics had, in the main, never accepted Leo XIII's sound advice to make their peace with the Revolution, and Catholic antipathy toward the Popular Front government of the thirties was partly at fault in the debacle of Vichy.

9.54 The Church in Spain and Portugal

During the papacy of Pius XI there were two violent outbreaks of a kind of anti-clericalism which had become a periodic epidemic in Spain since 1870. Since the Revolution of 1848 Spain had a long history of political instability, and an even longer history of the alliance of the Catholic hierarchy with arch-conservative political and social forces. In 1870 anti-clerical revolutionaries had taken control, but they were incapable of governing the country and in 1875 the monarchy returned and restored Catholicism to its privileged position. In 1909 a workers' revolt flared in Barcelona and one hundred and thirty-eight priests were killed by the enraged workers—a clear signal of how the working class in Catalonia felt about the church. The revolt was suppressed and the country returned to the old clerical conservatism, with Spanish Catholicism remaining the most traditional in Europe.

In 1928 a conservative and rather secret society, *Opus Dei*, was founded, and it exists to the present day, as a blend of arch-conservative (if not Fascist) political theory with extremely traditional concepts of religion and Catholic duty. But in other sectors of society, there was much underground opposition to the church, and in 1931 the Socialists were able to win the election and they promptly declared a Spanish republic. They immediately enacted legislation separating church and state and confiscating the property of the religious orders. But in 1933 the Socialists lost the election, and the confusion which followed lasted until 1936, when an army officer, Francisco Franco, crossed from Morocco at the head of an army of Moorish troops and began the Spanish Civil War. The war was fought with unparalleled brutality on both sides, and in those areas which were controlled by Republican and Socialist forces, a large numbers of priests and members of religious orders lost their lives. Franco finally won, with the help of Hitler and Mussolini, and established an extremely conservative dictatorship which recognized Catholicism as the only legitimate faith of the country. As a result of these policies, Franco Spain was largely isolated from the rest of Europe and it was not until his death that Spain began to move into the community of western European nations. It is only in recent years that the government has taken steps to dissociate itself from the antiquated church policy of the Franco regime. Although the overall picture of the church in Spain is very conservative even today, there are a number of younger bishops whose views on political and social questions are progressive and who have distanced themselves from the semi-feudal society of Spain's past.

The story of the relations of church and state in Portugal is similar to that of Spain. In 1910 a republican regime forced the separation of church and state, and in 1911 it became frankly anti-clerical and dedicated itself to de-Christianizing the country; its program was not stemmed even by the conservative revolt of 1918. In 1926 the confusion finally came to an end when Antonio Salazar assumed control. Rather than favoring the church, Salazar used it as a pillar of the arch-conservative state which he created as he proceeded to hermetically insulate Portugal from the rest of Europe. In general, all of these events on the Iberian peninsula took place without much reference to the papacy, and Pius XI had little influence on the church in either country during the period in which Franco and Salazar were in control.

9.55 The Lateran Treaties

In Italy, on the other hand, Pius XI's political initiatives were very successful and in 1929 he brought to an end the confrontation of the papacy and the Italian government which had lasted for fifty-nine years. The new Fascist regime of Benito Mussolini had come to power in 1922 and the dictator was eager for a settlement with the church. He was enough of a realist to see that his dreams of glory for himself, and for a resurgent Italy which he longed to lead, could not be achieved without at least the passive cooperation of that church to which virtually the entire population nominally belonged. Neither could it be done without the cooperation of the papacy which had been practically an Italian national institution for eighteen centuries. After long negotiations, the Lateran Treaties were signed in 1929. They set up Vatican City as papal territory within the city of Rome and arranged for the one-time payment of a large sum of money to the papacy by the Italian state, in compensation for the loss of the Papal States. In the treaties it was also affirmed that Catholicism was the state religion of Italy. In general, the relations of the church with the Mussolini government were quite good, and most churchmen urged loyalty to the dictator up to the time of his death in 1944.

9.56 The Church in Germany in the Twentieth Century

In Germany the situation was far more complicated and troubling. Catholics had been loyal and patriotic during the First World War, but they had never been very enthusiastic about the so-called Weimar Republic which replaced the Second Reich after the German defeat. This was strange, because during the twenties the church in Germany enjoyed more freedom and showed greater vitality than at any time in the past, and the younger clergy and the university chaplains had great success with young people. A Catholic youth movement, embodying strong emotional elements of the Romantic period, gripped the imagination of young Germans as never before.

As the Weimar Republic was rent by one economic crisis after another, the National Socialist movement gained strength, and increasing numbers of voters longed for the security which only an authoritarian regime could bring. In the late twenties and early thirties, church authorities resolutely opposed the Nazi movement. However, when Hitler was elected Chancellor in 1933, he arranged for a meeting with high church officials, and he explained his position and program so cleverly and persuasively that in March 1933 the German bishops withdrew all of their prohibitions against the National Socialist movement. In July of that same year, the papacy signed a concordat with Nazi Germany, which regulated the relations of church and state there. In the four years which followed, it became more and more evident that Hitler had concealed the real nature of the Nazi program from the bishops, and the Pope complained repeatedly about violations of the concordat—finally in the form of an encyclical letter, *Mit Brennender Sorge* in March 1937. Although in this letter the Pope attacked the pagan Nazi mythology in courageous and forceful terms, the strongest passages of the letter were reserved for violations of the concordat by the German government, and the letter had virtually nothing to say about the appalling violation of human rights in the Third Reich (probably because of the conciliatory policy of Pius XI's Secretary of State, Eugenio Pacelli—the later Pius XII). From 1937 to 1939, relations between church and state in Germany were tense and the Nazi government became increasingly hostile. This situation came to an end only with the outbreak of war in 1939, when the Nazis apparently felt that any further anti-Catholic episodes would hurt national unity.

9.57 Pius XI and Internal Church Affairs

On strictly religious terrain, the papacy of Pius XI was less successful. In matters of marital morality he was extremely conservative. He had been much irritated by the action of the assembled bishops of the Anglican church at Lambeth in 1929, in which they gave their approval to contraceptive practice on the part of married people, and in 1930 he issued an encyclical, *Casti Connubii*, which asserted the uncompromising opposition of the papacy to what was referred to as "artificial birth control." It was this letter, reaffirmed again and again by Pius XII almost up to his death in 1958, which constitutes what has become known as "the official Catholic position on birth control" up to the present day, and which no one in the church questioned publicly until the time of the Second Vatican Council. It was Pius XI's hard line position, essentially reaffirmed in a quite different context of questions and problems by Paul VI in 1968, which has precipitated the greatest crisis of authority in the Catholic church in modern times.

Finally, although Pius XI was as interested as his predecessors in restoring and strengthening ties with the Orthodox churches of the East, he really had no grasp whatsoever of what Catholic-Protestant dialogue might mean. He turned a cold shoulder to all requests for Catholic participation in the ecumenical movement which had developed within European Protestantism and which had found expression in the great international conferences on Faith and Order of the opening decades of the twentieth century. Like Popes before and after him, Pius XI found it virtually impossible to apply to his judgments about the world at large any standards less narrow than those he used in dealing with the Italian church.

9.6 PIUS XII (1939 to 1958)

Eugenio Pacelli had been nuntius in Germany and Secretary of State for Pius XI and no one was surprised at his election when Pius XI died in 1939. His pontificate will probably always be judged, especially by non-Catholics, on the basis of what he did or did not do to oppose the Nazi campaign of extermination against the Jews. It seems clear that in the mid-thirties he advised Pius XI against any condemnation of the National Socialist Movement as such, because he felt that this would lead to the political isolation of the papacy. This was not an unrealistic assumption, since at the time Mussolini was forming an alliance with Hitler and England and France were pursuing policies of appeasement. Once the war began, Pius XII's attitude on the Jewish question is more difficult to evaluate (and to defend). In 1943 the bishop of Berlin made an urgent request to the Pope to intervene on behalf of the Jews, but Pius apparently felt that such action would constitute violation of the concordat and would expose the church in Germany to reprisals on the part of an enraged dictator. However, it also seems clear that Pius XII's hatred of communism was so obsessive that he was quite careless in welcoming as allies all those who opposed Russian Bolshevism, for whatever reasons.

9.61 Eastern Europe

Pius' policies toward the communist states of eastern Europe after the Second World War were unrealistic and counterproductive, and they showed that the papacy had not learned its lesson from the loss of the Papal States in 1870— that it is a good thing to come to terms with the facts, no matter how unpleasant those facts may be.

As a result of allied agreements at Yalta near the end of the war, much of eastern Europe was given to the Soviet Union as its sphere of influence, and the satellite communist regimes which came to power there in the late forties were uniformly hostile to the church. The church in Poland had suffered appalling losses to both Russia and Germany during the war—twenty-six hundred priests had been murdered by the Nazis alone. Then in 1950, the communist government confiscated church lands and did all in its power to hamper the work of the church, particularly among the young. However, Polish nationalism had long been associated with the Catholic faith and it was the loyalty of Poles to the faith of their fathers against the Orthodox Russian East and the Protestant German West which nourished Polish national feeling during the long years when the country as such had disappeared from the map of Europe. The result was that loyalty to the Catholic faith in Poland was a political statement, not unlike loyalty to the Catholic faith in Ireland. But for this same reason, the church in Poland has had a rather conservative appearance up to the present day.

In Czechoslovakia the situation was very different. The Hussite movement of the fifteenth century had smoothed the way for Protestantism in Bohemia and Moravia. Far from being identified with the Catholic faith, Czech nationalism had run its course entirely outside the church's sphere of influence and it had developed its characteristic forms in opposition to the Austro-Hungarian Empire—the leading Catholic power of the day. As a result, the Communist assault on the church in the years after 1948 was incomparably more successful than it was in Poland, and today the church seems to have no influence at all on public life in the country. Judged in purely human terms, its chances of survival seem minimal.

In Hungary, the Communist campaign against the church began in 1948 and peaked in 1952 with the show-trial of the primate of the Hungarian church, Cardinal Mindszenty. There was a problem in Hungary and in many other parts of eastern Europe which a number of American Catholics never recognized: some of the very churchmen who were heroic defenders of the rights of the church were committed to an outdated social and economic order, and were arch-conservative, not only in church matters, but in political matters as well. After the death of Pius XII, Rome's policy toward the communist East became much more flexible, and Vatican diplomats have been able to secure a measure of toleration for Catholics in most countries outside Czechoslovakia.

9.62 Pius XII's Earlier Encyclicals

Pius XII was the "Encyclical Pope" par excellence, and although he does not hold the absolute record for the number of these general letters to the church, the forty which were issued in his name sum up the meaning of his papacy and his own understanding of the papal office. As was the case with other Popes, Pius XII did not write these letters himself. Individuals or committees were told, in general terms, what the

Pope wanted to say, and they then prepared a draft on which the Pope did varying amounts of editorial work.

Because the Catholic church during the reign of Pius XII remained very much the papal church (to a far greater extent than is the case today), these encyclicals are important historical documents. It is not simply that they indicate which way the winds were blowing, or, even more, who had the Pope's ear at any moment during his pontificate. Viewed in retrospect today, the most important of these letters show that this authoritarian Pope was well aware of powerful centrifugal tendencies which were on the move in his church, and that he did all in his power to bring pastoral innovations and what he regarded as an overly adventurous theology firmly under his control. Four major encyclicals give a clear indication of where the church was moving during the reign of Pius XII, and of what he did to control that movement.

In 1943 Pius issued an encyclical on the Mystical Body of Christ (*Mystici Corporis*). During and after the war, it was greeted by many as a bold initiative which broke with the sterile juridicism of Bellarmine's definition of the church as a "perfect society." But the encyclical is better understood as an attempt by Pius to domesticate theological tendencies which he regarded as dangerous. Biblical, patristic, and historical work in France and Germany during the twenties and thirties had already shown that Bellarmine's definition lacked a good scriptural pedigree, and many theologians felt that Paul's image of the church as body or organism might be the key to understanding its mystery. But Paul had asserted that *all* Christians are members of the body, although all are called to play different roles in the body. And there was another point which was calculated to make Rome nervous: the more one based a theology of the church on Paul's writings, the greater would be the emphasis on the universal priesthood of all Christians, and this would lead inevitably to a more egalitarian view of the church. This was inevitable, because in the communities which Paul founded, or to which he wrote, ministerial priesthood (that is, a separate priestly office) had not yet appeared, and the hierarchical and juridical elements of Bellarmine's definition were entirely lacking. In the Encyclical *Mystici Corporis*, Pius XII dealt with this problem in an interesting way. He asserted that the church was, to be sure, the Mystical Body of Christ (the word "mystical" in this sense was not a Pauline term), but he then asserted that the Mystical Body was to be identified with the hierarchical, juridically organized church. He thus accepted the Pauline image, but firmly subordinated it to another view of the church which was traditional but not biblical. This subordination of scripture to the papal teaching tradition was a characteristic of all of Pius XII's major letters.

In the same year, an even more important letter appeared; it bore the Latin title *Divino Afflante Spiritu* and dealt with the study of the Old and New Testaments. By the time of the Second World War, it had become clear to intelligent Catholic theologians that some way would have to be found to break with the primitivity and naiveté of the anti-modernist period. Catholic biblical scholars were still officially tied to positions which were hopelessly and even laughably outdated (and which had been articulated in the arch-conservative decrees of the Biblical Commission during the last decade of Pius X's reign). But the memory of the anti-Modernist witch hunts of that same period were still quite fresh in everyone's mind, and no one was willing to commit to writing positions which deviated from those which were officially prescribed. Exegesis and biblical theology in the church (with some exceptions in Germany) still lagged far behind what Lagrange had achieved in the nineties of the last century. Especially in France and Germany, theologians were becoming restive about a policy which rejected views about the character of the biblical writings which had become commonplaces in competent Protestant scholarship of the day.

Pius XII's encyclical in 1943 cautiously made room for scientific exegesis, and admitted that the scriptural writers had used literary forms different from those in use today, and that an understanding of those forms was necessary if the scriptural message was to be heard and understood. Pius clearly preferred evolution to revolution, and in the letter he staked out a moderately progressive position; he set more realistic parameters and then ordered Catholic scholars to remain within those parameters. But responsible scholarship follows its own rules and not those of an authoritarian system. Even more important, scripture follows its own rules; it has a dynamism all its own which will not allow it to be domesticated and put at the service of such a system. The biblical scholarship which had been suppressed in the church after 1910 was now claiming its right to be heard, and Pius XII's attempt to bring it under control was not successful (although this became clear only after almost twenty years).

Something quite similar happened with respect to the liturgical movement. During the twenties and thirties, developments in scripture and in the history of liturgy had taken place, and they brought in their train a new appreciation of the universal priesthood of the laity and a new sense of the importance of the participation of the laity in the liturgy. The word "liturgy" itself underwent a change in meaning. Formerly it had meant "the rules for performing an act of worship with ritual perfection," but now it came to mean "the public act of worship of the entire Christian community." By the early forties, liturgical experiments were taking place in France and Germany, and many observers felt that it was only a matter of time before they were sharply censured by Rome. But in his Encyclical of 1947, *Mediator Dei*, Pius XII gave a cautiously positive welcome to some of these experiments, and even allowed the use of the vernacular, not for Mass, but for the administration of some of the sacraments. In the years that followed the Encyclical, the ancient liturgy of Holy Week was restored. Pius had staked out so liberal a position that his attempt to get control of the liturgical movement appeared, for the moment, to be quite successful. It was not until the early sixties that it became clear that this Encyclical, too, had been a defensive, holding action on the part of the Pope.

9.63 The Encyclical "Humani Generis" and Pius' Final Years

The most significant event in the church in 1950 was the publication of the papal Encyclical *Humani Generis*. To understand this strange document, we will have to look briefly at developments in theology in the thirty years which preceded the publication of the Encyclical. In the twenties, theological leadership had passed to Germany. Romano Guardini's popular writings and lectures on scripture and liturgy advocated a return to those sources of Christian life which antedated the scholastic period by many centuries. In Tübingen, Karl Adam was developing an understanding of the church as a living and organic unity—an understanding which was a great improvement on the counterreformation's emphasis on the hierarchical and juridical elements in the church. But when Hitler came to power in Germany, this meant the end of the influence of the church in university circles and the youth movement, and for a time theological initiative passed to France.

In France, neo-scholasticism was so strong that it was evident that changes in Catholic theology would have to originate within the neo-scholastic movement itself, and this is precisely what happened. During the thirties and forties and especially after World War II, a number of Dominican and Jesuit scholars led a movement back to the sources—biblical, liturgical, and patristic—in the attempt to enrich the scholastic synthesis. The Dominicans Chenu and Congar and the Jesuits Daniélou and de Lubac were the leading figures of this revival. They developed a view of theology and life which was later to be called "la nouvelle théologie" ("the new theology"). All of these theologians had a good sense of history and of the extent to which history conditions our understanding of God, of our world, and of ourselves, and of the way we speak about all three. These theologians felt a deep respect for the biblical and patristic sources of Christian faith, and they urged a return to these sources in order to avoid the sterility into which Catholic theology had fallen again and again since the scholastic period. Their interest in the sources led them to see the chasm which separated the thought of Thomas Aquinas from that of his so-called interpreters. Finally, these theologians saw that divine grace was not something added to human nature from the outside, as though it were a piece of clothing, or

even a foreign body, but that it was the fulfillment of everything for which human nature was always longing in a silent
and inarticulate way.

These theological theses were not without influence on
church life, because they made people aware of how far the
institutional church of their day had moved from the church
of earlier periods. In France, this led to the honest admission
on the part of even some bishops that the country had become
largely unchristian. It was this awareness which led to the
"priest worker" movement, in which priests went into the fac-
tories to share fully the lives of the workers, so that they might
bring them a Christian faith which had never really been offered to them. (This priest worker movement, which began
in 1941 and received official approval in 1943 as the "Mission
de France," functioned effectively during the latter years of
the war and for about seven years after it. But conservative
French Catholics were infuriated by the radical positions
taken by many of the priests in the movement. Conservative
influence was strong in Rome at the time, and in 1953 severe
restrictions were imposed on the activities of the worker
priests and the movement was crippled. In 1965 the restrictions were largely removed.)

The movement back to the sources led to the insight that
Protestantism had taken with it much of the Christian patrimony at the time of the Reformation, and therefore it led to
a new understanding of the ecumenical task. Further, it led
some French Catholics to suspect that the opposition between
Marxism and Christianity was not fundamental, but was
rather the result of social conditions peculiar to the nineteenth century, particularly the involvement of the church
with the bourgeois social order. Some people even began to
suggest that Christian Marxism was a possibility. All of these
events provide the background for the Encyclical *Humani Generis* of 1950.

By the time the Encyclical was published, the final, quite
conservative period of Pius' reign had begun, and the influence of Curial reactionaries on the Pope was strong. Pius
probably sensed that his efforts to control what were, to him,
dangerous movements in the church were failing, and he be-

came very critical of those who wanted to break out of the rigid patterns of scholastic thought. When he condemned what he called "the new theology," he did so because he thought that the commitment of the leaders of this movement to scholasticism was only lukewarm, and he was very troubled by their desire to return to the biblical and patristic sources. He sensed that such a return to the sources would threaten the teaching authority of the church, as it was understood in his time (that is, as virtually identified with the teaching authority of the papacy!), and this led to what is undoubtedly the most remarkable statement of the Encyclical. Pius actually asserted that it was the task of the Catholic biblical scholar, when he writes on any biblical teaching, to take as his point of departure the most recent statement of the teaching authority of the church (that is, of the Pope!), and then to show that the content of that statement is *already* contained in scripture and that it is contained there *with the same meaning and the same sense.* This attempt to make scripture itself a tool of the teaching authority of the papacy represented the very summit of papal claims to absolute authority in the church.

It is not at all surprising that Pius XII was the first Pope after Vatican I to make use of the infallibility granted there. This was the second major event of the year 1950, and at the time many theologians felt that it had dealt a death blow to Catholic/Protestant ecumenism, although it merely climaxed a process which had been underway for some time. We have already seen how Marian piety developed during the nineteenth century. This development continued into the twentieth century and peaked in 1917 with the reputed apparition of the Blessed Virgin at Fatima in Portugal. The revelations at Fatima were in many respects a typical manifestation of rural, Latin piety, but in time the Fatima movement took on many of the trappings of an anti-communist crusade, which may have been a major factor in its winning the support of Pius XII. In any case, he felt that early in 1950, while walking in the Vatican gardens, he had experienced a rerun of the Fatima apparition, and this may have inclined him to promulgate the dogma of the Assumption of the Blessed Virgin— that is, to demand of all who wish to remain Catholic that they accept the fact that after Mary's death she was taken directly into heaven, body and soul. This definition showed to how great a degree Pius was living in another world and how little sympathy or understanding he had for the ecumenical movement.

It was not until twelve years later that it became evident that the Encyclical *Humani Generis* was simply the final salvo of an integralist, anti-Modernist movement, whose day had come and gone. In the fifties, partly as a result of this letter, theological initiative in the Catholic church passed to Germany again. In 1939 the Jesuit, Karl Rahner (1904–1984), had published a brilliant reinterpretation of Thomas Aquinas' theory of knowledge, and on the basis of that reinterpretation, a seemingly endless series of essays had proceeded from Rahner's typewriter, criticizing those elements of church life, from indulgences to private Masses, which lacked a firm basis in the public revelation of the church. Rahner has been extremely effective, because he never demanded that any practice be abolished outright. He simply reinterpreted the practices, isolated those elements in them which were genuine, and then suggested that these elements might be better preserved in another context and in different terms. Furthermore, Rahner was a Jesuit and therefore not suspect to Rome as he would have been if he had a chair of theology at one of the German universities (he was offered one in Munich rather late in life and accepted it). In addition, he was well-versed in the methods of neo-scholasticism, and he was able to make use of them in a very subtle way to topple the sterile edifice which had been the inevitable result of Leo XIII's attempt in 1879 to make Thomas Aquinas the court philosopher and theologian of the Catholic church (certainly an insult to a man of Thomas' depth and brilliance!).

Other factors worked to the advantage of German theology during this decade as well; Catholic exegetes there continued to do good work; neo-scholasticism had never been strong in Germany and it was virtually absent from the universities; in Tübingen, Geiselmann was reevaluating the post-Tridentine notion of tradition as a separate and competing source of faith and was suggesting that there was nothing contained in genuine tradition which was not already present in scripture. Finally, the Curia (central administration of the church) at the time was much less international in make-up than it is today—in fact, it was almost exclusively Italian. The work of these German theologians was not being translated into Italian, and although the Pope could read German (and occasionally did become quite irate at some of the things Karl Rahner wrote), the conservatives in the Curia who would have been interested in stamping out these trends were quite unaware of their existence for a number of years.

Pius XII had made a valiant attempt to hold the line, but he seemed to sense that control was slipping from his hands. But when he died in 1958, no one seemed to realize that the church was on the brink of a new epoch which would bring changes more profound than any that had occurred in more than a thousand years. The Second Vatican Council, which the new Pope announced less than a year after Pius' death, was an event of epoch-making importance in the life of the church, and it shook the foundations of Catholic life. Surprisingly, it was an event for which the church had been preparing, quite unconsciously, at least since the apparent triumph of ultramontanism in 1870.

10

From Vatican II to the Present

10.1 JOHN XXIII AND THE SECOND VATICAN COUNCIL

Pius XII's successor took the name John XXIII, and reigned from 1958 to 1963—a relatively short pontificate for popes of modern times—but in those five years the new pope put his unique imprint on both the church and the papacy. Most of the cardinals who chose Angelo Roncalli as Pope probably thought that they were electing what is euphemistically called "a transitional Pope"—a man of advanced age who would occupy the papal throne for a few years without rocking the boat. The real function of such a figure is to hold the papal office open for another cardinal, who needs a little more time to become better known, to gain support, or, simply to age, so that he will be eligible in the next election, which will presumably take place in the not-too-distant future. In this sense, Roncalli may have been the candidate of the Curia (even though Curial cardinals were outnumbered in the College of Cardinals by 1958). The cardinals in the papal bureaucracy had felt somewhat slighted during the later years of Pius XII, because he had kept the reins of power firmly in his own hands and delegated little of importance to the Curia. The Curia was now ready to reassert its power, but its leading candidates needed a few more years of aging, and of making more contacts, before they could be considered "papabili"—appropriate candidates for papal office.

If this surmise is correct, then never in history did the Curia make a more serious error in judgment (from its own point of view). The new Pope was a man of peasant origins, blessed with an engaging manner and simple piety, shrewd, observant, and, although trained in the stifling atmosphere of an early twentieth century Italian seminary, nevertheless the beneficiary of years of experience which had broadened his perspective and given him a deep understanding of the real world and its needs. In the twenties and thirties he had worked in the papal diplomatic service, in Bulgaria, Greece, and Turkey—countries in which non-Roman Catholics, and, in the latter case, non-Christians, were in the majority. (He had apparently been relegated to what the Vatican diplomatic service regarded as relatively unimportant backwaters because Curial officials did not feel that this rotund peasant would cut a proper figure in the centers of European power.) However, in 1944 he had been sent to Paris to deal with the delicate question of the "Vichy bishops"—that is, the French bishops who had supported the policies of the puppet regime at Vichy during the Second World War. The new French government wanted them removed, but Roncalli charmed the authorities into allowing a few bishops to resign "for reasons of health," while the others, whose support of Vichy had been less whole-hearted, would be allowed to remain.

On January 25, 1959, John announced that an Ecumenical Council would meet in the not too distant future. In June, 1960, the Curia was told to begin preparatory work for the Council, which would be called the "Second Vatican Council." Already at this early stage, many members of the Curia were worried about the coming council, and some were beginning to wonder if they had not made a serious mistake in electing John XXIII. Actually, no one knew just what to make of the coming meeting; even some leading Catholic theologians had been certain that Vatican I would prove to be the last ecumenical council; once the Pope had been declared infallible, it seemed difficult to find any role for such a council to play in the life of the church. Furthermore, those parts of canon law which dealt with councils (canons 222 to 229 of the old Code of Canon Law) made it clear that such gatherings were merely consultative bodies. They were to so great an extent tools of papal policy that on the death of the Pope who summoned it, a council automatically ceased to meet and juridically ceased to exist. The general feeling in much of the church in early 1959

was that the Second Vatican Council would be a largely ceremonial demonstration of unity in the church and of support
for one or two pet projects of the Pope. However, before the
end of the year, the coming council had gripped the popular
imagination, triggered wide-ranging discussion, and awakened
hopes, in a way which indicated that powerful forces, profoundly spiritual because rooted in scripture, had been latent
in Catholicism and were now ready to break into the open and
to transform the church. It was John's call for "aggiornamento"
(bringing the church up to date) which inspired enthusiasm in
some and fear in others, because it implied that the church
was, in some significant ways, out of date.

Some have wondered how the Curia could have been
ignorant of Roncalli's reforming tendencies, his up-to-date
ecclesiology, modern ideas about liturgy, etc. The answer is
that his theological ideas were not particularly up to date.
(After all, the instruction *Veterum Sapientia*, mandating a
return to Latin as the language of instruction in seminaries,
was issued over his signature in 1961.) It was rather that he
sensed that the church had lost contact with the modern
world, and that he was convinced that things would work out
if the Holy Spirit was allowed to speak through the bishops of
the world. If John XXIII had a "pet project," this was it.

10.11 The First Session of the Council

On October 11, 1962, twenty five hundred bishops came
to Rome for the first session of the Council. They heard the
Pope give an opening address which emphasized the pastoral
character of the Council and clearly indicated that, in his view,
the church needed to be brought up to date. John's opening
address also implied that a rerun of the old condemnations of
the modern world was not the result which he wished from his
Council. Curial officials were most troubled by John's obvious
willingness to allow the bishops full freedom of discussion
and to welcome their initiatives.

But the Curia still held what looked like a strong card.
The direction which the Council would take depended very
much on the *Commissions*—that is, committees of twenty-four
members each which were to prepare the outlines which

would serve as a basis for discussion and debate. The Curial party already had lists of candidates for these positions prepared and hoped to have them rubber-stamped by the bishops. But when they met, the bishops demanded time to prepare their own lists. More than anything else, this set the tone for the Council. In addition, the Curia had already prepared initial *schemata*—outlines of decrees which it wanted the bishops to approve. These documents were extremely conservative and amounted to a rehashing of Vatican I, differing only in the fact that they reproved and condemned developments in theology, church life, and the world at large, which had come into being since 1870. These schemata were very much in the spirit of Pius IX and Pius X, and eventually *all but one* were rejected by the bishops at the Council.

The first thing that the bishops did, taking their cue from the Pope, was to vote a group of moderate and even progressive bishops into power in the commissions which were to prepare the outlines for discussion. It soon became evident that the Pope was behind this new coalition, and this was the first time in many centuries that the Pope and the Curia were not united in taking a common stand in the face of, if not against, the worldwide episcopacy. John XXIII was apparently the first Pope since the fifteenth century who did not fear the specter of conciliarism.

At the first series of meetings in the fall of 1962 the bishops held long discussions on the question of liturgy—the only one of the prepared schemata which they allowed to stand as written. For years, although the Mass was theoretically the center of Catholic piety, it was actually the Eucharist, *not as the action of the community, but as an object of adoration,* which played this role. The liturgical movement in France and Germany from the twenties on had made a number of bishops aware of this dangerous imbalance in eucharistic piety. Many of them apparently saw that the ceremonies of this piety, with some vernacular hymns and devotions, were able to engage the laity, to involve them, in a way in which the celebration of liturgy did not. It was probably this insight which generated strong support for the use of the vernacular languages in the celebration of the liturgy itself, and which has led to the greatest visible change in

Catholic life in modern times (although the council itself was far more cautious in permitting the vernacular at Mass than papal instructions of the post-conciliar era would prove to be). In any case, vernacular liturgy was inevitable because it was an inevitable consequence of something else which was the heart of the matter: the call for the laity to make the eucharistic celebration their own, and for close integration of the sacramental action with the scripture readings and the homily.

On November 14, 1962 the bishops began discussion of a document on the sources of revelation—one of those schemata which had been prepared by a commission of Curial theologians. It immediately became clear that a number of the council fathers were very dissatisfied with the negative tone of the document, with its outdated scholastic terminology, and with its resolute rejection of recent theological work on the relation of scripture and tradition. When a vote was taken on what to do about the outline, just short of the required two-thirds majority of the bishops wanted to reject it outright and to send it back for fundamental revision. Very significantly, at this point the Pope cast the deciding vote on the side of the majority and ordered the document returned to its authors for revision. This was merely a face-saving formula for the Curia—the document was rejected and it was to be replaced with an entirely new one.

When the bishops adjourned on December 8, planning to meet again the following fall, they did not know that their deliberations would continue under a new Pope. John XXIII died before they were to meet again, and he was mourned by a larger percentage of the population of the world—Catholic, Protestant, Jewish, Muslim, agnostic, and atheist—than any Pope in the entire history of the church. He was a thoroughly engaging individual, and a truly humble man who was able to move with equal ease among the mighty and the lowly. He was a man of simple piety and of great trust in God, and a man free of all dogmatic narrowness and defensive anxiety. He realized that the church was in many ways out of date and incapable of dealing with the challenges and opportunities of the modern world. But he also felt that in an atmosphere of free and open discussion, God would move him and his brother bishops in the right direction, if they gave the Holy Spirit sufficient elbow room.

In his rather short pontificate, John XXIII gave the modern world a totally new definition of the word *Pope*. His notion of papacy was not authoritarian but pastoral. He emphasized that he himself was a bishop, and he did all that he could to associate the other bishops with himself in the leadership of the worldwide church. He decentralized church administration and insisted that bishops be recognized and treated as successors of the Apostles and not merely as local ambassadors of the papacy or representatives of the Curial bureaucracy. Finally, he brought an entirely new approach to ecumenism, and suggested that separated Christians should not be asked to return as penitents to Catholic unity, but that all Christians, including, first and foremost, Catholics, should put their own affairs in order and should atone for their past arrogance and bigotry. He seemed to feel that if Christians did this, they would find out that they were far closer to each other than they had realized. When he died on June 3, 1963, he had already been able to put the stamp of his humble but powerful personality on the Council and its work.

10.2 PAUL VI

Cardinal Giovanni Battista Montini, the Archbishop of Milan, succeeded John XXIII, and took the name, Paul VI. He had worked in the papal Secretariat of State under Eugenio Pacelli (the later Pius XII) in his earlier years, but as a result of a (never clarified) dispute within the Curia, and involving Pius XII, he had been sent to Milan, somewhat pointedly without the cardinal's hat, and his curial career was obviously at an end. Montini was the first cardinal chosen by John XXIII—just in time, as it turned out, for him to be at the conclave which followed John's death. The new Pope was sincerely committed to continuing the Council—and in any case by this time it had gathered such momentum that any attempt to terminate it would have caused havoc in the church. At the same time, it is possible that Paul VI was already beginning to worry about the direction the Council was taking, and to wonder if the bishops might not be making too great use of the freedom of discussion which John XXIII had urged on them.

10.21 The Second Session of the Council

The second period of discussion and debate took place from September 29 to December 4, 1963, and centered on three important questions. The first was a new understanding of the church as the *people of God*–a concept which had strong biblical support but which had been neglected during the entire counterreformation period. This new notion implied a very different view of the role of the hierarchy in the church: they were not a privileged caste, endowed with the God-given role of ordering the laity about, but were a group called to serve the people of God while remaining, themselves, a part of that people. The second question discussed was that of *collegiality*–the theory that the bishops, together with the Pope, formed a group like that which was constituted by Peter and the other Apostles in the early church. This theory also implied that leadership and decision-making in the church should be the work of this body, this corporate group, and not simply the work of an isolated individual. The bishops were beginning to balance Vatican I's extreme emphasis on papal authority by pointing out that the Pope ordinarily should not act in isolation, but should act as the leader of (and a member of) the college of bishops. In the third place, at these meetings in the fall of 1963, the bishops also decided on the renewal of the *diaconate*–that form of the sacrament of orders which endowed its recipients with virtually all priestly functions short of the authorization to celebrate Mass and to grant sacramental absolution. In an important move, they recommended that this form of the sacrament might, under the proper circumstances, be granted to mature married men. Finally, during this same period there was much discussion on the question of ecumenism. It seems certain that it was during this second series of meetings that Paul VI began to fear the direction that the Council was taking; and in the interim between the second session in the fall of 1963 and the third in the fall of 1964, these fears took concrete shape and form, as we will see.

10.22 The Third Session of the Council

The third session of the Council took place from September 14 to November 21, 1964. This session saw the important discussion of the Constitution on Divine Revelation, which led to a strong assertion of the primacy of scripture as a source of Christian faith—an assertion not readily reconcilable with the views of Pius XII in his Encyclical of 1950, *Humani Generis.* During this series of meetings, the bishops began to search for compromise formulas which would express the results of their discussions in a mildly progressive form, but one temperate enough to win the allegiance of the overwhelming majority of the bishops of the world.

When the document on the church (which had been discussed during the second session) was presented in reworked form (which supposedly reflected the earlier discussions), a number of bishops were irritated to find that the Pope himself had made changes without consulting them—changes which lessened the significance of collegiality and strongly re-emphasized papal primacy. (And, of course, the very fact of the Pope's intervention was itself a repudiation of collegiality.) Changes had also been made in the proposed decree on ecumenism which had the effect of weakening it, and this also annoyed many of the bishops of France, and even more, those of Holland and Germany. During this third session, some leading churchmen (among them Cardinals Alfrink, Suenens, and Léger) asked publicly for a discussion of the so-called "official" position on birth control. At this juncture, Paul VI showed how different his approach was from that of John XXIII: he simply removed the question from the agenda and ordered the assembled bishops not to discuss it. He announced that he would appoint a commission of his own to examine the question and to report directly to him (after the Council was over!). Although these papal initiatives created some resentment, there was little the bishops could do. The Catholic Church was still the papal church, and the bishops at the Council had too deep a sense of their common responsibility for the unity of the church to take any action which might compromise that unity.

10.23 The Fourth Session of the Council

When the bishops met in the fall of 1965 for the fourth and final series of meetings (September 14 to December 8), their task was largely that of editorial work—that is, the preparation of the documents for the final voting (although they did manage to give their approval to a strong statement on religious liberty). It is clear that by this time the Council had lost both its élan and its momentum, and it is significant that, in the final document on the church, less emphasis is given to the church as people of God, and more to the church as sacrament—that is, as the effective sign of the presence of God on earth. Some found this change unfortunate, but it did provide some needed balance. The church is not simply a human community; it is a mysterious entity, which incarnates God in human words and actions, and the new image, joined to that of the people of God, and not replacing it, makes that important point very clearly. And the linking of the two images represented a vast improvement over Bellarmine's approach (church as a "perfect society"), which had dominated the counterreformation era (see §9.61 above). It also became clear in this fourth session, both from the form and content of the decrees, that the era of neo-scholasticism in the church had come to an end, and it was evident that a new era of international cooperation among Catholic theologians had dawned. For the first time, theologians began to feel that they constituted a body with a recognized task in the church, and that they had a divine commission to fulfill that task in an atmosphere of freedom and mutual cooperation similar to that which characterizes scholarly work in all other areas of human endeavor.

The Council had shown that many bishops were aware that the church had lost contact with the modern world. The first two sessions had given them a deep sense of their own collegiality, and of their common responsibility, with the Bishop of Rome, for the universal church. The meetings themselves had provided the format for such cooperation, while John XXIII had offered (for the first session) papal stimulus, encouragement, and approval. But it became evident in the later sessions of the Council and in the years which followed it, that without the proper forum (provided by the Council itself), and when papal encouragement was cautious and restrained, the bishops were unable to act as a body, and collegiality retreated to the realm of theological theory.

The initiatives of the Second Vatican Council have put their stamp on the church since 1965. The conciliar decrees were generally well-received, but they were implemented unevenly and, at times, superficially. In some areas (notably the liturgical changes) there was resistance, and that resistance has grown in recent years, with significant support from Rome. Publications such as *The Latin Mass,* and *The Adoremus Bulletin* have attacked Paul VI's liturgical reforms, and the indult of 1984, allowing the Tridentine Mass in certain circumstances has, in the view of a number of bishops, left liturgical reform and renewal in disarray. Some developments over the more than thirty years since the Council came to an end could not have been foreseen (most notably the changing role of women in the world and the church, and the resurgence of conservative forces in the church), and these developments have led, at times, to bitter confrontations.

It is becoming clear that the Council was a far more complex event than many suspected. It was the expression of a pastoral vision which saw that the church is there for the world (and not for itself), but it was, at the same time, a perhaps overly optimistic vision, which was not fully aware of the recalcitrance of the world, and of the world's resistance to adopting the ideals of the kingdom of God. The Council tapped hidden sources of life and power (for example, the new roles of the laity which followed from the perception that the Spirit is given in Baptism), but it also set the stage for intense polarization in the church (particularly, again, in matters of liturgy, but also on questions of the nature and limits of dissent). As was to be expected, the term "the spirit of Second Vatican" has had different meanings for different groups in the church.

The problems that have surfaced during the decades which followed the Council stem from a simple fact which is not often noted: unlike their predecessors at Trent, the bishops at Vatican II had too much of a sense of history to try to fashion a church which would remain unchanged into the indefinite future, and had too deep an awareness of the fact that human beings are not simply observers of a changing world, but that they themselves are constantly changing in the process. The popes who reigned during the twenty years of sporadic meetings which we refer to as "the Council of Trent," wanted to achieve clarity about what traditional teaching had been, presumably from the beginning, so that the church, armed with immutable truth, might confront and vanquish the Reformation. (This was most evident in an event which followed the Council: the promulgation of the revision of the Mass by Pius V, which was to be in vigor *"in perpetuity"*–words which liturgical conservatives never tire of citing.) But the bishops at Vatican II were not thinking of four centuries of immobility; they wanted to bring about renewal by a return to the sources and, in their view and intent, this return would power that renewal into the indefinite future.

In the rest of this chapter we will be examining some of the events of the years since Vatican II, and looking at the reciprocal relationship of these events to the Council and its documents, seeing them as events which reveal the complexity of the initiatives of the Council and of hidden motifs in the conciliar discussions, of which even their authors were not fully aware. It was often these hidden motifs which made it possible in the years after the Council to raise some questions which could not have been broached before: questions, for example, about the possibility of a full sacramental life for the divorced and remarried; about the possibility of women being ordained to the priesthood; and about the wisdom of retaining the law of celibacy for priests in the Latin rite. However, although some groups welcomed these questions, others thought they should never have been raised, and this led to conflict.

Even as we turn to the effects of the Council on the church in the decades which followed, it is good to remember that the understanding of the church and its mission which prevailed there was not as radically new as many thought; the best initiatives of the Council derived their content power from the work of theologians who sometimes paid dearly for their attempt to restate the ancient truths in language men and women of this century could understand. The continuation of the work of the Council demands the same kind of commitment from theologians and the same kind of cooperation between the bishops and theologians which was such a remarkable fruit of the sessions of the Council.

10.24 The Pontificate of Paul VI after the Council

In the years after the closing of the Second Vatican Council in 1965, Paul VI seemed more fearful of the new currents which were moving in the church and more indecisive about how to control them. In accord with the wishes of the Council, in 1965 he created the Bishops' Synod—an arrangement in accordance with which representatives of the world episcopacy would meet periodically in Rome. But Paul was ill at ease with the concept of a Synod, and he was at pains to underline the fact that the bishops who met at the Synod were in no sense a legislative body, but were merely a group of consultors, whose advice he could accept or reject. It seems clear that the Bishops' Synod has not fulfilled the hopes of those at the Council who urged its formation. Paul's conservative tendencies were apparent in other ways too: in that same year (1965) he published an Encyclical entitled *Mysterium Fidei* (Mystery of Faith) which was theologically very conservative and, in some respects, almost anti-Modernist in tone.

Liberation Theology

Paul VI was much more successful in dealing with social questions, and the two encyclicals, *Populorum Progressio* and *Octogesima Adveniens,* broke new ground in this area (see §10.47 later in this chapter). He took the initiative in pushing the bishops of South America to meet at Medellin, in Colombia, in 1968, and in approving the program hammered out at that meeting. (The meeting is often referred to as CELAM II—the acronym for "Conferencia Episcopal Latinoamericana"). Since the principles approved there embodied what many saw as a "liberationist" agenda, some comments on what came to be called "liberation theology" will be appropriate here, even though they will bring us to a time after the pontificate of Paul VI.

Although its full development came only after Vatican II

(the Council's document *Gaudium et Spes,* §§26,27, provided much of the impetus), liberation theology had already begun to take shape before the Council and, although there are African and Asian (and even North American) varieties, it was Latin American theologians who provided much of the theory and set the tone. It was there that theologians (some of them trained in major European centers) began to reflect on the relationship between the Christian message and the oppressive social and political structures which held so many in their grip. They began to argue that the Christian message itself demands structural changes in the political, social, and economic orders. Gustavo Gutiérrez of Peru was the best known, and it was his book, *A Theology of Liberation,* in 1971, which popularized the term; but others took up the cause and were influential in the 1970s and 1980s: Juan Luis Secundo in Uruguay, Leonardo Boff in Brazil, and Jon Sobrino in El Salvador. (It was in the same year, 1971, that the Synod of Bishops produced the document *Justice in the World,* echoing liberationist themes.)

Liberation theology was not monolithic. What all its protagonists agreed on was that Jesus Christ brings us a liberation which touches all dimensions of human existence, and demands change in the oppressive structures which dehumanize our lives. They also agreed that real theology could be done only in a situation of solidarity with the poor, and that, for this reason, "base communities," where the poor gathered to reflect on the Gospel from their own perspective and made plans for social transformation, should become a fundamental structure of church life.

There was another element which appeared in some (by no means all) of the writings of liberationists, and which led some to question their Christian credentials and gave others a pretext to do the same. This element was the use of Marxist social analysis as a tool for understanding the oppressive structures of society, and for devising ways of overturning these structures. Those who were opposed in principle to any linking of the Christian message with economic and political liberation found a pretext for their opposition here, while many of those who were favorable to the basic liberationist agenda asked why some liberation theologians were borrowing anything from a system which had demonstrated its efficiency in only three respects: producing tyranny, shortages, and ecological disasters. Rome's wariness of liberation theology found expression in a document of the Congregation for the Doctrine of the Faith in 1984 entitled "Certain Aspects of the Theology of Liberation," and in the silencing of Leonardo Boff in 1985.

On the other hand, while rejecting themes such as Marxist economics, class war, and violent revolution (which were never part of the mainstream of liberation theology, but could be found out at the fringe), John Paul II has been favorable to the liberationist agenda, and he made his own the key phrase of CELAM III, which met in Puebla, Mexico in 1979—the church's "preferential option for the poor." And many of the points made in his encyclicals, *Laborem Exercens* and *Sollicitudo Rei Socialis*, provide the basis for a profound theology of liberation.

It is probably too early to draw up a balance sheet on liberation theology. The collapse of the former Soviet Union and the movement of China toward a market economy have left the world with basically one economic system, and this has made the core Christian elements of the liberationist program more relevant than ever, while rendering the ideological aspects of that program passé. Furthermore, the appointment of politically and ecclesiastically conservative bishops in Central and South America in recent years has clouded the picture. Archbishop Rembert Weakland's comments in an article in *America*, March 22, 1997 may be very close to the truth: "There has been a definite weakening of interest in liberation theology....The question must be asked if liberation theology has spun itself out....I sense that, in spite of what theologians have written about the popular church, the people in those countries want what people everywhere want, namely a higher standard of living like that which they believe is found in the United States."

Reforming the Liturgy

Vatican II had laid down the principles of liturgical reform, but it left the execution of its initiatives in the hands of the Pope. And Paul VI did implement those decrees, clearly and decisively, in a series of actions between 1964 and 1972. In 1964, Paul announced that the Tridentine Mass was no longer the official rite of the Latin church. In 1966 the furniture moved: altars were brought out toward the congregation and the priest began to face those in whose name he was presiding. In 1968 three new canons (that is, three new options for the central prayer of the liturgy) were introduced, and in 1969 a new *ordo Missae* (a set of instructions for the celebration of the liturgy) was introduced, in which the laity were mentioned for the first time. In following years the altar rails were removed, and bishops' conferences were given permission to authorize receiving communion in the hand and under both species. In fact, in view of what he achieved in these eight years, Paul's title to be honored as one of the great liturgical reformers in the history of the papacy is secure.

The year 1972 saw the introduction of a program which had a potential that few grasped at the time. It bore the somewhat cumbersome title of "The Rite of Christian Initiation for Adults," and was issued to fulfill a decision of the Council that was expressed in the document *Sacrosanctum Concilium,* §64, which called for the reintroduction of the catechumenate—a period of preparation for the reception of baptism for those who come to the sacrament as adults. Although the official title of the RCIA seemed to destine it for the relatively small audience of those who would be baptized at the Easter Vigil liturgy, the new rite had a hidden potential which has been realized in many parishes only during the past two decades: the rite is functioning as a catechumenate for those already baptized—that is, as a way in which Christians can come to a deeper understanding of the meaning of baptism, and of the commitment and dedication which the sacrament demands and empowers throughout their lives. There are riches here still to be exploited.

A Crisis of Authority

Paul's appointment of a commission to reexamine the birth control question caused him serious difficulties. In 1967 word leaked out that a majority of his own commission favored some basic changes in the "official" position on birth control, as that position had been articulated by Pius XI and Pius XII. But after long delay, Paul issued an encyclical in the summer of 1968 entitled *Humanae Vitae,* which reiterated earlier papal condemnations of contraception and went on to include the newly marketed contraceptive pill in the condemnation. (In the encyclical there were elements of a new and very positive teaching on the union and communion of the married couple, but few paid any attention to this teaching, because all interest was concentrated on a possible change in the earlier condemnations.) The teaching of this encyclical was rejected by the overwhelming majority of Catholics (in a survey conducted by Andrew Greeley the figure given was 94% of those for whom the encyclical had immediate significance—that is, Catholic couples in their child-bearing years) and by a large number of priests and bishops. The annoyance and disappointment of the Catholic laity was so great that even some bishops' conferences (groups of bishops from a single country who meet periodically to discuss questions of local interest) felt that it was important to demonstrate publicly their less than enthusiastic support for the theology of the encyclical. (The words of the Canadian bishops were typical: "Since they are not denying any point of divine and Catholic faith, nor rejecting the teaching authority of the church, these Catholics [who cannot accept the teaching of the encyclical] should not be considered and should not consider themselves, shut off from the body of the faithful.")

It is arguable that *Humanae Vitae* did more to undermine the foundations of papal authority than any event in the entire history of the church, and, sadly, the shadow of this fiasco hung over the final ten years of Paul's pontificate. He traveled widely—more than any Pope before him—and made some ecumenical gestures of great symbolic import, particularly in the direction of Eastern Orthodoxy, but also toward Protestants and toward the churches of the Anglican Communion, and he gave the church a politically and socially progressive image which won much praise from liberal elements throughout the world. But in the face of dissension within the church, he became ever more indecisive, as he realized that the Council had unleashed forces which he could not control. Paul VI was a brilliant man, and he was deeply concerned about the welfare of the church, but he had neither the strong personality of Leo XIII and Pius XII, nor the winning charism of John XXIII, and his final years were not easy.

Paul came to the end of his life as a troubled and almost tragic figure, whose attempt to preserve papal authority had led to the greatest crisis of authority in the modern church. In addition, he encountered criticism from both the left and the right. Liberals faulted him for the restrictions on collegiality which he imposed at and after Vatican II, and conservatives never forgave him for abandoning the Tridentine Mass. But history will be kind to Paul VI. Solutions will be found for the problems which shadowed his final years, and his great achievements—recommitment of the church to structural changes in society when demanded by justice, and reform of the liturgy—will loom ever larger as historians assess the meaning of his pontificate.

10.3 JOHN PAUL II

Paul VI died in 1978; his successor, John Paul I, lived for only one month and was succeeded in the same year by the Polish cardinal, Karol Wojtyła. The new Pope's style and program were clear from the beginning and, although advancing age and an attempted assassination in 1981 have taken their toll, his style and program have remained essentially unchanged. He combines profound concern for doctrinal unity with great personal charm and with a masterful use of the media. He is less committed to scholastic categories of thought than any of his predecessors have been for hundreds of years (and in fact he is quite at home with the personalist and existentialist philosophies which are typical products of the twentieth century). Some feel that his overall approach is restorative, but he sees his task as that of bringing to an end the period of confusion which followed the Second Vatican Council, and it is difficult to fault a Pope who is concerned about unity in doctrine and moral teaching.

10.4 HISTORY AT TOO CLOSE RANGE?

Despite the proverbial phrase, hindsight is never really 20/20. However, it is true that the very distance from a historical period which makes it difficult to gather the needed data compensates for that difficulty by making it possible to discern directions, trends, and historical movements, and to make judgments which have been refined and corrected in the great experimental laboratory of history itself. As we approach our own day and time, such judgments become more difficult, and it is easy to feel overwhelmed by the sheer number of disparate and apparently unconnected events, by the fragmentation of secular and religious life, and by the constant and accelerating rate of change in every sector of life. To understand what is happening at the present moment, we look for patterns in the past which might guide our assessments, but there is an intensity, a vividness, an immediacy, in our experience of the present which reminds us that nothing exactly like this moment has ever occurred on the planet before. And the laws of time itself award to the present a degree of reality which the past has irrevocably lost and the future does not yet possess. This obviously creates problems as we try to write the history of the past two decades.

We can't deal with the problem of "history at close range" by simply chronicling events. We need to concentrate on those events and developments which are typical of this moment in church history—those which reveal the deeper problems and confront us with the most difficult challenges, but also manifest the vitality of the church and suggest unsuspected possibilities in our present situation. Many of these events and processes touch the whole church, but, where possible, they will be illustrated by looking at events which have taken place in the American church. Some of these events and developments were a direct result of initiatives taken at Vatican II. All of them have been profoundly affected by the theology of the Council. The very fact that John Paul II asserted (January 25th, 1985, on the occasion of announcing the eighth Synod of Bishops) that "the Council remains the fundamental event in the life of the modern church...and it is the constant reference point of my every pastoral action" makes it imperative to examine the events of the past decades in this light.

10.41 Explosive Growth for a New Apostolate

In 1962, the year that the deliberations of the Second Vatican Council began, there appeared a book with a prophetic title. The author was Donald Thorman, who went on to become the third publisher of the *National Catholic Reporter,* and the title of the book was *The Emerging Layman.* Some of Thorman's proposals raised eyebrows at the time, although they were fairly mild and tame in comparison with the *Decree on the Apostolate of the Laity* which was to emerge in the final session of the Council in 1965. But it would be hard to find a better way of characterizing the church in the years since Vatican II than to speak of it as the time when the laity *emerged.*

In the years since the Council, lay ministers (the term had been virtually unknown) appeared at every level of church life. In the parishes, laypersons took their places on the altar as lectors and eucharistic ministers. On the diocesan level, Departments of Catechetical Ministries (or, as they are often called, Offices of Religious Education) were either newly formed or took on new and vastly expanded responsibilities, and these offices and departments were often staffed by laypersons or sisters. From the early seventies on, diocesan religious education congresses brought together thousands of participants who wanted updating on the meaning of Vatican II, and who, through that updating, were brought into contact with the theology of the laity which had been formulated by men like Yves Congar, Edward Schillebeeckx, and Karl Rahner. And, fulfilling a wish expressed by Cardinal Paul Emile Léger of Montréal at the Council in 1963, laypeople began to appear as students in the seminaries, sometimes outnumbering those studying for the priesthood. In other cases, seminaries which would have had to close because of a shortage of clerical candidates, were transformed into graduate schools of theology and ministry for lay students. Some of these were so successful that they led to the establishment of campuses in other cities. Interest in the lay apostolate on the national level found expression in the National Center for Pastoral Leadership, the National Association for Lay Ministry, the National Conference of Catechetical Leadership, and the National Federation for Catholic Youth Ministry, to mention just a few.

The new visibility of laypersons in roles which had been reserved to priests coincided with a serious and growing shortage of ordained clergy in Western Europe and North America (the shortage had been a fact of life in most parts of South America for centuries). But the initiatives of Vatican II did not see the development of the lay apostolate as a stop-gap measure, intended to cope with the priest shortage. Rather, chapters two and four of the Council's Dogmatic Constitution on the Church *(Lumen Gentium)*, and the whole *Decree on the Apostolate of the Laity* (AL), opened up new vistas because they saw the church, the people of God, as a priestly community, in which all members have a priestly office in virtue of baptism and confirmation. Chapter sixteen of AL insisted that the laity have an active share in the life and activity of the church, and chapter twenty-four affirmed the importance of their roles in catechetics, liturgy, and pastoral care. In fact, when the Council spoke (in AL) of the fact that laypersons would have to be present at times and in places where priests could not be present, they were not thinking precisely of the shortage of ordained clergy, but rather of the structures and conditions of modern life which, because of the professional training of laypersons, make it possible for them to make contact with their peers in professional groups and to reach an audience to which priests would have no access.

However, it remains true that the great expansion of the lay apostolate has come at precisely the time that large numbers of priests resigned from the active ministry, and the number of candidates entering the seminaries underwent exponential decline. And, although the expansion of the lay apostolate has theological and scriptural grounds which are valid independently of the priest shortage, the hyper-development of the lay apostolate in the past three decades is undeniably connected with this shortfall. This makes a brief glance at some statistics appropriate here. The figures vary only because some comparisons deal with the absolute number of priests, whether active or retired; others count only priests actively engaged in parish ministry. Some include priests who are members of religious orders, while others do not. Some surveys try to estimate results of the decline for the years 1992 or 1996, or even for a period a decade or two into the future. A distillation of the most reliable figures shows that there were about 35,000 active diocesan priests in the United States in 1966, and that the figure will drop to about 21,000 by the year 2005. (The statistics on seminarians are hard to evaluate, because earlier figures included men studying in minor or "prep" seminaries, the overwhelming majority of whom never continued to ordination. A practical estimate indicates that enrollment in major seminaries in 1998 had decreased by 65% to 70% since 1966.)

These figures contrast dramatically with the numbers we find active in lay ministry and, even more, with the numbers preparing for lay ministry. According to figures released by the National Association of Lay Ministry, there were, in 1996, over 26,000 lay ministers in the church who were working twenty or more hours a week, and of these, over three thousand were functioning as pastoral associates and therefore involved in some form of decision-making in the parish. In an even more telling figure, by 1998 more than 20,000 members of the laity were preparing to exercise such ministry, and were following courses of study in scripture, the theology of the church, and practical courses for directing parish programs; and many of those planning careers in lay ministry are getting graduate degrees in the field.

The development of the lay apostolate has not been spared controversy. Some have pointed to the danger of "desacramentalizing" the church, precisely because lay ministers cannot celebrate eucharist, and others have pointed to the communion services (with distribution of preconsecrated hosts), presided over by the laity, as obscuring precisely that fact. Many have observed that the shortage of priests should not be advanced as the reason for granting ministerial roles to the laity, since the laity already have the right and duty to exercise the common priesthood of all the faithful, which includes the call to pastoral ministry. On November 13, 1997, a document was issued in Rome which bore the title "Instruction on Certain Questions regarding the Collaboration of the Non-Ordained Faithful in the Sacred Ministry of the Priest." Signed by the heads of eight Vatican agencies and approved by the Pope, the instruction clearly intended to underline the difference between the ministry of the ordained priesthood and the ministry of the laity, which the latter have in virtue of the priesthood of all the faithful. However, the document went on to state that the involvement of the laity in the pastoral ministry of the priest is permissible only in cases where an adequate number of priests are not available, and this provoked some strong reactions.

On the very day it was issued, the document was attacked in unusually harsh terms by the president of the German Bishops' Conference, Karl Lehmann, Archbishop of Mainz. He found that the document echoes "a climate of mistrust for the laity" who might "get the impression that their participation is wanted only as long as there is a shortage of priests." Lehmann took particular exception to the fact that the instruction relegated diocesan and parish councils "to a consultative role only and denied that they could in any way become deliberative structures." In the United States, laypersons and sisters who have been functioning as hospital and prison chaplains for years were disappointed because the document asserted that only priests could use the title of chaplain. These lay chaplains pointed out that using the title of "chaplain" is not a matter of prestige or position within the church, but touches on questions of law and state financing of such ministries, as well as the question of their acceptance by those whom they serve.

10.42 The Pastoral Letters of the American Bishops in the 1980s

The American bishops produced two remarkable pastoral letters during the 1980s. The first, dubbed "the Nuclear Pastoral" (its real title was "The Challenge of Peace"), was issued in 1983, and it called into question the reigning doctrine of nuclear deterrence. The second, "Economic Justice for All," issued in 1986, suggested that there were elements in the American economic system which could not be reconciled with Catholic social teaching. Although the collapse of the Soviet Union left the world with only one superpower and has, on one level at least, lessened the threat of nuclear war, many of the bishops who wrote the original letter on the American economy feel the concerns of the pastoral are even more important today than they were in 1986.

At least as remarkable as the content of what came to be called "the Economic Pastoral" was the way it was written. Extensive hearings were held, and different positions along the economic spectrum were heard and questioned. (So extensive were the hearings and so open were the bishops to listening to different opinions, that some bishops felt their authority to speak as interpreters of the church's positions on social justice was compromised and that they would appear too dependent on those outside the hierarchy.) The bishops also avoided the temptation to lay down the law. They wanted to address men and women of good will, and they wanted to share the results of their reflections as Christian teachers, but they admitted that people of good will might disagree with the practical solutions they proposed. The approach of the bishops had been profoundly influenced by Vatican II's respect for the laity and by its perception that *we are the church.*

The long letter touched many areas of both the American and the global economy, but its thrust and purpose can be summarized in the four moral principles which were enunciated in §258. First: The demands of Christian love and human solidarity challenge all economic actors to choose community over chaos. They require a definition of political community that goes beyond national sovereignty to policies that recognize the moral bond among all people. Second: Basic justice implies that all people are entitled to participate in the increasingly interdependent global economy in a way that ensures their freedom and dignity. Third: Respect for human rights, both political and economic, implies that international decisions, institutions, and policies must be shaped by values that are more than economic. Fourth: The special place of the poor in this moral perspective means that meeting the basic needs of the millions of deprived and hungry people in the world must be the number one objective of international policy.

The principles stated here and in other parts of the pastoral met with general acceptance, but the applications received a mixed reaction. Catholics (and many others) on the liberal side of the political spectrum saw in the letter a prophetic critique of American capitalism, while those of a more conservative bent felt that the document failed to appreciate the capacity of the American economic system to extend prosperity more widely than any system ever devised.

Here, too, the collapse of communism has complicated the issues. There is now not only a single superpower, but a single economic system—free-market capitalism—which seems as attractive to former communist states such as Russia and China as it does to the countries of the First World. For precisely this reason, as the millennium draws to a close, many feel that the critique of unbridled capitalism, found in "Economic Justice for All," has lost none of its relevance, but is even more needed today because of the possibility and the reality of massive abuses of human rights in the global economy.

10.43 The *Catechism of the Catholic Church (CCC)*

There had been calls for a new catechism (a concise statement of Catholic belief) as early as Vatican II, but it was not until 1985 that the process of preparing such a document began to take shape. It was at the Extraordinary Synod of Bishops in Rome in that year that Cardinal Bernard F. Law of Boston requested that an international catechism be drawn up (the first draft was referred to as the "Universal Catechism"). It was assumed that he did this on his own initiative because, at this same synod, Law complained about theologians at Catholic universities who dissented from the teaching of the magisterium. In 1986 the Pope named a commission of twelve cardinals, under the direction of Cardinal Joseph Ratzinger, Prefect of the Congregation for the Doctrine of the Faith, to supervise the writing of the catechism. The actual writing was done by seven bishops who consulted theologians from around the world (although it was never clear exactly who these theologians were, or how broad a spectrum of theological thought they represented).

A provisional draft of the future *CCC* was sent to the bishops of the world in late 1989, with instructions that corrections and suggestions concerning this document were to be sent to Rome by June 1990—a very short period, given the length and complexity of the document. The commission of writers took note of the 24,000 suggested amendments and emendations. The first draft of the catechism received some stinging criticism from a number of U.S. bishops (probably from about thirty-five American bishops, since this was the number that helped Thomas Reese, S.J. publish his *Universal Catechism Reader*) who said, among other things, that the text quoted scripture out of context, that it failed to distinguish between peripheral doctrines and central truths, that it relegated the laity to a passive role, overlooked ecumenism, and set up a false separation between science and faith. Other comments were even more negative: Reese referred to the sharp and, at times, biting criticism by 938 bishops—one quarter of the world episcopate (again, the [mis]use of scripture seems to have caused most of the problems).

The Pope read the final draft early in 1992, and it was issued with his formal approval in the fall of 1992. John Paul II, in speaking to the Dutch bishops, promised that the catechism "will reassure and strengthen the faithful who were disoriented by the theological ferment of recent years and will bring back to the genuine sources of faith those who were led astray by false prophets." The French original was published in November 1992; translations into the other languages and the preparation of a normative Latin version began. Unspecified problems with the English translation delayed its publication. (It turned out later that these problems were the result of disagreements about inclusive language.)

The *Catechism of the Catholic Church* is one of the most significant events in the life of the church since the Second Vatican Council, and in many respects it is a splendid summary of Catholic faith. In every one of its four parts (the profession of faith, the celebration of the Christian mystery, life in Christ, and Christian prayer) there are moving and inspiring summaries of the faith (and this is true of the section on prayer virtually in its entirety). However, at least two criticisms were voiced by a number of American bishops—the fact that scripture is used decoratively and not in its proper context, and that no attempt is made to distinguish central from peripheral doctrines—and these have been echoed by a number of theologians, particularly in Germany and the United States.

10.44 The Difficult Road to Reunion

The Second Vatican Council's Decree on Ecumenism *(Unitatis Redintegratio)* demonstrated an openness toward the Protestant churches which no one would have thought possible even a decade earlier, and it had raised high hopes on both sides of the ecumenical divide. These hopes grew with the publication, in 1983, of a book by Karl Rahner and Joseph Fries *(Church Unity: A Real Possibility)*, because the book showed that ecumenical fervor had gripped some of the best minds in the church, and it proceeded to set out a practical program for the development of "partner churches," with full mutual recognition. Optimism grew in the early years of the pontificate of John Paul II, and well into the 1980s. Discussions with Anglicans in Europe (at the highest level: John Paul met with Archbishop Runcie of Canterbury five times during the eighties); with Lutherans in Germany; and with Episcopalians, Lutherans, Methodists, and Presbyterians in the United States, had led to agreement on dogmatic and liturgical questions which would have been inconceivable in the years before the Council. The discussions brought a sense of shared unity on essentials to a point which Rahner and Fries (in the book mentioned above) clearly thought was sufficient for what is often called "pulpit and table fellowship"—that is, shared eucharist, and shared preaching of and hearkening to the word of God. Notable here was the Catholic-Lutheran Report, "Facing Unity," which summed up the results of meetings between the two groups in the United States in 1985, and called for joint exercise of the episcopal office, including joint ordinations.

The publication on May 30, 1995 of John Paul II's encyclical, *Ut Unum Sint,* heartened many supporters of ecumenism because of its statement that "ecumenism belongs organically to the church's life and work." (Incidentally, it is interesting to compare John Paul II's *Ut unum sint* with Pius XI's *Mortalium Animos,* published in 1928. The latter encyclical rejected practically all of the initiatives of the ecumenical movement as they had been voiced at the First World Conference on Faith and

Order in Lausanne in 1927, and forbade Catholic participation in ecumenical gatherings.) But John Paul's encyclical went on to list five areas in which deeper agreement had to be sought and found, and therefore established the parameters which would have to be respected if there were to be any progress in ecumenism during his pontificate. The five areas: the relationship of scripture and tradition, the understanding of the eucharist, the sacrament of orders in its three grades, the magisterium, Mary as Mother of God and icon of the church. Oddly enough, the encyclical did not mention the bilateral discussions between Catholics and various Protestant churches, which had made great progress in the first three of the five areas.

This absence of any mention of the bilateral discussions with Protestants reflects the fact that the principal concern of the encyclical is reunion with the Orthodox churches of the East. But on this front, although the dogmatic obstacles are minimal, historical and emotional factors are not, and the disintegration of the Soviet Union in 1989 opened the field to turf battles between Orthodox and Eastern Rite Catholics, which have made prospects for reunion seem remote indeed.

One final bittersweet note: the momentum generated by the Council's decree *(Unitatis Redintegratio)*, and by the Catholic-Protestant discussions of the two subsequent decades, may have done more in bringing various Protestant groups to the point of shared table and pulpit fellowship than it did in lowering barriers between Catholics and Protestants. Many Lutherans, Presbyterians, Reformed, and members of the United Church of Christ are now in full communion.

It seems clear that the hopes of Vatican II for reunion of the Christian churches have not been fulfilled, and for each step forward toward forging agreement on eucharist and ministry, new obstacles have appeared, such as aggressive evangelization by Pentecostal groups in South and Central America and, most of all, the 1992 decision of the Anglican Church to ordain women. It is true that in many places there is a good deal of sharing, not simply in social ministries, but in eucharist and preaching, and Protestants and Catholics (including candidates for priesthood and ministry) are attending each other's graduate schools in unprecedented numbers. But there has been little movement in the higher echelons of the Catholic Church, and for the moment, at least on the official level, Catholic-Protestant ecumenism is stalled.

10.45 The Role of Women in the Church

There is another area, replete with problems, challenges, and some stunning successes, which reveals much about the state of the contemporary church and the tasks which face us: the role of women in the church. It was inevitable that the changing and expanding roles of women in society would lead many people, men and women alike, to ask what consequences this new situation would have for the church. Specifically, questions were raised about whether the exclusion of women from positions of authority in the church was an anachronism, and whether Jesus really intended to restrict the ministerial roles of diaconate and priesthood to men alone. (As we noted in the first chapter of this book, we might just as easily ask if he intended these roles, *as they are understood today,* for men.) As early as 1976, a document issued in the name of Paul VI *(Inter Insigniores)* had tried to remove the question of ordaining women to the priesthood from the area of possible discussion, although not with the solemnity with which Rome would address the question in subsequent decades.

The Women's Pastoral

We can understand some of the problems connected with this issue by examining the fate of the so-called "Women's Pastoral," which the American bishops tried to write in the late eighties and early nineties, and this will tell us a great deal about the relationship of the American church to Rome, about divisions within the American church itself, and about the unsolved problems, and challenges still to be faced, which have confronted the church in the late eighties and through the nineties.

The first draft of the intended pastoral was ready in 1988, and its title ("Partners in the Mystery of Redemption") showed that those who prepared it did not want to lecture women on their proper roles in church life, but wanted to listen attentively to what women were saying. The approach was not deductive—drawing theoretical conclusions from principles enunciated in papal encyclicals—but inductive—trying to develop a picture of the real-life frustrations and hopes of women who love the church, but who are frequently annoyed ("appalled" would be more appropriate) at being treated like second-class citizens—welcomed as envelope-stuffers, but denied any roles in decision-making.

Furthermore, on what was to become a major issue in the following decade, the first draft wanted further discussion of the question of the ordination of women to the priesthood, and noted, somewhat wryly perhaps, that not all exegetes, church historians, and dogmatic theologians had found the arguments listed in *Inter Insigniores* convincing (a situation which had not changed as the end of the millennium approached). On this and on other questions concerning women, the pastoral took its intended audience very seriously, and its authors felt that they could not teach authoritatively and responsibly until they had listened to the concerns of women themselves.

Two years passed between the first and second drafts, but the document of spring 1990 was quite different from its predecessor. For example, instead of calling for further discussion of the issue of women's ordination, the second draft positively rejected such a possibility. By the time the third draft appeared, a year later, the reasoning was largely deductive, and drew on traditional ways in which the papal magisterium had dealt with the roles of women in church and society. The blunt criticism of sexism found in the first draft ("sexism is a moral and social evil") had been dropped and, in fact, sexism was given an entirely different definition, with the emphasis put on pornography and abortion as its manifestations. The first draft's sympathy for more inclusive language in biblical translations and liturgical texts had given way to warnings about erroneous developments which might be fostered by imprudent use of inclusive language. The fourth draft, which was ready for the bishops' vote in the fall of 1992, differed from the third in two respects: the section on sexual ethics had undergone enormous expansion, and a lengthy rationale had been added for rejecting the possibility of ordaining women to the priesthood. The document had changed profoundly in moving from the first draft to that text which failed to muster sufficient support when the vote was taken in 1992. By then, many of the authors of the first draft, as well as those who were sympathetic to its inductive and pastoral approach, were probably among those who voted to reject the final draft.

Perhaps the key to understanding what happened during the four-year debate on what was intended as a pastoral but finally became only a "report" (as well as the key to many other problems and conflicts among the American bishops) is to be found in two contributions which appeared in the *New York Times* on December 6 and December 10, 1992—the first written by Archbishop Rembert Weakland of Milwaukee and the second by Cardinal John O'Connor of New York. Weakland called for a fundamental change in the attitude of the church toward women, and warned of a new "Galileo case" if the church retreated to the medieval model. He argued that the church could and should accept the new insights of anthropology, psychology, and sociology, and that, if it did, it could assume a leading role in creating the new global culture. Writing four days later, O'Connor reacted negatively to most of the points Weakland had made. And he closed his letter by noting that he and Weakland looked at the world in fundamentally different ways. Weakland, said O'Connor, is optimistic, and thinks that cultural harmony between the church and the world is possible. He (O'Connor), on the other hand, is convinced that the church is and must remain a counter-cultural force, and that this will continue into the indefinite future, because the church teaches almost the exact opposite of what the world teaches. Regardless of which judgment is the better assessment of the relationship of the church and the world, O'Connor's remarks about the basis of their difference were very perceptive.

Of course, the question of the role of women in the church is not just an American problem. Admittedly, it is not a major issue in the Third World, where women are faced with far more fundamental problems in society, and where the church is more often one of the only places where women's fundamental human dignity is respected. However, in Europe the question is being raised as insistently as it is in North America, as is clear from the following events. In 1992 the German bishops commissioned the Allensbach Demoscopic Institute to do a survey of the views of Catholic women about various questions connected with church life, and the results of that survey were available by late spring of 1993. Interestingly enough, the survey evoked some of the same kinds of answers which many of the American bishops were probably looking for when they wrote the first draft of their Women's Pastoral, but it did so in a format which was not subject to Roman editorial work. The survey documented massive shifts in the attitudes of women. In 1993 just 25% of the women surveyed felt "very close" to the church, down from 40% in 1982. The number of Catholic women with no connection to their parishes had jumped from 12% to 20% in the last twenty years. The survey showed that 45% of all Catholic women, and 54% of the 30 to 44 age group think that the church is holding on to an antiquated image of women, and two-thirds feel that the church is one of the areas where the claim of women to equal rights is least respected, while only 20% think that the church understands the reality of their lives.

A Quiet Revolution

The story of the Women's Pastoral and of the survey commissioned by the German bishops document some of the problems women have experienced in the church throughout most of its history; that is, they speak of the present as the heir of the past. But there is another dimension—the present as it points to the future—and here the picture is very different. With the exception of the sacramental ministry in the narrower sense (that is, the administration of the sacraments and presiding at liturgy), women are present and active in ministerial positions at all levels. They proclaim the word and give communion at liturgy; they direct RCIA programs; they are in charge of religious education in most parishes; and in many dioceses they not only staff the departments of religious education, but run them as well. They serve on diocesan tribunals, and when communion services are scheduled because of the unavailability of a priest to preside at the liturgy, 80% of these services are led by women. With their husbands, they have virtually taken over marriage preparation sessions in many parishes. More and more, contact with the church is mediated through women, from childhood (when religious education outside the family begins) to the verge of death, because women bring eucharist to the sick and accompany the dying as hospital chaplains.

And if the changes in the church to which these facts attest are striking (although they have come with so little fanfare that many are still unaware of them), they point to a future where women will be even more prominent in ministry. According to figures released by the National Center for Pastoral Ministry, of the 20,000 persons now studying and preparing for lay ministry (and mentioned in §10.41 above), 85% are women. The historic prominence of women as churchgoers is being repeated and surpassed by their prominence at every level of church life.

10.46 Social Justice and the Modern Encyclical Tradition

One of the most profound and positive initiatives of the church in modern times has been the engagement of a series of Popes with social and economic problems, and the development of proposals which apply the scriptural message to contemporary problems. Although a late starter, Catholic social thought has developed rapidly since the papacy of Leo XIII (1878 to 1903). It started with the encyclical *Rerum Novarum* in 1891, which voiced a principle that would be paramount in all future papal documents: human dignity is the norm and standard by which the political, social, and economic structures of society are to be judged. This was new; the common view was that these structures were there to preserve the nation, and the stability of the social order and the class system; and millions would be slaughtered on the field of battle to preserve these pseudo-values.

Pius XI (1922 to 1939) and Pius XII (1939 to 1958) continued the tradition, and the latter elaborated a concept of *social justice* which implied that human dignity might demand structural changes in society itself. His 1944 Christmas

address was a landmark: he argued that the power to participate in the political process, and thus to shape one's own
future, was essential to the preservation and development of
human dignity. This was the first papal statement supporting
the democratic political system.

John XXIII developed this theme in his 1961 encyclical,
Mater et Magistra. He felt that because of the size and power of
economic and political institutions, people in both East and
West were losing confidence in their power to shape their own
futures, and that this represented an assault on human dignity
because human dignity includes the power to shape the
future. In his 1963 encyclical, *Pacem in Terris,* there is more
emphasis on life in community as the context in which human
dignity can be protected and expanded. A noteworthy and
refreshing feature of this encyclical is that it represented a
definitive break with the incredibly tortured, pretentious, and
antiquated jargon which had been common in encyclicals—
speaking about former Popes as "predecessors of immortal
memory," etc.

The Second Vatican Council's document, *Gaudium et
Spes,* built on the encyclical tradition, but represented an
advance in two respects. First, it moved away from a concept
of natural law as an unchangeable norm, and recognized that
human institutions and persons are not static, but change in
history. (Up to that time, much Catholic moral thought had
been based on an analysis of human nature, on the assumption that the latter was constant and unchangeable, and that it
was a simple matter to discern the finality of its various functions.) Second (and dealing with precisely this problem), it
adopted an explicitly theological point of view: human dignity
does not consist in conforming to an abstract reality called
"human nature"; rather, it is identified with the power to exist
as finite beings who are called to absolute transcendence. We
are made in the image and likeness of God, and we are called
to dialogue with him. We are made to "know the one true
God, and Jesus Christ whom you have sent." Our dignity is
rooted in God's fidelity, and not in some immutable quality
which we possess on our own.

Paul VI's *Populorum Progressio* introduced the concept of

integral development and affirmed that human dignity is protected only by promoting the development of the whole human being by realizing each person's potential for knowledge, responsibility, and freedom in every area of life, political, social, and economic. *Octogesima Adveniens* (1971) was even more theological: it made the point that absolute value and truth have taken historical form in Jesus, because, in him, God's reign has entered history.

In 1981 (on the ninetieth anniversary of *Rerum Novarum*), John Paul II issued the encyclical *Laborem Exercens*. This encyclical continued the theological emphasis: the source of our conviction about the dignity of work is the revealed word of God and the transcendent destiny given by the living God; we are called to know him and love him. Because work is a *personal action* (and the person cannot be understood without God), it is only through faith in God, hope in God, and love of God that work can be given the meaning that it has in the eyes of God.

His next encyclical on social questions *(Sollicitudo Rei Socialis)* was published in February 1988, and had more clearly political overtones. He protested against the restriction of initiative in the social systems of the communist bloc and in much of the Third World, and he bluntly asserted that those regimes should be replaced by democratic and participatory ones, because "the free and responsible participation of all citizens in public affairs is the necessary condition and sure guarantee of the development of the whole individual and of all people" (§44). In 1991, *Centesimus Annus* summarized a century of Catholic social thought and made some important additions. The encyclical deals with the problem of alienation, in noting that, as human beings, we need a distinctive set of relationships to the world around us and to others. If those relationships are disturbed we become strangers in our world, and strangers to ourselves (§41). Alienation is a reality in Western society as much as it was in those lands under the communist yoke. When people are enmeshed in a web of false and superficial gratifications, rather than being helped to experience their personhood in an authentic and concrete way, they lose it. And finally, in §54, there is an interesting connection made between evangelization and the church's social teaching: the church's social teaching is a valid instrument of evangelization because it is a practical form taken by preaching, and it constitutes an offer of faith.

The modern encyclical tradition on questions of social and economic justice is a splendid chapter in the history of the church in the last hundred years, and it is a fine example of the indispensable moral authority of the Petrine office, when that office is defined in terms of John 21: "Feed my lambs and feed my sheep."

10.5 COPING WITH THE CHALLENGES AND CAPITALIZING ON THE POSSIBILITIES

The lesson of church history for us today is the same as it has been since the church first defined itself in accepting the Old Testament and writing the New, and since it committed itself to live under the judgment of both Testaments for all of the years that it would exist on this earth: we will cope with the real challenges of the moment to the degree to which our understanding of the church as both task and reality is constantly nourished by the scriptural word, provided this word is correctly, and that means *critically,* understood. We will be able to cope with these challenges to the degree to which we strive to discern the intentions of Jesus as these can be found in the gospels, and strive to fulfill these intentions.

There is clearly a certain tension between the self-understanding of the church which was articulated at Vatican II and that which had gone before, and that tension has continued to the present day. The serious and quite objective differences which distinguish the self-understanding of the church, as spelled out at Vatican II, from that of the pre-Vatican II church, can be reduced to the question of *authority* and its bases—not simply to the old question of whether bishops and Popes have the power to make laws binding in conscience (the question of jurisdiction), but to the deeper question of the ultimate norms and criteria of Christian faith and life. Vatican II represented an epoch-making shift in direction here, even though few of the bishops who were present there were fully aware of this (although several of their *periti* or theological advisors were). For the first time in history, the church in council stated that "The magisterium (teaching authority) is not above the word of God but serves it...because it draws from this one source of faith all that it presents for belief as revealed by God" (*Lumen Gentium*, c.10). It is eminently clear from this same document that the Council fathers (at least the overwhelming majority of them) had no intention of calling the autonomy of the magisterium into question, for the same chapter contains these words: "The task of giving an authoritative interpretation to the word of God has been entrusted solely to the living magisterium of the church." But there are unreconciled and unreconcilable assertions in this document and I believe that Oscar Cullmann was right when, after lamenting the fact that the church at Vatican II did not clearly subject itself to scripture as a norm, he noted that his reservation applied only to the theory as presented in the conciliar text, and added: "In the final analysis, perhaps the Second Vatican Council as a whole made submission to the Bible its guiding principle" (*Die Autorität der Freiheit, Munich*, 1967).

An epoch-making shift took place at Vatican II, even though this was not the intention of the Council fathers, as the unreconciled antitheses of the Constitution on Divine Revelation makes clear. The document is a symptom of the fact that a new way of hearkening to the word of God has begun to make itself felt within the Catholic church, and that scripture has, in principle, vindicated its right to be a *norma normans non normata* (an ultimate norm of faith and life which is subject to no other norm). Nothing will ever be the same again.

10.6 SUMMARY: THE CHURCH ITSELF AS TASK

Paul spoke of the church as the body of Christ and he and some other New Testament writers also talked of it as the work of the Spirit of God, who is effective in baptism, eucharist, and preaching. In this sense, they are all speaking of church as that which Jesus intended as the continuation of his word, his work, his very self; they are speaking of the *deep reality* of this new community, and they are speaking of that which is essential to this community and gives it its identity. In the best sense of the word, they are talking about church as an *ideal reality*—not an unrealizable dream, but as that which already exists in a hidden way within the community and which summons it to become what it should be. For most of the New Testament, "church" could be defined as God's call and the response of human beings, precisely insofar as they hearken to that call.

But what came to call itself "church" in history is not simply God's call and the wholehearted response of human beings. The church which exists at any moment, the church as visible and tangible, always falls short of the ideal. It is a human church and a church of sinners; it is a sinful church. Church in its profound reality (the ideal reality spoken of above) is a *vocation* for the existing, visible church in every age. The existing church in every age is ambiguous, and within it different and competing elements coexist: human sinfulness resists the saving will of God; human ignorance and stupidity choose inept and counterproductive ways of preaching the gospel. The real problem for Christians in any age is that of discovering the deep reality of the church—the church as vocation and ideal—and of seeing it as a call to the existing church, that church which falls short of the ideal and which is a tragic mixture of good and evil.

In every age, the church must become institution, organization, establishment, society, in order to discover and employ forms of preaching and sacramental life which will express appropriately, in the language of a given age, the new life brought by the Lord. But these institutional and social structures cannot themselves be absolutized, because then they would be exempt from reform. Certain exaggerations of papal and conciliar infallibility pose serious problems here. Scripture alone can judge these institutional structures because, as preached and heard, it is virtually identical with the deep reality of the church—identical, paradoxically, with the normative church of the first generations and with Augustine's "church of the future." Scripture is not an element of church life which is at the disposal of the institution, and Vatican II stated this clearly.

Our task and vocation today, like that of Christians at every moment of history, is to become, under the power of God, that church which is the visibility of Jesus Christ here and now. We will never be fully successful in this. The attempt to succeed at it involves both a hearkening to the word of God *and* a grasp of the possibilities and dangers inherent in the "raw material"—the historical situation of Christians and non-Christians at a given moment of history. Our grasp of this situation can be much helped by reflection on the concrete reality of the church in the past, on past successes and past failures, and on the causes and effects of both. This is the relevance of church history as a theological discipline, and this is the role which it can play in our faith and life as Christians today.

Index